That's How It Was

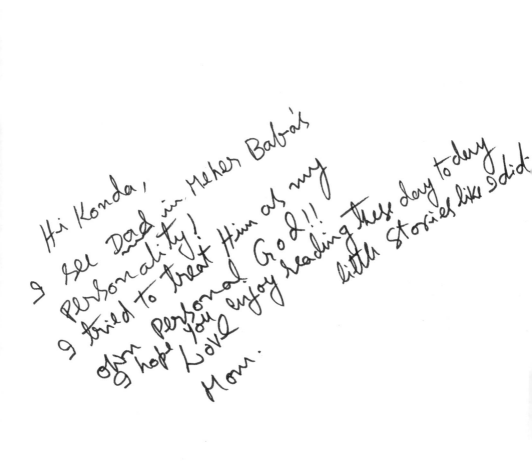

Hi Konda,

I see Dad in Meher Baba's
Personality!
I tried to treat Him as my
own personal God!!!
I hope you enjoy reading these day to day
little stories like I did

Love
Mom.

Meher Baba with Eruch in India in the 1950s

That's How It Was

STORIES OF LIFE WITH MEHER BABA

ERUCH JESSAWALA

2010

SHERIAR
FOUNDATION

C O N T E N T S

⚛ A C K N O W L E D G E M E N T S

FIRST AND FOREMOST, a supreme debt of gratitude is due Avatar Meher Baba whose love created these "stories," whose presence keeps them ever fresh, and whose Reality gives them significance.

Next, Eruch's astonishing patience, tolerance and forebearance throughout the compilation and editing of these three volumes must be acknowledged. To sit in Mandali Hall and tell the same stories year after year because people are so eager to hear them is one thing, but to have someone try and write those same stories up and be forced to listen to them once again and make corrections, knowing all the while that invariably some confusion, controversy and complications will ensue because of this, is of another magnitude of resignation to His Will altogether.

Many thanks are due, and happily given, to Bill LePage and Judith Garbett who compiled, edited and transcribed many of the stories in this volume. Thanks also go to Davana Brown, Laurel and Glenn Magrini, and Daphne Klein for editing and proofreading suggestions. Anil Nori and Jeff Ives generously contributed their computer expertise. Lastly, I lovingly acknowledge the help of Jimmy Mistry who not only made the previous publication of some of these volumes possible, but whose ever present sense of humor made the whole, sometimes infuriating process, fun.

Over the many years that the compilation and editing of these stories has taken place, quite a few people have come forward to help. It is entirely possible that I have neglected to mention some-one in this acknowledgement who rightly deserves to be publicly acknowledged. If that is so, I apologize and assure one and all that this omission is entirely because of my failing memory and not because of the insignificance of the contribution.

Steve Klein

⚈ INTRODUCTION

THIS IS THE THIRD COLLECTION OF STORIES Eruch tells in Mandali
Hall which I have edited. The two earlier volumes, *Determined to Be
His* and *Is That So?*, are included in this present volume. In the original volume, I note that I assured readers of the accuracy of the stories presented therein. Yet the stories in that volume are usually presented in isolation and in only a minimal sort of context.

My sense after talking to Eruch was that he did not feel this
was the best way to present the material. These incidents from
Eruch's life with Baba are not told to simply pass the time, but to
help people get a better understanding of how to live with God and
for God. Therefore, in *Determined to Be His*, an effort was made,
not simply to relate a story, but to recapture the "feel" of a morning
or afternoon spent in Mandali Hall listening to Eruch. The stories
were put into the kind of context in which they are sometimes given,
and oftentimes several stories on one theme are strung together.

At the time, I felt the overall effect was more realistic and
somehow more "authentic." Paradoxically, however, because more
editing was necessary, there was more scope for the editor's point of
view, conscious or otherwise, to intrude. For example, although the
stories are given in relation to some point Eruch is making, at other
times he will use the same stories to make a different point. In fact,
I have often teased Eruch that someday we are going to bring out a
book which will simply contain all the different versions he has told

over the years of the same story. Obviously choices have to be made, and each choice reflects my way of hearing the stories and my way of interpreting them. At the time, I did not worry overmuch about this, perhaps taking refuge in the thought that if I went too far astray, Eruch would correct me when I read the stories back to him.

I have subsequently come to the conclusion that this is not Eruch's way, that while he might correct an obvious factual error, or an expression which was more in my words than his (and often did so) he will only hint at those places where I may have misinterpreted his meaning. Some of these hints I am able to pick up on; others, undoubtedly, I miss. If I do, Eruch will not insist upon making changes. His view seems to be that it is up to him to tell the stories as honestly as he can, but it is up to each listener to interpret the meaning as they see fit. Thus no one view is right, no one view is wrong, they are all true, but, as he is fond of saying, they are only part of the truth, they are not the whole Truth. The end result is that these "more authentic" stories were perhaps also more influenced by my personal perceptions, limitations, and biases and represent perhaps more of my "truth" than of Eruch's.

Realizing this, I wasn't sure what approach to adopt as I set about preparing this group of stories. I won't bore you with the complete set of rationalizations I came up with to justify the final decision. I think Eruch will be pleased, however, and my conscience will be satisfied if I can simply state that the material presented in here is my *version* or my *interpretation* of Eruch's stories as recorded or jotted down in Mandali Hall.

If there is anything in any of the stories which you don't find helpful in your pursuit to live with and for God then simply discard it. It is my hope that you will enjoy the material as much as I do and that you might hear a new note or two, or a few notes more clearly, which will help in learning to dance to His tune.

Steve Klein

THAT'S HOW IT WAS

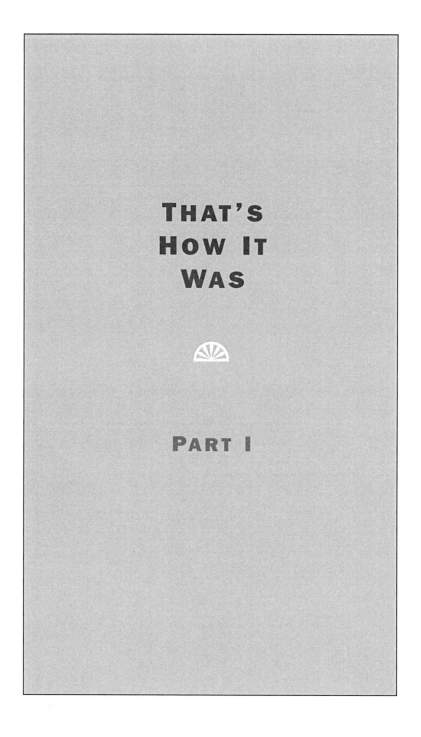

PART I

⁂ A L O N E

IT'S TRUE THAT BABA WAS IN SECLUSION during the later years quite often; people were even told they shouldn't correspond with Baba. They couldn't see Him and they weren't even supposed to write Him, and yet Baba was never alone. There was always someone with Him. Not necessarily in the same room, but right outside His door. We would sit there, and when Baba clapped, only then would we enter. In my whole life with Baba, I know of only two instances when Baba was left completely alone. Of course, there may have been some instances before I came to Him, but in my life I only know of these two.

One I have already told you: the time at Vengurla, after we both got dumped into the filthy water, and I left Baba alone while I ran back to get some clean clothes for Baba. The other time occurred when we were staying at Mount Abu. Baba had gone there with a small group of men and women. I don't remember exactly who was there but I think it was Baidul and maybe Vishnu. Donkin I know was there. I remember that because he got so sick. You see, Baba and the women had a small house where they were staying, and we men lived in the town nearby. We lived in what you may call a slum area. We had two small rooms, and Donkin was housed separately. Baba must have felt that our quarters weren't proper for Donkin; after all, he was not used to such things. He was a well-bred Englishman. So he had his own place. But even so, the town was so primitive there was raw sewage lying about, and Donkin got sick. He was laid up in bed.

Baba wanted to make a flying visit to a *mast*, so just He and I went. When the women knew we were going out, they gave us a shopping list. Mount Abu is a remote area, and the town, as I have been saying, is very small. It wasn't possible to buy good vegetables there. So when the women heard that we were going out, they gave us a list of things to get.

So Baba and I left Mount Abu and contacted the *mast*. On our return, we stopped and bought all the vegetables the women wanted, and they had been put inside a large box. We were at the Abu Road Train Station. We were going to take a train from there to Mount Abu. We were on the platform with our box of vegetables, and we didn't have any tickets. But to get the tickets I would have to leave Baba alone. Some of you have traveled by train here. You know what the rush at the ticket window is like. I couldn't have Baba stand in line with me, so I said, "Baba, I am going to have to leave You for a few minutes to get the tickets. Is that all right?" Baba indicated that He would be fine. "Are You sure, Baba?" I asked. "Yes," Baba gestured. "It is better this way because I can stand here and keep an eye on our box while you get the tickets."

"Okay," I said, "but don't move. Stay right here."

Baba said He would, and I went off and got into the queue for a ticket. As I stood there, I heard the bell ringing announcing an incoming train. I became very nervous. Our train was arriving, Baba was all alone, and I still hadn't gotten tickets. Somehow I forced myself to the front of the line and quickly bought two tickets and then hurried back to Baba. But when I got there, Baba wasn't there.

I looked around, but no Baba. Our box of vegetables was gone too. Everywhere people were rushing to get on board the train, and I felt this sinking sensation in my stomach. What had happened to Baba? I looked around, and then I spied our box of vegetables bobbing up and down in the distance. I ran after it and saw that Baba was carrying the box on His shoulder. He was looking for an empty compartment so the two of us could get on board.

I ran up to Baba and took the vegetables, and, since we had tickets, we both got onto the train. That was the second time I can remember when Baba had been left completely alone.

🌿 B E R R I E S

YOU HAVE HEARD ME SAY SO OFTEN, "Don't try to fathom Him, don't try to understand His ways, just remember and love Him." Why is this? Why should this be? Let us, for a moment, leave aside anything spiritual, let us forget about the mystical and just look at the practical side of it.

What is the Avatar? The Avatar is God in human form, the God-Man. So let us take the man side first. There are so many psychologies, so many different ideas as to why people act the way they do that it is impossible for anyone to say, "Yes, I understand it all." We have people coming here who practice therapies we've never heard of. I say, "What is this?" And they say, "I'm a psychologist," and then they give some long title. And I say, "What's that?" and they explain that's the branch of psychology they practice.

It is all Greek to me. Now, don't misunderstand me, I am not saying that these therapies do not help. I am not talking about that at all, that's a completely different thing. I am only saying that there are so many different psychologies today. And why? Because it is so impossible to fathom what makes a man act the way he does. So that every day it seems someone comes up with a new explanation, a new way of trying to understand man, and that is only man, mind you. We haven't even gotten to the God part of God-Man.

And Baba is both. He is the Lord of Lords, and He is Man amongst men. So how can we understand Him? We obviously cannot understand God, and we cannot understand man, so how can we expect to understand the One who is both, simultaneously? Clearly it is impossible.

But I can give you an example of how Baba, in different situations, demonstrated His God-Manness. How, in one case as Man amongst men, Baba set an example of how men should behave towards each other and, in the other, how, as Lord of Lords, Baba gave a guideline for how man should relate to God. Would you like to hear them?

The first incident happened in Hamirpur. I have told you before what it was like when Baba first went there, how the masses were ablaze with the fire of His name. I won't dilate on that now. This story concerns something quite different. It is not about the masses and their spontaneous adoration and worship of Baba as God in human form, but concerns those who were traveling with Baba, His mandali. We were in Inghota, I think, but whether it was Inghota, Icchaura, or Nauranga, it doesn't matter. Everywhere we went people could not do enough for Baba.

Our hosts would completely turn their homes over to Baba for His disposal. You had the feeling that at a word from Baba these new lovers of His would have jumped into a fire for Him. That was the impression we got, that nothing was too much for them to do for Baba. I say this because it has some bearing on the story. It is important that you understand this background so you can appreciate Baba's meticulousness.

You see, where we were staying there was a berry tree. A "borr," I don't know what you call it in the States, or even if you have such trees. They are something like cherries. And it was that season, November, when the tree was full of berries. Not only was the tree full, but the ground was also covered with the berries because they were so ripe they were falling off the tree. Now, Gustadji was with us, and he happened to be walking by and he picked up a berry from the ground and ate it, and this was followed suit by the other mandali who were with him.

Now, see the fun. Baba came to know of this. And Baba was not pleased, in fact He was very upset. "What are you all doing?" Baba demanded.

"Baba," the mandali replied, "we were just eating some berries that had fallen."

"Did you have permission to eat these berries?"

"But Baba, they had fallen to the ground and we were just picking them up."

"You should have asked first," Baba insisted. "Who owns this tree?"

It turned out to be our host, so Baba said to call him. And Baba had all of the mandali and our host and his family come into the room with Him, and it was obvious from one glance that Baba had not called everyone together for some sweet words on love. On the contrary, Baba was fiery.

And He began to upbraid Gustadji for stealing the berries. When the host heard this he got very upset and tried to pacify Baba. "Baba," he said, "I am Yours. This house is Yours and even the berry tree is Yours. The mandali are also Yours. So the berries they ate belong to You, not to me." And what he was saying was true. That is what we had felt, that he was all for Baba.

But this answer did not seem to please Baba, although it was made in a most loving manner. Baba continued, "Yes, the whole creation is Mine, and yet the world's laws must be followed. It is not right in the world to take something that does not belong to you without the permission of the owner. This is true in the world. And it applies even more so with those who are living with Me. They should not think they are above such laws."

This was the point Baba was bringing home to us. I have told you before how particular Baba was about any money that was raised in His name. Once Baba even said that for each penny one raised wrongfully in His name, one would have to take a million births. Baba was most particular that those of us who lived with Him be very meticulous in our observance of such things. Yes, it is true that being with Baba gave us a feeling that we did not care for the world, that we were with the Emperor so what did we care what kings or presidents might think. That was there, we did not care what the world thought, but Baba trained us to be very careful about what we did in the world. And this was an opportunity for Baba to stress this once more to all of us. And, of course, not just to us, but to the host and his family and all the new lovers of Hamirpur. Baba was indirectly teaching them that although their enthusiasm, their zeal, their love was very great, still they must learn that did not excuse them from obeying the conventions of the world.

So when Baba said all this, there was a tremendous silence in the room. And then Baba did something which was most unexpected, and most touching. He stood and joined His hands together and on behalf of His mandali, Baba asked the host's forgiveness. See how perfect Baba is as man. He did not just tell us what we should do, how we should behave, but He took our faults upon Himself and begged for forgiveness. And this was not just a show for our benefit. Baba did it in such a way that all there felt Baba's absolute sincerity, His humility. That is what I mean when I say Baba was a Man amongst men. And as such, He demonstrated for all who aspire one day to become men, how we should act.

That is one side of it. That happened up North. Now, see the other side. This particular incident happened only a few weeks later, down South in Andhra. Once again our host was doing everything for us. And not just for us. He was feeding all the poor of the community as well. He was a wealthy man, one of the village elite you may call it, well respected, and he was pleased to be able to do this. Only Baba knows what is inside the heart of another, but it seems there was some sense of pride in this feeding of the poor. I say this not only because it is common sense – after all, it is only human nature to feel some sense of pride, of satisfaction with yourself for feeding so many, for doing such a good deed – but also because of what transpired next.

This man was Baba's host. And it so happened that there was a river, a wide river that ran alongside the town. This man used to run launches from one side to the other, to ferry people across. And he put those launches at Baba's disposal. There was a launch for Baba and the few who stayed with Him, and then there were two other launches for the rest of the mandali.

This arrangement worked out very well. The previous year, was it one year or a little longer? Yes, our first visit was in '53 and this was '54. I don't remember the exact date but I know we celebrated Baba's sixtieth birthday in Andhra, so it most likely was in February. Anyway, whatever it be, the year before when we were in Andhra, we found that the people's love for Baba was so great that they would come to wherever Baba was staying and sing love songs to Him all night long. It was impossible to sleep. Even when we told the people to stop, they continued. And why? It is the oppression of love. Their love for Baba made them insensitive to the comforts of their Lord, their love made them senseless, I should say, and to express this love, they sang songs to Baba, not thinking that this out-pouring of love was preventing Baba, their Beloved, from getting any rest. It is because of love, it is all because of love.

And perhaps it was because our host didn't love Baba in quite that way, he respected Him, he admired Him, but he didn't love Baba in that passionate way, and perhaps it was because of this that he used his common sense and decided to house Baba and His party on his launches. You see, once we got on, the launches were then taken across the river, almost to the other side, so that it was impossible for anyone to get near Baba. Baba was able to have some privacy and quiet this way, and we all appreciated this.

And it was something new for us as well, to spend the night on the launches. Well, the next morning, our host put our food in a launch and sent it with a man so that we could have breakfast. This man had been feeding all who came to his place for days, so to feed Baba and His party was easy for him, and the launch brought basket after basket of food, and the mandali took the food and had a good feast.

Now, Baba had had His launch moored at a little distance from the two launches of the mandali. This was Baba's way; if He could, He would tend to sleep apart from the mandali. He would have a watchman with Him, but it was His way to always sleep away from the mandali. And with the launches this was easy to do.

That morning, Baba had His launch taken over to where the mandali's launches were. In fact, all three were taken to shore, and Baba asked everyone if they had slept well. How had they enjoyed the night on the river? Then Baba asked if they had had breakfast yet. And several of the mandali replied that they had, that it had been delicious.

"So," Baba gestured, "you have been enjoying your breakfast while I have gone without." I was interpreting Baba's gestures, and I said this with displeasure in my voice because that was what Baba wanted to convey. He was not pleased. His mandali had not been thinking about Him, they had just been thinking about themselves and had enjoyed themselves while Baba had had to go without food.

To be fair, it wasn't really the mandali's fault. How did they know Baba hadn't been given any food? They had nothing to do with that. It was Savak Kotwal who had been put in charge of seeing to Baba's food, and he was the one whose duty it was to see that such things didn't happen. But when Baba would express His displeasure this way, even those who had done nothing wrong would feel the sting. All would be quiet, their heads hung, in guilt. Why? I don't know. I think there were two reasons. Even if we hadn't personally committed the fault Baba was upset at, what was the nature of the fault? It always came down to thinking too much about ourselves and not enough about Baba, and we were always guilty of that. Even if Baba was focusing His displeasure on Savak Kotwal, we all knew we were equally guilty. And there was something in Baba's manner, the way He would express Himself at such times, the way His eyes would flash, that brought this home to us.

And the second thing is that people were unhappy to see Baba displeased for any reason. Baba's moods were so overwhelming that it was like clouds had suddenly blotted out the sun. Naturally you want the sun to reappear, you are upset at the sudden storm that had arisen. Some say this is because of the mandali's love for Baba, but I don't know about that. I didn't have that love and it doesn't seem necessary to me to bring love into it.

When Baba was in a good mood it made us happy. Not because we loved Baba, but because His good spirits were infectious. You've seen that, how someone comes into a room with a big smile, their eyes twinkling, and it makes you feel good. Or if someone comes into the hall with a long face and sighing deep sighs, it dampens the atmosphere. This is just human nature.

At any rate, whatever it be, Baba was expressing His displeasure over the fact that He hadn't been fed. Our host was called over and Savak was called and Baba started demanding to know why He hadn't been given any breakfast. Baba turned to the host: "You feed all the poor, you feed My mandali, but you don't feed Me!" And Baba gestured that this man was worthless and should be thrown in the river.

As I said, our host had respect for Baba, perhaps in his own way he had some feeling for Baba, but at these words, he was completely taken aback. His only experience of Baba had been during public *darshan* programs where Baba had seemed all loving and infinitely compassionate. He had never seen this fiery side of Baba before and it gave him a shock. His mind started wondering how Baba could act this way. This didn't seem to fit his conception of how God should behave. And so when Baba gestured that he should be thrown into the river, he was astounded and frightened. One of the mandali, I forget now which one, moved towards him to throw him into the river and, without thinking about it, he moved away, and then turned and began running down the beach with the mandali member chasing after him. Our host was a big man, dignified, stout, and I still remember the sight of him running down the beach being pursued by one of the mandali.

This sight amused Baba, and He clapped His hands and called them both back to Him. "Why did you do this?" Baba asked in a gentler tone, and the host explained that he had sent food for Baba. It had been put into one launch and he had given instructions to the boatman which baskets were for the mandali and which was for Baba. But the boatman must have gotten confused and delivered them all to the mandali.

So Baba turned to Savak Kotwal and asked him what had happened. He replied that the launch had brought all the food to the mandali, but he had assumed that it had already taken Baba's food to Him. The boatman hadn't said anything about some of the baskets being for Baba.

This answer did not please Baba. "You assumed I had had My breakfast? Why didn't you ask? It is your job to see that I am fed. Are you trying to kill Me? You love only My mandali." I remember Baba saying that, "You love only My mandali," and "Are you trying to kill Me?"

And then Baba turned to our host and said, "Get a big stone, tie it to a rope around Savak's neck, and throw him in the river so he drowns."

Once again the poor host is completely taken aback. Now what to do? And Baba is snapping His fingers and gesturing, "Hurry up, do it." But the man is so stunned that he just stands there. So Savak starts telling him, "Hurry up, man, do it. Didn't you hear Baba's order, what are you waiting for?"

And Savak is now the one scolding this man for being so slow in obeying Baba's order. And what is the order? That this man should drown Savak. See the fun? So the man starts looking on the shore for a big stone, and Savak follows along urging him to hurry up.

But as it turns out there are no big stones on that section of the shore, and finally Baba tells him to forget it because there isn't time. We have to take the launches to the other side of the river so Baba can begin His *darshan* program.

Now, see the difference. In one instance, just for the sake of a few berries, Baba humbly apologizes on behalf of His mandali. But here, just because He didn't get His breakfast, Baba orders that our host be thrown in the river and that Savak be drowned. Some people when they hear stories like this might think that Baba was some sort of tyrant, but it wasn't that. Baba was demonstrating to us His role as Lord of Lords. As Man amongst men, Baba took all faults on Himself and humbled Himself as an example to us of how we, as men, should behave. But as Lord of Lords, Baba was demonstrating how much care we should take when serving Him.

What did Baba care about breakfast? Baba fasted for months on end; you mean to say He couldn't miss one breakfast? It was not that. Baba was merely using this as an opportunity to bring home to us how we should serve the Lord, with what care and meticulousness we should see to His needs. How we should always think of His needs before our own.

And see the effect this lesson had. Our host was stunned by that morning's happenings. As I said, his conception of God had been destroyed by Baba. But equally shocking was Savak's willingness to drown because Baba had ordered it. This type of devotion made him realize that his feeding of the poor was nothing in comparison. Here he had run away rather than be thrown into the river, yet Savak kept berating him for not finding a stone with which to drown him. That kind of obedience, devotion, love, call it what you will, was something new to him. As was the Lord who demanded it.

Somehow it made him realize that Baba was not just another guru or Master, but was indeed God in human form. And this man's relationship to Baba, his attitude towards Baba, his whole demeanor changed completely. That pride which seemed to be there got burnt away in his love for Baba, the Lord of Lords.

And Baba later used him as a means of bringing home a lesson for all of us about how we should worship Baba. This is now somewhat off the subject but since it has come up, would you like to hear this story?

As I said, after this experience, this man's whole attitude towards Baba changed and he became completely devoted to Baba. Years passed, and it seems that this man's sister-in-law had a vision of some sort which convinced her that a temple should be built for Baba. So this man, when he heard about it, decided to build a large temple in a field across from his home at the very site where Baba had given *darshan*. But now a temple means what? In India, as you have seen, temples always have statues of the deities inside. So in this man's mind, if he wanted to have a temple for Baba, he had to have a statue of Baba inside. And he wrote Baba for permission to build the temple and put a life-size statue inside so that all the people in his area could have the blessings of Baba's *darshan* whenever they wanted.

I was the one who had to see to the correspondence, and I would write this man back and say that this was not a good idea, that Baba had come to do away with all rites, rituals, and ceremonies and the only temple Baba wanted was the temple of the heart or some such, I don't recall exactly what I said. But something along these lines. But this answer did not satisfy the man. He felt that Baba wanted him to build this temple, and he wanted to do it on a grand scale so that people from all over could come and worship.

Now, when I was writing to him, trying to discourage him from doing this, why was I doing that? Because Baba had indicated to me that I should try to talk him out of this idea. But I wasn't allowed to say, "Baba says you shouldn't do this." So the man thought I was just expressing my own opinion, and he became quite angry with me. After all, who am I to tell him what to do? He thought I, on my own, was trying to interfere with his love for the Lord. So he would write back to Baba, and again Baba would tell me to answer the letter in my own name, and I would say something to the effect that the important thing was our remembrance of Baba in our heart, not the outward expression of devotion through temples and the like. And I remember he got quite indignant in his letters. He would write back that that was easy for me to say, since I was living with Baba. That it was easy for me to sit with Baba and criticize his idea, but if we changed places, if I went to Andhra and he came to live with Baba, then we would see who wanted a reminder. I had Baba's physical presence twenty-four hours a day, so naturally I could talk about inner remembrance. Let's change places, he suggested, and then we'll see who wants a statue. And he went on and pointed out that Baba lovers had Baba buttons, they had photographs, and Baba permitted this. In fact, Baba even blessed photographs, and had them distributed. And what were these but reminders of Baba, symbols of Baba's presence. A statue was the same thing, only even more life-like and so on.

Eventually a delegation from Andhra came to put their case before Baba directly, and Baba finally gave His permission, provided this man met certain conditions. I don't remember all of the conditions, but I know he had to pay for the construction entirely out of his own pocket, he wasn't allowed to ask for even a paise from anyone else. The man readily agreed to this, and there is a long story about the coincidences and happenings which made it possible for this man to raise the money in time. But that's a different story and we won't go into that now.

And the second condition was that this man had to prominently display a series of messages which Baba dictated, messages to the effect that "I am only here when your love brings Me here," "Rites, rituals, and ceremonies expose me to the cold winds of ignorance, it is only true love which clothes me." As I say, I forget them exactly, but there is a book, a magazine which had been put out which is dedicated just to the inauguration of this temple. Davana, could you go get me that special issue of the *Divya Vani* please? And this man agreed. He agreed to every condition Baba imposed.

So now that permission had been given, Baba took an interest in the project. As long as there was going to be a statue, He wanted it to be a good one, so the best sculptor in Bombay was contacted and he came to Poona when Baba was there.

Let's see, the temple was inaugurated in February of '63, so this must have been the summer months of '62 or possibly even earlier. And the sculptor came and Baba sat for hours while this man took careful measurements of Baba's head from every conceivable angle. You may be knowing the way they do that, they measure from here to there, and from there to here, very precise measurements, and it is necessary, after all. A bust is not a two-dimensional affair, and they wanted it to be perfect, so Baba sat there very patiently while all the measurements were being taken. And then they took a plaster cast of Baba's hands and feet, and eventually a life-size sculpture in bronze was finally completed of Baba sitting in a chair. There are photographs in the magazine, and you can pass it around later.

And then there began a long correspondence about how they were going to inaugurate the temple. Whether they should do Vedic rituals and of what sort and so on and how they should install the idol. Baba had me write back, and I said if they thought they were installing an idol there was no point to it, they didn't understand at all the proper perspective. I remember I wrote that Baba's form was itself the real Idol of God and no other idol could replace it. And there was lots of correspondence back and forth. It's all there, it's in the special issue. You may read it later if you like. But eventually it was all settled and the inauguration took place. It was a big affair. Adi went there, the Maharani of Baroda went, Bal Natu went, Baba sent many of His close ones to go and represent Him. Baba took this very seriously.

Ah, here it is. First, read out those eight messages because really, I tell you, they are good ones. Read it slowly, loudly. Do justice to the messages.

One. "Tear the curtain of set ceremonies and rituals and you will find that I am the Worshipped, the Worship, and the Worshipper."

Two. "To clothe simple Worship with the garments of ceremony and ritual is to expose Me to the cold winds of ignorance." You follow, to clothe simple worship with the garments of ceremony is to expose Him to the cold winds of ignorance. Good. And the next one.

"To faithfully love God-Man is to truly worship God."

"To find Me here in Mehersthan . . ." That's what the building was named. Not to be confused with Meherastana. That is in Hamirpur. This is Mehersthan. I'm sorry, read it out again.

"To find Me here in Mehersthan, search the depths of your heart." You see what Baba is saying. No matter where we search for Him, He is only to be found in the heart. But that is His game. Here you are, you have come halfway around the world to find Baba, and it is good that you have come, but what do you find, you find that Baba has been in your heart the whole time. All right, next?

"Mehersthan has been built for Me with love, but I may only be found here by My lover who brings Me here in his heart." How true, how true. Only when we bring Him with us in our heart do we find Him.

"As the heart is, so is the house; as the eye is, so is the Image within the house."

"The heart of man has always been the ancient temple for the worship of the Ancient One."

That's seven, and the last?

"Nothing can house the Ancient One that does not house love." Read that one again. "Nothing can house the Ancient One that does not house love." That is why Baba says it is the strangers in our heart that drive Him away, the strangers of lust, anger, and greed.

Anyway, those are the messages. You see how it is. This man's love for Baba was such that Baba permitted him to go ahead and build this temple. Despite the fact that time and time again Baba said He was against all this, that He had come to do away with all these rites and rituals, He allowed this man's love to express itself in this way. But at the same time, He added these messages to guide people to the truth behind the outward expression. So it is good that this man built the temple so that Baba had the excuse to give us these messages. And they are still there, they are prominently displayed on the walls of the temple. Because this man did learn his lesson and he obeyed Baba one-hundred percent. And because of his obedience and his love, we all today have been blessed by hearing Baba's messages read out.

RULES

YES, THERE ARE QUITE A LOT OF CHILDREN here right now. But this is nothing. Last summer I think we had forty children here at the same time. But why not? It is good for them to be exposed to a Baba atmosphere at such a young age. Of course you cannot be accommodated at the Pilgrim Center unless your child is at least seven, but that is a different matter.

Every now and then someone asks us about this, and there is

a reason for it. You people seem to think that we make up rules just to impose our will on you, but it is not that. Nobody likes rules, but they are necessary. If we all had common sense, if we had a certain amount of respect for each other, rules would not be necessary. But we find that we do not always use our common sense.

Let me give you an example. There was a family who loved Baba very much. And Baba would tell them time and time again to love Him more and more and still yet more. And He would tease the husband and wife about whether they loved Him or their partner the most. Baba would often do this with couples who were close to Him. I always say that Baba is a very jealous God. He always tries to see that He has first place in His lovers' hearts. Of course, this is for the lovers' own good, but that is a different story.

Baba would tell us that God alone is real, but that didn't mean that we were to totally ignore the world. Now, see what happens. The wife takes Baba's words very seriously and she tries to spend all her time thinking about Baba, remembering Him, praying to Him, in an attempt to love Him more and more. She spends more and more time each day in her prayer room, being with Baba.

When it is time for her children to go off to school, she is not there to see them off. She has no lunch prepared for her children or her husband when he goes to work. To make a long story short, she forgets her own family, you may say, in her remembrance of her Lord. And the next time when she came to Baba, He told her that her love for Him made Him very happy. And this woman was very happy herself to hear this, but then Baba added, "Your love for Me has made Me very happy, but your neglect of Me has made Me sad."

"What! How have I neglected you?" she asked, since she thought she was spending all of her time just thinking about Baba and loving Him. "I think of You all the time," she said. "Yes," Baba said, "but I am in your husband, I am in your children, and you are neglecting Baba in them."

You see, this woman was honestly doing her best to obey Baba, but she failed to use her common sense, to realize that it wouldn't please Baba if she concentrated on Him and completely neglected her family.

And because we don't use our common sense, rules eventually become necessary. Let me give you another example. In the early years, after Baba dropped His body and people started to come here, we had no rules. We thought, these people love Baba, they will know how to behave. But then we found people wearing outfits that shocked and outraged those living here. I don't mean the mandali – what do I care if you all come naked? – but Ahmednagar is a very conservative community. The people were not used to foreigners, to their ways, and they didn't understand that in your country you can dress and act that way and not mean anything by it.

Of course it is not your fault either. You weren't familiar with Indian customs, with Indian ways. You couldn't know that no respectable Indian woman would wear her long hair loose, it must always be braided or tied up in some fashion. You couldn't know this, so we found it necessary to advise you of our local customs. But now how can we meet every single person coming and take them aside and tell them this? In the first few years we could because there weren't that many coming here. It was possible for us to do this and we did it, we did it happily. But then the numbers became so great that we found someone might have been here for several days already before we spoke to them, so it seemed best to let people know when they came to the registration office.

But then we found some people would come here and wouldn't register right away. Or they would be traveling through India first and, without intending anything, they were upsetting the sensibilities of the populace. And they were wearing Baba badges, buttons, and this was giving Baba a bad name. So we had an information sheet printed and sent to the West so you would know our customs, our ways, before coming. These were not rules, this was friendly advice, because we knew people would have the common sense when they understood the situation not to do such things. But then we found that some people, not many, I am not suggesting that, but there are always a few who decide that such things do not apply to them, that Baba wants them to be natural and it is only natural for them to act in this way. And therefore, to avoid trouble for you, we turn such advice, such recommendations, into rules. And there was trouble in the early years; I am not just throwing out words.

Some of you were here back then, you can bear out what I am saying. But it is true. Things reached such a point that the children used to throw rocks at our Baba lovers when they walked through town. Sarosh had to intervene and talk to the Superintendent of Police to get some protection for the Baba people. You weren't all staying at the Pilgrim Center then, it didn't exist, and people used to stay in town on their own. And troubles did arise. Women were being subjected to abuse, to rude propositions when they walked to the bazaar, so eventually we made it a rule that women should not walk alone in town. Why? For your own protection. That is what I am trying to bring home to you. These rules have come about not because anyone likes making rules, but to make it easier for you come and not be harassed, to be able to come and just think about Baba. It is for your sake that these rules are there.

And it is the same with the rule about children, that they must be over seven. Because Baba Himself made this rule. Baba used to have large *darshan* programs and people would bring their children. It was only natural, whole families would come. You must have seen in the films, mothers putting their infants on Baba's feet. And you've heard the story about Baba's nazar. That beautiful explanation Baba gave was because a woman had brought her infant here to have Baba's *darshan*. But then, when planning the '69 program, Baba said people should not bring children under the age of seven. Why? Because it would be a distraction. It would be a distraction for the parents and it would be a distraction for others as well. Baba wanted people to concentrate just on Him.

Of course, some parents come and say they can't concentrate on being here because they are thinking all the time about their children back home. This is only natural. The same thing would happen time and again with Baba. People would come but their minds would be back home with their family, or with their business, or some worry they were having. But Baba didn't want that. He wanted people to leave everything behind and just think about Him when they had this precious opportunity to be with Him. Baba used to tell people, "Don't worry about your family, just think about Me and I will take care of your family for you."

And we have heard story after story from people who have experienced this. Of people who were experiencing so many problems at home when they left, but they gave them all to Baba and came here and returned home to find that Baba had taken care of everything better than they had been able.

Haven't I told you all the story about the time Baba called one of his lovers to be with Him? This man loved Baba but at the time he had so many business worries that he felt that he couldn't dare leave his business. And so he didn't come. When Baba saw him next, He asked why this man hadn't come when called, and the man explained. Baba said, "I am God. I manage the entire creation, and you don't think I could take care of your small business for a day or two while you are with Me?"

We have heard countless stories of people coming here without their mate, where the husband or wife had to stay behind, because there wasn't enough money, or someone had to take care of the children, and the one who was here would sometimes feel guilty, would feel sorry for the one who stayed behind and wasn't able to experience Baba's atmosphere here, and they would return only to find that the one who stayed behind had seen Baba, or felt His presence to a greater degree than the one who came.

But now please, for heaven's sake, don't go home and tell everyone that Eruch says we should forget about all of our responsibilities and come to India and just think about Baba. It is not that. But when you are here, you should try to concentrate on Baba. What good will it do you to worry about your family? Your worrying about them will not help them, on the contrary, not only will it not help your family, but it will prevent you from getting what you have come all this way to get, an intimate contact with your Beloved. Baba used to quote Hafiz, "If you want your Beloved to be present, do not absent yourself." Baba is always here, it is we who are absent ourselves. And worry is one of the main causes for us to absent ourselves. And whether we are worried about our children back home, or whether we are worried about the children we have brought with us, we are absenting ourselves from Baba's presence.

And because they might prove a distraction, Baba himself asked that children under seven not be brought. We did not make this a rule but, when asked, we would share with people Baba's wish. Still many people brought young children, and then what did we find? Time and again we found that the children got sick, they weren't used to the food, the climate; they would be covered with mosquito bites, they were unhappy, and they used to cry and beg to go back to America. That is why we made a rule for the Pilgrim Center for Westerners.

It is not that we are against children, or that all children are a distraction. Any child can be, but it is so much harder for the Western children. There is so much here that is hard for them to adjust to. They don't have the things they are used to, they don't have the games, the TV's, that goes without saying, but they can't even bathe every day, there are no hot showers, the food is so different, it is hard for them to sleep at night, and they come down with diarrhea, or fevers, or they are cranky and irritable. But the parents don't want to leave and they come and sit in Mandali Hall and there is nothing for the children to do but sit outside and be miserable, or run around and create a disturbance, because this is not a playground here. This is an old folks' home now.

We are all geriatric cases here. We have put up a swing and a what do you call it, a see-saw, but it takes more than that to keep active children happy. And even then, how many times has a child come in here in tears because they have hurt themselves. We cannot look after the children properly. We cannot even look after ourselves these days. Eventually, someone, out of the goodness of their heart, will take the children up the Hill, or play a game with them, but in the meantime there would be quite a distraction. And there would be many complaints from other pilgrims.

And Dr. Goher would be worried because she was the one seeing to these children, caring for their health. Although she is overbusy with the clinic and has no time for such things, still people would come to her. They could easily see a doctor in town, but they would come to her and say, "My child is sick, what should I do?" And you all know what a soft heart Goher has. She is already overburdened with work because she not only runs the clinic but manages the household, too. She has to see to so many things, she takes care of all the mandali, and believe me that is no easy task. We are all old and frail now. One of us can't eat this because it upsets his stomach, and another can't eat that because it makes him constipated, really, it is more like an old folks' home than an ashram, and poor Goher is old herself, yet she sees to all of us, she tends the household, she orders supplies, she sees what needs repairing and so on and so forth, and she also manages the clinic and she meets with the Baba lovers when they come, and on top of all this Baba lovers come and want her to treat them. For simple things, for an aspirin or a throat lozenge. All of this is available at the Pilgrim Center. But people tell us, "Goher treated Baba and so we want her to treat us, too." And it is true. Goher's treatment is different. The villagers say this, too. Not because she prescribed different medicine but because she treats all her patients with such love. But it is too much now. And that is why we say by all means meet Dr. Goher, sit with her, share her love for her Lord, Meher Baba, but do not go to her with your medical problems.

There are so many other doctors and nurses here, living here as residents, there are allopaths, homeopaths, chiropractors, doctors of all sorts who will be most happy to treat you. And they even have regular hours for appointments and in case of emergency you can call on them anytime. So where is the need to burden poor Goher further?

Of course, she would be furious with me if she knew I was saying this, but it is the truth. It is common sense after all. That is what I am saying. If we used our common sense, we wouldn't need rules.

We have nothing against children. On the contrary, we love children. Baba told us all we had to become childlike, not childish, but childlike. And Baba loved children, children and venerable old men with long beards.

And it is a delight when the children come. They have such innocence, such purity. And we learn quite a lot from them. I remember one day Mani was telling the story of Baba's niece, who had come and was asking Baba questions. She couldn't understand why, since Baba was God, He had allowed awful things like scorpions and snakes and lizards to be created. She had a real fear of such creatures, she could not tolerate their sight even, and so naturally when she asked Baba about the bad things in the world, this was the example she used. It was a child's example. Grownups ask why is there suffering, why is there disease, why are there wars, but this child wanted to know why Baba had permitted these noxious creatures.

Baba looked at her and commented on how pretty she was, and it was true, she was pretty. And then Baba went on, "And yet, each morning when you go to the toilet, don't you bring out filth from inside? You are beautiful, yet every day you produce such filth that you do not want to have anything to do with it. Isn't that so?" And the girl agreed. "It is the same with Me," Baba replied. "The creation has come out of Me, and though you see Me as beautiful and loving, there came out of Me some things which seem like filth to you, which you would like to avoid just as there is filth which comes out of you, although you are beautiful. And it is that filth coming out of you which keeps you beautiful and healthy."

And the girl was satisfied with this answer. It made sense to her, she could understand it and she was satisfied. Mani told that story in the hall one day, and as it so happened there was a young girl here with us at the time. So I was trying to think of what story I should tell for her. I knew she wouldn't be interested in discussions about free will, or planes of consciousness, and Mani's story reminded me of another one involving Baba's niece, and I thought this young girl, since she was about the same age as Baba's niece had been when she was here, might be interested. So I went on to relate how this niece looked at the photo of Baba and asked why in the photos there was often a sort of halo of light around Baba but in real life that halo didn't exist. And Baba replied, "With your eyes you are able to see the halo in the photo, but it takes another eye," and Baba pointed to His forehead, "to see the halo in real life. If you were to look at Me with that eye, you would see a halo around Me."

And no sooner had I finished this story than the girl spoke up and said, "But I see the halo." "Yes," I said, "you can see it in the photograph, but that's not really a halo." "No, no," the girl said, "whenever I go to the tomb I see the halo around Baba's marble slab." "You do?" I asked. For this was news to me. I have never seen such a halo. And so I asked her many questions, thinking this must be a child's imagination, but she was quite definite. I suggested it was the sunlight from the door, or she was merely seeing the light reflected in Baba's photograph behind the marble, but she was very definite, she told me where she stood and how the light was all around the slab and so on and so forth, and she was quite surprised because she assumed that everyone saw this light.

And this was a good lesson for me to not underestimate Baba. To not assume that just because I do not have a certain experience that Baba might not give it to someone else. It is impossible to limit Baba. And since then, we have heard many such stories, and it seems that Baba often appears to the youngsters in ways which are not given to us. You've heard about the two girls who used to have tea parties and Baba would attend. They would see Baba physically with them, playing with them. There have been so many stories like this, and it makes me understand a little of what Baba means when He says we should be childlike but not childish. In the innocence and purity of the youngster, they can see Baba in ways we do not.

But not all youngsters. Just the other day there was a youngster here who was sitting by my side. It seemed she wanted to ask me something but was too shy. When I turned to her and said, "Is there anything you want to ask?" she just looked down and shook her head, but I had the feeling that there was something on her mind. So when everyone went out for lunch I stayed behind and asked her again if there was something she wanted to ask, and she said, "Eruch, if God is everywhere, why can't we see Him?"

Now, what to say? This was a good question, and I hadn't given it any thought before then. What should I tell her? And she was very serious, I couldn't just say something lightly, she really wanted to know. So Baba came to my rescue and made me say, "It is because He is infinitely compassionate."

"What do you mean? How can you say He is compassionate when I want to see Baba and I don't see Him?"

I said, "Yes, that is true, but do you really want to see Him? When you really want to see Him, you will, but until then it would be an intrusion on His part. And because He is compassionate, He does not want to intrude on your privacy."

"Oh yes, I want to see Him more than anything else in the world," she replied. "How would it be an intrusion?"

"Well, just think," I said. "Think about all those times when perhaps you are doing something you really should not be doing. Let us say your parents have some toffees – do you like toffee?" and she said yes, so I said, "What if your parents had some in a jar and you are tempted to take one? What do you do? Do you take one when your parents are in the room?"

"Oh no," she said, "I wait until no one is around, when no one can see me, and then I take one."

"And what," I asked, "if just at that moment Baba were to appear, what then, how would you feel?"

"I would feel embarrassed," she said.

"That is what I mean," I replied. "You would feel uncomfortable, it would be an intrusion on Baba's part to interfere with your privacy at that moment. And throughout the day we are doing things and thinking things which we really would not feel comfortable doing in Baba's presence. I may be sitting here thinking how nice it would be to see Baba, I may be longing to see Him, but the very next moment some unworthy thought passes through my mind and if Baba were to appear just then I would feel very embarrassed. So, out of compassion, Baba restrains Himself. Actually He is most anxious to reveal Himself. He is more anxious to let you see Him than you are to see Him, but He restrains Himself out of compassion for you, and for all of us, because He knows we do not really want to see Him. Or rather we want to see Him, but only for a moment or two, we do not want to have Him before us each moment. So, until we are ready to really want His company, until we want to see Him more than we want to snitch that toffee, or indulge some unworthy thought, until then, in His infinite compassion, He withholds from us that sight."

This is what I told that little one. Whether it satisfied her or not I don't know. But afterwards I thought, that was a good figure Baba had given me. And that is what I mean when I say we learn so much from the children. I had never thought about this before, but because of that little one's question, Baba gave me this figure. Do you like it? What do you think?

◈ DESHMUKH

THE OTHER DAY I TOLD YOU MY STORY of coming to Baba, and you remember I said, "By Your grace anything is possible." I don't know what put those words into my head. As I told you, I was not a spiritual aspirant. It was not in my nature to run off and seek out every person reputed to have some spiritual status. I enjoyed the world too much for that. My preference was for sports, or going to the movies with friends, or having a feast. As I told you, from my earliest days, from my infancy I was a glutton.

But life in India was such that at our mother's knee we learned the stories of the saints. We heard spiritual stories, and it was ingrained in us that we should behave a certain way with our elders, with those in authority, and with those whom the world regarded as spiritual personalities. Perhaps this is why, when Baba asked if I could stay with Him permanently, I blurted out, "By Your grace anything is possible."

But over the years with Baba, one thing I learned is that by His grace anything is possible. With Baba we found that the possible became impossible, but the impossible became possible. I have already told you about the New Life, how we would ask complete strangers to buy train tickets for a party of twenty and, without hesitation, they would agree to it. Or we would ask someone to provide food for our party on the condition that they never come to visit or try to see the very people they were serving. And they would say yes.

For some, like Kaikobad, or Dr. Deshmukh, this was accepted as a matter of course. But they were not worldly persons. Even though Deshmukh had been to England and received his Ph.D., even though he was a professor at Nagpur and head of the department of philosophy, he was not worldly. He was very innocent, I should say.

You've heard of how Dr. Deshmukh came to Baba? He was in England at the time. He was studying. You know, he was a great philosopher, and he was in England for his postgraduate studies, for his Ph.D. And he saw an advertisement that said Shri Sadguru Meher Baba was coming and he thought, being a philosopher, that he would go, and he did and he saw Baba and he fell madly in love with Him.

Then he returned to India, to his home place, which was also my home. I was a student at the time. Deshmukh was a lecturer at Morris College, and I was attending the Science College. Now, at that time, there weren't very many Baba lovers. He must have written one of the mandali when he was in England, maybe Chanji, and was told that when he was in Nagpur he should go to Mary Lodge and the Jessawala family would tell him more about Baba. So Deshmukh came and met my mother, and he told her about the planes, you know how philosophers are, how he had seen Baba in the subtle sphere and the mental sphere and whatnot; I don't know what it all means. And then my mother told him about her times with Baba, and it was a good day for both of them.

But then, as Deshmukh is sitting there, he glances up and he sees this photograph of Baba. Just like the one that's over there on the wall near Baba's chair, with Baba sitting and the kerchief tied around His head. And Deshmukh sits and looks at it, and looks at it, for that was his way, he would lose himself looking at Baba, and he said, "I like that picture very much. Do you have a copy of it?" My mother said no. There were very few photographs of Baba in those years, '31, '32. "But you can take it to a photographer and they can make a copy for you." Just then I returned from school and my mother said, "Eruch, get that picture." So I stood up and got the picture down, and my mother said, "This is Dr. Deshmukh," and I folded my hands and greeted him, and then she told me to give the picture to Dr. Deshmukh, who was very happy. He promised to get a copy made and return it as soon as possible, and then he went away.

A day or two passed, and my mother got a telegram from Baba which said, "Why have you driven Me out of our house?" Now, my mother couldn't understand this. "Driven Him out of our house? What have I done?" And she was very upset thinking she must have done something terrible, but she couldn't figure out what it was. For several days she was upset and depressed at this cable. Why did Baba say that? "How have I driven him out?" But then one day she was sitting in the sitting room – it was a large room, bigger than this room – and she noticed a gap on the wall and she thought, "Something used to be there. What was it?" And then she remembered the photograph, and she thought, "Perhaps this is what Baba means." So when I came home from school she said to me, "Eruch, go see Dr. Deshmukh and ask him for our photograph of Baba back. Whether he has made a copy or not, please get the photograph and bring it back."

So I did. In the meantime Deshmukh had made a copy and he very lovingly returned the photo, and I gave it to my mother, who put it back on the wall. She still has it. Ever since then she kept the photograph, and it hangs now in her little sleeping cubicle at Bindra House.

One day when Baba came to Bindra House – for that was His custom, He used to visit there whenever He felt like it, – He looked at this photograph and then turned to my mother and said, "Come on, let's do *arti*." And they all did *arti* to the photograph and when they were finished, Baba then took *darshan* of the photograph, bowing to His own feet. Baba said, "I really like this photograph. In this photograph I am depicted as I really am." And then of course, my mother told Baba the whole story about Deshmukh and the cable.

You know, it was thanks to Deshmukh that we have the

original *Discourses*. He was the one who compiled them. He was a great philosopher, but he was also most innocent and simple when it came to Baba. During his lectures at the university, his students used to find that he would stop periodically and gaze at a book which he kept with him. Naturally the students began to wonder, what is this? Who is he looking at so intently? And so one of them managed to sneak down and station himself behind Deshmukh. The next time he stopped and opened the book and looked at it, the student sneaked up and looked over his shoulder, and what did he see? He saw there was a photograph in the book, a photograph of a beautiful face with long flowing hair, so he reported to all that their professor had a girlfriend. Of course, it was really a photo of Baba, but the students didn't know that.

Once one of his former students came here. He was a retired district judge and he came here and told us this story. He said that Deshmukh used to sometimes take his class for walks. And while they were walking he would discourse on philosophy. Now this day they were walking across the fields and came to a small farmhouse with dung patties smeared on the wall. Have you seen this? Here the women collect the dung and they pat it into a big circle, and then they stick it on the side of a wall to dry. When it's nice and dry they use it for fuel. Anyway, this is a common sight in India, and all know it. But Deshmukh stopped and stared at this farmhouse, lost in deep thought.

The boys looked, but they couldn't see anything there to prompt such speculation, so they all stood and waited to hear what profound philosophical idea had occurred to their professor. After a while, Deshmukh returned from his reverie and turned to the boys and said, "I wonder how the cow could have dropped his flops on the wall like that?" This was the sort of person Deshmukh was. Although he lived in the world, he not only was not of it, he didn't even seem aware of most of it.

So one day Baba decided to have a little fun with Deshmukh.

Deshmukh didn't live with us, but he would come every chance he got during his school holidays. And this time, when he was coming it happened to be April Fool's Day, so Baba, on His own, decided to play a joke on Deshmukh. Somebody had given Baba a big basket of fruit or something, all nicely wrapped up and tied with a ribbon. So Baba asked me to fetch the basket and the wrapping paper and the ribbon and everything, but, instead of fruit, he had me get a large stone and put that inside, and then wrap it up so it looked like some very fancy gift.

Baba told us, "When Deshmukh comes, we'll give him this present." And we all thought this was a good idea. It seemed like it would be a funny joke, and we anxiously looked forward to his coming. That was how we got our entertainment. We didn't watch TV or videos the way you do. We don't go to movies or have readymade games to play with, so we used to entertain ourselves with such innocent mischief. For example, let us say that I know Aloba feels very strongly about Iran; I might let slip some little comment about Iran in his presence. You know Aloba's nature. He will flare up, "What's this you say! What's this about Iran?" and this would be our amusement.

So Deshmukh comes and he very reverentially greets Baba, bows to Baba, and then sits at His feet. Baba then makes a big show of presenting Deshmukh with the present, and with great reverence Deshmukh receives it, places it at his side, and then sits there gazing at Baba with adoration. Baba gestures, "Aren't you going to open it?" "There's plenty of time for that, Baba, after you've gone to the women's side," Deshmukh replied and just sat there staring at Baba. You see, all those months that he had been away he longed to be with Baba, and now that at last his opportunity had come, he didn't want to waste a second of it by looking at anything except for Baba's face.

Now Baba doesn't know what to do. He is God, He is omniscient, but He doesn't know how to play His joke on Deshmukh. If

Deshmukh waits till Baba leaves and the mandali disperse, where will the fun be? Baba doesn't want that. So He gives me a look and makes a little gesture to me, so I start needling Deshmukh.

"Doctor," I say, "is this the way you honor Baba's gift, by ignoring it completely?"

"I am not ignoring it," Deshmukh insists, "but why pay attention to the gift when the Giver is here before me?"

Now the other mandali were also anxious to see Deshmukh open it, so they also start pressing him to open it. But even though they plead with him to open it then and there, he is adamant about waiting. Someone says, "Doctor, don't you want to see what it is?"

And Deshmukh says, "The mere fact that my Beloved has remembered me is something most precious. It doesn't matter what the gift is."

So I see my chance here and I say, "You're saying you don't care that Baba went to so much trouble to choose something specially for you? What kind of rudeness is this? Is this the way to honor your Beloved by being so indifferent to His gifts?" and so on and so forth. The whole time, mind you, Baba is secretly urging me on, gesturing that I should give him another little prick and another until finally Deshmukh relents, and to everyone's relief, including Baba's, Deshmukh opens the package. We all stand around, waiting expectantly for the moment when he will discover it's a rock and we can all laugh. Baba's eyes are twinkling in anticipation. But even here Deshmukh keeps us waiting because he unwraps the package so slowly, admiring the ribbon, admiring the wrapping, and then he can't seem to get it unwrapped. He's fiddling with the paper and fooling with it, but he's not making any progress at all, so in desperation Baba signals me to help, so I just go over and rip all the paper apart and then at last Deshmukh reaches in and pulls out the rock.

But what does he do? He bows to Baba and we can see that tears of happiness are starting to stream down his face as he exclaims, "Baba, thank you, it is the perfect present."

We are all wonder-struck. What kind of man is this? He gets a rock and he says it's a perfect present. So one of the mandali says, "Doctor, it looks like you've just been given a rock."

"Yes," Deshmukh agrees, "but just think, if I had been given anything else, eventually it would have been used up, or decayed, or fallen to dust, but this, this is an eternal present. Baba has given me something which I can always keep, and this will be my most precious treasure from now on," and with that Deshmukh puts it on his head and starts dancing about in ecstasy.

What can we say to this? Baba just wanted to have a laugh at Deshmukh's expense, but his love was so great that the laugh was on us.

And yet Deshmukh did have a weakness. He was very tight with his money. There was no question about his love for Baba, but for some reason he couldn't bear to part with his money. Deshmukh came from Nagpur, and Nagpur is famous for its oranges, at least in those days it was. But when Deshmukh would come he would bring as a present for Baba the smallest, hardest oranges you've ever seen. He would go to the market and he would pick the best oranges and ask how much. And let us say they would say six rupees for a bushel. Then Deshmukh would hesitate and say, "So much? Can't you give me something cheaper? And they would point to some oranges which weren't so big and weren't so juicy, and they would ask only five rupees for those, but still Deshmukh would hesitate and he would haggle and bargain until he got oranges that were oranges in name only.

And Baba would enjoy this eccentricity of Deshmukh's and would always make a big show of the gift and wonder aloud about how much this must have cost Deshmukh and how great his love was that he would be willing to spend such a sum.

It was a joke we all enjoyed, but Deshmukh never seemed to realize what was going on. I remember one time Baba was giving *darshan*, and He hadn't visited Nagpur in quite some time, so the Nagpur lovers were requesting Baba to come and bless them with

His presence. If I remember correctly, Baba had agreed to visit Delhi, and now His Nagpur lovers were asking Him to extend His itinerary and visit Nagpur. With a smile Baba agreed, saying, "I will come, but only on condition that Deshmukh agrees to pay the fares for Me and the mandali from Delhi to Nagpur."

Deshmukh was taken aback. "Baba, what will my wife say?" he stammered. "I will have to check with her." And he began to make one excuse after another. Meanwhile the other Nagpur lovers are screaming at Deshmukh, "Just say yes, we will pay for the trip, don't worry, it won't cost you a cent, just say yes," but Deshmukh was so panicked at the thought that he refused to commit himself, and so Baba's visit to Nagpur was postponed.

Of course, this was what Baba wanted in the first place, but this way we all had a good laugh about it. But really, Deshmukh's love for Baba was marvelous. It may seem like we're having fun at his expense, but it is not that. He was a character and we enjoyed his eccentricities, Baba enjoyed them, but that had nothing to do with his great love for Baba. And that's what really counts and that's how he endeared himself to Baba.

You know, there were many characters amongst the mandali, and I am including myself foremost in this category, and sometimes we would get annoyed with one another. Sometimes there were even those with us who did not seem completely scrupulous. In fact, a few who were with Baba for a while were finally asked by Baba to leave. Yet even then, in a few cases, Baba would remind us of the work they had done for Him. I remember a meeting Baba held at Meherabad. I think this was just before the New Life, and Baba on His own brought up two of the men who were living with us. Baba said, "I know if you," meaning the mandali, "had your way, you would drive these two out, but none of you knows the work they have done for me that only they could do."

And it's true. We cannot judge another's love for Baba or have any idea how Baba might be making use of that person's weakness for His cause. This is slightly off the subject, but speaking about Nagpur and about being unable to judge another reminds me about a Baba lover, from Nagpur. At least this fellow proclaimed himself a Baba lover, although all of us who knew him felt this was stretching the truth a bit, for he was a rascal, a scoundrel, I should say. Whenever he was home he never seemed to think about Baba at all. In short, he seemed to do only those things which he would hesitate to do in Baba's presence, to say only those things which he would hesitate to say in Baba's presence, and we suspected he thought only those things which he would hesitate to think in Baba's presence. But whenever he came to see Baba, he put on very pious airs and tried to pass himself off as a great lover of the Lord.

Now, I knew all this. I would hear stories about this man from people I knew. He was from our hometown after all, and I had even had some direct experience with him, so I wasn't taken in, but it seemed that Baba was. Whenever he came, Baba would make a big deal of it. He would praise this man to our face, hold him up as an example of what His lovers should be like, and He would always have this man sit at His feet and would pat him on the back and stroke his chin and act as if this man was most precious to Him.

Finally one day I couldn't take it. You all know I have a temper, and after the man left, I just blurted out to Baba that this man was a hypocrite, that Baba shouldn't be taken in by his pious manner, that I knew this man well and I knew he was a scoundrel.

Baba instantly turned to me and I could see that He was very displeased at what I had said. "It seems you know more than I know!" Baba gestured, and then with great authority added, "You don't know the man at all." Baba then held His hand in front of the wall so that a shadow was cast and asked me, "What do you see?"

I said, "I see the shadow of Your hand on the wall."

Baba continued, "That's all you see, you just see the shadow of the man, but I see directly into his heart, and I tell you he is a great lover of mine."

What could I say? I realized it was true. That I didn't know this man, that I couldn't presume to know this man the way Baba knew him and so I kept quiet. And over the years this man changed. Until, just judging from his behavior, anyone would look at him and say, yes, he really does love Baba very much. But I have never forgotten the lesson Baba taught me that day, not to judge anyone, because we can't see their heart. Only Baba knows the true value of a person.

◬ E I N S T E I N

DID BABA EVER MEET EINSTEIN? No, not to my knowledge. Somehow the rumor has gotten around that Baba did meet Einstein but, as far as I know, from my own experience, this is not so. But Einstein's daughter did meet Baba, and perhaps that is what people are thinking about. Would you like to hear about that?

Baba was meeting with the public at a hotel in New York. I was not with Baba at the time, but I heard this from those who were with Baba. I think it was Norina or Elizabeth who first told us this story, I am not sure which, but I remember the story itself.

It seems Baba had finished meeting with people and now there were no other people left for personal interviews, but Baba asked Elizabeth or Norina to go check in the lobby and make sure that there were no others left waiting to see Him. She went and looked and there was no one there. So she reported this to Baba, but Baba said, "Look again, make sure." So she went again, and again there was no one there. Why should there be? Baba must have given the timings for the program, and it was past time now and all knew that and they had left, but Baba sent her three times to check to make sure that no one was waiting for Him.

So she thought, "Baba must be expecting someone." So the third time when she went to the lobby and there was no one there, she had the prompting to go to the door of the hotel itself and look out and, sure enough, there is a woman looking up uncertainly and then looking down at a scrap of paper in her hand as if to ascertain whether this was the right address or not. Seeing this, she thinks this may be the one Baba is waiting for and she says, "May I help you? Did you come here to see Meher Baba?" And the woman replies yes.

"Come in, Baba is waiting for you," and she ushers this woman into Baba's presence. And it turns out that this is Einstein's daughter. Baba met with her, and at the end of the meeting Baba asked one of His mandali to give her some of His books. She was given quite a stack of books to take with her.

Of course we have no way of knowing, but from that we may assume that she talked to her father, perhaps she even shared the books with him, so maybe Einstein read Baba's books, but as far as I knew he never met Baba. But Baba would refer to him now and then. He would make the gesture for large head, great intellect, very brainy, and whenever He wanted to give an example of such an intellect He would say, "Einstein," because he had that reputation, as being the smartest man, the greatest intellect on earth, so Baba would use the name when He wanted to indicate something about great intellects.

But I remember another occasion when Einstein was mentioned in Baba's presence. And it led to a very nice discourse Baba gave. I remember it very well. I was reading the paper to Baba. You know how I used to read it. I would read out the headlines, one after the other, until I got to one that seemed to interest Baba, and then He would gesture, "Read on," and I would read the first few lines of the story and usually Baba would say, "Okay, enough, go on with the rest," and I would then go back to just reading out the headlines. But every now and then Baba would get interested and would want me to read more, and one story I read in its entirety had to do with Einstein.

I was reading the paper one day to Baba and this one headline said, "Einstein takes a vacation." And this intrigued Baba, so He gestured to read on and I did. It seems one day Einstein went to the ocean with his grandchildren. And they played on the sand and had a good time, and at the end of the day the children called to Einstein to come and watch the sun set with them. So Einstein went and admired the sunset.

And that was the story. It was just a little filler, you may say. The idea of Einstein, this great intellect, playing on the beach with his grandchildren struck someone as amusing and they wrote the article. But when I finished Baba looked at me and gestured. "What do you think? Einstein knows very well that the sun does not rise and set. This is merely an illusion caused by the earth's rotation around the sun. He knows this, yet still he can admire the 'sunset' with his grandchildren. He does not try to explain to them about astronomy and physics. He plays with them and joins in the game and admires the sunset just as they do.

"It is the same with the Avatar," Baba continued. "Whenever I come, I come down to your level. I am omniscient, but I come down to the level of humanity, and on your level I admire the creation, although I know fully well that it is just illusion."

So those are the only two incidents I know of which connect Baba with Einstein. But I often think of the figure Baba gave, that just as the great intellect can play with his grandchildren on the beach, so too the Avatar, the one who knows all, comes down to our level. And, speaking of sunsets, this reminds me of another figure Baba gave one time when I was walking with Him. It was noon and we were walking and it was very hot and Baba gestured like this, "Do you feel the heat? It is very hot, isn't it?" And I said, "Yes, Baba. I feel it."

Then Baba suddenly asked me, "Which is more glorious, the sunrise or the sunset?" And I said, "The sunset, Baba." Baba said, "Yes, it is so." Then He asked, "Do people ever come out to admire the sun when it is at its zenith?" I said, "No, Baba." Baba said, "People do not even see the sun then, they are not aware of it. They feel the heat, but they do not even look at the sun. It is only at sunrise and sunset that people glorify the sun." And then He continued and said, "It is the same with My advent. When I am about to come, there is great anticipation. It is the sunrise. But then, when I come, now that I am in your midst, it is like the midday sun. But when I drop My body, that will be the glorious sunset and then all the world will become aware of My advent."

That is what Baba told me.

◈ G I N D E

BABA HAS HIS OWN WAY OF DRAWING HIS LOVED ONES. Doctors are a prime example. And Dr. Ginde, you may say, is a glaring example of this. Baba was suffering from excruciating pain in His face. He had what is called trigeminal neuralgia. Our Feramji who just died this last June, also suffered from it and the pain was so bad that he used to come out of his room and bang his head against the pillars of the verandah to get some relief. Baba hadn't been able to eat for several days because of the pain, and naturally we were all worried about Baba's condition. Nariman was living in Bombay then and he contacted Dr. Ram Ginde.

Dr. Ginde was the top neurologist in the country at the time, a renowned doctor, and Nariman went to Beach Candy Hospital to see if Dr. Ginde would travel to Ahmednagar to examine Baba, because he knew that Baba would not come to Bombay to be treated. In a way, it was a preposterous request to expect such a big person who was so famous and so busy to go all the way to Ahmednagar, but, of course, where Baba was concerned, no task was too imposing for Nariman to take on.

How can I explain this to you all? It wasn't that we weren't aware of how preposterous some of the things we asked people to do were – we were intelligent people, Nariman was a man of the world, he knew very well how important people had to be handled – but there was an air of freedom around Baba. Baba was the Emperor, the whole world was His, everyone in it was merely one of His vassals, so what did it matter to us if the world thought this one was great or that one was a VIP, or this one was a Maharaja – it was all the same to us. We were in the world but we truly were not of it. We were free men who had chosen to become His slaves, and by becoming His slaves, we became totally free from bondage to the values of worldly people. So Nariman didn't hesitate for a second to go and ask this famous neurosurgeon to see Baba.

I remember Nariman telling us about it later. It was amusing the way he described it. Instead of having an interview with Dr. Ginde in his office as he expected, he found that Dr. Ginde was too busy for that. Nariman ended up following Ginde around the hospital as he made his rounds, talking to him in between patients. Dr. Ginde was very abrupt, almost rude, but it was just that he didn't have time for the social niceties. So Nariman followed Dr. Ginde around and explained the situation, and Ginde agreed to come. Dr. Ginde had never met Baba before and, of course, at first wanted Baba to come to Bombay, but Nariman told Ginde that Baba couldn't come to Bombay and that Ginde would have to go to Ahmednagar. "How?" Ginde asked. Nariman said that he would arrange a car and driver to be put at Ginde's disposal, and eventually Ginde agreed.

A certain date had been set up, and on that day the car containing Dr. Ginde arrived at Meherazad and I went to receive him. As soon as he got out of the car he said to me, very curtly, "Do you have anyplace to piddle?" "What?" I was a little taken aback. And the question surprised me because we used to piddle wherever we wanted to in those days. We didn't have the latrines you see now. There were just a few buildings here, and we were completely surrounded by fields, so whenever we had to ease our bladders we would just wander into one of the fields and go. So I told Dr. Ginde, "Yes, just this field."

Ginde walked off into the field where Falu's rose garden is now, and I showed him the water tap and the soap and he said to me, "Do you know how to wash your hands?" I don't remember what I said to that, but he went on, "Most people don't have any idea how to use soap properly to wash their hands. You don't just rub some on and then immediately wash it off." And the whole time he's talking he's rubbing his hands with the soap, making a rich lather. And he gave me a lecture on the proper way to wash your hands. I don't remember it now, but it had something to with working up a good lather and letting the soap bubbles stay on your hands for a while so that a catalytic agent had time to work, and it was the reaction caused by this agent which actually got the hands clean.

I don't remember exactly what he said, but I'll never forget the way he immediately started lecturing me on the proper way to wash your hands. He was like an army general ordering his troops about, showing them how to do this or do that. After coming into Baba's contact he was a completely different person, but this was how he was with us in the beginning. Very abrupt, very curt. In the meantime, Dr. Goher had come to tell Dr. Ginde that he could see Baba.

So Dr. Goher led him to Baba's room, and Ginde began his examination and he quickly diagnosed the problem as trigeminal neuralgia.

"I can give you some medicine for the pain, but there's nothing else I can do," Ginde said.

"There's no cure?" Baba asked.

"Yes, there is a cure, but it is worse than the disease."

"What's the cure?" Baba asked.

"I can give you an injection which will relieve the pain in an instant, but I don't recommend it."

As soon as Baba heard that, He wanted the injection given, saying that the pain was unbearable, but Ginde kept insisting that he couldn't recommend it. I remember Ginde said at one point, "If my own father were suffering the way you are, I would not recommend that he have the operation."

But Baba wouldn't be put off, so finally Ginde said, "Well, if you want it done, you will have to go to the hospital."

"Hospital?" Baba made a frown to show that he didn't like the idea. "Why not do it here?"

"But Baba," Dr. Ginde said, "it is a delicate operation. It has to be done in a hospital."

"Do it here," Baba gestured.

"Baba, that's impossible. First of all, the room must be completely antiseptic and . . ."

Baba turned to Dr. Goher, "Can't you make the room antiseptic?"

"Yes, Baba. We can do that, and in the meantime Dr. Ginde can have some breakfast. By the time he's finished, we'll have everything ready here."

"No, no, it's not possible. It's a very delicate, intricate, and sensitive operation. You need a special screen to make the proper measurements." And Ginde explained that you had to insert a needle into the brain through the temple. You had to make the most exact measurements so you would know where to inject the needle and how deep to position it so that it would be situated at the very end of the trigeminal nerve. Then you released a drop of alcohol on the nerve end and it deadened the nerve so that there would be no more pain.

"Do it," Baba gestured.

"But Baba, even if I could do it here, which I can't, I don't recommend it. The pain will stop but that whole side of Your face will be permanently desensitized, numb. You won't be able to feel any normal sensations like heat or cold. Better to live with the pain, which is only periodic, than the loss of sensation, which will be permanent. You will have no feeling on that half of Your face" – I think it was the right side of Baba's face – "You won't feel Your tears, Your saliva will dribble, Your eye will droop. Better to live with the pain, which is intermittent. I will prescribe some medicine to make it more tolerable." You see, already Dr. Ginde had developed some feeling for Baba. He didn't want to see Baba looking that way. That's why he had pleaded with Baba that even if it were his own father, he wouldn't want that.

But Baba was adamant. "No, I want you to do the operation," Baba indicated. "I will take full responsibility for it."

"But Baba, without a screen it is not possible to measure accurately. There is no way of knowing whether the needle is in the right position."

"I have been hearing," Baba gestured "that you are the top neurosurgeon in the country, and you can't do the measurements properly without a screen?"

"It has to be exact, Baba. You don't want to deaden the wrong nerve."

"But surely, with your experience, you would be able to make the measurements."

You see how the conversation turned. Baba started playing on Dr. Ginde's pride. Buttering him up, as it were, emphasizing how skillful he was reputed to be. And though Baba was supposed to be the patient, see how He is the one who leads the doctor in the conversation. Baba conducts it all.

Dr. Ginde admitted that he could do the measurements without the screen. "But how is it possible for me to do the operation here? You will have to be anesthetized."

"Why?"

"Baba, You must not move. This is a very delicate operation. The slightest movement of Your head could result in my hitting the wrong nerve."

"I will sit very still. I won't move."

"But I have to inject the needle to just the right depth and then release one drop of alcohol. How will I know if I have found the right spot, how will I know whether the pain has subsided? You don't even speak."

"I'll raise my finger."

"How?" Ginde demanded, and Baba gestured, "I'll do this," and showed him how He would raise His finger without moving His head at all.

"But will you be able to bear the pain without moving at all?"

"I will bear it."

"Your head mustn't shake at all."

"I won't shake."

And Baba indicated this with such calm authority that Dr. Ginde believed it and eventually was persuaded that he could do the operation here.

He went and had breakfast, which the women sent over while Dr. Goher supervised the cleaning of Baba's room. She turned it into an operating theater. And when it was ready Dr. Ginde came back inside and began taking the most precise measurements of Baba's head and forehead. He spent a long time with calipers measuring from every angle. Finally he was ready, and he inserted a large needle into Baba's head, here, at the temple. You could hear the needle as it pierced Baba's skull – you may call it a long, thin nail, not even a needle. As I recall, there was another needle inside this, with a drop of absolute alcohol. Dr. Ginde inserted this into the hole made by the larger needle.

"The instant you feel relief, raise Your finger," Dr. Ginde instructed Baba. Baba sat absolutely motionless. And when Dr. Ginde found the right spot and released the alcohol, without moving at all, Baba just raised His finger, like this.

Dr. Ginde withdrew the needle and then applied a dressing to the temple. Baba was very happy because the pain was completely gone, and Dr. Ginde was also very happy and very proud because, really speaking, the operation should not have been done like that and it required great skill on Dr. Ginde's part to be able to do it.

Ginde asked Baba to walk. He wanted to see if Baba's balance had been affected, but I still remember the sight because Baba took Ginde's hand, and the two of them, hand in hand strolled up and down the room. Baba turned to Dr. Goher and gestured that they should give Ginde some food. "Bring some rice and dal for him," Baba ordered, and when the food came, Baba fed the first morsel to Dr. Ginde Himself.

Ginde said, "But Baba, You have not eaten for some days, it is better if You have some food and Ginde tried to persuade Baba to eat.

"I am very happy," Baba declared.

"But I am not," Ginde answered.

"Why not?"

"It's not good, Baba. You should not have done it." He was glad the pain was gone, but he was unhappy that one side of Baba's face would now be permanently without feeling or sensation.

But, as usual, Ginde was in a hurry, so he wanted to leave right away now that the operation was over. And only a minute or two after, the car drove off. It was just at the end of the driveway, or the top of the hill, you may say, when the pain returned. Baba told us to immediately call Adi on the phone in Ahmednagar and tell him to stop Dr. Ginde's car and tell Dr. Ginde the news that the pain had returned. So we did. We didn't have a phone here, but we cycled down to the pumping station and called Adi and told him to stop the car when it came through town. So Adi did.

"What is it?" Ginde asked.

"I just received a phone call," Adi said, "that the pain has returned. What should we do now?"

Ginde replied, "Tell Baba that I am very happy to hear that the pain has returned."

And this was how Dr. Ginde was caught. It seems as if Baba suffered this excruciating neuralgic pain only to have the excuse to call Dr. Ginde to Him. And after the contact was made, which was the important thing, the pain came back and Baba's face was not affected. And Baba stopped complaining about the pain as well.

In subsequent years, Dr. Ginde saw Baba many times, but not as a doctor, and grew to love Him very deeply. You know that at the very end, on the 31st of January, Dr. Ginde was the last person Baba remembered. He had called Dr. Ginde and given instructions that he should come to Him at Meherazad before noon on the 31st, and throughout that morning Baba would inquire whether Dr. Ginde had arrived yet. Finally, just before noon, Baba told us to call Adi and leave word that as soon as Dr. Ginde arrived, he should be brought to Meherazad at once, without any tea or refreshment first.

And Ginde arrived just after Baba dropped His body. But you know that story, don't you, you know why Ginde was late? As I've told you, he was a very busy man. He was always in a hurry, so when he would come to visit Baba, he would drive from Bombay, spend a few hours with Baba, and then rush back to Bombay. But the whole way here, he would be instructing his driver to go faster. "Can't you go faster, why are you taking so long, don't dawdle." And he would instruct the driver to pass cars without regard for whether the road conditions permitted it or not. It used to terrify his wife, and she complained to Baba. "How often have I been telling him not to back-seat drive, but he doesn't listen to me. But if You were to tell him, Baba, he will listen to You."

Baba agreed and told Dr. Ginde that from then on he was not allowed to say anything to his driver. He had to let his driver drive at his own speed and not insist that he try to pass every vehicle on the road. Dr. Ginde didn't like it, but his love for Baba was such that he obeyed. But now see the situation. He had been called to Meherazad on the 31st by Baba, and Baba had emphasized that he must be there by twelve noon at the latest. So Dr. Ginde had left early that morning, in plenty of time. But for some reason, his driver went even slower than usual. Of course, Dr. Ginde didn't know just how critical Baba's condition was, but he was beside himself, and yet he couldn't say a word to his driver. And then, to make matters worse, the driver suddenly pulls over to the side of the road and gets out of the car. Dr. Ginde thought the driver had to piddle or something, but the driver just stood there for quite a while, resting, and Dr. Ginde, bound by his obedience to His lord, had to remain silent. And it was because of that that he was late. He arrived at Adi's office just in time to hear that Baba had dropped His body. The shock was so great that he had a heart attack right there in Adi's office.

But after only a minute he and Adi drove to Meherazad and he was able to pay his last respects to Baba. "Where were you?" we asked. "Baba wanted you here by twelve, Baba kept asking for you." And poor Ginde, it wasn't his fault that he was late, but how he must have felt it. I told you, the shock was so great that he had a heart attack as soon as he arrived and heard the news.

But then he stayed and was with us while Baba's body was lying in the crypt at Meherabad. It was Dr. Ginde who kept urging us to inter Baba's body. We hadn't planned to keep Baba's body for seven days in the *Samadhi*. We had no such plans at all. We weren't able to think ahead that way. We simply were following Baba's orders. We took Baba's body to the crypt at Meherabad because He had told us all many times how important it was that His body be placed there after He dropped it. And we played "Begin the Beguine" because Baba had told us to do that as well. But we had no idea so many of Baba's lovers would come to pay their last respects to Him. To have one last glimpse of His face. And with so many lovers coming, and from distant lands, how could we deprive them of this last *darshan*? We couldn't, so we got blocks of ice and kept Baba's body surrounded by ice blocks.

Even so, Dr. Ginde was upset. "Eruch," he would tell me, "Baba is God, but His body is human. It will decompose just like any other body; you must inter it." You see, Ginde was afraid that Baba's body would swell up and burst. "You can't keep His body indefinitely. This is a desert climate, you must inter it as soon as possible."

And we said we would as soon as there was the first indication that Baba's body was starting to deteriorate, but the days passed and we still hadn't interred the body and Dr. Ginde couldn't take it anymore, he decided to go back to Bombay. But before he went, he asked Don Stevens, who was there, to come and see him in Bombay on his way back to the States to tell him exactly what occurred during the next few days.

And you know, Baba's body stayed fresh the entire seven days. But after a week it was decided that the time had come to inter Baba's body and so, on February 7th, on His birthday by the Zoroastrian calendar, the ice was removed and Baba's body was covered up. A wooden coffin had been made with a lid and earth was put on top of that and then a cloth was placed at the top. The marble slab wasn't installed until sometime later.

Don Stevens left and went back to America. But he remembered Dr. Ginde's request and so he went to visit him. He went to Dr. Ginde's apartment and opened his arms to hug Dr. Ginde when, to his utter astonishment and surprise, Dr. Ginde bent down and lowered his head on Don's shoes. Don didn't know what to say, he was so taken aback at this. Here was this man, this famous doctor, falling at his feet and wiping the dust off Don's shoes and placing it on his head. "You've just returned from Meherabad," Dr. Ginde explained, "so the dust on your shoes is sacred."

That is the degree to which this famous neurosurgeon came to love Meher Baba as the Lord. Dr. Ram Ginde, truly a great lover.

And to net this lover, Baba used the excuse of trigeminal neuralgia. At one time or another, I think every part of Baba's body suffered from some sort of ailment. And in each a different specialist would be sought out, and whosoever came to see Baba, they ended up by surrendering to His love. The Avatar suffers, but through that suffering His lovers are drawn to Him. And through our suffering for Him, not for ourselves, our love for Him is increased. And the more we love Him, the more we feel we don't love Him and the more we suffer for Him, until that love and that suffering reaches such a height that the Beloved falls in love with His lover and the game is over. The Beloved becomes the lover and the lover becomes the Beloved. That is called realization.

🜲 GUSTADJI

REALLY SPEAKING, YOU ARE BOTH RIGHT. Your father is right when he says we simply have to love Him and you are right when you say we have to obey Him. Obedience is very important. Meher Baba put great emphasis on it. But what will you obey? First and foremost, Baba left us with one standing order—to love Him as He should be loved. So your father is right. But who of us can obey that? So, failing to obey Him in that, there is a second course open to us, and that is to obey Him in lesser things. And that's where the type of obedience that you're talking about comes in.

It is the same with the breaking of His silence. Remember our discussion yesterday? Those who say Baba's breaking of His silence will be a dramatic event like the bursting of a thousand atom bombs are right, because Baba said that. But Baba also said that His voice speaking in our hearts is the breaking of His silence, so that must also be right. Baba has said both, so they must both be right. I tell you brother, over and over again I tell you, whatever it is, it is true, it is part of the truth, but it is not the whole truth.

And that's the way this world is, everything you see or experience is part of illusion. Now, illusion means what? Illusion means it's in the realm of duality. So no matter what you say, the opposite will also be there. If you have hot, you also have to have cold. It cannot be helped, there is no way out of it, because that's the nature of duality, of illusion. But the truth, the whole truth, is beyond duality. And that is why Baba stressed love. Because love is the experience of unity in the midst of duality. Do you know that quote of Muhammad's I like to say, are you familiar with it? "Harmony is the imprint of oneness upon multiplicity." Baba once said we should strive for union or real harmony, which is union in diversity.

As long as we try to understand things with our minds, we are dealing in the realm of duality. But when the heart experiences love, we get a taste of the unity of life. Perhaps that is why Baba said understanding has no meaning and love does have meaning. But then you raise the question of obedience because Baba said obedience has most meaning. But what was that obedience Baba wanted? It was to love Him as He should be loved. So to obey Baba is our attempt to love Him. This is the difference between the two. Real love implies obedience, obedience is part and parcel of it. When your Beloved asks you for a favor, do you refuse? Of course not. In fact, when you love someone, you do not even wait for the Beloved to ask, but you anticipate their needs and see to it first. That is what I mean when I say love implies obedience.

So why did Baba stress obedience? Because He knew we can't love Him as He should be loved. That is what He wants. But we cannot do it. So Baba says, well if you can't do that, then obey Me. And that is where the following of those standing orders comes into play. What did you say those orders were? No taking of drugs, no sex outside of marriage, the how to love God message, and so on and so forth. Those are all good, what you say is right, they are His standing orders if you take them that way. But then your father is also right to concentrate on simply remembering Him, thinking about Him, for those are the primary lessons in learning to love Him. And they are also the secondary lessons too. The lessons don't change, but the way we go about it changes. It becomes more natural. More automatic and spontaneous, but we still find ourselves thinking about Him, remembering Him. After all, when you obey what you call His standing orders, what happens, you are also thinking about Him, remembering Him, isn't it? So it all comes down to the same thing. It is as if we are all stationed on the circumference of an infinitely large circle. No matter from where we start, as we approach the Lord, our paths converge until, when we find Him, there is no difference at all, there is unity.

But this hall is not meant for that. It is not meant for talks about unity, because when one experiences that, there is no need of talking. Talking implies separation and duality. So let me tell you a story which is all about duality, and separation and obedience and love. An epic, you may call it. And if it sheds any light on what we've been talking about, well and good. If it doesn't, well, that is also well and good, for that is the nature of our life in duality.

This story concerns our travels with Baba. There were just a few of us. There was Gustadji and Vishnu and Baba and Chaggan and Baidul and myself. Baba was doing *mast* work, and we were traveling with Him towards Calcutta, and the journey was long and exhausting. You know how it was with us when we traveled with Baba. It wasn't even so much the fact that we rarely slept, it was the anxiety, the nervousness we felt because we were also so worried about taking care of Baba's physical body. For ourselves we didn't care. I was young and strong and I could easily shoulder people aside and get on a train no matter how crowded. I could also go long periods without sleep or food – what of it, there is nothing in that. I could make myself comfortable on a train no matter what, sitting on top of someone's baggage, standing the whole way if need be, but with Baba it was a different matter. It was our duty to see to His comfort, and so we always were anxious as to whether we would be able to find space for Baba. Would we be able to protect Him in the mad crush on the platform, and then, would we have enough time to get all the baggage Baba always traveled with on the train before it left? It was this sort of anxiety which made our traveling such an ordeal for us. And then, to make matters worse, there was Gustadji. I said before how those of us with Baba were all characters, and Gustadji was no exception.

His duty was simply to be with us, to entertain and please Baba with his presence. But the journeys were very long. I had so many things to see to, and Vishnu was looking after all our luggage, counting it at every change, making sure that nothing got left behind, Chaggan would cook for Baba, Baidul would help contact the *masts*, everyone had some duty except for Gustadji; he had no duty of this sort at all. And this made life very difficult for him. Maybe it sounds like he had the easy role to play, but believe me, it is much easier to be kept busy than to be given nothing to do. So how would Gustadji pass his time, how would he keep himself busy? He would pick up bits of string and newspaper and collect them. This was his habit. He was a little like Katie: nothing ever got thrown away in his presence, but he would swoop on it like a hawk and save it. And what would he do with all this junk? He would collect it in big piles and then send it to town and he would get a few paise, a few rupees in return. And this became his spending money. He would buy sweets, because he liked to suck on sweets and he would see to it that he had a nice supply by collecting and selling all this trash. But such was his habit that even when we traveled, Gustadji would continue with it. So not only did Vishnu have to see to all our baggage, but he had to see to all of Gustadji's packages, and these were mostly rubbish—bits of string he had picked up out of the gutter, old newspapers, and the like. He would tie them all into big bundles and carry them with us. So as we traveled and we got more and more tired, Vishnu had more and more luggage to look after.

And he had a lot to look after to begin with, because whenever we traveled with Baba we always had a lot of baggage. Why was this? Was it because Baba liked to travel with lots of baggage? You've seen pictures, perhaps of how when we traveled in the blue bus, how overloaded the bus was. It used to be piled up so high that we had to be careful when driving under anything with a low clearance, but that's a different story. You know in the early years, sometimes the mandali were referred to as Baba's spiritual baggage, because it seemed that it was Baba's way to always take with Him not only more baggage than was needed, but many more people than were needed. But there was a reason for this luggage. It wasn't that Baba ordered us to carry so many bags; it was our desire to have everything He might need in the course of His travels.

When we traveled with Baba we didn't have regular hours, we didn't eat regular meals, but every now and then Baba might get hungry, He might express the wish for something to eat or drink, and so we wanted to be ready. So we carried drinking water with us. I always carried a special container with clean water for Baba because we could never be certain of the water we would get when we traveled. And this water was kept in a brass container, so it would get hot. You know what it is like here in the summer, even now it gets hot during the days, and of course the trains were not air-conditioned, and the container would get warm to the touch, and Baba would express His desire to have something to drink, and I would feel the container and see that it was warm and so I would want something else for Baba to drink. And then, if we were lucky, we would come to a station and we would be able to get some green coconuts and give Baba the coconut milk, the juice, to drink.

Have you ever tasted that? It is most refreshing, delicious, and it is very pure, because it can't be contaminated, the coconut protects it, nothing can get inside. The man who sells them hacks a hole in the top right there before you, and then we would pour the juice into a glass for Baba, or sometimes he would drink directly from the coconut.

But if Baba wanted food, then the problem became more difficult because it wasn't always possible to get food at the stations, and Baba was very particular. He liked plain rice and dal, and when He decided to eat, He would want His food right away, so we would take all of our cooking utensils with us, the pots and pans and whatnot, so that we could cook a meal for Baba if need be. Even if we never used it on a trip, we would have it with us, just in case. And so it went. That is why we had so much luggage with us, not because Baba wanted it, but because we who served Him wanted to be ready to meet any wish of His. To see to His comfort means what, after all? It means to be ready to be able to satisfy His wishes, and that meant carrying extra blankets along in case it got cold, in carrying extra clothes for Baba, in carrying all the cooking paraphernalia, in carrying water and soap and special basins and towels in case Baba decided to bathe the feet of poor people and lepers. We had to have that with us also. If we are traveling and Baba decides to bathe the feet of five lepers, we can't go out begging ourselves for soap and water and towels and basins. We had to carry all this with us.

And it was good that we carried such things with us. It served us well in serving our Lord. To digress a little, I remember one time we were traveling with Baba and there had been a cyclonic disturbance – a bridge had been washed away and we were stranded for hours together. But we had tea and sugar and milk with us, so Baba said we should have some tea while we waited. And we had playing cards with us, so we could pass the time easily. But when we got out our little cook stove, it had, what do you call it, a kerosene canister, but it turned out it was exhausted. We didn't have any more fuel with us, so now how to heat the water?

Baba told me to go to the engineer. Our compartment was right behind the engine and I went to him. Now, at this time it was common that many of the engineers were Zoroastrians. My uncle was an engineer, and it turned out that this engineer was also a Zoroastrian, so I spoke to him in Gujerati and I borrowed some hot water from him. We got it right from the train's boiler. You know, the trains of that day were steam trains. And steam trains means what, it means they have a huge boiler full of boiling water which becomes steam which drives the train. So he gave me some boiling water and we made tea.

In talking to the driver, I must have told him about my uncle and somehow or other we got friendly and he gave us the water, so Baba said, go and give him some tea. So I did this and he was grateful and he too had nothing to do to while away his time, so he came back to our compartment and Baba permitted him to sit with us and even to play cards with us, which was most unusual. He must have been with us for hours, and yet in all that time he never noticed that Baba was silent. Gustadji he noticed right away. Gustadji's gestures were very obvious, but the expression on Baba's face was so eloquent, His gestures so natural, so easy to understand, that the man never realized that Baba wasn't talking.

Anyway, to cut the story short, Gustadji had to go to the toilet. We were in a forest area, so Gustadji simply went out into the woods. But as it so happened, just then the engineer gets the signal that the rails have been fixed, the track is clear and he can begin. So he lets out a loud whistle. Now, by this time, we were all very friendly with him, so I went running up to the engine and said, "Please, please, Gustadji has gone out. Do not start the train yet, we must wait till he returns."

And the engineer, who had become very fond of Gustadji, said, "Oh, when will that dumb one return?" And he starts playing all the more with Gustadji by pulling his whistle repeatedly as if the train will now leave any second. And then we see Gustadji hurrying back from the woods and the engineer calls out to him, "Hurry up, you dumb man, hurry up or we will leave without you."

But the point I am trying to make is that it was good we had all of our supplies with us, so we could have tea, so we could make Baba a snack of some sort, that we had the cards with us to pass the hours and so forth. It was a headache for us to carry all this luggage, because we were not the ones to hire coolies. Everything we took we had to carry on our backs, and we knew this. So we always wanted to travel as lightly as possible, but by the time we took everything that was needed, we had mountains of luggage, you may say, but time and again it came in very handy.

Still, for poor Vishnu it was an ordeal because he was the one in charge of seeing to it that it all got loaded and unloaded whenever we got on or off a train, and we changed trains frequently, because Baba would go to out of the way places to contact *masts*. This meant switching trains a lot, and getting down from the trains and taking buses and bullock carts and whatnot. And it was always a hectic time for us, because at these little stations the trains do not stop for long. At a big junction the train might sit for half an hour, but at some little station, it would stop for five minutes at most and the crowd would always be so heavy that it was a struggle to get on or off the train in that time, never mind the luggage.

To give you an idea of just how much luggage we had, I remember an incident from this very trip I am telling you about. For one part of it we were in two different cars. We had managed to reserve a coupe for Baba, and there was an adjoining unreserved four-person compartment for the mandali. As the train pulled in, we all had our duties. I saw to it that Baba got on safely and was comfortable in the two-person coupe. Meanwhile Vishnu was seeing that all the luggage got on. And that was quite a job. He would count it all ahead of time, get it piled just so before the train pulled in, and then he would work as fast as he could to get it piled on board in time. Then he would count it all again to make sure he had everything. Only then would he rearrange it, stow it under the seats and so forth, so that the mandali could be comfortable.

Well, this time, as I said, we had a reserved coupe. So Vishnu put the luggage in the coupe. That was easier for him because he didn't have to worry about other people fighting to get on or lots of people getting off with luggage, and since we were at a small station and the train wouldn't be stopping long, Baba said Vishnu could put the luggage in the coupe. So he did, he piled it up and managed to get it all inside and quickly counted it, and it was all there, and he heaved a huge sigh of relief. We all did. After the crisis had passed once more, Baba was safely on board, all the luggage was on, and we could relax slightly.

So Vishnu went back to be with the others and I stayed with Baba in the coupe. But at the very first stop, Vishnu comes running to our compartment and asks if Gustadji is with us. We say, "No. Isn't he with you?" Vishnu says, "No, we can't find him anywhere, we must have left him behind."

Now what to do? Gustadji is an old man and, not only that, he is silent. So what will he do if he's been left behind? He has no money with him, he can't talk, he can't explain anything, and he has no way of catching up with us. So this is a real problem. Baba says, "Are you sure?" And Vishnu says, "Baba, he is not with us. I was hoping maybe he was with You." "But where can he be?" Baba asks. "Wasn't he with us at the station?" "Yes, but maybe he wandered off to piddle and didn't make it back in time." You know that was Gustadji's way. His bladder was not good, and he had to piddle a lot and it would take him some time. He was slow, and it seemed whenever we needed to go somewhere, he was always off piddling. Haven't I told you about the day Baba stepped out of the New Life for a few hours and the meeting at Mahabaleshwar, and how some strangers got into the meeting place because Vishnu kept the gate open after Baba had told him to shut it? And why did he keep it open, because, as always, Gustadji had gone off to piddle and was slow coming back. So Vishnu said maybe Gustadji went off to piddle. "But why did you let him go off like that?" Baba asked, and Vishnu replied that he was too busy with the bags to be able to notice where Gustadji was and he just assumed that Gustadji would get on the train.

All of this transpired very quickly, you understand, because the train was starting to roll again. So Baba gestured, "Go back, check through all the cars, because maybe Gustadji got in the wrong car by mistake, and then report back."

So Vishnu rushes back to his bogie just as the train pulls out and Baba turns to me and wonders what's happened to Gustadji and what are we going to do now.

Just then we heard a knock coming from the wall. "That must be Vishnu signaling us," I said. And we decided it was Vishnu's way of telling us that Gustadji had turned up after all. Because there was no connecting passage. There was no way for him to get us a message until the train stopped and he could run outside and approach our compartment. So we felt relieved that everything was okay. But Vishnu kept knocking. Every few minutes he would knock against the wall, and I felt, "Yes, we understand, we know Gustadji is with you. There is no need to keep knocking, we are not deaf." Because I was thinking this noise would disturb Baba. He was lying down on one of the berths and He was resting, and I thought there was no need for Vishnu to keep knocking on the wall every few minutes or so. So when we reached the next station and Vishnu came running up, I was taken aback when he blurted out, "Baba, Gustadji is not anywhere. I checked every other compartment and he is not on the train."

"Not on the train? So that is why you have been knocking on our compartment so often."

"What do you mean? I haven't been knocking on your compartment."

"Then who has . . ." And just then we heard the knock again. So we investigated, and what did we find? Behind all the luggage which was piled up in our compartment was the door to the toilet and Gustadji had gone there to relieve himself when the train pulled in, and without realizing it Vishnu had piled up all the bags in front of the door and then poor Gustadji had found himself trapped inside. He was on silence so he couldn't say anything, so he was banging on the door to get our attention, but I hadn't looked because I thought the whole time it had been Vishnu banging on the wall to let us know that Gustadji was with them.

This is just to give you an idea of how much luggage we had and how hectic it was when we were getting on or off the train. In fact, one time, on this same trip that I have been telling you about, it so happens that after getting all the luggage on board, Vishnu counts it and discovers one bag is missing. That he has left one on the platform somehow in all the hustle and bustle of getting on the train in time. But we've already pulled out of the station. It is too late now to go back and get it.

Baba became very upset with Vishnu for this. And it becomes too much for Vishnu to take. He tried so hard to please Baba and now this happened and Baba is expressing His displeasure and Vishnu can't take it and he turns and starts getting wild on Gustadji. "It's all his fault, Baba," Vishnu says. "It is hard enough seeing to all of the luggage, but most of the luggage is Gustadji's rubbish which we are carting about with us. How can I keep track of our bags when every day he makes some new bundle of trash which he insists we carry with us? It is too much now, Baba." And with that, Vishnu picks up one of Gustadji's bundles of trash and starts to throw it out the window. But Gustadji grabs it and is holding on to it so Vishnu can't throw it and they are pulling the bundle back and forth between them like a tug of war and, of course, Gustadji can't say anything but he's red in the face and holding on to his bundle for all he's worth and Vishnu is ranting and raving and all of this right before Baba, mind you, and finally Baba claps and makes them both sit down.

Now, it seems funny, but at the time they were both very serious. But this is not what I wanted to tell you. All of this has just been
background to give you some idea of what our traveling was like and
how the tensions would build, the little irritations would get on our
nerves, and suddenly we would just explode. As always, it was Baba
who would bring us to our senses and help us regain our poise. And
now my story really begins. For one of the ways Baba would help us
calm down was to hold out in front of us, like a carrot dangling
before the dumb ox, the notion that once we finally reached Calcutta
we would stay in a nice hotel and would get plenty of rest and have
a good meal and generally relax and enjoy ourselves.

So when our tempers started to flare up, or we got to grumbling about our traveling or whatever, Baba would distract us by
bringing up what a wonderful stay we would have once we reached
Calcutta. And so we started looking forward to it. It is only natural.
We were exhausted, we never got proper sleep, we ate at odd hours
when we ate at all and even then it wasn't a proper meal, and it did-
n't take much coaxing on Baba's part to make the picture of spending time in some hotel in a quiet locality where we could rest and get
good food very appealing to us.

And finally we did pull into Calcutta. We had been there before
and we had stayed at a nice hotel in a quiet locality, so we went
there. It was not a posh place, not a five-star hotel, a one-star, you
may call it, but it suited us. We had a good meal and then we retired
for the evening. Now, whenever we traveled with Baba, we would try
to get three rooms. Baba would stay in the middle room, and the
other two rooms would be kept empty. This was because Baba did
not like any disturbances at night, and the noise of people sleeping
in the next room would be too much for Him. So we would get one
room for Baba, one room for the mandali and then we would try to
see to it that we could have an empty room on the other side of
Baba's room. Now, Baba wouldn't want to pay for this if it was pos-

sible. We would just ask the manager if he had a vacant room and then try to get the two adjoining rooms.

And we did this, we were able to do it. Although it was a busy season, we were able to get three rooms in a row for Baba and we were all happy. I unpacked Baba's bedding, spread it all out for Him, and Baba lay down to rest. I was sitting in the room with Him, and the mandali unpacked their bedding and were sleeping in the corridor.

It must have been about ten o'clock at night now and we were all very pleased that at last our traveling was over. But what we hadn't realized was that in hotels like this, people eat very late. They also drink and there were waiters pushing trolleys with food and drinks up and down the halls to take to people.

"What's that noise?" Baba asked, because the trolleys make a lot of noise, you know the way they clatter, and the silverware and the plates rattle with the vibration. And I looked outside and saw what it was and reported back to Baba. "Baba, it is just some trolleys taking food to various people."

"It won't do," Baba gestured. "It is too noisy, we will have to leave."

"Baba," I said, "it is after ten now. People will be going to bed soon and the noise will stop. Let us just wait a little while and all will be quiet." I said this, and I was hoping it would be true, but to be honest I must admit that it was also that I didn't want to have to pack up everything again. Baba agreed, but almost immediately another trolley rolled by our room and Baba sat up and said this was no good, we would have to leave.

So I said, "Baba, stay here and I will go out and find another hotel for us." Because I thought even if it was noisy, it would be better for Baba to wait comfortably inside rather than take a rickshaw through the streets of Calcutta while we searched for another hotel.

And I went out and after an hour or so I did find another hotel. An even better one, in a nice locality, and again they had three rooms in a row which were vacant. So I went back and packed up Baba's bedding and the mandali packed up their beddings and we helped poor Vishnu carry all the bags and we all went downstairs to leave for the next hotel. But then Baba gestured, "Get our money back." So I went to the manager and demanded our money back. I told him it was too noisy and we couldn't stay there and we wanted our money back.

Of course, he did not want to give us our money. He said he did not rent his rooms by the hour and we had taken two rooms and we should have to pay for two rooms. After all, other patrons had come and he had turned them away, and if he had known he could have rented them our rooms, so he lost money because of us. And I said if other patrons had come he would have shown them to the room next to us because it was empty and so, to cut it short, we haggled and haggled and finally we paid some reduced rate for the hour or two we had been there and then we left for the new hotel.

We got there and once again I had to unpack Baba's things and make Him comfortable. Baba lay down and after a minute or two there is a thud. Baba sits up and looks at me. After another minute or two there is another loud thud reverberating, echoing in the air. I got up and went to see what it could be. And what do you think? It turned out there was a blacksmith shop next to the hotel and he was beating something on his anvil. I told this to Baba and He said, "Is this the time to be working? Come, let's go to a different hotel." "Wait, Baba. Let me talk to him," I said. And I went outside. I don't recall what I said. I think this was one occasion when I lost my temper. I stormed at the man, asking him what he was doing making so much noise at this hour of the night, and so on and so forth. The man said that he was sorry but he had a job to do and he wanted to finish it while his fire was still going. After all, he was a poor man and he couldn't afford to go to bed whenever he wanted to, but must do the work as his customers demanded. "But there is no customer here," I said. "The work can wait until tomorrow. You will be lighting your fire again tomorrow and you can continue the work then." And so it went, back and forth and finally he said, "Give me five more minutes, just give me five more minutes and I promise I will stop."

So I went back to Baba, and I remember, even as I was walking back and entering Baba's room I could still hear him working. "Baba, he will be quitting very soon now. He is almost done and then there will be no more noise." And in a few minutes he did quit and it was quiet. At last, I thought. But within a few minutes there was a noise in the vacant room next to us.

Baba sat up again, looking very displeased. "What's this?" He gestured. "I thought you had arranged for this room to be vacant?" "I did," I said. "There must be some mistake." So I went to see the manager and I said, "What is this? You have put people in the room next to us." "Yes," he replied. "What else can I do? This is a busy season and I cannot afford to turn customers away. And you were not paying for the room." "Yes, but I told you when I engaged the two rooms that if anyone came and wanted the room to turn them away and that we would pay for the room then." You see, Baba did not want us to waste money. So He would have us try to only pay for two rooms. But this made us nervous because we knew Baba wouldn't like it if the other room was occupied, so what I did was make an agreement with the manager that we would pay for the two rooms but if someone came, rather than rent them the room, at that point we would pay for it. But the manager hadn't done this. It seems he wasn't sure we would agree to pay, although I had told him that, so when a couple came and gave him the money on the spot, he led them to the room. After all, he figured, they are not using the room. Maybe he thought he could even collect for the room twice, once from them and once from us. So again there was a big argument. And I went back upstairs to tell Baba what had happened and I told Baba I was sure I could have the manager remove the couple.

"No," Baba said. "My mood is spoiled, this is no good, let us move again. be quick, I am not happy here." So once again we had to repack. Now it is well past midnight at this point. It must be closer to one or two in the morning and we still haven't had any sleep, and Baba is not in a good mood and is urging us to be quick about it, so I am hurriedly trying to tie up Baba's bedding and Gustadji comes to me and starts gesturing something to me.

It seems a shoelace of his had rolled under the bed and he wanted me to get it for him. But I was so preoccupied with tying up Baba's bedding that I couldn't pay any attention to his gestures, because to see what he was saying I would have to really look at his hands, and if I did that then I couldn't see to pack up Baba's things, and it was too much for me and I said to him, "It is bad enough that I have to care for one dumb person, but I can't cope with two." I was completely exasperated and I just blurted this out. I didn't know that Baba was standing right behind me at the time.

But the next thing I knew, Baba had grabbed my ear and twisted it and said, "Who are you calling dumb? I am not dumb, I am silent."

I felt so embarrassed. "Yes, Baba," I said. "I am sorry," and I apologized. Now I can laugh at it, but it was really a humiliating episode at the time. Poor Gustadji, it always seemed he took the brunt of our ill humor. But what could he do? It was very difficult for him being on silence. And he was also much older than the rest of us, so he needed our help. If we had been more rested, if we had had the time, we would have realized this, we wouldn't have acted this way, but that is what I am trying to share with you, I am trying to give you a glimpse of what it was like on our travels. It was so hectic, and our nerves became so frayed. And once again we had to pack everything up, and once again Baba told us to not pay the full amount, and I had to haggle with the manager to get some money back.

But the most embarrassing and humiliating part was still to come. As we loaded all of our luggage into a horse carriage, the blacksmith saw us and came up to me and said, "I thought your elder brother was sick! You made me stop my work and now you are leaving?" And again I had to say something to pacify him. I had to apologize and make up some story and the whole time Baba is in a hurry and so we go to another hotel.

It is almost morning now by the time we find one and again we unpack everything and I smooth our Baba's bedding and make Him comfortable and at last we sleep. We are so tired, so exhausted, we oversleep, and it is daylight when we get up. Even Baba oversleeps and He is still sleeping. The mandali are sitting quietly so as not to disturb Him and Baba sits up and gestures, "What's the time?" I said "Ten o'clock, Baba," and Baba seemed upset. "How did we oversleep like this?" Baba asked. I said, "Baba, we were all exhausted." Baba sat on His bed and He still looked very solemn, He was not in a good mood, and He asked, "Did you have your tea and breakfast yet?" I said, "No, Baba, no one has had anything yet." And then Baba said, "Lucky that you have not taken anything." And then His mood seemed to brighten. But He would have really been upset with us if we had had something to eat without waiting for Him. It was lucky for us that at least that time we had the common sense to wait. So whether this was love or obedience, I can't say. Whatever you want to call it, it was simply our life with the Lord, dancing to His tune.

〰 H E A L T H

"DO YOUR BEST, AND LEAVE THE RESULTS TO BABA." How many times have you heard that? But what does it mean? Do you think that just because you have done your best, there will be no difficulties, that everything will go smoothly? Not at all. Sometimes, despite your best efforts, despite your best intentions, the results will not be what you want. It is easy to say leave the results to Baba, but it is no joke to do this in your life. Let me give you some examples from our life with Baba.

We looked upon it as our duty to see to our Lord's physical well-being. Whatever work Baba did on the inner planes, whatever Baba's spiritual work was, we had nothing to do with that. Perhaps, unwittingly, we helped Baba by obeying Him, but we had no understanding of what He was accomplishing on a spiritual level or how He was doing it. We were not the people for such things.

What we could do, and what we did do, was attend to practical matters, worldly duties. And one of these was seeing to it that Avatar Meher Baba's physical body was protected and well cared for. Really speaking, Baba did not need our help, but He gave us the opportunity to feel as if we were doing something for Him. His compassion allowed us the scope to think that we were rendering service to Him. And yet, our very enthusiasm to see to Baba's well-being came in our way time and time again and ended up causing Baba pain.

As you may have heard, Baba lost His teeth fairly early. Some say this was because they were loosened during the period when He used to bang His head on the floor. Whatever it is, He did lose some of His teeth early and, despite the best care we could provide, eventually He lost all of them. This was before the New Life. Baba was always impatient over food, impatient over the time spent in eating, and so He tended to eat very quickly. As a result of all this, He suffered from stomach discomfort. The doctors thought that Baba should have dental plates and that these naturally would help Him chew and digest His food better.

Knowing this, I went to a Dr. Bharucha, a very good dentist in Poona, and persuaded him to come to where Baba was staying. After two or three visits, the plates were completed and fitted. In the course of the visits, the dentist was drawn to Baba and he had Baba's blessings. But afterwards, Baba complained that the plates were too heavy, were too awkward in His mouth, and finally He stopped using them.

Now the New Life came, and Baba continued to complain about indigestion. This distressed me but there was nothing I could do. Later we moved to Hyderabad and we stayed there for some time with Baba. Hyderabad at that time was a princely state ruled by the Nizam. The Nizam was well known as one of the wealthiest men in the world, and I knew that such a man would be used to having only the best of everything. And it occurred to me that his dentist must be a man of exceptional skill. I wondered what sort of plates he had made for the Nizam. Were they of special material?

Without telling Baba, I found out who the Nizam's dentist was and, still dressed in my New Life attire, I managed to get an interview with him. My kafni was shabby and I must have looked like a beggar, but the dentist agreed to see me. I told the dentist that I was interested in getting some plates made; I explained that I wanted them to be extremely lightweight. I asked what kind of material the Nizam had used for his.

The dentist looked at me suspiciously. "You want the very best?" he asked. "Yes," I replied. "But will you be able to afford it?" he asked. I explained that the plates weren't for me but my elder brother and that he had many friends who would want to see him comfortable. I assured the dentist that no matter what the cost, he would get paid.

Then I asked how quickly he could do the work, for it was always possible that Baba would suddenly decide to leave Hyderabad. The dentist must have wondered about this whole transaction but he expressed his willingness to do the work, and I returned to Baba.

I told Baba about the dentures and, by emphasizing the light, transparent nature of the material used, I managed to persuade Baba to accompany me to the dentist.

The job was done, both plates, top and bottom, and they were very fine. They cost 1,000 rupees and this was paid, with Baba's approval, by the Arrangementwallas of the New Life. I was very happy. I felt that I had really accomplished something for Baba's health.

It was only a year or so afterwards that Baba had His first car accident, in Oklahoma. At the time, Baba was wearing only His upper dentures, and the force of the impact caused the teeth to become embedded in the lower gums.

When I heard about this, I was very penitent. Baba hadn't wanted the plates, but I had persisted and finally He had acquiesced, and see what trouble they had caused. Why did I insist? I asked myself. Why did I force this extra pain and suffering on Baba? But what could I do? It was my duty to try to attend to Baba's health. And I had to do my best in doing my duty, yet it was a paradox that my best efforts only brought Baba more pain.

After the accident, Baba never wore the plates again. Also, because of this accident, Baba injured the septum of His nose. Because of this, He became extremely sensitive to dust and wind and you must have seen films of Baba where He is holding a scarf over His nose. You see, the least little bit of dust or a strong breeze would cause Baba acute discomfort, so He would have to hold scarves around His face for protection.

We knew this. We knew how Baba was suffering, so naturally we wanted to do something. One time when we were staying in Poona, the thought came to me that we should take Baba to an eye, nose, and throat specialist to see if there was anything that could be done. This thought surfaced and, on my own, I emboldened myself and I went and found such a specialist. I described Baba's condition and suggested that this was due to His accident and the injury to the nose and wondered if something could be done. The doctor said, "Yes, I accept what you say, but I still have to examine the patient for myself."

I explained that the patient was my elder brother and that He never went out, except for short drives in a car. The doctor insisted, however, that he could do nothing without examining my brother and that there was no recourse but to bring Him to his office. He said he could give me an appointment for such and such a time on such and such a date.

"If I can persuade Him to come, will you take us immediately?" I asked. "Without our sitting around for half an hour in your waiting room or anything like that? As soon as we come, can we go directly to your office for the examination?"

You see, knowing Baba's nature as I did, I had to take such precautions. This is what my life with the Lord was like. The doctor assured me that if we came at the appointed time, he would see us immediately and there would be no need to wait, so I said I would do my best to persuade my elder brother to come, and then I left the office.

As this was after Baba's second accident, He was having difficulty walking, so once or twice each day Baba would go out for a drive for some fresh air. I would drive Baba, and we would go for some distance, not in the city, but on the outskirts, for half an hour or so. So, on the appointed day, I took Baba out for a drive as usual. I hadn't told Baba about my visit to the doctor because I knew He'd refuse to go, so I just kept quiet. But once we were in the car and I was driving Baba, I took a route which brought us to the area of town where the doctor's office was. Then, all of a sudden, I took a turn and pulled in through a gate to the doctor's compound.

"Where are you going?" Baba asked me.

I stopped the car and told Baba that I had made an appointment for Him with an ENT specialist. Baba gestured, "Why?" and I explained that I thought maybe the doctor could do something to alleviate His suffering. Baba kept quiet. Why, I don't know. Whether it was because He was so amazed at what I had done, so astonished at my impudence, or so irritated with me, I don't know, but without a word, Baba got out of the car and walked to the doctor's office with me. Most probably not to let me down.

I introduced Baba as my elder brother to the doctor, who then examined Him. "Oh, it's a simple thing," he said. "Have you had an injury to your nose at some point? There is a small nodule growing at the base of the septum. That is what is causing all your problems. It needs to be cauterized."

When I heard that, I thought the doctor meant that some sort of operation would have to be done and my heart sank because I knew I would not be able to persuade Baba to come back for another visit. I asked the doctor how long this operation would take and he said it was very simple, it could be done in five or ten minutes. It's not really an operation, he explained. You just put an electric wire on the nodule and you run a current through it. The wire heats up and you burn a small cross on the nodule. That way it won't grow anymore and, after a while, it shrinks and just withers away.

So I looked at Baba. Baba looked at me. "Well," I said, "now that you have come so far and the doctor is so confident and it's such a simple procedure, why not just get it done now and get it over with?"

Baba very lovingly acceded to my request, and the doctor began. First he cleaned the nostril with an alcohol swab and then he inserted the cauterizing gun – you know it's something like a soldering iron – and he put the current on. Soon I could get the stench of burning flesh. It must have been very painful.

After a moment or two, the doctor had finished burning the cross and appeared very satisfied. He plugged the nostril with some cotton and said, "For a couple of days you will feel pain, it will be inconvenient, but then it will heal and you will be perfectly all right once again." He gave us some nasal drops to lessen the pain, and that was the end of the visit.

But to be fair to the doctor, I should mention that he recognized Baba and he never charged us. That pleased Baba, and, of course, I was very happy about it, too.

So that's how it was. In the car Baba, of course, started expressing His disapproval of everything that had just happened. I should have informed Him beforehand, He insisted. Once I pulled the car into the doctor's compound, how could He refuse after all my efforts? So He allowed Himself to undergo this torture for my sake, but it wasn't right. I should not have placed Him in that position, and so on.

And I answered back. I said, "Baba, in the long run this will help You. I know it must have been very painful for You, but as it is You suffer so much now because of Your sensitivity to dust and wind. Now, in a few days, You won't have that problem anymore, so it will be worth it."

"That remains to be seen," Baba said, and that was the end of our conversation.

And you know what the result of the operation was? There was no effect at all. In spite of the torturous experience I had made Baba undergo, there was no improvement in His condition. You can see in the movies that Baba continued to use the scarves, that He still suffered. Once again, my efforts to do my best, to do my duty, to see to Baba's health, only resulted in my causing unnecessary suffering for Baba. It seems it was always this way.

I remember one time which had a humorous tint to it. We were in a rustic area with Baba. There were just a handful of us, and we were not even in a village or anything; it was the outback, you may say. We were traveling with Baba in a bullock cart. Some of you may have seen bullock carts, but unless you've ever been in one, you can have no idea of the jolting you get inside. There are no springs, of course, no shock absorbers, nothing to cushion the ride. And because we were way out, away from everything, we were not on a road. We were on a sort of track, and it was all uneven and the cart was lurching and jolting as we slowly moved along. That was the only saving grace, I may say, that the cart goes so slowly, otherwise it would be too much to bear.

I spread Baba's bedding out in the cart. We call it a hold-all, maybe some of you have seen it, it not only holds a mattress, but it has flaps on each side in which one can put one's clothes, one's sandals, everything in fact, which is why it is called a hold-all. So I spread Baba's out in the cart and Baba was able to lie down on that while the rest of us sat perched on the railing with our legs dangling down like monkeys.

The area we were traveling was hilly. There was a succession of hills and we were going up one, like our Seclusion Hill. The poor bullocks were straining to make it up that steep grade, and the driver kept calling out to them to urge them on. Finally we got to the top of the slope and started down the other side, and the driver, as if to get his revenge on us for forcing his bullocks to work so hard, suddenly threw the reins on the bullocks' horns.

Now, going downhill is when you need the reins, to check the bullocks' progress. But the driver just threw the reins away and the bullocks began to gallop down the slope unchecked.

"Hey, hey," I called out. "What are you trying to do? Check the bullocks."

"No, I can't" he replied. "If I try to check them on this steep slope, they will only stumble and I will injure them and then the whole cart will be endangered."

You see, the reins pass through the bullocks' noses. The driver felt that with the steep grade, if he tried to check the bullocks, the pulling in on the reins would come as such a jolt that it might injure the bullocks, or they would lose their balance and stumble. Whatever it is, he did not try to do anything and we started going faster and faster downhill. The bullocks practically galloped, and of course while this was happening we were bouncing around like popcorn. We were trying to hang on, but even this was difficult, we were being jolted so much. It felt as if our bones were being broken to pieces.

When we finally got to the bottom of the slope Baba gestured to us, "You were lucky. You only bumped your fannies, but I was lying down, so My whole body had to bear the brunt of the jolting."

And when I thought about it, I realized that what He said was true. Here we had tried to make Baba more comfortable by having Him lie down while we sat on the railing, but see, even here, it had ended up only causing Baba more pain.

There was only one time, in all the many occasions I had to see to Baba's physical needs, when it seemed that I was able to actually help Baba. This concerned Baba's eyes.

Starting in Dehra Dun, Baba developed a problem with His eyes. He had an irritating, scratchy sensation in His eyes, as if something, a particle of dust or something, had blown into His eyes which caused Him considerable discomfort. For the next two years, during our wanderings, Baba continued to be plagued by this problem. Periodically we would persuade Baba to allow some doctor to see Him, but they could never find anything wrong. We were sometimes in big cities, and we would consult the top doctors, the specialists, but they could never find anything wrong. Some would prescribe drops, some would suggest that Baba needed glasses or should wear dark glasses, but none of this brought any relief and Baba continued to suffer.

Finally we were in Satara. This must have been 1951. I remember we were staying at Muttha's bungalow, so you can figure out the exact date because we only stayed there once. At that time Satara was a small town and it had the reputation of being a pensioner's retirement town. And it was true. In the streets, at the bazaar, you only saw old people, carrying little bags, tottering along. There wasn't any trade to speak of. The whole town just sort of dragged along at a slow pace.

One day as I was walking through the town I noticed this sign board for an eye doctor. I don't know why I noticed it, because it was such a crude little sign. Not at all the sort of sign to inspire confidence, but for some reason I went inside and there was this shabby, dilapidated little clinic. I don't know why I went in. Maybe it was because we had already gone to so many big doctors, so many specialists, and none of them had been able to do anything for Baba, so it occurred to me that maybe some small doctor might see something the bigger ones had missed. Anyway, what did I have to lose?

So I went inside and talked to the doctor, and he agreed to come to our bungalow and examine Baba. Why shouldn't he agree? As it was, he had so little business, he didn't insist that Baba come to his clinic. So he came to our bungalow. But see what kind of doctor he was. When he came, he didn't even bring anything with him.

He pulled Baba's upper eyelid up and back and said, "See, see those tiny white specks there?" They looked like crystals. "They are what are causing all the problems. Do you have a forceps?"

He hadn't brought anything with him, so he asked Dr. Goher for a forceps. Then he asked Goher for some antiseptic solution. He had to ask her for everything. Then he started plucking the tiny white granulations off Baba's eyelids. In no time he was done. There was a little bleeding from where he had used the forceps, but within a couple of days Baba was all right. The problem was completely gone. For all that time Baba had suffered and none of the big-time doctors had been able to do a thing, and here this little doctor in a run-down clinic in a small backwater sort of place was able to diagnose the problem and cure it.

But this was the exception. Usually our very efforts to help only resulted in causing Baba more pain. Why this should be I don't know. Are we especially clumsy people that our every effort should miss the mark, or is the fate, you may call it, the role of the Avatar such that when He comes He must suffer and therefore even our attempts to reduce His suffering only do the opposite? I don't know, brother. But what can we do? We still must try our best. And that is what I mean when I say that it is easy to say do your best and leave the results to Baba, but it is no joke, I tell you, to do that.

⚛ IMPOSSIBLE

THIS MORNING WE HAD STARTED A TOPIC and we got sidetracked talking about Dr. Deshmukh and I never told the stories that Susan had wanted to hear. Do you remember what we were talking about? No? Well, at least I remember. I had started to tell you how one thing I learned from my life with Meher Baba was how, with His grace, anything was possible.

Oh, now you remember. What kind of memory is that? That only remembers something after you've been reminded of it? Baba would tell us something and He would expect us to remind Him of it. With a memory like yours, what would you do? But, no, it is good that you can't remember, I am only teasing you, it is good that you have forgotten because this gives me the opportunity to remind you, and in reminding you I am reminded of how I would remind my Lord, Meher Baba. You see how easy and natural remembrance of our Lord is? This is what I was trying to bring home to you the other day. You do not need to sit and stare at His picture for hours at a time, you do not need to repeat His name ten thousand times a day. I am not saying that you shouldn't do these things. If you can lead an ordinary life, attending to all of your worldly duties and family responsibilities, and still find time to stare at Baba's picture, that is wonderful. But for most of us this becomes unnatural, we do not have the time or the scope for such remembrance. But in the midst of our everyday life, there are countless reminders of Him. And this is easy and natural.

But now you remind me about this and we will talk about it later because if we get into that now, we will never get to the stories I wanted to tell you. By His grace, anything is possible.

It is easy to say that, and many of you think that with that assurance in our hearts and minds, life with Him must have been easy. But this doesn't give you the right picture of our life with Baba. Really, our life was most embarrassing, most humiliating. That assurance came with time, it was not something that developed overnight. And Baba did not make it easy for us either. Baba would ask us to do something for Him and He did not want us to have the attitude, "Well, Baba has asked us to do it, so I don't have to worry because if He wants it done, He will do it." No, Baba wanted us to try our best, to make every effort, and when we didn't succeed He would express His disappointment, His displeasure, and if He knew we hadn't really tried with all our heart, His anger. Baba did not want us to worry, that is true, but He did want us to take every pain possible to see that a task we were given was accomplished. And this was not easy.

On top of that, Baba would ask us to do things which we knew were impossible. That's what I was starting to tell you this morning. For someone like Deshmukh, who seemed unaware of the world, who was so innocent in his love, he had no way of knowing what was possible and what was not. But I was a worldly person. So when Baba would give us these orders, I knew well that they were impossible. That nobody would ever agree to them. And yet we were ordered to carry them out.

And we couldn't go about it with hesitation, you understand. If we had gone up to someone like this, very timidly, apologizing and speaking softly like Davana here, we never could have gotten the work done. We had to be bold, we were emissaries of the Emperor, after all, and even though we may have felt in our heart of hearts that the order was impossible, we had to act as if we fully expected the other person to accede to the request, no matter how strange it might be.

I have told you many such stories. I told you about the coriander and the fan in the dak bungalow, but here are two more which
just came to me the other day and which I haven't shared for some
time. Would you like to hear them?

The first was during a phase of Baba's work when He was giving away money to poor people. Perhaps this was during the New
Life, because Baba did a lot of such work then. Remember, He
stepped out of the Old Life for one day and He raised money during
that day. And then we spent months traveling across India giving that
money away.

Whatever it is, Baba had sent me to Kanpur. And I was to
arrange for one hundred and fifty poor but deserving folk to come
together so Baba could give them money. Of course I couldn't use
Baba's name, I just said, "my elder brother." And I couldn't mention
anything about Baba bowing down to them because then no one
would have agreed. That we would leave to the actual day itself.
Once they were there and had the prospect of the money before
them, as it were, then I would explain that my elder brother wanted
to bow down to each of them and they must not step away, and it
was too late, you may say, at that point for them to refuse.

Now I had come to Kanpur and Baba was going to come in two
days, so I had to make all the arrangements in that time. The first
thing I had to see to was where this could take place. You know, we
just couldn't do this in a public street or anything like that. And as I
went round the city I saw a small building in the middle of a park. I
thought that will be good, it's not too public, it is a little secluded and
that will be the best venue for this program.

Next I had to find one hundred and fifty poor people, and Baba
was always most particular. We could not just round up any hundred
and fifty people, they had to be really deserving. There is no shortage of poor people in India. But by deserving Baba meant people
who were not on the streets begging, who were not looking for a
handout. On the contrary, the hallmark of these people is that they

are reluctant to accept help even when it is offered. This may make them deserving, but it also makes them very hard to find. Now, I knew that in two days I would not be able to find one hundred and fifty such people in a locality I was not familiar with. So I contacted some like-minded people in the area, and with their help we started going from place to place interviewing people. This was not two days' work. This was a week's work but we kept at it twenty-four hours a day, and I would hear about people who were working hard, who were really struggling to get by but, for various reasons, could not make ends meet, and I would be touched and I would give them a ticket as one of the one hundred and fifty. And so it went. By the afternoon of the second day, I had selected all one hundred and fifty. I had given them all tickets and told them to be at the park the next morning at such and such an hour and my elder brother would be there and would give them the money.

So now I went to the park to make sure I could use the building, and I asked the caretakers there who owned it. They said it is a municipal building so if you want permission to use it you must approach the municipality, we are only caretakers.

So I went to the municipal authorities and put my case before them. I told them my elder brother had arranged for one hundred and fifty poor people to meet at the park and he wanted to give them a substantial sum of money, and could we use the building? It is now the afternoon before Baba is arriving and I have already contacted the one hundred and fifty people and told them all to be there the next morning. You see the situation I'm in. It's too late to make any other arrangements, and now the municipal authorities tell me that I can't have the building.

"Why not?" I want to know. "It's too dangerous," they say. "How is it dangerous?" And they explain that there have been communal tensions, riots, and an order has been promulgated that people are not allowed to congregate. Of course, people who just happen to come to the park and are walking there, that is okay, but to specifically call one hundred and fifty people together, that is now against the law.

Naturally, I argue with them, but they refuse to give me permission. But what can I do? I have to keep arguing, so finally they say, if you still want to try, you will have to see the mayor. He is the only one who can give you permission, because we will not.

It is now about six o'clock in the evening. The mayor will not be in his office. Baba is coming the next morning and there will be no time to see the mayor tomorrow, so I find out where the mayor lives and I go to his home. I knock at the door and I announce that I have important and urgent matters to discuss with him. You see, this is the way we had to be. Otherwise I would not even have been let in. His servant would have turned me away or told me to go to the mayor's office the next morning. But I sounded as if I really had something very important to discuss, and I was shown into the house.

And I begin the argument with the mayor. "It's impossible," he says. "The order has been promulgated, it is too dangerous." "On the contrary," I say, "this will help ease the tension. These people will be less likely to be swayed by any rabble-rouser because they will have had their immediate needs met for the next month." You see, Baba was going to give each person one hundred and fifty rupees, and in those days, that was a considerable sum.

But the mayor wasn't convinced. I said we are not involved in politics in any way, this is purely a philanthropic venture. And then I went and blamed everything on Baba. I said, "But my elder brother has already contacted the people, he has already arranged for the program to be held tomorrow morning in the park, it is too late now to change the program." "But who is your elder brother to make such arrangements without consulting the authorities first?" the mayor asks. "But who are you to stand in the way of one hundred and fifty of your citizens receiving such timely aid?" I replied, and so it went.

Several times he said, "No," very forcefully and indicated that our interview was over and I should leave. But I just kept on arguing with him, pleading with him, pointing out that this wasn't going to cause any trouble, on the contrary it would help the situation, it would make the people in town feel better, it would rebound to his credit that such a program took place, and so on and so forth. I don't know how long I stayed there. It must have been quite some time, hours, you may say.

Finally he stood up and came around his desk. I also stood up. After all, he was the mayor and I had to show him some respect. I thought he was going to throw me out, but as he approached me he put his arms out and embraced me. "Never have I met such a persuasive and persistent man in my life," he said. "If your elder brother wants to have His program, go ahead, let Him have it."

And so the next morning when Baba arrived, the program went off without a hitch. And every time, it happened this way. Whatever Baba wanted would happen. But we couldn't just have faith in that and then not try wholeheartedly. We still had to try our best, we had to make Herculean efforts, I may say, and even though it always worked out, that didn't mean that I wasn't anxious. I tell you I was perspiring like anything, I was so afraid he would say no, and then what would I tell Baba.

Let me give you another example. We were traveling with Baba and He was contacting *masts*, and I remember one time we were in Madras, walking down a busy side street when we saw a *mast* sitting on the verandah of a building. Baba indicated that He wanted to spend some time alone, secluded with the *mast*. Now what to do? How to arrange this? Sometimes we could coax *masts* to come with us and meet Baba wherever we were staying, but here we weren't staying anywhere, we were traveling, we had no place to take the *mast* to.

Sometimes the *mast* would be in a semisecluded area to begin with and we could simply stand watch while Baba sat with the *mast* but here the *mast* was sitting on the verandah of a bank of a busy city street. And we didn't have any time. Baba was always in a hurry. There wasn't time to make any elaborate arrangement, so Baba gestured to me to go inside the building and get permission for Him to meet with the *mast* inside for fifteen minutes.

But it so happened that this was a bank. True it was not a huge bank, it was a branch office, but it was still a bank. Now I knew this was an impossible request. What bank manager is going to allow two people to sit inside his bank alone? – because it was Baba's condition, not just that He and the *mast* sit inside, but that everyone else had to leave the bank while Baba met with the *mast*. I knew this was impossible. At least part of my mind could register that, could register that this was an absurd request and it was humiliating to have to go inside the bank and make it as a straightforward proposal. But the other part of me registered simply that this was what Baba wanted and so I had to do it, and I had to do it in such a way that the bank manager agreed.

So I went inside and demanded to speak to the manager in a very authoritative manner. You see, our manner had to be very forceful because our attire was not very impressive. You know how it is. If we had walked in all booted and suited, wearing expensive watches and Western-style clothes and the like, those in authority would have been inclined to listen to us. But we always were dressed in rags, you may say. We usually hadn't slept or bathed properly or washed our clothes in days, and looking like ragamuffins, we had to demand to see the bank manager, the mayor, and so on. You see what I mean when I say we couldn't be timid? The way we looked, if we had acted diffidently, no one would have listened to us for a moment. So with great authority I ask to speak to the bank manager.

After a few minutes the manager comes and I explain that I am there on behalf of my elder brother, who has a most delicate and urgent matter to attend to which only he can help arrange. Naturally this piques his curiosity and appeals a little to his vanity as well, so he asks what it is. I say that we were traveling, we just happened to be passing through Madras, and as we were walking down the street

He happened to see an old old friend of His. Someone He had lost touch with, and now after a long time He saw him again. The only problem is that the friend is not responding to Him and my elder brother would like to be able to sit with him for a few minutes. As it so happens this man is sitting on your verandah, so it would be ideal if my brother could come here and sit with his friend for a while inside this bank, to spend some time with him, away from the hustle and bustle of the street, and maybe then this man would respond.

"Yes, but what do you want of me?" "Well, sorry for putting you to so much trouble, it is very good of you to do this, but what else can I do, how else can my brother sit with this friend?" You see, I was apologizing for putting him to so much trouble as if he had already agreed to my request. And I went on and explained to him that it would be best if everyone else left the bank.

"What do you want? You want me to ask the clerks to leave?" the manager asks me in some astonishment. "Yes," I reply, "but don't worry. They can stand on the verandah, and I will also stand watch at the door to see that no one else enters, so you have nothing to worry about and it will only be for a few minutes, and this will be such a wonderful opportunity for my elder brother," and so on and so forth.

The manager hesitates, as if searching within himself, but finally he agrees and he asks all the customers, all the tellers, even the guard to leave, and he lets Baba and the *mast* come inside and use the bank. I remember this so vividly because there was still money lying about. The manager just had everyone leave then and there, and all the bank's business was just left lying about. But the manager is still standing there himself, so I say, "Please sir, you too, come out. We will all stand on one corner of the verandah." And then I walk out with him again, you see, acting as I expected him to come with me, and he did. And then, without even asking his permission, I shut the doors behind us as if the bank belonged to me and I closed it up and we stood there while Baba contacted the *mast*.

The situation was an impossible one, if you think about it from a worldly point of view; it was preposterous of us even to suggest it, but, by His grace, it became possible. And, as it turned out, it was a good mast contact; I could tell right away when Baba came out that the contact had gone well, that Baba was very happy, so I thanked the manager and we left. But this presumption on our part, this assuming authority which we did not possess, at least in the worldly sense, was a necessary part of our lives with Baba. Because we were serving the Lord, we did have the authority, but it was still embarrassing for us to try and exercise it. Let me give you another example.

I remember one time we were in Surat somewhere. I don't recall exactly, perhaps Kawnpore. It had been a long journey and it was very hot and we had some hours to wait before our connecting train. We were all exhausted, so Baba said, "Where should we rest?"

It was a large station and there was nowhere on the platforms where we could rest, nor did we want to. But as we crossed over the raised walkway above the tracks – you may have seen how in India at the large stations they have walkways crossing the tracks so you can shift from one platform to another – from there we could see the surrounding town, and Baba spotted a quiet secluded cottage and said, "We'll go there."

So I studied the direction of the cottage because I had to figure out how to walk there once we got down, and I noted various landmarks so I could lead Baba there, and we started walking, carrying all of our luggage on our heads. It so happens the cottage was a P.W.D. godown, a storehouse. There was a nice compound there, some trees and grass, and it looked perfect, but the gate was locked. So I called out to the gatekeeper, "Hey, there, come on over here and open this gate." I acted as if I had every right to be there and it was his duty to obey. So he came over and I said, "Open up, we want to come in and rest for a while."

He said he couldn't do that, he couldn't let anyone in without proper authorization. But I told him there was no question of authorization, we weren't going to go into any of the godown rooms, we were traveling and we just wanted to rest under the trees for a while. "Don't keep us waiting here, that is not good, open the gate now so we can rest," I commanded.

And the poor gatekeeper, what could he do? So he opened up the gate and let us in. I remember it so well, because we had such a good sleep. I remember Baba lay down next to me under a tree, and the rest of the mandali were a little distance off, and we all slept. We were so exhausted.

The next thing I knew Baba was shaking me, "Eruch, get up. Look over there. What is happening?" Baba gestured. I sat up and I saw that some official had come to the gate and was loudly abusing the gatekeeper. He was shouting, "Who are these strangers? This is why the gate is kept locked, so that no one can get inside." And he was very angry. It turns out he was the executive engineer. He must have just stopped by for an inspection and seen all of us lying there in the compound sleeping and got wild on the gatekeeper. Finally he said, "You are dismissed," and then he drove off.

Baba turned to me and said, "You see what has happened. For our sake this poor fellow has been dismissed. Do something."

"But Baba, what can I do?"

"Go tell the officer that we are not ragamuffins. We are people of status. Tell him who your father is and see what you can do about this."

So I went to the gatekeeper and said, "Who was that?" And he said it was the executive engineer. "Oh, where does he stay?" "He does not live here. He is on tour." "But where would he be now?" "He has gone to the government resthouse, you can find him there."

So I went to the resthouse. I was still in my shorts, mind you. Baba had wakened me and told me to go and there wasn't time to get dressed, so I went to the resthouse and knocked on the door and got the executive engineer. I don't know what he must have thought seeing me, but I didn't give him a chance to say anything. I apologized. I explained that I had been one of those sleeping in the compound and that I was very distressed to have heard the altercation with the gatekeeper. "After all, it is not his fault," I said. "I asked for his permission to stay there and when he found out who we were he granted us the permission. He did not just open the gate to anyone."

"But who are you?"

"My father is the chief inspector of boilers and factories."

"Oh," the executive engineer said, and I could see that he was impressed. His tone changed completely because my father had such a high post. And I explained that a group of us had gone on pilgrimage and we had been traveling by train for a long time and were very tired and just wanted to rest for a few hours. I explained that we had assured the gatekeeper we would not be using any of the rooms. We just wanted to rest in the open for a few hours.

The executive engineer said it was okay, he hadn't understood. And that now that he did, it was all right.

"No sir," I said, "what about the gatekeeper? You dismissed him."

"Don't worry about that, I will see to it that nothing happens," he assured me. But I wasn't assured. I knew Baba's ways and I knew if I went back to Baba and reported, this He would not be satisfied, so I kept on. "Excuse me, sir, but the gatekeeper is really quite distressed about this." You see, it was Baba I was worried about, but I couldn't say that. So I blamed it on the gatekeeper and I said, "Please, sir, would it be all right if I brought the gatekeeper here so you could tell him personally that he is not being dismissed?"

"How long will it take?" "Not long. I can have him here in fifteen minutes or so." And he agreed, so this is what I did. And only then did I feel relieved because I knew Baba would now be pleased. And we had a good rest in that compound.

So over the years, perhaps, when we saw that every time the impossible became possible we started to have that inner confidence that Baba would turn the key, but we still had to always do our best, to make every effort, and we couldn't become puffed up about it when we succeeded. And of course, even though I say it always worked out, that the impossible always became possible, we still had many experiences when the possible became impossible and we weren't able to accomplish something which on the face of it seemed quite simple. So we couldn't ever relax, there was always that tension, at least for the first so many years. And when we did succeed, we couldn't feel puffed up. I told you the story about the time I had done some very difficult work for Baba and felt a little sense of pride that I had accomplished such a difficult task and how Baba deflated that pride by ordering me to eat shit, so even though I never knew a time when Baba's impossible orders, by His grace, didn't become possible, still it was an ordeal for us to have to see that they were obeyed. And that is why I say you have no idea how embarrassing and humiliating our life with Baba was.

KIRPAL SINGH

THE OTHER DAY I MENTIONED HOW EMBARRASSING and humiliating our life with our Lord, Meher Baba, was. How Baba would routinely ask us to do something which was impossible, which was preposterous from a worldly point of view, and how embarrassing this was. Even though, as I said, by His grace, it would become possible. But this doesn't give you a true picture of our life with Baba either. It is like our discussion the other day. What I said was true, but it was only part of the truth.

So today I am going to give you another part of the truth, a picture of our life with Baba from a slightly different angle. Someone was asking earlier about Guruprasad. Well, the incident I am relating took place there. There was a retired army major in Poona who used to come and see Baba occasionally. It is easy for me to remember him because he took to wearing a long ocher-colored robe of renunciation. The robe was quite colorful and printed all over it was a mantra, "Ram Sita, Ram Sita," or something like that. As I said, he used to come periodically to see Baba at Guruprasad, but this one time I remember he brought his wife.

The program had already started, and the room was quite full. As usual, one side of the room was for men and the other for women with an aisle down the center. Baba was sitting at the far end of the hall in a chair, and I was standing off a little to one side so I could interpret Baba's gestures.

I was standing there when I noticed this retired army major enter the room. He was with his wife. And it seems he was very anxious to introduce her to Baba. But for some reason, instead of simply walking in front of her, or letting her go first and walking behind her, he came in walking backwards. He was talking to his wife, encouraging her to come and meet Baba, and, at the same time, he was bending over, trying to push people aside so the aisle would be wider, and in this manner he approached Baba.

I expected that as soon as he got a little bit closer he would straighten up and turn around, that he would face Baba, but he kept coming with his back to Baba. Not even his back, I should say, since he was bent over; he was really, unbeknownst to him, approaching with his bottom to Baba. He was shoving his fanny in Baba's face. At least, that is how it appeared to me. He came closer and closer and I was afraid, since he couldn't see where he was going, that he would actually bump into Baba. Now, it was my duty to see that Baba's body was protected, because after the second accident Baba's body was very sensitive to physical contact, even a little jarring would be very painful for His hip joint.

Baba was in a chair. His leg was damaged. He could not get up easily. I knew that. I knew Baba would have to remain sitting there while this man backed right into Him, so I stepped forward and put my hand out, to stop him. To let him know that he had come far enough and that he should now turn around.

But, at the same time, to be perfectly honest, I admit I was also upset that this man had so little common sense that it never occurred to him that this is not the way you approach the God-Man, the Avatar, with your fanny stuck up high in the air. So I stepped forward and I put my hand out, like this, to see that he kept his distance, so he would realize he had come far enough and that it was time to turn around.

But even though I just put my hand out, because the man was bending over and was turning this way and that, as he tried to clear people from his wife's path, he lost his balance and fell forward into the crowd. But what made it even worse, he sprawled into the lap of one of the women that was sitting there.

He picked himself up and he was furious. He turned around and started abusing me like anything. He started a long tirade, the gist of which was that I didn't have proper respect for him, that I had been rude, that I had been the worst sort of scoundrel to push him into those women, that I had no sense of decency. But not in such mild terms, mind you. I'm telling you the gist of it, but he expressed himself much more forcefully.

And Baba was upset. "Why did you push him?" Baba demanded. "I didn't push him, Baba," I said. "I merely put my hand out so he wouldn't back into You." "No," Baba gestured. "You did the wrong thing. Apologize to this man. Bow down to him and ask his forgiveness." I was upset at this man for his rudeness in approaching Baba the way he had, and I was completely out of mood now that he had abused me so much in front of everyone when I was not at fault. You know that I have a temper, that it is not my nature to meekly accept such abuse without giving back a tongue lashing of my own, and now Baba was telling me to apologize.

So I bowed to this man and said, "Please forgive me, it was my fault." But still the man wasn't satisfied and he continued to abuse me. In fact, the next time I saw him, I happened to meet him one day in Poona, he began abusing me all over again. I only met him a couple of times after that, but each time he would start in again about how rude I had been to him.

But because it was Baba's order, I had to willingly submit to his abuse. After all, what was our duty but simply to obey Baba's orders, no matter how embarrassing or humiliating the situation? And it was. That is what I am trying to bring home to you. It is not that we did not have faith in Baba. That was our refuge, as it were. But if we were anchored in the safe harbor of obedience to Him, that doesn't mean that we didn't still feel the strong winds of the world's opinions. We were not of the world, but we were in it, and our minds registered these things, or at least, my mind did, I cannot speak for the others. It is possible to become immune to the stings, the mosquito bites of the world, but the droning that mosquitos make in your own mind, that is very irritating, that is much more difficult to block out.

That is why I say, over and over, that we are all in the same boat. Because we all have the same mind, the same heart. Just because we were with Baba does not mean that our minds would not register irritation or annoyance or embarrassment. In fact, Baba seemed to put us in those situations all the more. But one thing I have marked is that when we think of ourselves less, we tend to be less distracted by such thoughts.

Some of you have asked about Kirpal Singh and whether he ever met Baba. The answer is yes, he met Baba on several occasions. Baba used to refer to Kirpal Singh as a "saint," and treated him very affectionately, and Kirpal Singh, whenever I was there at any rate, always used to show great respect for Baba. I remember one time, in Guruprasad, that Kirpal Singh came to see Baba.

This was not one of the large *darshan* programs. I don't recall the occasion, but it was held in the room where Baba used to meet with the mandali, so it couldn't have been a very large program. There was a chair for Baba to sit on, and there may have been some chairs at the sides of the room for some of the elderly folk to use, but most people just sat on a carpet on the floor in front of Baba. I was near Baba when Kirpal Singh and a small group of his followers entered.

Baba was very happy to see Kirpal Singh and greeted him warmly. Then Kirpal Singh went to sit on the carpet in front of Baba. One of his followers, however, thought it wasn't fitting that his master should sit on the ground with the rest of them. So he went to get a chair so that Kirpal Singh could be higher than the rest. I don't blame him, because in a way he was right. How could they, as disciples, sit on the same level as their master? It isn't right. But when he went to get the chair, Kirpal Singh was not pleased. He refused to sit in the chair and insisted on staying on the floor.

After all, how could he sit before Baba on a chair? He knew that it was only fitting for him to sit on the ground before Baba's feet. Of course we all have different ideas, according to the depth of our understanding, of what constitutes the proper amount of respect which is due us and which we owe to others. But just see the difference. Here is a man whom Baba refers to as a saint, and he would not even sit in a chair before Baba, and here is this retired army major who insisted on his right to put his fanny right in Baba's face. Almost always, it is those who insist on privileges who are least worthy of them, while those who truly deserve our respect are very humble and self-effacing. At least this is what I have found. And that is why I say that it is when we take ourselves too seriously that we are especially susceptible to the mosquito bites of our mind. If we think more of Baba, it is like a net that surrounds us, and we won't get bitten. However, we will still be bothered by the buzz, that is what I am saying, but over time and by His grace, we can learn to ignore that too.

But it is not easy. And our obedience to Baba's orders time and time again placed us in very awkward situations with respect, not just to the world, but to Baba's lovers. For example, it was a standing order that we were to see that Baba was not disturbed when He was in seclusion. We had to act as if we had hearts of stone when people used to beg us to be permitted to see Baba for only a moment. But we couldn't be soft-hearted, no matter how much we might be moved witnessing the plight of those sincere ones who loved Baba and only wanted a glimpse of Him. Of course, from time to time we would give in to our feelings and try to help these people, and it almost always ended up causing trouble for Baba. So we learned to harden our hearts.

Not that we would be rude to people when they came. That would not have pleased Baba either. We would sympathize with people, and it was no lie, we did feel for them, we understood their plight, their longing, but we were helpless; there was nothing we could do for them. Baba's "orders" means what, after all? We couldn't just disregard them, so we would explain the situation, our helplessness, and beg the people to have patience, to be resigned to His will.

Usually people understood and took it well. Sometimes, however, people used to get wild with us, accuse us of being jealous, of not wanting anyone else to see Baba. They would abuse us like anything and we had to accept it. What else could we do?

And if such altercations came to Baba's attention, He would always take the other person's side. He would express surprise and astonishment that we had been trying to keep someone from Him, and make that person feel that of course it was all right that they had come to see Him. That He had been waiting for them for a long time. Baba might even turn to us and gesture, "What! My lover came and you didn't even tell Me!" And we had to keep quiet. Baba might have told us only ten minutes before that even if God came to the door we should keep Him out, yet here He was rebuking us for keeping away one of His lovers. But we would just accept it all. That was our duty. To accept whatever Baba gave us, whether it be abuse or praise. And that made it easier for us to learn to accept whatever the world gave us, whether it be abuse or praise. It is that acceptance of Baba's will, of His whim, that ultimately allows us to ignore the buzzing of our minds. And I'll tell you something else, the secret to real happiness lies in that acceptance as well.

⚜ M O N E Y

THIS MORNING I WAS TELLING YOU SOME STORIES that concerned money. Well, I just remembered another amusing incident. It concerns Gustadji. As I was telling you earlier, Baba used to tell us periodically that He had no money. If the mandali complained about the plain food we were getting, or the fact that we were only allowed one little piece of bar soap to use, Baba would gesture, "What can I do, I have no money." And often Baba would pull out His pockets to show us that they were empty.

And it was true. Baba had no money for Himself, or for those who lived with Him. The money that people used to give Him was given away to others. You have no idea how much money Baba used to give to other people. There were so many families Baba used to support, so many individuals, and this, of course, was in addition to all the *masts* that Baba used to provide for.

I think I've told you that whenever Baba would contact a *mast*, or even when one of the mandali would contact a *mast*, Baba would usually see that we also contacted the person who was taking care of the *mast*. You see in India, *masts*, even people who are only mad, are regarded as holy. And usually wherever you find a *mast*, unless it's a wandering *mast*, you'll find someone in the community who sees to the *mast's* welfare. And we would have to find this person and then arrange for them to feed and clothe the *mast* with the money we would give them.

Whenever Baba was finished working with a *mast* and sent the *mast* back home, He would also make arrangements with the person who used to look after the *mast* to continue to do so. And if there was no one in the community who was already doing so, then often Baba would have us make some arrangement with a chaiwala or someone who stayed near where the *mast* tended to spend his time to take care of him.

Nowadays people have computers to do everything. You people are always telling us we have to get computers for the office, to keep the books, to file papers, to organize things, but Baba used to keep track of all this, of the hundreds and hundreds of people He was responsible for, without any computer, without writing anything down. Baba's perfection was such that He would never overlook even the tiniest detail of anything.

Anyway, getting back to our story or we'll be late for tea and Aloba will be upset, the mandali often had to do without. I remember at one time we had toothbrushes but no toothpaste. We used to rub our brushes on a little piece of bar soap and brush our teeth with that. We had no bathroom soap. We would be given one little piece of bar-soap and that had to do for all of our washing, not just of ourselves, but our clothes too. We didn't have servants to do things like that, we had to do our own wash, and we had to find the time to do it.

This wasn't easy. So, often it was only at the end of the day, just before bed, that we would have a spare moment, and then we would gather around a well and do our wash. In the early years the mandali used to look forward to this moment because it was the only chance we got all day long to be together, to talk with each other. You just have no idea how busy Baba used to keep us, what our life with Him was like.

And on top of this, the manager, whether it was Kaka or Pendu, whoever was put in charge, the manager would always complain that we were using too much soap. We would go at the beginning of the month to get the tiny piece of bar soap which had to last for the whole month, and often before the month was out the soap would be gone, and if you tried to get more, the manager would begin complaining. "What have you been doing that you want more soap? You got your one piece, now go." And we would say, "Yes, one piece is fine if you've been sitting inside keeping accounts all day, but I've been working on the pump and my clothes can't be cleaned with just that one piece." "No," the manager would say, "you've been wasting the soap, you don't get any more."

Wasting it, we wouldn't even bathe properly! We would just rub a little on us and then spread it all over. We were so careful, so frugal in our use, and then the manager would accuse us of wasting the soap. All of this fuss, mind you, over a piece of soap that didn't even cost a rupee, a few annas only. Not only that, but we were all living together. The manager knew we weren't being extravagant, but he would refuse to give us extra soap, or he would finally give it to us, but only after a big argument and yelling and haranguing us.

It used to make me mad. After all, it was not as if we were asking for some luxury item, only a little soap so we could keep our clothes and ourselves reasonably clean. And why did we want to do this? For ourselves? No. I didn't care what I looked like, or smelled like. I would have been content to look like one of those people who sleeps out in the street, but because we were with Baba, we wanted to keep up our appearances at least to some modest extent. Because we were in Baba's company and others would see us and would judge Baba partly on how we, the mandali, comported ourselves, we wanted the extra soap. So I used to get wild when the manager wouldn't give it to me when I needed it.

And so, periodically, one of the mandali would complain to Baba. And Baba's answer, almost every time, was to pull out His pockets and shrug, "What can I do, I have no money." So one time this was too much for Gustadji. As I've told you before, Gustadji was really a delightful character. There was something very appealing about his looks – you must have seen him in the movies, with his round cheeks and his big smile. And, even though he was on silence, he was a wonderful storyteller. It seems, in the early years, he must have had the tendency to talk quite a lot, which may have been why Baba put him on silence. And the other disciples, the younger ones especially, seemed to have given Gustadji a lot of trouble. I don't know what it was all about because this was all before my time, but I remember Gustadji suddenly telling Baba about the old horse in the stable. That was after I came. Have you heard this?

As you know, Gustadji was a great storyteller and he used to amuse Baba very much with his accounts of his dreams and what not. Of course, being on silence, Gustadji used to use gestures. Not the same ones Baba used, he had his own alphabet and his own system of gestures, but I learned to read them as well, and I used to translate often for Gustadji. Of course as I read out the gestures to Baba, I used to add my own embellishments, and Gustadji would like that, and Baba would be amused by the end result.

So one day, out of the blue as it were, Gustadji suddenly says, "Oh, now I know why I have been treated this way."

Baba looked surprised. "What?" He asked.

"When I was a kid in Bombay, Baba, I used to walk to school every day," Gustadji explained. "On my way I had to pass a stable, and whenever I went by I would look at the horses." And here Gustadji described the horses he had seen. "And I couldn't help noticing that these horses used to come and go but that there was one old horse that was always there. No matter how often the other horses changed, he was always there. And I used to notice that sometimes a carriage would be hitched up and this old horse was always one of the two horses pulling the carriage. Because he was old, he tended to be slow and steady, but the younger horse with him would be prancing around and would want to go very fast and the driver would beat the old horse to urge him to keep pace with the younger one. Time after time this old horse was paired with one of the young horses and every time, although the old horse was well trained and knew the correct pace to use, he would be maltreated by the driver, whipped and beaten to force him to keep up with the reckless gallop of the younger horse.

"As a child I used to wonder about this. Why did the owners of the stable keep that old horse if they were only going to abuse him? If they didn't think he went fast enough, why didn't they get rid of him and only keep the young horses? After all, it seems that they never kept the young ones for very long. Why was he the one horse that always remained in the stable while the younger ones came and went? I never understood that, Baba. It didn't make sense to me. If he was too old, why didn't they put two young horses together to pull the carriage? I used to walk by the stables every day, and every day, I would see this, and I could never figure out what was behind it all.

"And I used to notice that the young horses got the best treatment. They always had nice feedbags filled with oats and hay, but the old horse had to feed himself from whatever old hay he could find on the ground. The young horses were always well groomed and looked after, but no one seemed to take any care for the old horse. Even when the young horses did something wrong, it was the old horse that got whipped. And I would see this and I would wonder about it.

"Then as I got older someone explained it to me. The old horse belonged to the stable. He was used to break in the young ones, to train them, to teach them the proper way to be. Other people, wealthy people, would send their horses to this stable to be trained. That was why they were well fed and looked after properly. Once they learned from the old horse how to behave, they would be sent back to their owners. That was why the young horses used to come and go but the old horse always remained.

"Now I understand, Baba, why I have had to suffer all these years. It was to properly train all these young horses around you that you have done this to me. I have been abused and mistreated so that they might learn."

Baba laughed. We all laughed, because Gustadji would say all this with great good humor. He had that capacity so that even his complaints brought a smile to our lips. He had perfected the art of entertaining Baba with his complaints.

So this one day, when Baba again complained about having no money, Gustadji gestures, "Baba, You always say You need money. Well, I have a plan and if You'll follow it, we won't ever have to worry about money again."

"Oh?" Baba immediately looks intrigued. "What's that?" And with that Gustadji launches into the following story. Of course, I was the one actually talking, because I would look at Gustadji's fingers and speak out what he was "saying."

"One day," he begins, "there was a famous con man. He was not just a con man, but a master con man and he had his own bunch of disciples who lived with him and who practiced the art of fraud and deception under his guidance. This man was so famous, so well known, that eventually it became impossible for him to make any money where he was living. Not only he, but even his disciples were well known. When anyone saw them coming they would avoid them, because they knew that if they got involved with them at all, somehow or other it would end up costing them money. Even the children, when they saw one of the con man's disciples coming, would run and hide.

"And this happened not just in the village where they lived, but in all the villages in that district. Every day they made less and less money, and it was obvious that if this kept up much longer, the day would come when they wouldn't make any money at all and they would starve. So one day the master con man calls his disciples together for a conference.

" 'I've been thinking about our situation,' he begins, 'and it seems obvious to me that we will have to move to another place. But what will happen there? Eventually the same thing will happen and after a few years we will again have to move. We could do this. India is a big country after all, and we could simply move and settle down again every few years, but that doesn't appeal to me. I have given this a lot of thought and I have come up with a plan. If you all agree to follow it, we will move this time and, within a few months, not only will we have enough money to live on for the rest of our lives, but we won't ever have to move again. Does that sound good to you?' "

"Of course, everyone said that sounded fine. 'But this will not be easy,' the con man warned. 'It will be hard work, but if you trust me and promise to do whatever I say without asking any questions, I promise you that within a few months we will have more money than you have ever dreamed possible. What do you say?'

"Well, he was their guru, their master, and they had faith in him, so all agreed. Then the master says, 'We still have some money left in our treasury, and whatever you have privately I want you to give me now.'"There was a little grumbling at this, because although they always gave the money they earned to the master, he would always return some of it and tell them that that was theirs and no one had any right to it. It seemed now as if he was going against this principle, but he reminded them, 'I told you this would not be easy, but trust me and I guarantee that you will not regret it.'

"So they all give over their money to the master, who then says, 'Now, before we end up starving, we will start searching for a new place to live. But remember, wherever we go, you must do whatever I say with no questions and no arguments. Take an oath that you will obey me and I promise you that you will not be disappointed.' So they all took the oath and set out on their journey.

"After traveling for a week, they had left their old district behind and were now entering an area where no one knew them. And the disciples start looking at the villages they are passing, judging them as to whether they look like good places to settle down. And how do they judge? They don't look to see if the land is fertile, they don't look to see how available water is, they don't look for any of the signs that ordinary people look for; they look to see what sort of opportunities there seem to be for them to practice their craft. And a few of the villages they pass through seem promising, but their master insists they keep going.

"After a few weeks of this the men start grumbling. Their money is slowly getting exhausted, they haven't earned any new money the whole time, and there is no sign that they will ever settle down. But all the master says is, 'Trust me.' Finally they came to a small village and the master announces, 'This is where we will settle.'

"The men can't believe it. Not only is the village poor, but it happens to be a particularly devout and religious village. The master says, 'This is it, now we just have to walk a few furlongs out into the country to find the perfect spot.'

"None of the men could figure out what he was talking about. The perfect spot for what? It doesn't make any sense to them. Especially since they had already passed what seemed the ideal village—a newly prosperous settlement, full of flourishing businessmen, the sort of place where people only seemed interested in one thing, making money. And, as all con men know, the easiest people to cheat are those who are interested in becoming rich themselves. But they had passed that village by, and only when they came to this poor and devout village does the master declare that this will be their new home.

"That night, after selecting the spot a few kilometers outside of the village, the master calls his disciples together. 'It won't be long now,' he tells them. 'But now it is more important than ever that you all must do exactly what I say. I want you to dig a pit right here, four feet by four feet by four feet.'

"This didn't make matters any clearer for them, but the master kept reassuring them that now their golden days were not far off, so they spent the night digging the pit. At last, when it was done, the master said, 'Now put the loose dirt back inside and put a mat down over the whole area.'

"Some of the disciples began to suspect that their master had gone mad, but he seemed so sure of himself that they obeyed. 'Now clear off an area twenty feet by twenty feet and sweep it clean,' he ordered.

"Once again, with some grumbling under their breath, they did as they were told. But the most astonishing order was yet to come. When they were finished, the master seemed delighted with their preparations and, as dawn was just breaking, instead of allowing them to sleep, he declared, 'Wonderful. Soon we will all be very rich. But from today onwards you must all sit along the outside of the square you have just cleaned. Four of you should sit on each side, facing the center, and I want you to sit that way all day long.'

"'Doing what?' they asked. 'Doing precisely nothing. But look spiritual.' 'How will we do that?' the disgruntled disciples demanded. 'It's easy,' the master assured them. 'Just pretend you're constipated. Sit quietly and look as if you are preoccupied with something inside you and don't pay any attention to anything that happens around you. If anyone approaches you and says anything, don't answer them. No matter what, don't speak.'

"'And what will you be doing?' they asked.

"'I'll be sitting right here, in the middle.'

"It sounded utterly crazy, but they were all too tired from the digging to feel like doing anything anyway, except sleep, so they all sat in their respective places and waited to see what would happen. But, as far as they could tell, nothing much happened. They hadn't been sitting long when some young boys herding goats passed by. The boys, of course, ran over to see what they were doing. But they weren't doing anything, just sitting there. The boys called out to them and asked them where they were from, but they didn't say anything. In fact, no matter what the boys said, the disciples didn't answer, so the boys soon lost interest and went on their way.

"Some time after that, a few farmers on the way to their fields passed by. Like the boys, they too were attracted by this strange sight and came over to investigate. They too asked questions but, receiving no answers, after a while they wandered off to their fields.

"And that was all that happened, except that in the middle of the day, some of the farmers' wives came by carrying their husbands' meals wrapped in cloth. Being women, they didn't approach but they certainly looked at the men intently from the corners of their eyes and, as soon as they passed, started wondering aloud just who those men could be.

"After a little while, the women returned from the fields,

walking a little slower this time so they could get a better look at this strange group. And then, hours later, the farmers and the boys herding the goats and cattle passed by. Once again, a few of the farmers tried to strike up a conversation, but again the con men just sat there without saying anything. And that was it.

"The master, however, was delighted with the day's events. 'It won't be long now,' he crowed. 'That's good,' his disciples replied, 'because we can't keep this up much longer. Sitting still in this sun without talking is hard work.' 'Don't worry,' he assured them. 'The way things are going, we won't have to wait much longer. Just a few more days.' 'A few more days!' the men protested. 'We'll go crazy sitting here doing nothing for that long. And what will we eat, and when do we get to sleep?' and so the complaints started pouring out. But the master managed to console them by reminding them how rich they would all be soon and how then a few days' inconvenience would seem like nothing to amass such treasure. 'Besides,' he added, 'aren't I sitting here too?'

"The men didn't have an answer for that, because of course the master was also enduring everything they were, and so they stopped their grumbling. 'Now, tomorrow, do the same thing,' the master advised. 'Just sit quietly and try to look spiritual if anyone approaches. And don't say anything. But, if the village elders come, then point to me. No matter what they say, simply point to me, and let me do all the talking. Don't say anything. And another thing. No matter what I say, don't pay any attention to it. Just continue to sit where you are. Is that understood?'

"The men all said they understood, and then the master called two of them over and whispered some instructions in their ears. He reached into the bag of money which he carried, which contained the group's entire assets, and doled out a certain amount to the two, who then got up and walked away leaving the others sitting there.

"They looked questioningly at the master, but all he said was, 'Now go to bed, because we'll have to get up early tomorrow and do some hard work before sunrise.' But when the men tried asking him more, he wouldn't say a word. He just lay down and prepared for bed.

"Sure enough, a few hours before sunrise, they were awakened by the heavy rumbling of a bullock cart. To their surprise, their two companions who had left the night before were driving it. They wondered what could be inside and immediately thought that perhaps it was filled with the gold their master kept telling them would soon be theirs and so, tired as they were, their greed got them to their feet and they rushed over. Imagine their surprise when they saw that the bullock cart was completely full of chickpeas!

"'Hurry,' the master ordered, 'dig up the loose dirt from the pit and put the chickpeas inside. Then cover them with a few inches of dirt and put the mat back on top. Throw the dirt you remove far away so it's not obvious. Hurry, our fortune depends on this being done in the dark when no one can see.' There was so much urgency in the master's voice that even though it sounded insane, they got to work and began shoveling the loose dirt from the pit.

Meanwhile the master had others unload the bullock cart and, as soon as it was empty, he told the two disciples to leave at once and return the cart. Then he returned to his men and urged them to keep working as hard as they could. Under his constant prodding the men worked hard and, well before dawn, they had finished pouring in the last of the chickpeas and were putting the few inches of dirt on top.

"The master was so excited about what they had accomplished that they felt as if they had pulled off some great triumph, but there was still a lot of confusion and doubt in their minds. However, there was no time to ask any questions because it was just about sunrise, and they knew they had to take up their positions and sit quietly for the rest of the day.

"That day was pretty much like the day before. Only, this time, just about dusk, a group of men came walking slowly towards them. It was obvious from the way they held themselves that they were the village elders. They came forward and began questioning the men, but they refused to answer. They just sat there. Finally one of the con men pointed to the master, who was sitting silently in the middle of the square, on the edge of the mat which covered the secret pit."

Mind you, Gustadji is telling all of this to Baba. And every now and then Baba would interrupt and gesture "So? When are you going to tell Me how to make money?" And Gustadji would answer back, "Wait a minute, Baba, I'm coming to that," and then he would continue with this long story. It is a story, in fact it is a fairly well-known story in India, but Gustadji was making it into an epic. It's too bad none of you had the opportunity to meet Gustadji. Some of you say I am a good storyteller but to tell you the truth, I feel that I am just like a bee, droning away, throwing out words. But Gustadji knew how to tell a good story. He would do it with such enthusiasm and such animated gestures, acting it out as he went, that Baba was always entertained by the performance. The way I tell the story now is one thing, but the way Gustadji told it to Baba was something else entirely.

So Gustadji says to Baba, "Just wait a minute, I'm coming to that," and then he continues. "When the elders approached the master con man, at first he didn't say anything. He just sat there seemingly absorbed in his own meditation. But, after a while, he looked up, startled, as if he had only just then noticed that someone was talking to him. 'Forgive me,' he says and pays his respects to the elders. 'What can I do for you?'

"'You can tell us who you are and what you are doing here,' one of the elders replied.

"'That is simple. As you can see for yourself, we are a simple band of mendicants, and we aren't doing anything. We are just sitting here, remembering the Lord.'

"'But what sect are you? We have never seen any others like your group. And why are you sitting in this manner, facing one another?'

"'We are no sect, we simply love the Lord and, as to our sitting this way, it's, well . . .' and he hesitates as if unsure whether to divulge the reason or not. He seems to think it over and then only says, 'Well, let us just say that we prefer to sit this way.'

"But the very way he said it makes it obvious that there's some other reason for this peculiar arrangement. Yet, despite further questioning, it is clear that he is not going to reveal what it is. So, after some more conversation, the elders take their leave, and when they are out of sight, the master claps his hands together and laughs and announces, 'I tell you, men, it won't be long now. The money is almost ours.' But that's all he'll say.

"The next few days are pretty much just like the last few. They continue to sit there, saying nothing, and in the evening some of the elders come by to see if they can learn the secret of their sitting in that manner. But there is one change, and for the men it is both a most important and most welcome change. Now, when the women go to the fields with food for their husbands, they tend to stop for a moment and leave something for them to eat as well, a few rotis, some rice and dal mixed, sometimes even a cooked vegetable. And the boys will offer some curds and milk in the morning when they head out to the fields with their herds.

"But there was no sign that the villagers were going to part with a pie, and even the food they gave them was plain and not particularly plentiful. Now that they knew what had been in the master's mind and could see that it wasn't working, they got very upset, and that night they began to complain in right earnest. 'Fools,' the master retorted. 'Everything is going exactly according to my plan.'

"But what is your plan?' they all wanted to know. 'Ah, that's a secret which I can't divulge,' the master admitted, and disappointed though they were, there was nothing to do but continue to sit and wait and see what would happen. They were slowly becoming almost as curious as the villagers to see where this would all end. So they were all terribly excited when one day the master whispered to one of the elders, 'There are too many others here now, but come back later this evening, alone, and I'll tell you why we're here.'

"The elder came back alone that night, and the master, after looking around in all directions to make sure that they couldn't be overheard, confessed, 'We are here to serve the Lord.' ' But we already know that,' the elder replied. 'No, I mean we have come to this spot, specifically, to serve the Lord,' the master explained.

"' But why this spot?'

"The master looked around again to make sure that no one else was around and then replied in a low voice, ' Because it is on this spot that the Lord will appear.'

"' What?' the elder exclaims. 'The Lord will appear here! How do you know?'

"Again the master seemed reluctant, but finally he blurts out, 'Promise not to tell anyone else, but the truth is that the Lord appeared to me and told me He would manifest here, and so we are simply waiting for our Lord to manifest.'

"'To manifest here!' The elder can't believe his ears, and as soon as he can politely take his leave, he goes hurrying off to share this astonishing news with everyone else in the village, even though he has pledged himself to secrecy.

"The next day they found that the food offerings were more generous and that more of the villagers started to come round to see them. They always had some excuse, they had to go see a neighbor about borrowing a bullock, they were going to a different well because the water was sweeter there, some excuse or other to pass by and spend some time in the company of the con men.

"That night, the master called one of his men to him. 'There isn't much time left now, so we had better prepare the final stage while we still have a little privacy. Soon the villagers will be hanging around here all night long.' And he gave his disciple the bag of money and whispered some instructions in his ear. 'Remember,' he called out, as the disciple prepared to leave, 'travel by the lesser-used paths and stay in the woods on your return until it is safe for you to enter our camp.'

"When the con men saw that the last of their money was being given away, they had mixed emotions. On the one hand, they were a little nervous, because if this plan didn't work they would have nothing. But on the other hand, they knew this meant that the end of the plan was now in sight and soon they might all be rich.

"The next day, as usual, various villagers found excuses to visit the con men and, at different times throughout the day, the elders would come and privately sit with the master con man, trying to find out from him exactly what the Lord had said. The master pretended to be very reluctant to talk about it, and once even snapped at an elder, 'How can I sit here and remember my Lord if I have to answer questions all the time?' The elder was properly abashed, paid his respects, and left, holding the con man in greater reverence than before.

"But that evening the master confided in an elder, 'I don't know what to do. Perhaps you can help me. The Lord has come to me again, and He has told me that He will be manifesting here soon.'

"'What! Soon?' he exclaimed, unable to believe this good fortune.

"'Yes, but here is my problem. As you can see, we are but poor mendicants.' At this, all the ears of his companions picked up, thinking that at last they were getting somewhere. And the elder too seemed to sense this, for a curious reserve immediately molded his features. But the master continued, 'Nor do we want any money, for of what use has our Lord for money? He is the king of wealth, so He does not expect us to offer Him what is already His.' The elder looked relieved to hear this, and his companions felt disheartened, but both tried to hide their true feelings.

"'I've been thinking. This spot is undoubtedly holy, because it is here the Lord has chosen to manifest, but it is also rather barren. Wouldn't it be fitting if we planted some flowers around this square so it would be a little more beautiful for our Lord? Doesn't it behoove us as His devotees to try and do that?'

"The elder agreed that this was a good idea. "'But,' the master continued, 'we have no money and have no seeds or bushes with us. Do you think it would be possible for some of those in the village to donate a few flowers and shrubs for us to plant for the Lord? We will tend to them, and water them and care for them. But if they could donate some from their fields and houses and gardens, we would be very thankful.'

"The elder, relieved that he was not being asked for money, instantly agreed and said he would go back to the village and personally order everyone to donate at least one plant.

"'No,' the master begged, 'don't do that. This is for our Lord, so the gifts must be gifts, they must be given out of love and not because you have told people to give.'

"The elder bowed his head in submission to this superior understanding of devotion and went away with a new respect and regard for the master who seems so eminently sensible and devout in all things.

"The villagers were tremendously excited to hear the news that the Lord would be manifesting there soon, and very little work got done that day in the fields or the homes as the entire village came out to plant flowers and shrubs to create a suitable garden spot for the Lord. It was only with the greatest difficulty that the master convinced them to leave them alone that night. They didn't want to miss the chance of seeing the Lord manifest, and it was only when the master promised them that the Lord was not going to manifest that night that they reluctantly agreed to go.

"'Please,' he pleaded. 'The Lord is for all and we certainly have no intention of trying to keep any away, but He will not come in the night like a thief. Do not worry. And please, allow us to have a few hours to ourselves so that we may practice our devotions in private. The Lord indicated to me that He would come to me one more time before completely manifesting, and He will not do that if there is a large crowd here. So if you want to see the Lord, then please go. You are all welcome to come back in the morning.'

"Finally, all the villagers left and the con men heaved sighs of relief, because it was not easy having to act spiritual all day long in front of so many people. But they liked their new chore of gardening because it gave them a much-welcomed break from the more onerous chore of sitting still the entire day.

"'Tomorrow,' the master said, 'it will be even easier for you all because there will no longer be a ban on your talking.' A muffled cheer went up from the companions at this. 'Of course,' he continued, 'you will have to spend the time singing the Lord's praises.' There were some scattered groans at this, but even so the companions felt that singing bhajans was still, all in all, better than keeping silent, so they didn't complain too much. However, one of them said, 'But master, I don't see how our life now is any different from what it would be if we really did become sadhus. I know it is all pretend, but our discipline is just as great and, no disrespect, when is the money coming in?'

"'Have patience, we're getting very close now.'

"Just then, they heard an owl hooting from the forest, and the master hooted back, twice. Soon, their brother con man who had been sent away with the last of their money emerged from the wood with a huge pack strapped to his back. In whispers the master instructed them to remove the few inches of loose dirt from the top of the pit and to scoop out as many chickpeas as necessary to make room for the bundle.

"As some of the men set to work digging out the pit again, the others helped unwrap the large bundle, and what did they discover inside, but a carved wooden image of Lord Krishna. 'Bury it so the top is six inches below the surface,' the master instructed, 'and then pack the dirt down hard around the edges of the pit. Only leave it loose right above the statue.'

"This done, they smoothed the area over the whole pit and made it seem as natural as possible. Then they planted a tulsi plant just behind where the statue was now buried. 'Well, boys, that's it. Now we are all rich men,' the master declared.

"The next day, when the villagers came by, they found all the con men singing away for all they were worth. The master was in the middle, leading them, clapping his hands and swaying back and forth in time to the music, as if lost in his adoration.

"'What is it?' the villagers wondered. 'Why this sudden celebration?'

"'Because the Lord revealed last night that it won't be long now, He will manifest any day now.'

"When the villagers heard this, they became overwhelmed with devotion and they wholeheartedly joined in the singing. After a few hours, however, the master seemed to become aware of his surroundings and he looked suddenly embarrassed. 'What?' he exclaimed. 'Have we forgotten to take care of the Lord's garden? We must water all the plants so that they are blooming and in perfect health for the Lord when He manifests.'

"Instantly the villagers rushed to get water, and throughout the day they sang bhajans and took turns watering the plants, especially the tulsi planted in the center of the square. All night long the singing went on. And not long after dawn the next morning, a huge gasp went up from the assembled crowd because there, right in the center of the square, right in front of the sacred tulsi, they could see what looked like a peacock feather, growing up from the ground.

"The fervor and devotion unleashed at this astonishing sight was amazing. And somehow, as these things happen, word seemed to spread immediately and, before long, villagers from the surrounding villages also started to appear. By now, it could clearly be seen that it was a peacock feather and, what is more, the top of Lord Krishna's head had now thrust itself up from the earth.

"The villagers were beside themselves, prostrating before the idol, singing, bringing offerings. As the day progressed, the idol slowly, inch by inch pushed up from the ground until it was nearly completely uncovered. Only the very base was still underground. 'It's a miracle, a miracle!' the villagers exclaimed, and there was no one to contradict them either.

"All who came were amazed at this manifestation of the Lord and stayed to worship. After a day or two, however, the initial fervor had cooled enough for the villagers to begin to think about what this all meant. 'It's not enough that we bow down and make offerings,' they decided. 'We must build a house worthy of the lord.'

"'But what sort of temple should we build?' they asked the con man. 'Now that we are so blessed to have the Lord Himself manifest near our village, we don't want to offend Him by building the wrong sort of temple.'

"'That's right,' the other villagers agreed. 'If we can keep the Lord happy, our village will be permanently blessed.'

"'Build any sort of temple you wish,' the master con man told them. 'The lord is pleased with your devotion. He will be pleased with the love with which you build Him His home.' This of course made the villagers very happy, and work was begun immediately on the temple.

"But word of the Lord's miraculous manifestation continued to spread, and people from all parts of the country began coming on pilgrimage. Amongst these were prosperous businessmen, lawyers, and accountants, and on their advice it was decided that a trust should be established to manage the temple. Naturally the master con man and his disciples were asked whether they would consider being trustees of the temple since, after all, it was to them that the Lord first appeared.

"'No,' the chief con man answered. 'We are simple lovers of the Lord. We do not know anything about administering. All we ask is that we be allowed to live near the temple and that we be able to have free access to worship our Lord whenever we want.'

"These requests were quickly granted, and the con men's reputation for piety was enhanced. Soon houses were built around the temple for them. Every day lavish food was prepared for the Lord and they partook of it as *prasad*. And, without having any of the responsibility of looking after the property or managing its affairs, they managed to see that a considerable portion of the incredible amounts of money that were offered found its way into their pockets.

"Thus the master con man's prediction came true. They were well fed, and had nice homes and as much money as they wanted for the rest of their lives. Not only that, but they were respected and revered as holy men on top of it all.

"So Baba," Gustadji gestured, "just give us the word and we can do something like that, and then our money problems will also come to an end."

Baba was greatly amused at Gustadji's story and the way he had told it with so much feeling, but it seems Baba decided not to heed this advice, and maybe that's why Baba, and we who lived with Him, had to do without until the very end.

☙ *P A R V A R D I G A R*

WHAT YOU SAY IS RIGHT. The "Parvardigar" prayer does seem to contradict itself. In the first half it says, "You are without attributes," and then in the second half it says, "You are the one with infinite attributes." So what? Do you mean to say that it is not true? Doesn't He have infinite attributes? Whatever adjective you can think of to describe Him, He is that.

Look, you have been here how long now, two weeks, three

weeks? Something like that. And you go to *Arti* at the *Samadhi* every morning and every evening. At least that is what I have been told. Of my own I have no idea who goes to *Arti* and who does not. Nor do I care – what do I have to do with that? But someone was mentioning yesterday in the hall that you go regularly and you sing. Now, how many different songs have you heard, have you sung, during this time? No, no, I do not need a number, this is just to give you an idea.

And all those songs have so many verses, and each verse is a different way the poet has thought of to describe Him, to describe His attributes. And there are an infinite number of songs written to Him in His Praise, and still people are writing songs. You heard the song Susan sung just now, and she wrote it. Is she here now? She's stepped out. Why is it that whenever we want someone they have always just stepped out. Are you people psychic or something that whenever I am going to call on someone they leave the hall? Whatever it be, no, don't fetch her, let her be. Anyway, if we ask her why she wrote the song, where was the necessity to write another song, she would say that the other songs don't suit her, they don't express her Beloved in just the right way, and so it goes, there is no end to it. No end to songs and poems and even paintings. You see this painting here, you know that a blind man painted it? But that is a different story.

What I want to say is that when he came to visit Baba, Baba told him to paint Baba's face and he started doing that, and I don't know how many portraits he did, but it seems that that is all he did for years and years until he became absolutely and completely blind. How could he paint so many portraits, some wondered. After the first dozen, the first score, the first fifty, what would be left to paint, and yet he never had any trouble because even the expressions on Baba's face were infinite, it seems. Baba's face itself is finite; it is a limited human form, and yet its expressions could not be exhausted by this painter, who painted nothing else for years and years together. And if this is true simply of Baba's face, then what of His other attributes? Surely they too are infinite.

You see how it is. And yet, whatever you say about God, He is also beyond that. It is impossible to limit God. If you say God is perfect peace, He must also be beyond that. For if God is only what you say, then you have limited Him, He is no longer infinite. So if you say God is infinite attributes, He must also be beyond that. But what is beyond that – without attributes. God simply Is. That is why the prayer begins by saying God is without color, without expression, without form, and without attributes. There is simply an ocean of infinite existence, but even to say ocean is misleading, because this ocean has no shore, it has no color, no shape, no boundary, nothing anywhere which isn't also ocean. It is beyond our imagination and conception to conceive of such an ocean. So how does God get His attributes? Baba Himself answered this question.

One day we were sitting here with Baba, and on His own He raised this very question. Baba then answered it for us. He said, "Attributes are given by humans who love Me and want to glorify Me. But who am I? I am Infinite and Eternal Existence. All the attributes showered on Me stem from My being Infinite Eternal Existence, infinite existence, infinite." Baba told us this twice, three times, to bring home to us the idea of infinity. Baba continued, "That means if I am Infinite Existence that there is no nook or cranny where I am not, so people give Me the attribute of being omnipresent.

"Now, My being omnipresent means that there is not a place where I am not. If I am everywhere, then nothing is hidden from Me, and if nothing is hidden from Me, then I must know everything so they give Me the attribute of omniscience, all-knowing. And when I become in their eyes omniscient, then I must know how to create. Doesn't it follow that if I know everything, I must know how to create? So I become the Creator. And I must know how to preserve, so I become the Preserver. I know how to dissolve so I become the Dissolver, so the Holy Trinity is attributed to Me. And if I am omnipresent, omniscient, and the Creator, Preserver, and Destroyer, then it is only natural for Me to be all bliss."

Then Baba turns to us and says, "What does it imply when I say I am omniscient, that I know everything? What must My experience be like?" So we said, "Well, You must experience that You know everything." "No, no," Baba said, "I don't want dictionary definitions, tell Me what My experience must be like." So we all tried in some way or other, but none of our answers satisfied Baba, so, as always, Baba came to our rescue and told us, "My experience is that there is nothing to know.

"Anyone wanting to know anything is a poor attempt to become it. But if I am anything and everything, there is nothing for Me to know, because I am that. I don't have to know it, I am already it. So My experience of being all-knowing is that there is nothing to know. I am everything. I am without attributes, that is My state, but mankind has showered attributes on Me, to glorify Me, to remember Me."

Do you follow? You don't have to study yourself to know all about you. I am not you, so if I want to know what your likes and dislikes are, what you're thinking, I have to study you, I have to ask you lots of questions, but you know all that because you are that. So if Baba is everything, then He knows everything, He doesn't have to study anything, He doesn't have to think about anything, because He automatically knows it because He is it. You see?

But you know, the other day I was telling this story to someone and a thought came to Me. How would you like it if I addressed you by simply shouting, "Hey you," at you? You wouldn't even know who I was talking to. And if I said "You" again, you would feel something, you wouldn't like it. But if I turned to you and said, "Tom," you would feel much better, that would suit you.

And it must be the same way with God. He must not like it when we address him as "You." But what else can we say when He is simply Infinite Existence, when He is formless, without attributes. There is no name for us to use. Of course we have enough sense to call Him "Thou," that much common sense He has given us, but that is still only a polite form of "You." And it doesn't carry the intimacy, the satisfaction for Him as when we call Him by name. So that is why we use His attributes. We say, "Thou, the Lord of Lords," or "the One with infinite attributes," and that is a little better. God must be a little better pleased with this. At least it is clear to whom we are talking. In the same way, if I say, "You, the one who is always tape-recording these sessions," Dara knows I am addressing him. But he still does not feel pleased about this manner of address as when I simply call him by name. But now what name can we give God? How will he get a name unless and until, in His infinite compassion, He comes in our midst as Man amongst men and gets a name? How God must love it to be called at last by such a name.

Even in the world we see this is true. Have you ever been around a couple who were in love? What do they do? They give each other many nicknames. They call each other "darling" and "sweetheart" and all sorts of endearments. And the lover might say to his beloved, 'You are the fairest in the land, your hands are so soft, your cheeks are so rosy, your eyes are like sapphires,' and so on and so forth. He is enumerating her attributes. But this is all in the play of courtship. When he really wants to declare his love, he does not bother with such flowery speeches, he simply gazes at his beloved and heaves a deep sigh and simply whispers her name. And this is the very thing his beloved has been longing to hear. Because there is something about a name which captures our innermost being. We do not want to hear someone extol our virtues, we do not want to hear a long list of our attributes, somehow even that is too impersonal. We simply long to hear another say our name with great feeling and love, and that touches us.

At least this is the way it is in the world. And the thought came to me that it might be this way with God too. So what He longs to hear is our calling out to Him His name. Yes, in a certain mood, He might enjoy our praise, He might enjoy our listing His attributes, but how His heart must feel delight when one of His lovers is overcome with love and without even thinking about it, sighs and softly calls out, "Meher Baba, Meher Baba."

⚜ BABA ARRESTED

NOW THAT YOU'VE MENTIONED PRASAD, that reminds me of a good story – would you like to hear it? This concerns Baba's visit to Andhra. As you know, after the New Life, Baba entered a phase of His work which He called "the Life." Most of you call it the "Fiery Free Life," but to be accurate, the Fiery Free Life was really just one of the three phases of the Life. But whatever it may be, it was during this time that Baba first went to Hamirpur and Andhra. And before that, while Baba was in America, Pendu and I went on tour throughout India. We also went to Hamirpur and Andhra and we were amazed that wherever we went, people were on fire to hear about Meher Baba. Most of the people had never heard His name before, but as soon as we arrived, they couldn't hear enough about Him. They would listen for hours as we talked and still they weren't satisfied, they wanted to hear more and more. And why? Because we were so eloquent? Not at all. Pendu was no speaker, and neither was I. We were two buffoons, really speaking. We just went to places because Baba had told us to go, but we had nothing to say. But we were bringing a precious gift, I may say, the gift of His name. And wherever we went, people were so receptive that as soon as they heard His name, they were on fire to see Him.

You may say it was like ripe fruit. We didn't even have to shake the trees. We simply entered the orchard and the fruit fell into our hands. But that's a different story. Anyway, when Baba returned from America He asked about our travels and we began to tell Him, but after a while He stopped us and told us to prepare a chart instead. And we did. I still have it. It's maybe half as big as this rug here, and it listed every place we went to and how much money we spent and all the details Baba might be interested in.

Sometime later, He suddenly asked to see the chart and then announced that He would be visiting those villages in Andhra and Hamirpur. I won't go into the story of that visit or we won't have time for the story I want to tell you today, but it really was an incredible time, a sight for the gods, I should say, to see how the fire of Baba's love just spread like a tidal wave and almost overwhelmed us during those days. There were so many touching incidents. But again, that's a different story. If you're interested, I wrote a brief account of Baba's visit. I think we have a copy somewhere, it's called "Baba's Mass *Darshan*," or something like that, I don't remember now. But even that can't do the scenes justice. There is no way I can bring home to you the fervor and love of the people for Meher Baba.

But, of course, despite this love, this fervor, there were those who in their enthusiasm would ask Baba to bless them so that they might have an issue. And Baba would bless them. Baba would give them bananas as His *prasad* and gesture, "I give you My blessings."

That is what reminded me of this story. The mention of *prasad* because I was struck at the time at the mounds of bananas that Baba used to hand out. You know, in Andhra they have plenty of bananas and Baba used to hand them out by the truckload, and that will give you an idea of the number of people who thronged around Baba. And He would give people His blessings that they would have children or jobs.

At the end of Baba's visit, on our arrival back, Baba said to me, "I want you to go back. I've been thinking about what I said.

Everything I have said will come true. There is no doubt of it, but it will take some time. I want you to go back and let the people know that they shouldn't expect My blessings to bear fruit immediately." I said, "Baba, they know that. It is common sense, after all. They won't expect to have children immediately."

"No," Baba said. "I want you to go back and tell them that My blessings will come true, but it will take time."

I tried to talk Baba out of this. That was the intimacy Baba permitted us. He allowed us to give our opinions, and this didn't seem necessary to me so I said that. I didn't feel like taking that long train ride back again to deliver a message which was so obvious. Surely no one would expect Baba's blessings to materialize like that. But Baba made it clear that He wanted me to go back, so I wrote to people and told them I was coming with a message from Baba and arranged for my visit.

I took the train and got down at my first stop. I was met at the platform by many Baba lovers who immediately bombarded me with questions, "Is it true?" "Was Baba really arrested?" "Why was Baba arrested?" "When was Baba arrested?" and so on and so forth.

"Yes, yes," I said, "Baba was arrested. But I've just arrived. I am hot and tired and dirty. Let me clean up first and get refreshed and then I'll answer all your questions."

So I did that. I had a bath and while I was washing my mind started working. What had happened? Why had I said that? I got a little fright. Why had I blurted out that Baba had been arrested? There is a limit to humor, after all, and I didn't know what I would say now. But I finished my bath and then I met with everyone and I said, "I'll answer all your questions, but first you must answer one question for me. Who told you about Baba being arrested?"

"The children," they said. "Which children?" And I kept asking questions until I discovered that the news of Baba's being arrested as soon as He left Andhra had emanated from the mission school. It seems Baba's visit had created such a stir that the missionaries felt threatened, so to counteract all the excitement about Baba in their schools, they had started the rumor that He had been arrested as soon as He left Andhra.

So I told the people, "Yes, it's true that Baba has been arrested. You shouldn't have to ask me that. Don't you realize that each and every one of you has arrested Him with your love?"

"You mean he's not behind bars?"

"Yes, He's being held behind the bars of your hearts."

"So, He wasn't really arrested?"

"No, of course not. What nonsense. Haven't I just come from Baba? I can assure you that your love has arrested Him, but nothing else has or ever can."

And the people were relieved. And that's why Baba had sent me back. The order about explaining that His blessings take time to bear fruit, that was just the excuse to send me back. Baba knew that these people, so new in their love for Him, might be shaken by false rumors, so He sent me back immediately so I could reassure them. That's why He sent me, but, of course, I didn't know that at the time. But what made me say, "Yes, yes, He's been arrested," when I first arrived, I still don't know. Baba put those words in my mouth. Otherwise I would have said, "Arrested? What are you talking about, I don't know anything about that." But instead I said, 'Yes, He's been arrested." Baba made me say that. On my own I wouldn't have. I am not such a quick thinker. But Baba put those words in my mouth so eventually the whole situation could be turned around in a humorous but telling way.

And it is true. Baba has said that He's a thief. He's the perfect thief who steals our hearts without our even being aware of it. And so we have to take Him prisoner, we have to arrest Him, and again it is only the heart which can do this.

◁▷ G O   H O M E   D I R E C T L Y

RULES, AGAIN WE ARE TALKING ABOUT RULES. Why do you keep asking about rules? How can I bring home to you that our life with
Meher Baba was not about rules; it was about learning to dance to
His tune. Rules implies coercion of some sort. It is a rule, so we have
to do this or that. Baba has not come to lay down a set of rules for
people, He has come to awaken love in their hearts so that they want
to obey the rules that are inherent in their hearts. Haven't I told you
all how Baba said the ten commandments are in people's hearts?
And even then, it is not a question of obeying these commandments
because they are rules; it is common sense. If I love you, then I have
no wish to harm you. What mother wants to harm her own child?
Does she restrain herself from killing her child because of the com-
mandment, Thou shall not kill? No, the very idea is preposterous.
She is not obeying a rule not to kill her child, she is simply loving her
child. If she is obeying any rule, we can say she is obeying the rules
of love. But the rules of love are not like ordinary rules. That is what
I am trying to bring home to you. Really speaking, they are not rules
at all. Perhaps a story will make this clearer.

Baba used to tell His lovers that they should go right home
after having His *darshan,* taking His love with them. That was Baba's
wish. Time and again He would tell His lovers this. Why this should

be, we didn't ask. Baba merely said it and His lovers would nod their heads and say, "Yes Baba," and that was that.

But it was not just with newcomers or people uncertain in their love for Baba to whom Baba used to give this order. He would also tell His close ones, people like Meherjee and Nariman who would drive here from Bombay to spend time with Baba. And then, when they were leaving, invariably Baba would say to them, "Remember, go straight back." Or sometimes, they would leave the hall and then Baba would gesture to me, "Go, tell them to go straight back." And I would leave the hall and catch up to them and say, "Baba says you are to go straight back." And they would say, "Yes, we know," and leave. But this began to prey on my mind. What was the need of Baba to keep reminding His close ones, time after time?

So one time I remember, when Meherjee or Nariman had left and Baba gestured to me to go and tell them this message, I blurted out, "But Baba, they know it. Where is the need to repeat it each and every time?" "Go and tell them," Baba insisted, and so I did. I went out and reminded them, "Baba says to go straight back."

But I couldn't understand why Baba was doing this. Where was the need? It annoyed me, I may say. You know, this was Baba's intimacy with us, His compassion. He allowed us to feel annoyance at His ways. I mean now it strikes me how presumptuous it was of me to even question such things, but at the time, I did question them, and Baba's insistence on repeating things we all knew and understood would annoy me.

Why? Because it meant more work for me. I already had enough work, and now Baba would make me drop whatever I was doing and go out and tell these people this message which they knew perfectly well. It is not as if they were infrequent visitors. It is not as if they were not dedicated to Baba. They had been with Baba for decades. These were people who were meticulous about following Baba's slightest command to the letter. So it was embarrassing for me to have to remind them every time to go straight back. They would look at me and say, "Yes, we know." And I felt it was a waste of my time to have to remind them each time.

You see how the mind works. Here I had come to live with Baba, to serve Baba. My time was at His disposal, and yet when He asked me to do this, my mind would register, "Oh, this is a waste of my time." Of course the reason it seemed like a waste was because Baba had given me so many other things to do and there wasn't enough time to attend to all of them, and here I was being given more work which was totally unnecessary. But this too is just an excuse of the mind. I am just trying to give you a picture of the way the mind works. Or, I should say, of the way my mind works, because all of you may not find your mind playing such tricks on you.

And Baba let me continue to feel this irritation for several years. I did not bring it up to Baba. I did not argue with Him again about giving this message and He did not say anything about it either. But then one day I was driving Baba to town. From here, from Meherazad. And we had gotten to the nulla at Shendi. It had rained and the nulla was full. Have you seen the way that a dry nulla fills up after a good downpour? It is something to see. Instead of the dry bed you see now, it becomes a river. After a hard rain the water floods the whole nulla, they completely fill up and there is nothing to do but sit and wait for the waters to subside. Because it doesn't last long. In no time the waters recede until there is only a trickle left. Of course, now there is a big concrete bridge, but back then we used to drive down into the nulla itself. So there was nothing to do but sit in the car and wait for the waters to recede. I couldn't risk trying to drive through because we might stall in the water, and then what would we do? So we sat there waiting and Baba suddenly asked me, "When a man loves a woman does he think about her?"

I said, "Yes, Baba."

"And if a man really loves a woman, but is separated from her, will he be anxious to see her?"

What do I know about love, so I said, "Yes, Baba, I believe that is the way it is in the world." And Baba continued, "Now if his beloved keeps the man at a distance, in fact is indifferent to him for years together no matter how much the man wants to be with his beloved, and then one day sends word that he can finally come, what will the state of that man's mind be?"

"He will be most anxious to go see his beloved," I replied. As I said, I do not have experience of such things, but it is common sense after all. So I said, "He will be excited, he will be delighted to get the word."

"Will he wait a few days before leaving to see his beloved?"

"No, Baba. He will leave immediately. He will be in a rush to get to her."

"Suppose he takes a train and the train has to stop at a station for a few hours. Will he decide to take in a movie?"

"No, Baba. He will pace up and down on the platform, just waiting for the next train so he can see her."

"He won't think about taking in some entertainment?"

"No, Baba. Not if he has any feeling of love."

"Would he stop and see a prostitute, then?"

"Of course not. That would be the furthest thing from his mind."

"If he did, and his beloved found out, how do you think she would feel?" Baba asked me.

"She would be revolted at such behavior, Baba."

Then Baba turned and said, "That is why I tell My lovers to go straight home after receiving My love. Imagine how I feel if someone comes to Me, professing to love Me deeply and I give them My love and then, only hours after leaving Me, they fritter away this love by stopping to see some saint or so-called holy person. Doesn't that belittle My love? They just fritter it away, such a precious gift and just thrown away. That is why I remind them time and time again that they should go straight home. Even My close ones I tell. Why? Because I think they are going to forget My order? No, it is because

I dare not care not for those who love Me. Once they come to Me, it is My responsibility to see to them, and I know it is not good for them to fritter away My gift of love, and because I dare not care not, that is why over and over again I tell them all, go straight home now, do not visit anyone else."

You see Baba's compassion. The other day we were talking about rules and I was trying to bring home to you that the rules we make are for your benefit and I should have told you this story then, because this is an even better example. Baba had made a rule, go straight home after receiving My love. But why, because it was for His lover's benefit. It was His compassion which prompted this rule because He dare not care not. And it was also His compassion that He shared this story with me. Because for several years the thought had been in my mind, "Why does Baba do this," but out of compassion for my confusion, Baba told me this story.

But now when I say this, someone in the hall blurts out, "But Eruch, I have a stopover in Europe on my way home, does this mean I should change my ticket?" And again there is confusion. And again the confusion is because of the word "rule." I said Baba made a rule that He wanted His lovers to go straight home after having His *darshan*. But I should not, really speaking, call this a rule. I should say this was Baba's wish, that He expressed over and over. Maybe this story will help make the difference clearer.

One day we were sitting here with Baba and out of the blue He tells us this story. He said there was an innocent woman who was convicted of adultery and sentenced to death. The law said she was to be placed in the middle of the market square and it was a rule that anyone who passed by had to throw something at her. So when anyone walked by they would pick something up, a stone, some rubbish, some filth, and throw it at her, but she endured all this without a word. She gave no indication that any of the rocks hurt her, she just stood there, looking beautiful and radiant.

Now it so happened that this woman's daughter passed by and, by law, she was required to throw something at her mother. She did not have the heart to throw a stone or anything like that, so she bought a rose and as she passed by she tossed the flower. When the flower struck her, the mother cried out in agony, even though no stone or filth until then had made her utter a word. She had stood smiling throughout the roughest treatment, but the slight touch of a flower thrown by her daughter brought forth this cry from the depths of her being.

"How much the mother felt the accusation when it came from her own daughter," Baba gestured. "How much more," He continued, "will I feel when My own ones hurt Me, even with the petal of a rose."

We didn't understand what Baba was driving at and we confessed to Baba that we didn't understand, and He explained, "You have all been with Me for many years. If now, in your ambition to seek more and more of the truth, you were to seek the blessings of a saint, that would be the equivalent of the daughter throwing a rose at her mother."

So you see it is not a question of obeying rules, it is a matter of being careful that we do not even throw a rose petal at Baba. This is the rule of love.

◈ SELFLESS SERVICE

WHAT YOU SAY IS TRUE. Baba did stress selfless service, but do you mean to say that there is no thought of your self in your service? There will be, brother, there will be. I am saying this not because I know you, but because I know myself. No matter how hard we tried to be selfless, some thought of ourselves would creep in—"Oh, I have done such a good deed today," and we would get a little puffed up at the thought. It is human nature. That is why I tell people do not think so much of selfless service, real selfless service is impossible until you are realized, but concentrate on doing those things which enable you to forget yourself. When you lose yourself in your work, when you become totally absorbed in it so that you forget yourself, that is selfless service, even if the work itself does not seem to be.

But this also is not easy. Even when we wake up from a deep, deep sleep, sometimes we may forget for a moment or two where we are, but we never forget who we are. When we were traveling with Baba I might wake up and for just a moment or two not realize where I was, but I never woke up wondering who I was; the thought "I am Eruch" was always with me. It is still with me, or I wouldn't be here this way talking to you at all. Anything and everything we do, all of our attempts at self-forgetfulness, at selflessness, they only succeed in creating impressions which bind us. There is no way out of this.

There are even people who seem to be great spiritual figures, yogis who can do all sorts of what we would call miracles, and they have not succeeded in forgetting themselves. Sometimes, in fact, their very advancement is the cause of them remembering themselves all the more. That is why Baba told us that true spiritual advancement is really self-effacement. But this too is not easy. It is impossible, I should say, so now what to do? If everything we do creates more bindings, how will we ever get ourselves freed from these impressions? Why, as Sonia asked, is there any point in doing good deeds as opposed to bad ones if they both are binding?

It is true they are both binding. Baba has said that bad deeds are like iron chains binding us while good deeds are like gold chains binding us. The difference is that the iron chains shackle our hands and feet while the gold chains only shackle our feet, our hands are free. And eventually, with our hands, we will be able to remove the chains from our feet. So there is a difference.

We should try to do good, we should obey the injunctions Baba has laid down for us. That much we can do, but this alone will not free us. It will help us, it will make it easier for us to eventually be freed, but it will not, by itself, free us. So what to do?

There is one way out. And that is to think about Meher Baba. To remember Him, to love Him. Why? Because He is the impressionless One. Anything we do creates impressions, and when we think of Him we also create impressions, but these are impressions of the impressionless One and as such they do not bind us. These very impressions help us to uproot the impressions of the impressioned mind.

This is the remedy Baba has provided us with. Otherwise it is very, very difficult. That reminds me of a story which shows how difficult it is to do a selfless deed, how rare it is. Would you like to hear it?

In India, many years ago, in one part of the country there was a long period, years you may call it, when the monsoons failed. Each year the people could grow fewer and fewer crops and they ate less and less. It was a famine, I should say, and the people were slowly starving. But this they could bear. Farmers are used to this in India.

They know how to subsist on very little. I am not saying this was an easy thing for them. It was very difficult, but if the monsoons came the next year and they had good crops and could eat well again, they would be able to pull through. But in the meantime what was happening was that all the wells were drying up. Now while they could go long periods without food, it is a different matter with water. If there were no water to drink, they would die, and by the time the monsoons came again, it wouldn't matter how much it rained because none of them would still be alive. They knew this. And they were very worried about what would happen now. In the entire area there was only one well left that had any water at all in it, and it had only a small muddy puddle, you may call it, at the very bottom. The people could see how much water was left and they could calculate how many weeks they had left before they all died of thirst, and they knew this was an extremely serious situation.

Now, it so happened that nearby was the seat of a Perfect One. The people all revered him, but you know how it is, when things are going well they would say it is because of His grace, but they did not take this too seriously, they did not visit him or pay him their respects. Only when someone wanted to be blessed to have a child, or wanted to see that his cow should have healthy calves or something of that sort. But now, in their calamity they all thought of this Master and decided they would go as a group, the whole village would go and beg this Master to intercede on their behalf.

And that is what they did. They had exhausted every other avenue. They had had prayer meetings in town, they had all fasted for days, they had done this and done that, all to no avail. He was their last hope, the last resort. And it is always this way. We only really turn to God when we realize, when we understand that He is the only way out for us. And so the villagers all went to see the Perfect Master to beg him to intercede on their behalf with the Lord to make it rain or else they would all be finished.

But the Master said, "I am sorry, I can't be of any help to you."

"What do you mean, you are one with the Lord, you are all-knowing, all-powerful, you can certainly make it rain if you wish."

But the Master said, "Although I have the power to do so, because I am all-knowing, I cannot make use of it."

"What do you mean?" the people said. "Why can't you help us? We will all die if nothing is done. We beg of you. What do you mean, because you know, you cannot help us. It is because you know all that we have come to you."

"No, because I know God is compassionate I cannot help you. I know what you all deserve. I know that justice demands that the world should open up and swallow you all, but it is His compassion that tempers this, that deems that you should only suffer from this lack of rain, so how can I do anything? I am powerless to help you."

"Then we are doomed."

"No, I cannot help you, but there is one and if you appeal to her, and beg her to supplicate the Lord on your behalf, He might honor her request."

"Who is this? Where does she live?" the villagers all asked, for again there was a glimmer of hope for them all. And the Master gave them the name of a woman and told them what village she could be found in and so on.

Now, as this village was some distance away, they decided to send only a group of elders to go, it was too far for the entire village to go. And so, without further ado, because the situation really was desperate, a contingent of the elders from the village set off. And they walked to this other town and when they got there they asked after this woman, and people seemed surprised when they asked for her. They say, "Are you sure this is the woman you want?" "Yes, yes." "But you are all elders, it is not for you to seek this woman out." "What do you mean, we want to see her, what does it matter that we are the elders of our village." And so on and so forth. For, to make a long story short, it turns out that this woman is a famous prostitute in this town.

When the elders find this out they are very disturbed. Surely there must be some mistake. But then the Master has been most specific in his instructions, so they go and they ask the prostitute are you so and so, who was born in this village and then came to this town some years back and whose parents were from this place, and they gave the whole pedigree, as it were, which the Perfect Master had given them so that there should be no mistake in identity. And she said, "Yes, I am that person. What do you want?"

"We have come here on a most serious mission. We would like you to pray to God on our behalf so that the monsoon might come and our village will be saved. Otherwise we will all die because we have no more water left, not only can we not irrigate our fields, but we do not even have any water left to drink."

The woman is surprised and she thinks they are making fun of her. "You want me to pray to God on your behalf? But don't you know what I am? You are all old venerable men, God is much more likely to listen to your prayers than to mine."

But they tell her about their visit to the Master and how he had told them that their only hope lay in persuading this woman to pray because God would listen to her prayers.

Well, if the Master said this, then she must honor his request. It certainly seems like an odd request to her, but there can be no harm in it, so the prostitute prays to God, imploring God to give the villagers rain, and even before she has finished praying, you may say, the clouds begin to darken and soon there is a torrential downpour.

The village elders, of course, are ecstatic, for they have been saved. For this is not just a local shower, it seems clear that it is a full-fledged monsoon. Now the wells will fill up and there will be enough to drink and life can continue. But the prostitute is very disturbed. What did the Master mean, sending these people to her. Was he mocking her way of life. Did he do this as a kind of joke? For she knows full well that she is entirely unworthy. Being a prostitute means what? After all, her life is steeped in sin. She has never given God a thought. So why should the Master say that God will listen to her prayers and no one else's. Surely the reverse is true, that God is less likely to listen to her prayers than to the prayers of anyone else. And the more she thinks about this, the more disturbed she gets, until finally she cannot contain it anymore and she herself goes to visit the Perfect Master.

And she goes through the same routine that the village elders did. "Are you sure you have not made some mistake, am I really the one you meant? How can this be, not only were they more worthy than I, but you are the most worthy yet, why couldn't you simply pray for rain?"

"Because I knew what justice demanded for them, I could do nothing to help them. But I also knew that on your record was one good deed, and this one shining deed gave you such merit that God would listen to your prayer if you made it."

"One good deed? But I am not aware of doing any such deed. On the contrary, I have always prided myself that I did not have to do such deeds, that my beauty was such that men would always forgive me no matter what I did or how I treated anyone."

"Yes, I know that," the Master said. "But I also know that you once saved the life of a starving calf, and that having saved one life, God's reward for you was that you would have the opportunity to save the lives of the entire village, and I knew that as well, and that is why I sent the elders to you."

"Saved the life of a calf? But I don't remember ever doing that."

"It was years ago, not long after you had just discovered the power your beauty gave you over people. You were young and haughty, arrogant in your beauty, and you delighted in making one and all do your bidding. Do you remember?"

"Yes, that describes me to this day. But I still don't recall the incident you mean."

"One day you were walking along. You were going to meet a man who had promised you gold ornaments if you visited him, and you took a walk outside the village so that you would not be on time, to keep him waiting and to prove your independence. And it so happened that while you were walking you came across a young calf that had been tied to a stake in the ground. But the rope had gotten twisted around the stake and the calf's hay now lay just outside the reach of the animal. The owners had gone off and there was none to see to this calf's plight. Without thinking about it, you kicked the pile of hay towards the animal and went on your way."

"Yes, yes," the woman said excitedly, "now I remember. It was just as you say. But, but," she faltered, "I don't see what was such a good deed about that. I was not trying to help the calf, I simply kicked the hay without giving it a thought."

"Yes, and that is what makes it such a shining deed, because you did it without any awareness of having done a good deed. You did it without expectation of reward, without any thought of your having done it or what merit you might gain by doing it. And as such it was a selfless deed, and this is what has enabled you to save the village."

You see how rare it is to do a selfless deed? But speaking of this, this reminds me of another story that one of you told me. I don't remember who it was now, but I remember this person came, for the first time, so I was asking him the usual questions I put, "How did you come to know of Meher Baba? What was it that drew you here?" and so forth, and this was the story he told me.

He said he had gone to Myrtle Beach for a vacation. He said it was the season. Do you have seasons there, too? I know there is a season for visitors to come to Mahabaleshwar, and he told me it was the same with Myrtle Beach. Whatever it be, he said, I am there, just roaming about here and there, having a good time and enjoying myself. One day while I am walking about I see a board that says Meher Spiritual Center. And I think, Spiritual Center in this area? Because you know Myrtle Beach is a center for parties and good times and all sorts of worldly entertainments. That is why I had gone there in the first place. So I am intrigued by this sign and I go inside. I had no idea where I was going, I just started walking. But I hadn't gone far when someone met me and asked me why I had come.

I said, "I have come for vacation." And they said, "Well, this is not a resort. This is not the place for that."

"What is this place?" I asked.

"It is a spiritual center."

So I said, "Well, can I have a look around?"

The person said, "Yes, but best is that you talk first to the person in charge because people are not allowed to come on Center without permission." This is what he is telling me, I didn't even know this.

"So we went to a nearby cabin where there was a phone and they called someone, a Kitty something or other, some woman named Kitty and it turned out she was not available for another three-quarters of an hour, but she said I could be taken around and shown the place for a while and then it would be time when she was free and I could see her.

"So my guide starts to show me around and he is telling me Meher Baba sat here and Meher Baba did this, and I don't know anything about this Meher Baba. I don't have any interest in it, but I am being polite and then he takes me to a cabin and says, 'This is the Lagoon Cabin. This is where Meher Baba used to have private interviews with people. Would you like to see it?'

"So I figure, why not? As long as I am seeing everything, why not see this too. So I take off my shoes because my guide tells me I should, and we go inside. And there is a chair there and a little sofa and the guide explains it all, he says this is where Baba used to sit, and people would stand here in front of him and so on, and I am not paying all that much attention, and then he says, 'Perhaps you would want to stay here for a while by yourself. We have to wait until we can see Kitty anyway,' and he goes out and leaves me alone.

"So I just sit there and look around. There's nothing much to see, it's a small room and there isn't much in it, but somehow my attention gets fixed on the chair. I start to stare at it, I can't take my eyes off it, and I see waves of love emanating from the chair. I don't know how to describe it, but it was like just wave after wave, and it gave me such peace of mind, I felt so happy sitting there, to such an extent that after a while I feel so grateful for what I am experiencing that I get the thought in my mind that I must give something to this place in return. But I didn't have anything. I had come directly from the beach. I didn't have anything with me, but I had a ring on my finger, and without thinking about it, it came to me, oh, I'll offer this, and I take the ring and there was a little table, next to Baba's chair and I put the ring there as an offering and I felt very satisfied and happy that I could give something.

"Then, after a while, it occurred to me that my guide must be waiting, that I shouldn't keep him waiting, so I got up and went outside."

Now the worst thing, he tells me, is the shoes. He had had very tight shoes on, and it wasn't easy getting them on again without a shoehorn. But he struggles into them and there is still time before the appointment, so the guide takes him across the bridge and they see the lake. The guide points out the gondola and then there is nothing left to see and there is still ten or fifteen minutes left, so what to do? And the boy asks, "Can I go back into the cabin?" The guide says sure. So he takes off his shoes again and he goes in with high spirits because he is expecting to have the same experience as the first time, and no sooner does he enter the cabin than his eyes fall on the table and there is no ring there.

"What a shock, I felt," he told me. "What kind of spiritual center is this? We have only been gone for a few minutes and already it's stolen," and all the joy he felt vanished with this thought. He says all that buoyancy, that delight, just collapsed and he became completely disillusioned. He left the cabin, struggled with his shoes again, and now they are going to see Kitty, but he had no heart for it. He has no heart to even mention the ring to his guide. He is just too crestfallen, too depressed to say anything. Really he doesn't want to see Kitty now, but he feels the appointment has been fixed, so he goes.

And as Kitty talks to him, some of that feeling starts to return, some of that happiness, and she ends her talk by telling him about the Lagoon Cabin, how Baba used to see people there, and that buoyant feeling starts to return. Then Kitty says, it was good of you to come, we are very happy to have met you, whatever it is that she says on meeting someone, and then she turns to the guide and says, "Well you have shown him around, so he can leave now. See that he finds his way out now."

And they leave Kitty's, but he turns to the guide and says, "Can I go once more to the Lagoon Cabin before leaving?" The guide says yes, so they walk back and again he has to take his shoes off and he goes in and, to his surprise, his amazement, he finds the ring on the table. He is shocked. What is this? he thinks. And he can't understand how this could have happened. He couldn't have overlooked the ring before, the table is too small, there is nothing else there, it is impossible that he wouldn't have seen it. So he sits there in a kind of daze and just looks about him, and then his eyes fall on the sign that says, "Things that are real are given and received in silence." And he leans forward and takes the ring back and leaves the cabin.

As he struggles to get his tight shoes back on, the phrase "Things that are real are given and received in silence" keeps going through his mind, and he is thinking about it, and suddenly the thought comes to him, "Oh yeah, when I gave the ring I didn't give it a thought, it was given in silence and Baba received it in silence, but when I went back and it was gone, I got suspicious, my mind was disturbed and I started thinking so many thoughts, so the silence of the love was broken and the ring was given back. Oh God, why did I do that? Why did I have to think those thoughts and make Baba give me the ring back again? Otherwise He would have kept it. And he kept wondering, Why did I do that? and this thought brought him here. He started to read Baba's books and he came here to find out, Why did I do that?

But you see how it is. He gave a present with no thought of himself, but he could not maintain it, his mind started working and vitiated it.

So you see what I mean when I say it is so difficult to truly be selfless. The second you are aware of having done a good deed, the instant the thought enters your mind, "Oh, that was a good thing I did," you have nullified it. Not that you should refrain from doing such deeds. Not at all. They may still be good deeds, but they are not selfless deeds, they will still bind you.

So the only way out is to create impressions of the impressionless One because these are the only impressions which will not bind us. Not only will they not bind us, but they will help to free us from our bindings.

△ S L E E P

DID BABA EVER TELL US THAT IF WE WOKE UP in the night it was bad for our health to go back to sleep? No. Not that I ever recall. You mean should we, if we happen to wake in the night, sit in meditation and repeat His name instead of trying to go back to sleep? No, that was in the early days. That wasn't for us. You see, in the early days there were youngsters with Him, and you know how it is with youth. There is so much energy, so much enthusiasm, that unless it is properly channeled, this will lead to mischief of some sort. So in those days Baba used to give instructions like that. But once those with

Him were older, once they were firmly established in His love, then all that sort of thing went by the side.

You know, Prophet Muhammad when He came used to have a standing rule that you shouldn't disturb anyone while they were sleeping. But then the next time He comes, as Meher Baba, He is known as the "Awakener." And it was true, even in a literal sense. Baba used to say, "Go give Peter this message." And we would go and we would find Peter asleep, so we would wake him up to give him the message. And what was the message? It was, "Peter, Baba wants you to sleep well." So we would wake Peter and tell him, and he would grunt and roll over and fall back asleep.

That is the way it was with Baba. Why? Why should He have been one way as Muhammad and just the opposite as Baba? It is just His whim. But no, Baba did not tell us that we couldn't go back to sleep if we woke up in the middle of the night. In fact, I remember one time we had been traveling with Baba and we hadn't slept for some time, days and nights together. You ask if this was normal? No, it wasn't normal. How can I give you a picture of our life with Baba? In short, nothing in our life was normal, I should say, but it was always most natural.

When you say normal, you are thinking of a routine. With Baba, His pleasure, His whim, if you want to call it that, was our only routine. And this changed in a most natural way. For example, let us say that there were three of us doing night watch. We would take turns. I would always have the first and the last shift, because that is what Baba wanted. I would be there to put Baba to sleep and to be there when He got up. So let's say my shift was from seven until ten. Then the next would do ten until one and then one until four and then it would be my shift again.

That's just an example to give you an idea of how it would be. The actual hours would depend on when Baba wanted to get up, whether we were traveling, what work Baba was engaged in, and so on. But this gives you an idea of how it would be arranged. Now let us say that Baba sent one of the three of us out to search for a *mast*, or out of station on some sort of work, then the two of us would divide the duty between us, which meant less sleep for us. And then it might happen that the other man would develop a fever, would be having diarrhea, and Baba would say, "Take care of your health, better you should sleep," and then I would do the night watch all by myself and wouldn't get any sleep.

When we went on *mast* tours with Baba we often got very little sleep. Sometimes we got no sleep at all. The particular time I am reminded of I had had no sleep for several days and nights. And now we were taking a bus somewhere, this must have been in the interior, and we were traveling by state transport bus. And you know how it is, the rocking motion of the bus, the rhythm, the heat, the days and nights without sleep, and somehow I succumbed, and the next thing I knew I woke up with a start. We were traveling on dirt roads and we must have hit a pot hole, a sudden jolt, and I woke up. But woke up from where? From His shoulder. In my sleep my head had fallen on Baba's shoulder, and I looked and I saw that I had drooled on Baba's coat. You know how it is when you're fast asleep, your mouth gapes open and the saliva collects and runs out. And I could see the stain on Baba's shoulder and I sat up feeling very abashed, but Baba just did this, He gently pushed my head back on His shoulder and gestured, "Don't worry, go back to sleep."

I couldn't disobey Baba, but how could I sleep? So I sat there with my head on His shoulder and my eyes closed for a minute or two to honor His instructions and then sat up. Baba seemed surprised. "So soon? Is that all you're going to sleep?" "It's all right, Baba, I feel refreshed now." And it was true. That deep sleep was such that I did feel completely revived, fresh, ready to go another week without sleep.

I don't know how long I must have been asleep, whether it was ten minutes or half an hour, but it was such a sound sleep that I did feel completely revived when I woke up. Baba said sound sleep is the original state of God. We are unconscious of it when we sleep, when we enter this original state of God, but the Avatar or the Perfect Masters are conscious of this state during their sound sleep. And I think I must have entered that real sound sleep, that original state of God, because I woke up so refreshed. Now don't say it was because of Baba's shoulder. Let's not get sentimental, it was because that's the nature of real deep sleep.

But anyway, to answer your question, you can see that Baba did not say to me, "Now that you're awake, stay awake and repeat my name." On the contrary, when I woke up, He on His own told me to go back to sleep. You cannot make rules for the Avatar. Do not try to limit Him by saying He always will do this or He will always do that. That would be to make Him a normal person, enslaved to habits and routines. Baba was not that, He was always most natural, and for us to become natural, not normal, we must simply learn to dance to His tune.

UNFATHOMABLE

DO YOU NOTICE ANYTHING NEW IN THE HALL? Yes, that big red badge. It came from the States, one of you sent it here. Read it out for me so those who are sitting on this side can know what it says. Yes, that's right, "Don't try to understand me, just love me."

Of course, Baba used slightly different words. How does the Parvardigar prayer go? What is the line at the beginning? "You are unlimited and unfathomable." Baba would tell us, "Don't try to fathom Me."

I remember one time, I think we were in Andhra, during Baba's visit there, but whether it was Baba's first visit or His second visit, that I don't know. I am no good with dates anymore. People come and they ask me about some incident and I say yes, that happened last year when you were here, and they say, "No, it happened five years ago," and I say, "Did it?" because I tell you the truth, I don't remember. The time just runs together in my mind now.

But I remember the gathering. I can still picture it in my mind. I think I must have told you all before how compassionate the Lord is that He used gestures with us. If Baba had talked, if Baba had given His messages orally, I wouldn't be able to remember them the way I do. But because we had to concentrate on His hands, His face, there is still a vivid picture in my mind of Baba's messages, the whole scene comes back to me and then I recall the words as well. So it is, I remember there were quite a few of the mandali with Baba and there were so many of Baba's lovers from the South sitting before Him and Baba was talking casually with them.

You know that even in public programs, when Baba would have a message read out, He didn't like the atmosphere to become too solemn or too worshipful. He liked the atmosphere to be lively, to have some humor in it. Baba had had some serious message read out, and one of the Andhra lovers couldn't follow it all and confessed to Baba that he didn't understand it and asked for an explanation. Baba replied that He was so unfathomable that even He couldn't begin to fathom Himself.

And it's true. The more you try to understand Baba, the more you will misunderstand Him. And it is this way with the Perfect Masters too. Let me give you an example.

There was a Master once who wandered from place to place. This is a true story, mind you. This isn't a made-up tale. I hope there isn't anyone from Iran in the hall today. Is there? No? Okay. Then I may proceed.

I say this because I remember when our dear Farhad was with

us. He used to get very upset whenever I used to say I was telling a story from our days with Baba. He would say, "Those aren't stories, Eruch. You are not making them up." "So what do you want me to call them, then?" I asked. 'You should call them truths, not stories," he replied.

And, in a way, he is right. They are truths, but somehow it doesn't seem right to call them that, so as long as he is not here, I will call them stories. But, in case anyone sees him, let him know that I am making sure to tell you that these are true stories.

Now, where was I? Yes, there was a Master who used to roam from place to place. And in one town, the Master had a couple who were very devoted to him. Whenever the Master came to that town this couple would come and join the crowd that would gather. For that was the Master's way. He would simply find a nice tree and sit under it, and soon word would spread that the Master had come and people would flock around him.

And it was a lively time. The Master would ask after those who had come, would wonder how they had been in his absence, whether they had stayed healthy, if anything interesting had happened, and so the time would pass. Perhaps one of his followers would sing a song for him or there would be bhajans or someone would ask him some questions and he would give answers and all were happy.

Then, as it started to get dark, the Master would say, "Well, now it's time for you all to depart. It's time for me to retire now, please go." And everyone would get up and leave. Such was the force of his personality that even though in some cases people had traveled long distances to be with him, when he told people they should leave they all got up and left. This couple, the ones who were so devoted to him, would also get up to leave, but the Master would catch their eye and give them a little signal, a gesture with his hand, "Wait, wait, don't go yet," and they would stay behind.

And then, after all had gone, the Master would call them near and start inquiring after them. How it is that this couple came to be so devoted to their Master, that part of the story I don't know. But whatever it was, they were entirely devoted to him and he, on his part, seemed to be especially close to them.

He would look at the wife and say to the husband, "My, she's even more beautiful than last time I was here, isn't it." And the wife would blush and the husband would feel so proud. And the Master would look at her as if he were seriously considering this and then, after seeming to give it some thought, would say, "It must be because of your love, you love her so much she is becoming more beautiful because of it."

And now it was the husband's turn to blush. "But there is one thing I don't understand, "the Master would continue. "I know she loves you very much, and I can see that you love her very much, so how is it that you have no children?" And now both the husband and the wife would blush. And then the Master would say, "Don't worry, there is still plenty of time." And he would ask about the husband's business, or he would clap his hands together with the excited delight of a child and, looking around as if to make sure that all the other people in town had left, he would say, "Now, what have you brought me?" For it was the custom that whenever the Master came, this couple would cook something special for him to eat.

Really speaking, it wasn't so special. The couple were not poor, but they were not wealthy either. The Master would wander from place to place and in some towns he had very rich devotees who would prepare elaborate feasts for him, but whatever this couple served him, he always acted as if it were the finest delicacy that could be imagined. He made the couple feel this. And so the night would pass. They would all enjoy the food and, in the Master's company, they forgot about the time and would spend most of the night with him, laughing and joking and just enjoying his company.

Each time the Master came to their town, this would happen. And each time he would make some reference to how anxiously he was waiting for them to have a child. And before long she did conceive, and the Master was very happy. He gave them all sorts of instructions as to what to do so that there would be a safe delivery. He was like a mother-in-law to the young woman; he told her what to eat and what not to eat and gave her advice on how much exercise to get, advice on everything. He was a Master, after all, and being a Master means what, it means that he would see to all these details.

Now, as it so happened, the next time the Master came to town was the very night that this young woman gave birth. And the Master was there and took the newborn child on his lap and admired her and told the couple how happy he was and declared that this child was his daughter, that she belonged to him and not to her parents. Of course the parents, devoted as they were to the Master, were overjoyed to hear these words and, if anything, their love and devotion only increased.

To make a long story short, the years pass. The daughter is brought up in a household which revolves around the Master. That is what their daily talk would be; they would recall his past visits. They would repeat the words he had uttered, they would remember so many incidents from their times spent together, and they would look forward to his next visit. Anxious for any news they could gather of his doings, if a neighbor returned from a visit to a different town to attend a wedding and would say, "Oh, did you hear, the Master was there?" the family would insist on all the details, how the Master looked, did he seem well, what did he say, and so on. That was their entertainment, as it were.

And whenever the Master did come to their town, it was always the same. "It is getting dark now, time to disperse, everyone should leave." But he would wink at the family and gesture for them to stay. And then after all had left, he would spend the evening with his daughter and her parents. The parents would bring out the food and he would play with his daughter and they all enjoyed themselves.

It is not too surprising to hear that this young girl grew up loving and respecting this Master. She loved her parents very much, but the Master became her real father and mother in one, and the whole family was very happy in their one-pointed love and devotion to the Master. To make a long story short, the years pass, and now this young girl is coming of age to marry.

Naturally the parents wouldn't think of marrying the girl to someone unless and until they had discussed it with their Master first, so the next time he is in town they go to see him. And they sit with him until it starts getting dark and then the Master calls out, "All right, it is time now, all should leave." And the people knew it. This was his way, so they all left except for this couple and their daughter, and the couple ask, "What should we do? Your daughter" – you see they never said "our daughter" because the Master had made it clear to them right from the start that although they were the parents, the girl was his, so they said, "Excuse us, but your daughter is getting of age now, and we wonder whether you want her to marry or not."

The Master turned to the girl and said, "What do you want? Do you want to get married?" And she said, "Whatever you say, I'll do."

This answer pleased the Master, and he said, "She should get married. Start making the necessary arrangements." Again, to make a long story short, a young man was found, brought to the Master for His approval, the arrangements were made, and the only problem was setting a date. Because naturally they wanted the Master to be there at the wedding, and it was impossible to know exactly when that would be. But the Master told them, "Don't worry. Pick any date you want and I will be there."

So they did and sure enough, no sooner does the wedding day dawn than they receive word that the Master is coming into town. And so a huge wedding takes place. As I said, they were not wealthy, but with the Master's grace, the couple had been able to save a little money.

Now, as it turned out, the groom, the husband to be, was not a follower of the Master. He was a good man, he had some spiritual feeling within him, but he was unaware of the ways of the Master. So, in addition to the happiness of the Master's company, and the wedding, the whole family was very happy because this was their chance for the young man to get to know the Master. You know how it is, when you love someone very much, you are always happy to bring your friends, your acquaintances, and have them meet this person. And because the Master had already approved of the boy, they felt totally reassured that he would be a perfect match for the daughter.

In short, all were very happy and the wedding went off very smoothly. But when it was over and the guests had departed, the Master called the boy over to him and said he would like to speak to him alone for a few minutes. Now, the couple and the daughter were delighted at this. For they knew there was no way that anyone could spend a few minutes alone in the company of the Master without falling hopelessly in love with him, and that's all they desired, that this new addition to their family learn to love the Master as they did.

So they were all very happy as the Master and the boy walked off and the Master bent near him and was whispering something in his ear. But they were completely taken aback when suddenly they hear the boy exclaim, "What?" in an indignant voice and then turn his back on the Master and march back to his new bride. His face was red with anger and fury and he grabbed his bride and said, "We're going. From today on, I never want to hear your Master's name mentioned in our household." And before anyone could say anything, he took his startled bride, you may say dragged her away, he was so enraged, and he loudly abused the Master, calling him a scoundrel, a rascal, and a charlatan the whole time as he stormed off.

The old couple, naturally, were astonished and they went up to the Master, but he didn't seem in a mood to enlighten them as to what had just transpired, so they simply accepted it. After all, whatever their Master did was right.

Still a burden, a pain grew in their hearts. For now, whenever the Master came, it would only be the two of them going to see him. The daughter never came. And when they went to visit her, she would meet them at the gate and make them stop and then she would ask all about the Master, what news they had, when they had last seen him, what he had done and said, but then she would warn them, "Now, when we enter the house, you must not say a word about our Master, for my husband forbids it."

But what else did they have to talk about, because their Master was their life. So the visits were very awkward and very painful, and although their daughter honored her husband's wishes, they could see how difficult it was for her. Not that she ever complained, but she had always been a carefree child, one who was naturally laughing and full of enthusiasm, and now she seemed to have aged so much. She walked with a heavy tread and her eyes seemed to lose their sparkle.

Some time passes, and now this daughter herself has a daughter. But this only adds to her secret grief, because she cannot take her daughter to see her Master. Her daughter must grow up without hearing his name or being allowed to worship him. But she is still a mother and she loves her daughter and she takes the best of care of her. She feels this is her Master's child, and so she treats her with the love she would have lavished on her Master, but she is still sad inside.

Again, years pass, and this girl's daughter herself is growing up. She has become a young woman and it is time to start thinking of finding a husband for her.

The Master, of course, knows this. He knows everything, but as always, he appears to know nothing. So the next time he comes to the old couple's town, he asks after his daughter and then he asks after her daughter. As if he doesn't know anything, he says, "How old is she now?" The grandparents give her age and the Master seems to consider this. "Is she married yet?" The old couple shake their heads.

The Master doesn't seem to notice their embarrassment and he continues quite innocently, "It seems she is at an age where my daughter and her husband should think of getting her married. I am surprised that this hasn't been done."

The old couple continue to sit there with their heads down. Finally the Master appears to notice their discomfort for the first time. "What's wrong," he asks. "Is something the matter?"

"What can we say? How can we tell you? It is not possible for her to get married."

"Not possible? Why not?"

Again there was an embarrassed silence, and the Master has to prompt and cajole until finally the husband whispers, "She has become a prostitute. No one will marry her. Your daughter and her husband are desolate. They are ashamed to show their faces in their community."

And it was true. The husband had had a thriving business, but now it was in ruins. Wherever he went people would point him out and whisper behind his back and he would hear the words "his daughter," and then the tale of her latest outrage. People would come by his shop, not to buy, but just to look at him, and he found doors that used to be open to him were now closed. When he entered a room, more often than not, the conversation suddenly stopped abruptly and people drifted away. It began to tell on his health. His whole mental attitude changed. He started dreading going out and hearing all the whispers behind his back. He started finding excuses not to go to work, and in his absence his business suffered. It got to the point where he didn't want to leave his house for any reason, and then his health broke down and he was almost unable to leave his house. His wife cared for him, but there was nothing she could do.

"Call them," the Master says. "Tell them I want to see them both."

"But Master, we are not even allowed to mention your name in his presence. How can we . . ."

"Call them. He is ready to come now."

And sure enough, when they relayed the message to the daughter, she emboldened herself and broached the subject to her

husband for the first time in all these years. "Why not go now?"
she asked.

"Okay, do what you want," the husband replied. He had been
crushed by circumstances, and he had no fight left in him.

"Will you come with me?" she asked. "Yes, if that is what you
want," he replied. And she helped him from the bed and got him
dressed, and together the two of them went to see the Master.

When the Master saw them coming, he hurried forward and
embraced his daughter, whom he hadn't seen for years now, with
such obvious tenderness and love that the daughter couldn't contain
herself and broke down and started weeping. "I know, I know," the
Master murmured compassionately and patted her on the back lovingly as she stood sobbing in his arms. Seeing the Master's love for
his wife, even the husband breaks down and begins to weep and
pour out his heart to the Master about his shame and embarrassment.

The Master looks at him very compassionately and says, "That
is why I told you what I did the night you got married. Do you
remember? Tell the others what I said to you that night."

The husband then, for the first time, revealed the secret of
their conversation. "He told me it would be best if that night I did not
spend it with my wife, but went to a brothel and slept with a prostitute. At first I thought this was some bizarre joke but then he even
tried to give me money to pay for it, and that's when I lost my temper and insisted that we leave."

"You see," the Master explained, "I knew your seed, your first
child, was destined for this. It could not be prevented. So I told you
to sleep with a prostitute and offered to pay so that you would not be
tainted by the transaction at all. That way the prostitute could have
conceived your daughter and the child would have grown up where
she belonged. When she became a prostitute herself, which was her
inescapable destiny, it would only be natural and there would be no
shame in it. That is why I told you what I did. Because of my love

for you and my daughter. I wanted to spare her this shame."

You see how unfathomable are their ways? It is impossible to figure out their methods. What can you say about someone telling a groom to spend his wedding night with a prostitute? Doesn't it seem preposterous? And yet look at how much suffering would have been avoided if he had only listened to the Master. And this is not a tall tale. In fact, it reminds me of a similar story that actually happened in Baba's time, that I was witness to. Would you like to hear that?

It concerned a family, like the couple in the earlier story, who were devoted to Baba. And like that couple, they had a child. This family was very close to Baba. They lived in Bombay and they came to see Baba whenever they could. Now, as it so happens, their son, for he was a boy, got sick. They were very worried, because although they tried to take care of him, he didn't improve. Now, in their love, their innocence, their first thought was to contact Baba to find out what they should do. This was nothing unusual. It had become their habit, after coming into Baba's orbit, of asking Baba's advice on any little thing, on anything and everything. There were many families like this. To some of us, at times, this total reliance on Baba was irritating. It seemed as if these families had lost all their common sense and were now incapable of making the smallest decision without bothering Baba about it. And, of course, this made more work for us. But it wasn't that. I see that now. It wasn't that they couldn't make any decisions for themselves, it was just that their love for Baba, the intimacy that that love created, made it only natural that as soon as any decision was there, they should turn to consult Baba. Their love was such that it never even occurred to them that this might be a nuisance to Baba, in the same way a small child in any and all situations automatically turns to its parents for help.

And this was not such a small thing. Their only son was sick and they were worried. Baba sent them a message to the effect that they shouldn't worry and should let their family doctor treat him.

So the couple did that. They kept the boy at home and treated him there, according to the advice of their family doctor, but the boy's condition did not improve. In fact, it got worse and worse. And the neighbors, seeing this, began to berate this couple, 'What are you doing? Are you trying to kill your child? Can't you see he is very ill and you must take him to the hospital at once?"

This was very hard for the parents. They had faith that Baba was God; that He knew everything, but it is the way with Masters that they appear to be ignorant. And so they wrote to Baba again and asked Him what they should do, explaining that their son's health was deteriorating. Baba made me write back that they should continue giving treatment through their family doctor. Of course, they couldn't tell the neighbors about Baba's instructions because the neighbors didn't believe in Baba and used to abuse Him.

Anyway, to make a long story short, the neighbors finally stepped in and forcibly took the boy to a hospital. The doctors immediately put him into surgery and operated on him. They did an appendectomy. And they berated the parents for waiting so long. If you had waited any longer, the boy would have died, it would have been too late to save him, they said. But they did manage to save him and the boy recovered and grew up into a healthy young man.

But then, as the boy became older, as he grew into a teenager, a young man, he started developing very bad habits. He began associating with a bad crowd and his behavior was such that he brought disgrace on the family to such an extent that the parents felt completely humiliated.

And a day did come, I happened to overhear it because I was with Baba when the parents came to visit, and I remember one time the mother confessed to Baba that she wished the boy had died in his sickness instead of being taken to the hospital and recovering. She said, "I prefer death for my son than this life he is living." Baba shrugged His shoulders.

And it was only then that Baba, just like the Master in the story, said, "I tried to help. Do you remember the orders I gave you? But what can I do, the neighbors interfered."

What exactly Baba meant by this we don't know. I have always taken it to mean that if the parents had kept the boy at home and let the family doctor treat him, he would have died and this would have been better for him and his parents under the circumstances. But you Westerners always object when I say this, and one time a boy came up to me and said, "Eruch, you know, maybe the boy wouldn't have died." I said, "What do you mean?" and he said, "Maybe if the neighbors hadn't interfered, the boy would have gotten very sick and would have almost died, and maybe, in that suffering the sanskaras would have been burnt away and his destiny changed. Just as when Baba asked a person to walk though the streets naked or something of that sort, as soon as the person showed a willingness to obey, Baba would rescind the order. So maybe, here too, if the parents had been allowed to obey Baba, Baba would have seen to it that the boy's tendencies died, but he would have survived."

Who knows? That too is possible; who can say? With Baba, anything is possible. But what this boy said is true of the way the mind works, trying to analyze and figure out meanings which are acceptable to us, but when we try to figure it out, we are doing exactly what these stories are supposed to teach us not to do, we are trying with our limited minds to fathom the unfathomable. Because it does seem rather harsh when I say Baba gave this order and the result of it was that the boy would have died, but the whole point is that whether the boy would have lived or died, it is impossible to fathom His ways. It cannot be done. Believe me. It is only love and acceptance of His wish which will ultimately lead you out of your mental confusion. That is why Baba says, "Don't try to fathom Me, just love Me."

⚅ W H O   I S   M E H E R   B A B A ?

AS YOU SAY, IT IS DIFFICULT SOMETIMES to know what to say to people when they ask about Meher Baba. You are not the only one who has had this difficulty. Even those of us with Baba didn't know how to answer people's questions. Haven't I told you about the time Baba sent me out to tell people about Him? I had never done any public speaking, and I didn't know what to say; I was not a philosopher like Deshmukh, who could discourse on lofty spiritual themes. What did I know about? I knew about looking after Baba, about packing His bedding so I could find whatever I needed in the dark, about sitting for hours without making a sound during night watch, about sweeping out His room and the like. That is what I knew. But now what to tell others?

As I have repeated many times, I was only here as an observer. I had no conviction that Baba was the Avatar, I was not a person who was head over heels in love with Meher Baba. Baba simply called me and I came and I stayed and served Him.

And Baba knew this. Without asking me what my thoughts and feelings were, Baba came to my rescue by telling me, "Even if you cannot say Baba is God, you can always say, 'Baba says He is God.'" So Baba has given us a guideline. We can always use His words. We do not need to have the personal conviction or experience to say, "Baba says He is the same Ancient One come once again in our midst." So this is one guideline Baba has given us. But Baba has also told us to be honest. If you take Baba to be the devil, then you should say you think Baba is the devil. If you take Baba to be God, then you should say that. Say whatever your heart prompts you to say. This is also a guideline Baba has given us. Why has He given us this? Because He is anything we take Him to be. He cannot be excluded from anything, as He is Existence Infinite and Eternal. Baba once said that if you believe hell exists, then it cannot exist without His being there.

But you already know this and still you don't know how to answer people when they ask, "Who is Meher Baba?" But did you know that Baba answered that question Himself? There is a story behind it. As you know, after the New Life, Baba suddenly released the treasure of His name. He told His lovers to share this treasure far and wide. Until then Baba would travel incognito. If someone asked, "Is that Meher Baba?" we had to pretend we were deaf because Baba didn't want people to recognize Him, to come to Him. All those years when He was so young and strong and energetic, He veiled Himself from the world. And then, after the rigors of the New Life, after the accident when Baba is still in a cast, that is when He starts announcing to the world His presence, that He is the Highest of the High, that He is God in human form, that He is the Avatar.

And His lovers began to do their part in introducing Baba to the world, in making His name known far and wide. Now it so happens, that there was a World's Fair in New York around this time, in the '60s. And some of the Western Baba lovers had a stall there and passed out Baba literature, and they would write letters to Baba telling Him about all the contacts they made and the humorous things that happened. And Baba was very pleased with their loving efforts. Especially so, it seemed, when there was an Eastern group of Baba lovers here. Baba would extol the virtues, the dedication, the hard work they were doing in the West. He would say, "Look at My lovers in the West, they hardly get a chance to see Me, and yet look at what they've done to spread My name and message. And you, all of you who have been given so many more opportunities to see

Me, to be with Me, to receive My love, what have you done?" And so on. You know how Baba would egg people on, how He would find occasion to put a little prick here, a little jab there.

And His lovers here took this to heart. They began to feel it was true, that they weren't doing enough. Now it so happened that not long after this there was to be a big industrial fair in Bombay. There were huge tents set up over acres of open land, and there were hundreds and hundreds of booths underneath and thousands of people coming each day, so the Bombay lovers thought, "Wouldn't it be wonderful if we could obtain a booth and have literature and information about Baba there so that all these people could hear about Him?" And that is what they did. How they arranged it all, that I don't know. You will have to ask one of the Bombay people, but somehow they managed and they set up a booth and the crowds did start coming. And the people who came were very curious to know about Meher Baba. But the ones who came kept putting the same question to them and they didn't know how to answer it. For the people would ask them, 'Who is Meher Baba?" and they didn't know what to say.

Some said, "He is the Ancient One." Others said, "He is the Highest of the High." The Bombay lovers said whatever came to them, whatever they took Baba to be, but they found that no matter what they said, it didn't satisfy the crowd. And they got desperate. How to answer this question? People kept asking it over and over and they didn't have any answer. So they called Baba. We were in Poona at the time, and I remember I answered the phone and they explained the situation to me and they said, "Eruch, what should we say?" So I said, "Baba is in the next room, hold on and I will ask Him." And I did.

Baba seemed amused at this situation, but He told me to tell them that when someone asked, "Who is Meher Baba," they should reply, "He is the one who provokes this question in you. The Being of all beings." Just that. So I repeated what Baba had told me to the

Bombay lovers and they eventually printed a little booklet called *Questions and Answers on Meher Baba,* and the very first question is, "Who is Meher Baba?" and their answer is what Baba had said, that He is the One who provokes this question in you. He is the Being of all Beings.

And that satisfied people. When the Bombayites told this to people, they felt astonished but satisfied. It made sense to them in a way that "Ancient One" and "Highest of the High" and whatnot did not. This, they could understand. Baba is the one who prompts us to seek Him out. Our curiosity to find out about God, or Truth, that itself is Baba. A Sufi saint once said that our very question to God, "Where are You?" is His answer "Here I am." That it is because we feel His presence that we are moved to search for Him and cry out in desperation, "Where are You?" When we don't feel His presence, we don't miss Him, we don't start looking for Him. What a game it all is.

A Perfect Master once said, "At the beginning I was mistaken in four respects. I concerned myself to remember God, to know Him, to love Him and to seek Him. And when I had come to the end I saw that He had remembered me before I remembered Him, that His knowledge of me had preceded my knowledge of Him, His love towards me had existed before my love for Him, and He had sought me before I had sought Him."

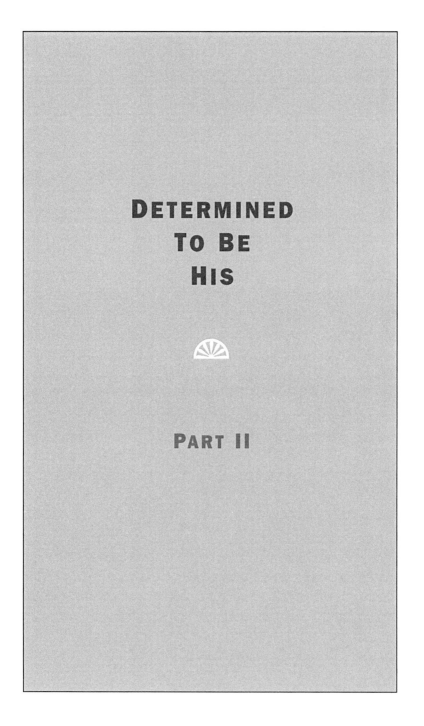

DETERMINED
TO BE
HIS

PART II

◈ NATURAL

HOW CAN I IMPRESS UPON YOU ALL how natural Meher Baba was? I've often said that ignorance is the God-Man's sharpest weapon to relate Himself to us. He must relate Himself to us only through ignorance, otherwise it is frightening. Baba is omniscient, He knows everything, but if He were to make us feel this, then what? You would feel naked. If you were going to meet someone and you knew that person knew everything about you, everything you had ever done, every unworthy thought you had ever had, you would run away.

So when someone came to Baba, He acted completely ignorant. "Who are you? What have you come from? Did you have a good journey?" Baba would appear not to know anything. So perfect was Baba's appearance of ignorance that sometimes when people would bring their newborn babies to Baba, they would put the child on Baba's lap, and Baba would play with it, pinch its cheeks, squeeze its fingers, and then He would look up at the proud mother and gesture, "Is it a boy or a girl?" The baby would be naked, mind you; Baba could easily have seen whether the baby was a girl or a boy but His not-knowingness was so perfect that He would look up innocently at the mother and gesture. This was Baba's gesture for a male child, and this was Baba's gesture for female. So Baba would gesture, "Boy or girl?"

Some people, when they think of God, automatically think of miracles. And there are many miracle stories associated with Baba, but Baba always insisted that He never did miracles, that it was the faith of His lovers that produced the so-called miracles. Certainly there have been instances when people have reported to us of being cured of some ailment after having Baba's touch, or of having a complete turnaround in their business affairs after receiving Baba's blessings, but where is the miracle in this?

What is a miracle, after all? The common conception of a miracle is of an event that is supernatural, that defies the laws of nature. But a miracle is itself part of nature, so how can it be supernatural? One time Kumar, Amrit's father, accused Baba of doing miracles. "You always say, Baba, that You don't do any miracles, but I have seen You do so many miracles with my own eyes that I don't understand how you can say this."

"What miracles?" Baba asked. "Well, for one thing, Baba, what about the time of our first meeting? My wife had made food for You and Your party, but I know there wasn't enough food there to feed all the people You gave it to. Not only that, but You gave everyone big servings and insisted they have second helpings, yet when I went to look into the pot before it was given to the women, I saw that only a small portion of the rice was gone. It was a miracle!"

"Why a miracle? You love Me. If you were to see that I needed something, even if I didn't ask you for it, you would try and get it for Me, wouldn't you?" "Yes, Baba." "Well, I have so many lovers. Not just those on this plane of existence; I have lovers on all planes. And these lovers try to help Me. They saw that there wasn't enough food to go around, so as it was dished out of the pot, they refilled the pot. But I had nothing to do with this. It wasn't a miracle. On their own, they saw that I needed something, so they supplied it. What's miraculous about that?

"It is like this. Let us say you were to visit a maharajah. You are a guest at his palace. The servants come and they carry your bags to your room and they even unpack for you. Now let us say one of the servants goes into your bathroom, and he sees that there is no soap and no towels. Will he go to the maharajah and disturb him to tell him that there is no soap or towels in the guest bathroom? No, he will simply go get the soap and the towels and put them in the bathroom himself. The maharajah won't even know any of this is happening. His servants will see to everything for him. Is this a miracle? In the same way, my "aides" see to My needs without telling Me about it."

Whenever people would tell Baba about some miracle He had performed, Baba would always look surprised and gesture, "This is news to Me," or "This is the first I'm hearing about it." Anyway, what is a miracle? Isn't the fact that the sun rises every day a miracle? Look out the door there, look at the trees in front of the clinic. See how many shades of green there are, isn't that a miracle? Isn't the very fact of our being a miracle?

But we don't consider these things miracles. They are miracles, I tell you, they are, but we don't ever think of them as miracles. Why is that? Because they are so natural that we take it for granted. That is what I'm trying to say about Baba. He was so natural, that even those things which others consider miracles also seemed so natural in His presence that it never occurred to us to think of them as miracles.

Let me give you an example. One time Baba was giving *darshan* in Poona. This was in the back of Guruprasad, and there must have been several thousand people there. We had rows and rows of seats, stretching way off into the distance, set up before the raised dais where Baba sat. You've seen this in films. The men sat on one side and the women sat on the other, and there was an aisle down the center which separated the two. There was a woman who had come who loves Baba very much. She was sitting way at the back, right next to the aisle. She always liked to sit on the aisle because that way she could lean out and get a good unobstructed view of Baba. Though she was way in the back, by leaning a little sideways, her head would be in the aisle and she could look at Baba and get a good view of Him sitting on the dais.

Now, when Baba gave *darshan* programs like this, He would often have a program in the morning and then there would be a break for lunch. Then people would return in the afternoon and there would be another program. Sometimes this would go on for a few days at a time. I don't recall exactly how long this particular program was, but I think it was for around three days. And each day this woman would sit in the same seat on the aisle at the very back of the crowd.

Similarly, there was a man who always used to sit on the other side of the aisle, right across from her. They sat in those seats every time, for several days. But as the days passed, the woman started to get a thought in her head, "I wonder if Baba even knows I'm here," she thought. "I can see Baba, but He is so far away, He seems so tiny up there on the platform, how can He see me when there are so many thousands here and I'm sitting at the very back; how can He see me over the heads of all those in front?"

It's only natural that she should have a thought like this. What she says is right, there were thousands there, so how could Baba be expected to notice someone sitting in the very back? But just then Baba had me call out a man's name. This was a man sitting in the back row, one seat in from the aisle. I forget who it was, but I remember Baba had me call out to this man on the public address system. When I did, he stood up. Such a tiny figure way way back in that huge crowd. And I said, "Baba says, 'What has happened to –.'" and I named someone. Again, I don't remember who it was, but I called out someone's name. "Baba says, 'What has happened to this person? Where is he? Hasn't he come today?'" At this, the man I mentioned stood up in the crowd, and shouted, "Here I am, Baba."

Baba looked at him and gestured, "Why did you change your seat? All these days you have been sitting in the back, why did you change your seat today?" "I wanted to be closer to You, Baba," the man replied. Baba gestured, "Go on back, take your old seat." So the man went back and sat in the empty seat on the aisle, across from the woman who had just been wondering whether Baba even knew she was there.

Baba didn't suddenly stop everything and announce to the woman, "I know what you are thinking, and I do know you are there." That would have seemed like a miracle, but it also would have been disturbing to everyone there. It would have created a different atmosphere. Baba wanted His lovers to feel relaxed in His presence. So in a very natural way, Baba inquired about someone who had changed his seat. And the woman felt reassured that Baba must know of her presence, as well.

Look, Mary has been sitting there, across the hall, under the window every day now this week, isn't it? If she were to suddenly come in today and sit next to Baba's chair, I would notice it. Even with my eyesight, I would look across the room and notice that Mary wasn't there today, and I would wonder, "Where's Mary, is she sick, why didn't she come today?" Didn't I just do that with John? My eyesight isn't good, so when he sat over there where he doesn't usually sit, I thought it was someone new and I asked him who he was. I couldn't see well enough to make out the face; it looked a little like John to me, but I knew he doesn't sit there, that's not his place, so I asked him who he was. I thought it was someone new, coming here for the first time.

There's nothing supernatural about this, on the contrary it is most natural. So it was with Baba. Even the hints He would give from time to time of His omniscience, or His omnipotence, seemed so natural that we didn't think about it. Now, in retrospect, we can look at it and say, "Yes, that shows that Baba is omniscient, He must have known what I was thinking," but at the time it all seemed so natural that our intimacy with Baba was not disturbed by any thoughts that He was reading our minds or anything like that.

Baba would be talking to one person in the crowd, and someone else would feel that the answers were meant for him. Baba wouldn't even look at that person, would give no indication that He knew what that person was thinking, but that person would feel the answers were for him. It was all so natural. Let me give you another example from my own life.

I've already told you, many times, of how I came to Baba for the first time, and how Baba used to come to my house when I was a boy, and about the telegrams Baba sent when I was working in the garden and all of that, so I won't dilate on that now. I'll just touch briefly on one small part of that story.

I was coming home from school on my bicycle and I saw Baba waiting for me at the front gate of the house. This was the first time Baba came to visit us in Nagpur. We had already seen Baba in Ahmednagar, but at the time we were living in Nagpur and Baba came to visit us. I jumped off my cycle and prostrated at Baba's feet and said, "Forgive me." Why I said that I don't know. I have no idea what put that into my head, other than the fact that I was a young boy and boys always have something they've done that needs forgiving. So perhaps it was just that, I had some guilty secret and when I saw Baba I spontaneously felt prompted to ask His forgiveness. Anyway, I went inside and Baba proceeded to play with me. But the games He played were all games for children. Find the middle finger, games like that. I wasn't at all happy. I was no baby to play games like that. I had my friends at school, I wanted to go join them to play cricket and football, not stay inside and play baby games with this man.

I was too polite to say anything, so I had to stay there and endure it, but I didn't like it and I made up my mind that I was not going to do this again. So the next day when I came home from school and saw, from quite a distance, Baba waiting for me at the front gate, I changed my route and went in by the back way. I parked my bike at the back entrance and quietly went in, had my bath, changed my clothes, and came out the back way again so I could rejoin my schoolmates.

When I returned that evening my mother was furious with me,

"Where were you?" she demanded. "Didn't you know Baba was waiting for you all afternoon? Why didn't you come home after school?" "But I did come home. I came home and changed my clothes and went out again." "How did you come? Baba was waiting for you at the front gate." "I know, so I came in the back gate."

My mother got furious at this. Some of you know what my mother is like, she is completely for Baba. So when she heard that I had deliberately avoided Baba, she became very upset with me. "Don't you know who He is?" she demanded. "He is Zoroaster come again!" "So what?" I thought. You see, at that time I loved Jesus the Christ. I was even shedding tears, wondering when Jesus would come again, and in answer to my tears, Jesus, in the form of Meher Baba, did come. He came right to my door, but I didn't know this. And my mother didn't tell me that Meher Baba was the Christ come again. She only said, "Don't you know who He is? He is Zoroaster come again!" So I thought, "So what if He is Zoroaster? I am not interested in Zoroaster, I only want Jesus the Christ."

Baba overheard the argument from the next room and came in and asked my mother what it was all about. She explained that I had sneaked off to play with my schoolmates instead of staying home with Him. Baba immediately took my side. He asked me about my friends, and I told him that we had football matches or cricket matches after school and my team was counting on me. Baba told my mother that I was right, that I must never let my side down, but should go to school and take part in the games. And Baba used to take an active interest in them.

When I would come home in the evening, He would always ask how my team had done. He never made me feel that I was doing anything wrong by not coming home right after school to be with Him. On the contrary, He made me feel that it was my duty to join my school friends and play in the outdoor games we used to indulge in.

And after that, Baba started a new game with me. When I came home after the match was over, He would sit with me and tell me stories on His board. Now this was a game I could enjoy. It was not a baby game like the others, it gave me an opportunity to utilize my intelligence. For it was a challenge, a puzzle to learn how to read Baba's board. It intrigued me and I used to enjoy trying to read it. For as soon as I learned how to read the board, Baba would speed up. In addition to hearing the stories which were interesting, there was the added factor of competition, for I would always try to keep up with Baba as He went faster and faster, tying to outdo Him as it were in this game. This was more like it, this was an indoor game which I felt was more suited to my age.

But the end result was that I became adept at reading Baba's board. When I joined Him many years later to live with Him, I already knew how to read the board. Recently, when I was telling this story one of you said, "See, Baba was training you for later on. He knew you would be reading His board so much, He made you an expert when you were still young." At the time I said, "Could be," but, to tell you the truth, I had never thought about it. It never occurred to me that Baba had taught me to read His board as a youngster because He knew I would need to know this later on. And when the boy said it, my first reaction was that it seemed too far-fetched.

But as I thought about it, I had to agree, it could be. At any rate, it had that effect, but even now, it seems so natural, the way it was done, that I just accept it. Baba is omniscient, so He certainly knew when I was a boy that I would be with Him in later years, but thinking about it in that way seems to add an unnatural element, at least for me. It makes what was very natural seem unnatural. And what I am trying to say is that everything Baba did, always seemed completely natural. That is the hallmark of the Avatar , His naturalness.

And Baba wanted us to be natural with Him too. He didn't like it when people would come and fold their hands and stand there lost in adoration. Baba had one very dear lover from the South. He was not an orthodox Hindu, in fact he was one of those speaking out against the evils of the caste system, but he was very orthodox in his ideas, I should say, about what constituted the spiritual life. He would never smoke, for instance, or use bad language. He always was very proper.

With Baba we were very familiar. Of course, there was always respect. We were free with Baba, but we never took license. There was always a line we would not cross. We could joke with Baba, we did not have to pretend to be spiritual, but we were never vulgar with Baba. Not that Baba ever told us, "Never say such things to Me, or never act in such a fashion to Me." We just felt it, within us, that it wouldn't be right to behave in certain ways with Baba. There was a natural reverence which we felt was due Baba, and so, naturally we observed this. It is common sense, after all.

So much of what I have to tell you all is just plain common sense. You people make such a mystery of it, but it's all really quite simple. You analyze everything and have so many questions, "What should I do in this situation?" "What about that situation?" "But if someone does this, then what should I do?" You make it all so complicated.

That's why I always tell everyone who asks, "First and foremost, just be determined to be His. Then everything else falls into place." Once you are determined to be His, you will only do those things which won't prevent you from being His. You don't have to analyze every single situation you find yourself in and try to determine what Baba wants you to do. You'll go crazy that way; just determine to be His and that determination will provide you with the answers you need. In a very natural way. It's not some complicated exam, with trick questions that you have to study and cram for. It's a question of just doing what naturally seems to be the right thing to do.

But people say, "How can we be determined to be His? What exactly does that mean? What do you mean, what naturally seems right?" So I tell them, if you can't simply be determined to be His, then it is still very simple, "Just do those things you would not be ashamed to do in His presence. Say only those things you would say in His presence, and think only those thoughts you would feel comfortable thinking in His presence." You see how easy it is?

And what is doing and saying and thinking only those things which we would do and say and think in His presence? It is keeping Him as our constant companion. It is living your life as if you are living in His company. That is why I am trying to bring home to you how natural it was to be in His company. Keeping Baba as your constant companion does not mean that Baba is always looking over your shoulder; it should not make you feel guilty or nervous or uncomfortable. Baba was our friend. He did not want us to feel distant from Him.

Yes, it is true that in His presence we would hesitate to do certain things. As I said before, we would not take liberties with His presence, but it was not a heavy or unnatural repression; it came naturally from our love for Baba. In His presence you don't want to do certain things. It's not that you refrain from doing them, but even the thought of doing them doesn't come up, because it would seem completely unnatural to do those things.

Or let me give you another example. When we were with Baba, sometimes Baba would get the whim to play cards. Baba always liked a lively atmosphere around Him and it was certainly lively when we used to play cards. In addition to the usual sort of banter that goes on when playing, we would accuse each other of cheating, and there would be protests and accusations, and a lot of argument and debate, in short, we acted completely natural with Baba. So much so, that sometimes Baba would suddenly stop and remind us, "Don't forget, I am God." And we would nod our heads, yes, and the game would continue.

We used to play at Meherazad, in Mandali Hall, and we would play in Guruprasad. And when we traveled on *mast* trips with Baba, sometimes we would play cards on the train with Him. Of course, then there was no question of the loser rubbing his nose on the ground, because that would have attracted attention to Baba and that was the one thing He didn't want when He was out on a *mast* expedition. Sometimes when we were traveling by train, Baba and I used to travel second class and the rest of the mandali with us would travel servant class. But they would come into our compartment and we would play cards. If the conductor ever came in, I would just tell him that these others were our servants and so they would be allowed to stay with us. Especially around meal time it was no problem having them join us because servants would naturally be needed then to serve the food.

But just as this lover from the South would not have understood our ways, there were many who would not have understood Baba's playing cards. Their concept of God was quite different. So when such lovers came, Baba would always act very serious and solemn, in short, He would act up to their concept of how God was expected to behave. Once I remember we were playing cards when suddenly a car drove up and some of these lovers arrived to see Baba. "Quick," Baba gestured, "sit on the cards." So we all slipped the cards underneath us and sat very straight, looking at Baba most attentively.

The lovers came in and Baba greeted them and then engaged them in some sort of spiritual discourse for a while. I don't remember what Baba said, but it was on some lofty spiritual theme which conformed with their preconceptions about what sort of subjects were suitable to discuss with the God-Man, and after a few minutes they paid their respects and left. "Are they gone?" Baba asked. I checked and made sure the car had driven away. "Yes, Baba," I said, "they have gone." Baba smiled and gestured like this with His hand, "Get out the cards." And we resumed our game.

That is what I mean by being natural with Baba, and yet not interfering with the natural relationship that another has with Him.

Sometimes people ask us, "But why didn't you ask Baba this?" or "Why didn't you ask Baba to explain why He was doing that?" but it just didn't seem natural to do that in His presence. Not that it was wrong to do such a thing, but it just never occurred to us. We just naturally lived our lives in a certain way in His presence, and it would not have seemed natural to suddenly start questioning Baba about why He was doing this or that. We didn't stop and analyze it and agonize over it, the way you do; we didn't wring our hands and wonder, "Oh, should I ask Baba or shouldn't I ask Baba?" No, we just naturally felt that sometimes it was appropriate to ask Baba certain questions and sometimes it wasn't.

Let me give you one example of a time when it was appropriate to ask questions. This was right before the East-West Gathering. The ground behind Guruprasad had been scraped clean and now thousands of chairs were going to be set up in rows for the *darshan* which was going to take place the next morning. Baba's health was not particularly good, and He had retired for the night, giving express instructions that He was not to be disturbed.

I was in charge of seeing to the preparations, and I had just lain down for an hour to get a brief rest when someone came to me and told me that the *darshan* ground was full of red ants. Apparently, when the ground had been scraped and dressed, the ants' nests were disturbed, and now there were millions of red ants crawling on the ground. Now, this was a real problem. Red ants are not like black ants. Red ants bite and their bite hurts. They are not big but the bite can be quite painful. We couldn't have so many thousand people sitting there and getting bitten the whole time by red ants.

On the other hand, I knew from my experience with Baba that He was always most particular never to kill ants. Mosquitoes we could slap. In fact, in the early years, Baba used to encourage the mandali to kill mosquitoes. In Manzil-e-Meem they each were responsible for killing a certain number of mosquitoes every day, by Baba's order. But ants Baba never wanted harmed. If we were walking along, Baba would sometimes suddenly alter His stride and then point down to the ground and gesture to us to go around. "Be careful," He would gesture, "there are ants here, don't step on them." And so we would take great care to step over them, to walk around them, so we wouldn't inadvertently kill any.

I knew this. I knew Baba never wanted us to kill ants. Of course sometimes it was unavoidable. You couldn't always be looking at the ground as you walked, and no doubt when I would drive Baba in a car we must have run over so many ants, but if we could avoid it, if we were aware that ants were there, then Baba always wanted us to make the effort not to kill them.

So I didn't know what to do. The program was scheduled to begin the next morning at nine; something had to be done right away, but what? And Baba had told me that He didn't want to be disturbed for anything. So what could I do? And yet I knew how important the *darshan* program was. I knew how important Baba felt it was, so I knocked on His door and woke Baba up.

"What do you want?" Baba gestured. "Didn't I tell you not to disturb me?" "Yes, Baba," and then I explained the situation. "So what's to be done?" "Can the ants be exterminated?" "Yes, Baba." You see, we were very lucky. The city engineer for Poona at that time happened to be a Baba lover and was helping us with the arrangements at Guruprasad. With his help we could get the exterminators that night to spray the ground and kill all the ants. And, by working all night long, we would be able to set the chairs in place before the morning *darshan*. I told all this to Baba. "But Baba, should we kill the ants?" I asked. "Why not?" Baba gestured. "Because I know You have always wanted us to avoid killing ants if we could," I explained. Baba made a dismissive gesture with His hand. "Kill them," He replied. "My lovers are more important than the ants."

And so we had the exterminators come in and spray the ground, and that cleared the area of the red ants. We worked all night long and by morning all those thousands of chairs were in place and no one ever knew what had happened. That's when I got an inkling as to the importance of Baba's lovers. It didn't mean that we should no longer try to avoid killing ants, but it put things into their proper perspective, a natural perspective.

The key word is natural. That's what I want to emphasize. And for this lover from the South, it was natural for him to feel that he should act a certain way, he was by nature very pious and he would not have understood the intimacy that we shared with Baba. So whenever he would come for a visit, Baba would remind us, "My lover is coming today, so any of you who want to smoke, better go out and smoke now because he would be upset if he saw any of you smoking."

Baba saw the humor in it. Baba would have a twinkle in His eye as He would tease us about the state of our dress, and tell us that we should put on better clothes, and should behave properly when this lover arrived. But Baba was very serious that we should not disturb this lover's natural relationship with Him. This man's love for Baba was very great, there is no denying that, but he would not have understood the way we related to Baba, and Baba respected that. So whenever he was coming, Baba used to remind us, "Better not do that when this man comes. Remember to be on your best behavior."

If you were to ask me, must we be pious around Baba? I would say, "No. Be yourself." This particular man was a very pious man and Baba didn't want his natural piety disturbed, but that doesn't mean that everyone has to act that way. I remember one time Baba was holding a *sahavas* program at Meherabad. Don't ask me what year because I can't remember years anymore. Perhaps it was 1955 when different language groups came from all over India to spend time with Baba. That is what *sahavas* means, to spend time in an intimate way with the Beloved. To bring this point home to everyone, on the very first day, Baba called everyone together and told them that they should feel at home at Meherabad, that He didn't want them worrying about anything; their minds should be free to concentrate entirely on Him. So if they felt even a little bit ill, they should contact one of the doctors instantly. They should just feel completely relaxed and at home at Meherabad.

Now it so happened that one of the men there was suffering from diarrhea. He was an old lover of Baba's and he came forward and said that he had so many medical problems and had to be careful about his diet, and Donkin and Nilu and the doctors talked to him and gave him specific instructions about what he should do to take care of his health. He was to avoid fatty foods, he wasn't to eat fried foods; I don't remember all the instructions he was given, but in short they told him very precisely what he could eat and what he couldn't eat so that his health could be properly maintained. And they saw to it that he got the type of food he needed.

See the care that Baba took. There were hundreds of people staying at Meherabad, but Baba would see to it that if somebody there needed a special diet, he got it. So the *sahavas* program started and everyone was very happy to get this opportunity to spend time with Baba. Baba was staying at Meherazad, but I used to drive Him every morning to Meherabad. Baba would go into that little cabin that's there, where Ted and Janet live now, and He would have His breakfast and then He would come out and mingle with all His lovers.

What Baba liked to have each morning was *malai*. Do you have that? No, your milk is homogenized and pasteurized and the cream has been removed and sold separately. But with us, we get milk directly from the milch cow. Then we boil it up and let it cool. After it cools, the cream rises to the surface and we scoop this off. This is what we call *malai*, and Baba used to like to have this for breakfast. Pendu, of course, knew this, so every morning he would send over a breakfast tray for Baba with a little dish of *malai* on it. Pendu was too busy seeing to everything to bring the tray himself, but he would have a boy bring it to Baba each morning as soon as Baba arrived at Meherabad.

But one morning when we arrived, there was only a tiny bit of *malai*. Baba asked, "Where is my *malai*?" "I don't know, Baba," I said. "Maybe there was an accident and it was spilled." "Call Pendu," Baba ordered, so I called Pendu and Baba asked him, "Where is the *malai*? Why did I get so little?" "I don't know, Baba," Pendu said, "the dish was full this morning." "Then who has eaten the *malai*?"

Pendu called the boy who was responsible for bringing Baba's tray but he swore that when he opened the *pindra* to get Baba's *malai*, there was only a little bit left in the dish. "Maybe a cat got into it," I suggested, and Baba said, "Be careful, and see that tomorrow there's no mishap."

But the next morning, again the *malai* dish was almost empty. Again the boy who brought the tray swore that he hadn't taken it. But the *pindra*, you know what a *pindra* is, don't you? One of those big wooden cabinets with a meshed door. That's where we used to store food, and they have a type of wooden latch that pivots on a screw and when you turn it, it sticks down in front of the doors so you can't open them. In addition to that, they would have a metal latch in the front of the doors, and each morning when the boy went to get Baba's food, the *pindra* would be closed and the latches shut.

So it didn't seem to Pendu that it could possibly be a cat. He thought that perhaps, in spite of his protests, the boy was the one responsible for stealing Baba's *malai*, because who else could be taking it? Everyone knew it was for Baba, so none of His lovers would think about taking it. Pendu resolved to catch the thief. So that evening he put the *malai* in the *pindra* as usual and then hid himself nearby where he could watch.

And what did he find? The next morning, while all were still asleep this one sahavasi comes and walks up to the *pindra*, opens it, reaches in with his fingers, scoops out most of the *malai* and eats it, and then goes back to bed. Pendu couldn't believe it. But the next morning, when Baba came, Pendu announced that he had caught the cat that had been getting into Baba's cream. And he told Baba who had done it. "Call him here," Baba said.

And you know who it was? It was the same man who had had diarrhea and had been told he had to be so careful about his diet. The doctors had told him he couldn't have fatty foods, and here he was getting up in the middle of the night and eating straight cream.

Baba said, "What are you doing? You have been told to avoid these foods; they are bad for your health and yet you are eating them? And didn't you know that cream was for My breakfast?"

"Yes, Baba," the man replied. "I knew, but what to do, I was only following Your orders." "My orders? What order did I give that said you should eat My cream," Baba asked. "Baba," the man replied, "when we first arrived, You told us we should feel at home. Well at home, whenever I can't sleep at night, I get up and have a little *malai*, and then I can go back to sleep. So when I couldn't sleep here, I did the same thing, because You told us we should make ourselves at home."

Baba laughed, and turned to us and gestured, "See, this is real obedience." And that morning, Baba called everyone together and told them this story and said that of everyone there, only this man had truly obeyed Him and made Him happy. The man's childlike innocence touched Baba. "That's what you have to be like," Baba would tell us. "You have to have the type of innocent faith that lover had."

And that man really was an innocent. He was just like a big child. You can't pretend to have that sort of childlike innocence; Baba would not have been pleased if someone else had used Baba's words as an excuse to do what he wanted, but this man took it to heart, there was no pretense here, no artifice, he honestly was making himself at home, and Baba liked this. This was being natural with Baba, and this was what Baba wanted and what He wants. We are not natural, we are most unnatural I would say, but Baba wants us to be as natural as children in His presence. Childlike, but not childish.

🕮 T A C T

THE OTHER DAY SOMEONE WAS ASKING ME, "Why don't you speak out when you see someone doing something wrong?" I said, "I do." But the other person insisted, "No, I see people over here and they're not behaving properly and you never say anything to them. You always treat them so lovingly. How will they learn if you don't teach them?"

"Who am I to teach others?" I said, but this person wasn't satisfied. But I tell you it's true. I feel it, I know my own weaknesses and I know I am in no position to try to teach others what to do. Of course, we do say things. If I see someone doing something which I feel is going to harm him, then I will say something. If I knew that someone here was taking drugs, I would take him aside and tell him he shouldn't do that. I would consider it my brotherly duty to say something. But if it is something minor, then who am I to say anything?

And more and more these days I feel that it is Baba doing everything. So how can I speak out, when it is Baba doing it? Every now and then someone will do something and it will bother me and I will blurt something out. You know my nature, I have a hot temper, and every now and then I will explode and say something. But it is Eruch who is blurting these things out, not Baba in me. My speaking out is my weakness, so how will you learn from my display of weakness?

And what is there to learn anyway? Baba has revealed to us that already within everyone, the Truth is. It is not a question of learning this Truth, but of unlearning all the falsehood we are accustomed to believing and what is this falsehood but our own selves?

When I say, "I am Eruch," that is not the Truth. That is a falsehood. But no matter how many times I say, "I am God," I will still feel that I am Eruch. In this case, it is also a type of falsehood for me to say, "I am God." It behooves me, until I truly experience it, to say, "I am Eruch," but always to keep in the back of my mind that this is not so.

It is a paradox, I know. It seems like a contradiction, I know it, and it is so. That is why the best solution is not to say, "I am God," or "I am Eruch," but "I am His slave." Perhaps that is not the ultimate Truth, but it is the truth, with a small *t*, which will most easily lead us to the Truth, with a capital *t*, of the "I am God" state.

You already know what you should be doing, everyone knows this. You do not need someone else to tell you. You have heard me tell stories so many times about how Baba would correct His lovers. He would not say, "You should do this and this and this," or "Never do that, or that or that." God has already given us such rules, that is what the ten commandments are. Isn't that so? For what else are they but rules of conduct?

But Baba said the ten commandments are merely the outward form of inner rules which are inherent in all people. It is not that God came to Moses and handed him a tablet with these rules on them. God has inscribed these rules on the tablet of every person's heart. That is the real significance of the story of the ten commandments. But just as the Israelis gave themselves up to drunken orgies and idol worship and Moses broke the tablets, so too we give ourselves up to our lower selves and we break the tablets, as it were, in our hearts. We know what is right, but we don't do it.

But that knowing gets stronger and stronger with our determination to be His, and eventually it becomes impossible for us to disobey any longer, and then, and only then, do we change our behavior. Not because someone told us to change, but because within ourselves we no longer could ignore what we know to be right. Baba has said in the *Discourses* something to the effect that it is not a question of teaching anyone anything, but of helping them uncover what they already know. And how do we do that? That is where we must use our intelligence.

I've told you before how when I was young I used to take pride in always telling the truth. I hurt a lot of people telling them what I took to be the truth. But you know what Baba told me, He told me, "The Truth when told is that which uplifts another. Anything which crushes another person cannot be true." So that too must be taken into account.

Sometimes, when Baba was in seclusion, someone would come to see Him. When Baba found out, He would express Himself very forcibly. But if this Divine Wrath were to be given full expression, it would mean *mahapralaya*. Baba would express His displeasure to us, but we were not to relay it so forcefully to the other person. Baba would not have been pleased with that. Even if Baba had just gestured, "The fool! Doesn't he know I'm in seclusion?" if we were to go out and say to the person, "You fool, don't you know Baba is in seclusion?" that would not be telling the truth, and Baba would have been displeased with us.

Why would it not have been the truth? Because that would have crushed the man's enthusiasm to follow Baba, who is the Truth. Also there would have been no expression given to Baba's love and compassion, which is an eternal Truth: God is infinite love and compassion. So if we were to only give expression to Baba's displeasure, we would not be expressing the truth. This doesn't mean that we would go and say, "Oh, we are so pleased you have come, it is wonderful and Baba will be delighted to see you." No, that also would not be the truth. We would have to let the people know that they had come at the wrong time, but we had to do so in such a way that they wouldn't feel hurt. We had to make them feel Baba's love and compassion for them at the same time that we let them know that Baba was in seclusion and couldn't see them.

Let me tell you a story which will perhaps make this clearer. There was a teacher in a certain town and he was well known and highly respected. Every day he would give discourses, and people would come and listen to him. Now once a year, at this town, there was a great festival, an *urs*, like our Amartithi, commemorating the passing away of some great spiritual figure. And every year, during this four day festival, thousands of pilgrims would flock to the town to take part. This year it so happened that a Master and his disciples came to the town. But because it was the time of the *urs*, there were no rooms to be had anywhere. All the hotels were full, all the guest houses, every vacant room had been let, there was no accommodation whatsoever, not even in a wayfarers' inn.

Wherever the disciples went, they were told the same thing: there is no room, but there is a teacher who owns much property and has many outbuildings where his pupils live, and it is just possible that somewhere on his property there is a room you can have.

So they went to see the teacher and explained that they needed a room, and the teacher told them that he did, in fact, have a room on the other side of his property. It was far from his residence, but they could have it for a short while. "Yes," the disciples said, "we only will want it for four days and then we will be going away."

"All right," the teacher said, "you can use the room for four days, but then you must leave." "Yes, yes," they assured him, "we will definitely be going after four days." So the Master and his disciples moved into the room on the teacher's property.

Now the next day the festival began and, as usual, many people came to hear the teacher deliver his discourse. But though the crowd was large, it was not as large as the teacher expected. "What has happened?" he asked his closest disciple afterwards. "Have fewer people come to this year's festival?" "No, more came than last year." "Then why was the crowd here so small?" "I don't know. Do you want me to try to find out?" "Yes, please do so."

So the disciple started asking questions and he found out that the Master had also given a discourse that morning and that many people had gone to hear him. He reported this to the teacher, who was not pleased. "Oh well, let it be," he decided after a while, "they have heard him speak now and so their curiosity will have been satisfied and this evening's discourse will be well attended."

But that evening there were even fewer people than that morning to hear the teacher. And the next day, there were fewer still. To make a long story short, each day fewer and fewer people came to hear the teacher. You might say that nobody came to hear him, they all flocked to the Perfect Master. The teacher was very upset at this. This had never happened before and he was furious. Out of the goodness of his heart, he had given the Perfect Master and his disciples a room to stay in, and this was how they repaid his generosity, by attracting all the crowds to themselves. Of course, he didn't express this, but such thoughts were going through his mind. And the only thing which kept his anger in check was the thought that at the end of four days the Perfect Master and his disciples would be leaving and then he wouldn't have to worry about it anymore.

So, as soon as the four days were up, he breathed a sigh of relief and went to give his discourse that morning with the expectation that he would have a nice sized crowd for once. But again no one came to hear him. The teacher couldn't restrain himself. "Go see if that man is still staying on my property," he ordered his disciple, "and if he is, tell him he gave his word that he would stay for only four days and tell him to get out immediately, as I don't want him staying here any longer."

The disciple went and approached the Perfect Master, who was still there. "Gracious sir," he began, "my master sends his greetings to you. As you know he has been very busy these last four days so he had not been able to greet you personally as he would have liked, so he has sent me to make sure that your stay has been comfortable, and to thank you for gracing his premises for these last four days."

"That is most good of him," the Perfect Master replied. "Please tell him that we are very grateful to him and that we understand his inability to greet us personally."

"My master also wants to know," the disciple continued, "whether there is anything you need now as you prepare to leave. Is there anything he can supply you which will make your journey more comfortable?"

"No, we have everything, thank you. Tell your master that we appreciate his extraordinary thoughtfulness, but there is nothing we need. As soon as we pack up our few possessions and say our prayers, we will be off."

The disciple went back and reported to the teacher that he had delivered the message and that the Perfect Master had replied that they would be leaving that day. The teacher was satisfied, but the next day the same thing happened. No one came to his discourse and he found out that the Perfect Master still hadn't left. "Go and order him to leave," he told his disciple. "He gave his word he would leave after four days. It is too much now. Tell him he has overstayed his welcome and he must leave at once or I will come and throw him out."

The disciple went and respectfully greeted the Perfect Master. "Gracious sir," he said, "my master has sent me because he's worried about your health. You told me yesterday that you would be leaving and he fears that you must have become indisposed because you are still here and he is anxious for me to find out if there is any medicine you need or if he should send for a doctor. He apologizes for not coming in person to attend to your needs, but he is very busy. But he was most particular that I come because he is sure you must have fallen ill for otherwise you would have left as you had promised to do. So he wants me to see if there is anything we can do to help you."

"Tell your master that, as always, he is most kind. But tell him not to worry, there is no illness here. It is just that this is such a beautiful spot, so peaceful and so sanctified by the countless pilgrims who have come and prayed here, that I could not bring myself to leave as I had planned. However, it is not good for us to stay here too long because then we might become attached to this place rather than the Lord Himself, so we will definitely be leaving tomorrow right after our morning bath and prayers."

The disciple went back and reported this conversation to the teacher. But what he said was, "Master, they apologized profusely for overstaying, but the circumstances were such that they had to prolong their stay. However, they assure me that tomorrow morning, after their baths and prayers, they will be leaving."

But once again the next morning the teacher discovered that although it was now ten o'clock, they still hadn't left. He grabbed a big staff and started to head out of his house so he could personally thrash these rascals who kept breaking their word and refusing to leave after promising to do so. The disciple knew what was in his master's mind, so he quickly interceded, "Master, wait a minute. There is no point in going there now, they won't be there." "What do you mean? It is precisely because they are still here that I am going." "Yes, I know that, but many have the custom to go out every morning for a walk at this hour. So why tire yourself with the long walk to their place when there is a good chance that they won't be there? Why not wait until they get back in an hour or so before going?"

This made sense, and the teacher put down his staff, muttering to himself how he would beat some sense into them when they returned. The disciple rushed off to the Master and again greeted him with every sign of respect. "Gracious sir, my master is very upset because he is sure now that you must be ill and that is why you keep postponing your leavetaking. On top of this, he feels very bad that he had not come to see you as he should have done long before this, and so he is coming to visit you personally to inquire about your health and to ask Your forgiveness for his rudeness in not greeting you himself as he should have done."

Hearing this, the Master stood up, gestured to his mandali to follow and said, "Your master should not come to see me, I am the guest, it is my duty to go personally to thank him for his kind and generous hospitality." And with that the Master leaves the room and starts walking to the teacher's house, which is at the other end of the property. Meanwhile, the teacher has gotten so mad thinking about the Master staying so long that he forgets that the Master is supposed to be out walking and he picks up his staff and rushes out of the house. So he is walking towards the Master as the Master is approaching him.

When the Master sees the teacher, he hastens forward and bows down before the teacher and then embraces him with great love and tenderness. And because he is a Perfect One, without a word being said, that embrace opens the teacher's heart. The Master begins thanking the teacher for his hospitality and praising his generosity and thoughtfulness and consideration to the skies.

The teacher is impressed. "Here I have said so many rude things about this man, I have ordered him off my property and have come now to thrash him, and yet he is able to greet me with such love. This is truly a remarkable man," the teacher thinks to himself. And he invites the Master to come to his house so he can personally serve him some tea before he leaves.

The Master accepts, and before long the teacher and Master are sitting comfortably, drinking tea, eating snacks and chatting as if they have been life-long friends. The more time he spends in the Master's presence, the more the teacher is impressed with him. And he begins to understand why people would flock to hear his talk, and in his own heart he can see now how shallow his talks were, how little he had to offer. For when confronted with love, the intellect realizes its irrelevance. In the Master, the teacher sees his dry discourses brought to full fruition, and he realizes for the first time that merely talking about spiritual topics can never satisfy the way a taste of Divine Love can.

When the Master finally takes his leave, the teacher is distressed to see him go and is now begging him to stay a little longer. But the Master says he must go, that his work here is finished, and he leaves with all his mandali walking behind. The teacher turns to his disciple and says, "There goes the most remarkable man you will ever meet."

"Yes," agrees the disciple, "truly he is one of the Great Ones." "And just think," the teacher says, "in spite of all my rude words that I sent through you, he is like this." The disciple doesn't say anything. After a few moments the teacher gets suspicious and says, "Tell me, did you convey my messages to him?" "Yes, every time I went and told him what you told me to tell him." "You gave him my message?" "Yes." "In the exact words and in the exact tone of voice that I used?" "No, not exactly in the same words or in the same tone of voice. How could I, a mere disciple, hope to achieve the same words and the same tone of voice as my master?" "Then what did you convey?" "Master, whatever I have learned from you in my long years spent living with you, that's what I conveyed to him."

The teacher turned to his disciple and said, "You have saved me from a great mistake. And in proving yourself to be the perfect disciple of my teachings, you have indeed become the master to the teacher."

This is how it should be. This is what Baba wanted and expected of us. And this attitude becomes second nature when you have determined to become His.

◁▷ M O N E Y

MANY TIMES PEOPLE ASK US, "What was it like living with Meher Baba?" What was it like living with God?" I have tried many times to answer this question, but I've found that it can't be done. There is no way I can bring home to you what it was like being in Baba's presence. Anything I say is just throwing out words. But being with Baba was really an overwhelming experience. In His presence, one felt His authority. Not in some mystical sense, but in a very natural way.

So often Baba would declare to the crowds of people that assembled to see Him, "I am the Ancient One, the same Ancient One come once again in your midst to give you My eternal message of Love and Truth." And it was my duty to speak these words out with authority. In those days I had a voice, not this reedy instrument you hear now, and I would say it out loudly, "Meher Baba says, 'I am the Ancient One,'" and people would accept it.

I think I've already told you about the time Baba declared that He was the Avatar and that He had come to do away with all rites and rituals, to an audience that was composed predominantly of orthodox brahmins. How nervous I was as to how they would react, because we were completely surrounded by people. There was no escape. I was the one who had to say out the words with an authority befitting Baba's status, but my mind was thinking, "What will happen when I say this out? It will cause a riot, and then what will happen to Baba?"

You see, our concern was always with Baba. Not with what people might think, but with Baba's physical body. And if any trouble started, I knew there was no way I could adequately protect Baba. There was no way out of that crowd, we would have been overwhelmed, but Baba reached out casually and pulled the edge of my jacket and then secretly gestured to me, "Don't worry, just say it out, everything will be all right." And of course it was. Even though we were in the veritable stronghold of orthodox brahminism, everyone accepted Baba's words. There wasn't even a murmur of dissent. Such was the power of Baba's presence. The power, if you will, of His divinity.

Sometimes Baba would give *darshan* to as many as seventy thousand people at one time. And most of these were not Baba lovers. Maybe you can call them "Baba likers" but to be perfectly frank, even that is going too far. For most were coming out of curiosity, or because they hoped in some way to be benefited by the contact. India is a land of spirituality, there is no doubt about it, but there is a materialistic side to this spirituality as well. People are eager to have the *darshan* of anyone who is reputed to be advanced spiritually; they may have never heard of the person before, but a neighbor will tell them, "Oh, didn't you know, Swami such-and-such is giving *darshan* today," and they'll drop everything and go for his *darshan*.

But why do they go? Most go in the hopes that they will get some benefit from it. That they will be blessed with children, or a good marriage, or a promotion or something of that sort. So, in that crowd of seventy thousand there were probably only a thousand or so who truly accepted Baba as the Avatar. And yet when Baba would declare, "I am the Highest of the High," or "I say with My divine authority that I am God in human form," the people, at least for as long as they were in His presence, accepted it.

You know, we have had visitors here, at Meherazad, who did not accept Baba, in fact who came to scoff, to show Baba up, to prove that He was a fraud of some sort. They would be here, right in this hall, sitting before Baba, and Baba would smile at them and embrace them, and they submitted like children. Baba would say, "I am the Avatar," and they would nod their heads in acceptance. Later, after leaving, they might sometimes again speak out against Baba, but while they were here, in His presence, they could not deny His divinity. And yet, paradoxically, our experience, the experience of those who lived with Baba, was not of His divinity but of His humanity.

Before a big *darshan* program, Baba's health would often not be good. He would be physically weak, He would be in pain, and He would look at us and gesture helplessly, "How am I going to be able to give *darshan*?" And we would say, "Don't, Baba. Postpone the *darshan*." But Baba would reply, "How can I? My lovers are coming from such long distances to see Me, how can I disappoint them by canceling the *darshan*?" And I would say, Baba, because they are Your lovers, they will understand." But Baba would always decide that He couldn't disappoint His lovers. Baba is the Lord of Love, but the Slave of the love of His lovers. He told us this, and how often we have seen it to be true. As the Lord, Baba could easily have told His lovers the *darshan* was canceled, but as the slave of their love, He would invariably give in and agree to give *darshan*.

Yet on the day of the program, even minutes beforehand, Baba would still look so pulled down, He would be suffering so much that even then we would beg Baba to cancel the program. Baba would refuse; He would simply put out His hand for me to escort Him to the dais, and as soon as He stepped onto the dais, what would His lovers see? — a radiant, beaming, healthy Baba. It was impossible for anyone to guess that just moments before Baba had been so ill.

And His lovers would look at us, the mandali, as if they had caught us out in a big lie. For we had been writing them that Baba's health was not good, that the program might have to be canceled, that no one should try to see Baba outside of the program because of His condition, and here Baba was looking absolutely fit, strong, healthy, smiling. And they felt we had been unjustly trying to prevent them from being with Baba. They thought we were jealous and were trying to keep Baba all to ourselves.

Even today there are some who still hold a grudge against the mandali, who blame us for keeping them away from Baba. But what could we do? We could see their looks, we knew what was going through their minds, but we couldn't say a word. We just had to accept their abuse, their ill feeling. And throughout the *darshan*, Baba would continue to appear full of energy, in good spirits, radiating vitality and love. So many have tried to describe what it was like to be at a *darshan* program. Some have said it was as if Baba opened the tap and let His love flow out freely. Francis Brabazon, in trying to describe the East-West Gathering, wrote that Baba let one of the veils which covered His divinity drop just a little and all were almost blinded by the radiance. Whatever it be, it is true that in His presence, people felt something.

And after the program, Baba would return to His room, and as soon as He got there, He would once again be weak. He would call Dr. Goher to do something, and we could see how He was suffering. And He really was suffering. Unlike a Perfect Master who pretends to suffer, when the Avatar takes a human body, He becomes human. A human body means what after all, it means suffering. That's what this body is. And the Avatar would suffer. We would see His suffering, but for the world, for His lovers, Baba would disguise it.

Of course I'm not talking about the early days. Even then Baba would often fall ill before a large *darshan* program, but we did see Baba's incredible vitality, His stamina, enthusiasm. But the later years, especially the Poona years, that is what I'm talking about. And at that time, it seemed that the world had the good fortune to see Baba in at least something of His divine radiance, while we, who lived with Him, saw His suffering.

In fact, once after one of these *darshan* programs one of the mandali asked Baba, "Why is it, Baba, that for Your lovers, for all who attend the *darshan*, You are so strong and healthy and radiant, and they all feel Your divinity, Your love, but for us, we see only Your suffering?" And Baba gestured, "What you say is true. The world now has the experience of My divinity, while you experience My humanity. But the time will come when all of you will experience My divinity, while the world will hunger to know of My humanity." And that day has come.

Not so much now, but in the early years especially, right after Baba had dropped His body, when people would come here, they had no interest in metaphysical discussions, in talking about the planes of consciousness or *God Speaks*, they only wanted to hear about Baba. And what did they want to hear about Him, they wanted to know everything we could tell them about His personal habits, — what was His favorite soap, what food did He like, did He brush His teeth with a toothbrush or His finger, did He shave, did He use an electric razor or a straight edge, did He sleep, did He snore, was He regular, in short, everything we could tell about Baba as a person they wanted to hear. They were hungry for His humanity.

And for us, we experienced Baba's divinity, seeing His children flock here this way. For we would ask them, "Why did you come? What brought you here?" and they could never answer. Oh, they might say, "I saw His photo," or "I read the *Discourses*," or "A friend told me about Him," but these aren't answers. Not really. You saw His photo means what? Is that any reason to travel halfway around the world to go to the place where the person in the photograph used to live? No, it's madness. There is no way to explain why these people were coming, except to say that Baba was bringing them. They themselves were not aware of it. They all had excuses for why they were coming, but we could see so clearly that they were coming only because Baba was bringing them.

And how was Baba bringing them? Was He chartering a plane, and buying them tickets and sending them letters telling them to come? No, Baba wasn't even in the body anymore, so it was His divinity which was bringing them. And so what Baba said was true, every day we would experience His divinity, while the young ones who came were hungry for His humanity.

For some reason, people today are not as eager as they once were to hear of Baba's personal habits. Now the emphasis seems to be more on Baba's Godhood. People come here and they say, "Since Baba was God, you must have experienced a lot in His presence." Or they wonder, "What was it like to live with God?" Their idea of God seems to involve occult experiences, or something of that sort. They know Baba is God so they want to know all about His perfection, but what can we say? Baba is God, there is no doubt about that, but our day-to-day experience of Baba's perfection was of His perfect humanity.

Meher Baba was the perfect sportsman, the perfect companion, the perfect friend, the perfect psychologist, the perfect teacher, the perfect philosopher. In short, in whatever field of endeavor you can name, Meher Baba was perfect in it. I say this to people and they still don't understand. But when I say Meher Baba was perfect in all things, that also means He was the perfect criminal, the perfect thief – yes, it's true. Haven't you seen the poster on the blue bus outside? Baba told us that, that He is the perfect thief, because He steals one's heart. And see the extent of His perfection, not only does He steal your heart, but He steals it so perfectly, so silently, so skillfully, that it may take you lifetimes before you even realize He's taken it.

Baba was also the perfect economist. Sometimes people are surprised to hear this. They know that Baba never touched money, and they have the feeling that managing money properly somehow is antithetical to spirituality, but perfection means what, it means being perfect in every aspect of life, not just one isolated fragment. And believe me, Baba was perfect when it came to managing money. Baba would plan *sahavas* programs when hundreds of people were coming from all over India to stay with Him. Housing had to be provided, latrines had to be dug, food had to be procured, and every detail had to be looked after so that Baba's lovers would feel comfortable, so they could relax and concentrate completely on Baba without worrying about anything else. And Baba would not only plan these programs down to the tiniest detail, but He would also allot a budget for them and make sure that every *pie* spent was accounted for.

Perhaps some of you who came in the early years have heard from Adi, Baba's secretary, how Baba used to drive him to distraction. Baba would call the mandali together and announce that He was running short of money, they would have to find a way somehow to spend less. And everyone would make suggestions. Some said, "We can have tea only once a day," or "We can have tea without milk," "We'll only have one vegetable," "We'll make do with one bar of soap for a month," all would try to figure out a way to economize. And Baba would consider all of these suggestions and decide what new austerity the mandali would live under.

And then Baba would tell Adi privately, "By the way, send a thousand rupees to this family up North, and send five hundred to this man in the South, and send three thousand here and fifteen hundred there," and Adi would be amazed. "But, Baba," he would protest, "we just barely have enough to pay our bills, how can I send so much to others?" But because Baba said to do it, Adi would do it.

To digress a bit, but to give you a good idea of what I mean, I remember one time, even in the later years, here at Meherazad. Baba's health was not strong and Mehera and the women thought it would be good for Baba if He could have some fresh fruit juice. So they ordered a few oranges from town and then squeezed the juice into a glass for Baba. They were so happy that they had been able to make this treat for Baba. I remember because Baba was sitting in Mandali Hall with a family from up North. This family was completely devoted to Baba but they were poor and were undergoing financial hardships of one sort or another. They hadn't come to complain; their dedication to Baba, their surrender to His will was so great that they wouldn't have said a word about their problems to Baba, but on His own, He had started asking them about their finances, whether they had enough money to manage the household properly. Baba always took a personal interest in the lives of His close ones. He was always completely practical and so, on His own, He would ask whether they could pay for schooling for their children, whether they could afford the books, whether they had enough to eat, how many vegetables they would have with each meal, and so on. Even in this, you can see Baba's perfection – He could have just asked, "Do you have enough money?" and they would have said, "Yes," and that would have been the end of it. But Baba loves His close ones, and love is never satisfied with such answers, so Baba would ask detailed intimate questions until the exact financial position of his family became clear. But

He did this in a natural way, not like some kind of interrogation; it was always apparent when Baba asked questions that He was doing so not out of curiosity but out of loving concern.

Anyway, to make a long story short, Baba was sitting with the family in this hall. They were sitting there, before Baba, and I was standing here, to interpret Baba's gestures, when Dr. Goher came with the glass of orange juice for Baba. Baba instantly became very stern. Instead of being pleased at the women's thoughtfulness, Baba wanted to know how they had gotten the oranges. And didn't they know how much oranges cost? How could they be so extravagant? And how did they have the temerity to order oranges from the bazaar without telling Him?

You see, before anything could be purchased from the bazaar, even if it was a bar of soap, or a bunch of coriander leaves, the manager would have to show the shopping list to Baba for His approval. But the women had prevailed upon Vishnu to get a few oranges in addition to the ordinary shopping. So Baba was very upset and gave Dr. Goher quite a dressing down about their extravagance. He made it seem as if, because of these oranges, the whole budget had been thrown off, and serious difficulties now faced everyone at Meherazad. Mani says that before Baba had finished taking them all to task for their extravagance they were all in tears. That's how seriously Baba treated the whole matter.

Of course, I wasn't there when Baba talked to Mani and Mehera, but I won't ever forget the incident, because I was the one who had to speak out Baba's words to Goher. But what really makes the incident stand out in memory was that right after impressing upon Goher that there was no money to pay for those oranges, Baba turns around and has one of the mandali give this family from up North five hundred rupees to help them out. That is what has made that little incident stick in my mind all these years.

Baba would always do things like that, and it used to make Adi frantic. You know how the mind is. Adi would do what Baba told him to, but he would worry, "What's going to happen now? We won't be able to pay our bills." Not that Adi cared particularly whether tradesmen had to wait for their money, or if someone came and repossessed something, it was just that he felt it wouldn't look good for Baba.

You see, that's how we were in those days. Maybe we didn't have enough faith, but we used to worry how Baba would look in the eyes of others. Now I can see how absurd this was, but then we were very protective. For example, take Baba's silence. For ourselves, we didn't care whether Baba broke His silence or not. We didn't care if Baba promised to break it every day for a year and never did, but we didn't like it when Baba promised to break His silence in public, when circulars were issued with a certain date given, because we used to think, "But what will others say, what will they think when Baba doesn't break His silence on that date?"

So Adi would worry about what was going to happen when he couldn't pay any of the bills. And then, at the last minute, every time, money would come unexpectedly from somewhere. One of Baba's lovers would donate a large sum which just covered all of the expenses, and Adi would breathe a huge sigh of relief. This happened every time. Baba was the true fakir. As He said, although He never handled money, except when giving it to the *masts*, poor, or the lepers, over the years *lakhs* of rupees flowed through His hands. But as soon as it flowed in, Baba changed its direction and it flowed out again. Baba didn't keep money, and He, and those living with Him, always lived very simple lives.

Adi was a very capable man, but he could never keep track of the finances the way Baba could. Baba would give money to so many different people, in so many different amounts, and not necessarily on a fixed schedule. Baba might hear of some needy person and spontaneously direct Adi to send a sum of money. And yet, somehow, the money coming in always equaled the money going out. It was a mystery and a marvel to Adi. Only Baba could manage it so perfectly.

Yet Baba always expected us to be very meticulous when it

came to money. Whenever we would travel on *mast* trips without Baba, He would always want a very exact accounting of how we spent our money. If we returned and said we spent thirty-five rupees contacting a certain *mast*, Baba would instantly gesture, "Why thirty-five? It should have cost you only twenty-eight."

So we would work it all out, so much for the bus, so much for the third-class train. Baba never cared how much money we spent on a *mast*, but when it came to our comfort, He was very particular. We always traveled third-class; we were never supposed to pamper ourselves. When we lived with Baba we lived very simply. So perhaps there was something of a temptation for some of us, once we were sent out, to live it up a bit, to take advantage of the fact that we were alone and could do what we wanted. But Baba was always very particular about our expenses and we would have to account to Baba for every *pie* spent.

So when we returned and Baba asked why we spent thirty-five rupees instead of twenty-eight, we would have to write out exactly what we spent the money on. And, sure enough, when we added up our travel expenses, rickshaws, everything, it would come to twenty-eight rupees. Baba would look at us, raise His eyebrows, and with His upturned palm gesture, "Well?"

And we would say, "Oh yes, Baba. I spent four rupees buying the *mast* tea and *beedies* and sweets." "But what about the other three rupees?" And then we would have to confess, "Baba, one night I was so hungry that I broke down and bought myself a big dinner and that is where the three rupees went."

"Three rupees for dinner? What did you have?" "Only rice and dal and a vegetable, Baba." "So why did it cost so much?" You know, those were the days when a rupee still bought a lot. And Baba would keep asking until it came out that instead of eating in the railway station where such a meal could have been purchased for half that amount, we had gone to a hotel which others had told us served excellent food.

Baba never objected to our eating, we didn't have to fast when we went out searching for *masts*, we weren't expected to impose austerities on ourselves; it was unnecessary indulgence which He never liked. And He was such a perfect economist that He could always tell when we had spent too much.

But this isn't the story I intended to tell you. This has all been the background for my story which just begins now.

This occurred back in the '30s. At that time Baba had several ashrams. The women stayed at Meherabad. Some of the men stayed at Nasik, and some stayed at Rahuri where Baba had a mad ashram. Baba used to take turns visiting each ashram, spending a day or two, or sometimes only a few hours, and then moving on to the next. There was no fixed schedule as such. Baba spent time in each place according to His work and what He had to accomplish.

One of the things Baba would discuss with the men mandali when He visited them at Rahuri was how to economize, as there wasn't much money. The manager was having a very hard time managing the ashram because there just wasn't enough money. The situation became so bad that finally it seemed the only solution was to disband the ashram entirely.

Now, one of the ashram members was Dr. Ghani. You have all heard me talk about Ghani in the past, about how clever he was, how witty. At this time, Ghani used to like to do the crossword puzzles that appeared in the paper. He also liked to avoid doing any work if he could. Not that he was allergic to work with the same intensity with which he was allergic to bathing, but still, if there was any way to get out of work, Ghani was sure to find it.

One day Ghani had a brainstorm. He knew that the ashram needed money. So he decided to enter the contest the newspaper held and win the prize money for correctly solving their crossword puzzle. The next time Baba's car arrived, Baba got out and looked around, He saw that Ghani wasn't there. This was unusual, because as soon as everyone heard Baba's car honk, they always dropped whatever they were doing and came rushing to welcome Baba. But even though the car had sounded its horn as usual, Ghani wasn't there.

Baba went looking for Ghani and found him sitting some distance away, absorbed in the newspaper. "What's this?" Baba gestured. "I've arrived and you don't even come to greet Me?" "Oh, Baba. Excuse me. I was just so engrossed in what I am doing that I didn't hear Your car pull up." "What are you doing?" "I am earning money so the ashram doesn't have to be disbanded, Baba." "You're earning money by reading the newspaper?" "No, Baba. I am solving the crossword puzzle. The paper is giving a prize to the one who can correctly solve the puzzle." "A prize, how much?"

Ghani told Baba how much the prize was for. I forget now but it was a considerable sum. Enough so that the immediate money worries of the ashram would easily have been taken care of. Baba expressed astonishment. "That much!" And then He got very excited and enthusiastic about the whole project. He told the others, "Now, don't disturb Doctor, let him work. He is going to make money for all of us. Don't try and make him do any other work. What he is doing now is the most important thing."

Of course there were some who were not very happy at this, for it seemed that this was just one more of Ghani's ploys to get out of working, but Baba got very excited about the whole thing. Whenever He could find some time, He would walk over and see how Ghani was getting along with the puzzle. "What a good idea," Baba repeated. And then He gestured, indicating how large Ghani's head was, "You are really most intelligent."

Baba kept complimenting Ghani on his idea and, in fact, took so much interest in Ghani's project that He decided to help him Himself. "After all," Baba explained, "with your intelligence and My omniscience, surely we will win the prize." So Baba would sit with Ghani and offer advice. He would gesture, "Show Me what you have done," and Ghani would show Baba the puzzle. Baba would look at the clues and see what Ghani had written and then say, "No, that isn't right. That's not the answer for that; this is the word you should use," and He would tell Ghani what the correct word should be.

"Are you sure, Baba?" "Don't I know everything? Put in what I tell you." And so, together, they finished the puzzle. Baba was so excited about it, He had Ghani send it off immediately and, as He left, He assured the mandali that their money problems were over now. "With Doctor's intelligence, and My omniscience, how can we lose?"

In a day or two, Baba returned and the first thing He wanted to know was whether the prize money had been received yet. When told that nothing had arrived, Baba seemed disappointed. "But Baba," Ghani explained, "we just sent our solution, it hasn't even had time to reach the editors yet, much less for them to reply." "Ah," Baba brightened at this, as if it had never occurred to Him. But even so, the very next day, as soon as the mail arrived, Baba asked anxiously if the prize money had come. I don't know why Baba was like this, but once Baba got involved in any project, He had no patience.

Sometimes Baba would send one of the mandali on an errand of some sort. And no sooner had the person left the room than Baba would become impatient and gesture to us, "What's taking so long? Where has he gone? Shouldn't he be back by now?" And sometimes Baba would even end up sending one of us out to find out what was keeping that person. But of course there was no way the person could have gone out and done the errand in that short amount of time. Baba must have known this too. As I said, I don't know why Baba was like this, but He used to say that although He had infinite patience, He was also infinitely impatient. Whatever it be, whenever Baba would come to the ashram, the first thing He would always ask about was the crossword puzzle and the prize money.

Finally one day, Baba arrived, and once again Ghani was not there. Baba went looking for him, and found Ghani sitting off by himself, sullen, morose, dejected. "Has the prize money arrived yet?" Baba asked. Ghani simply shook his head, "No," without answering. Baba went on asking Ghani questions, but Ghani never said anything in reply; just sat there looking despondent and shaking his head. At last, Ghani handed Baba the paper.

The paper was already opened and folded back to a page where the correct solution to the puzzle was given. There was also the name of the winner printed there. Baba looked at it in surprise and disbelief. "We didn't win?" He exclaimed. "But how can that be?" "Baba," Ghani blurted out, "look at the solution. We made seven mistakes! When I did the puzzles on my own, I would often make a mistake and sometimes even two. Once I made as many as three mistakes, but I have never made seven before! It's all Your fault, Baba! Because You helped me, we made seven mistakes!"

Baba couldn't believe it and He examined the solution. "But they are the ones who have made the mistakes," He declared. "The answers I gave were right, these aren't the correct solutions," and Baba continued to insist that His answers were right while the real answers were wrong. Ghani wasn't convinced, however. He was just disgusted and kept muttering, "Seven mistakes, Baba. I never made seven when I did it by myself."

Baba went away shaking His head in wonderment. And so ended Ghani's dream of getting money the easy way.

And speaking of getting money the easy way, that reminds me of another story. Would you like to hear it?

It concerns a couple who were very close to Baba. They were not living with us, but in a sense, you could say they were one of the family. Whenever Baba went to Poona, this couple would come and see Him at Guruprasad. And because they were so close to Baba, Baba would tease them. That was a mark of His intimacy. And how would He tease them? He would always tease the husband for not buying his wife bangles and ornaments and nice saris.

You see, this couple was poor. The husband used to do various odd jobs to make money and they were not starving or anything like that, but they were very poor. So when they used to come visit Baba, Baba would look at the wife and innocently inquire, "What, no bangles, no ornaments?" "No, Baba," she would say. Baba would turn to the husband, "How's this, your wife is so beautiful and you don't buy her any ornaments. Not even earrings! Every time you come she is wearing the same sari. Such beauty needs a little adornment to set it off properly. Why don't you spend some money on her?"

And the wife would be embarrassed and the husband apologetic and he would reply, "Yes, Baba, she is very beautiful, but what can I do? I would like to adorn her with gold bangles and all sorts of jewelry but I can't afford it." Of course Baba was not serious, He was simply joking with this couple. That was one of the signs of His intimacy with them, for Baba never would have joked in that way with someone who was not close to Him, who was not one of us.

And this couple really did seem to love Baba very much and so it went for several years. But then, I don't know what happened, but it seems as if somehow this man's head got turned. For one time when Baba was lovingly teasing them in the usual way, the man blurted out, "But Baba, what can I do, You don't give me any money. Bless me so I may get money so that Your wish may be fulfilled and I may buy my wife everything You want." Baba seemed surprised, "What, you want money?" "Yes, Baba, then I will be able to dress my wife properly." Baba looks at the wife and shakes His head pityingly as if the husband has taken leave of his sense. "What is he saying?" Baba asks the wife. "You are already dressed in My love, and he thinks that isn't proper!"

But the man could not be dissuaded. Even though Baba tried to turn it into a joke and make light of it, each time the couple came to see Baba, the husband would start begging Baba to bless him with wealth.

"Don't you realize," Baba would ask him, "that I was only teasing you? What need do you have for money? You have the greatest wealth of all, you have Me." "No, Baba, I want money. You have been telling me all these years that I should buy my wife nice ornaments and I want to do that now."

Baba would turn to the wife, "Do you really want bangles or ornaments or new saris?" He would ask her. "No, Baba, I only want You," she would answer. "See!" Baba would gesture to her husband. "Now forget this nonsense of yours." But the husband could not forget it. No matter how much Baba would try to persuade him to forget about it, he would insist that Baba bless him for money.

"What's this, all the time wanting money?" Baba would ask. "It is not good for you; *dal-roti* is good." *Dal-roti* is a way of describing a poor man's diet, one who can only afford to make a little *dal* and a plain *roti* to eat, and Baba would say, "*Dal-roti* is good," meaning, you don't need luxuries, the simple life is fine. But the man kept insisting and Baba finally ordered him, "Get out. Get out of here if you only want money."

But every time the couple came, the man would begin all over again. Baba told him, "I can give it to you, but do you want Me to soil My hands, to reach into a pile of shit to give it to you?" Baba turned to the wife, "Is that what you want? Do you want Me to have to soil My own hands so I can give you shit?" "No, Baba. Do whatever You want." "So can't you talk some sense into your husband?" "Baba," the husband spoke up, "whatever it is, I want the money." Baba looked at the wife again. "See what madness he's saying?" Baba did everything He could to convince the man to stop asking for this blessing but the man was deaf and dumb to all of Baba's words. Why it was that this man took something Baba said in jest and seemed determined to obey it, I don't know, but when Baba explicitly repeated over and over that it wouldn't be good to ask for money, that he should not do this thing, the husband paid no attention and insisted that Baba bless him so he could have money.

Finally, Baba said, "You have pestered me enough, I bless you, now go." And that was that. But next year when we were in Poona again, this couple came to visit us. And as soon as the wife walked in I noticed that she was wearing an expensive sari, and she had so many costly bangles and jewelry and ornaments adorning her. When

I saw her coming, I said, "Ah, now this is what your beauty needs. Before you were like a gem that hadn't been set, but now that the jeweler has set you, your beauty sparkles all the more." Not that I cared that she had ornaments, but this was something the husband wanted, and I was happy that financially they were doing better now. And, as I have said, they were very close to us, so we would indulge in this kind of banter. The husband seemed very happy. Not only was he dressed well, but he even had a paunch now!

When Baba saw them, He expressed surprise. "What is all this?" He gestured. "Baba," the husband explained, "by Your grace I am earning nicely now." And then the conversation moved on to other things and no more was said about it. And if we ever thought about it or mentioned this couple amongst ourselves, we would just express our happiness that they were now financially better off.

But the next year when we returned we discovered that now the husband had purchased a new car and a nice bungalow. All of this in a year and a half or so, mind you. And cars were not all that common back then. They were very expensive and only those who were quite well off could afford them. And a bungalow means what? So sometimes, amongst ourselves, the mandali would wonder, "How is this possible? How has he been able to earn so much money?" And I remember that Kaikobad would say, "Why not, with Baba's blessings anything is possible." "That's true," I replied, "but these blessings don't occur in a vacuum. How is he actually making the money?" It was a mystery for us, for even a good job with a good salary wouldn't enable you to save so much money in such a short time.

And then, one day while we were at Meherazad the newspaper came, and there on the front page was this man's picture. And the whole story came out. It seems he had started passing himself off as a relative of an important political figure. In those days there was still rationing on certain industrial equipment. To do certain types of business, you needed a license. To purchase equipment, you needed to be licensed by the government, and this man would go see businessmen and let it be known that as a close relative of this important official, he could procure the license for them. The businessmen would give him money then so he would use his influence. And then, having established all these connections with the business world, he would go to the government and tell them that he could easily arrange contracts and business deals for the government if they would give him a certain percentage. And so he was making money from both sides. I can't recall how he was caught, but he was and he was sentenced to prison. He lost his money, he lost his health, and I think he died not too long after that.

One of the mandali expressed their surprise, for it never occurred to us that he would resort to anything like that, and Baba replied, "What can I do? He forced Me to put My hands in shit and give it to him."

◭ P O L L U T E   T H E   O C E A N

THE OTHER DAY I TOLD THE STORY about the time someone was spreading the rumors, in the '30s, that Baba had been indulging in alcohol and women when He was staying in the Rishikesh-Hardwar area. Baba even issued a circular about it at the time. Well, this reminds me of a story that Baba once told us. I don't remember now what prompted it, but the story itself is so fresh in my mind. Baba was sitting with us and He told us this story.

He said that once there was a great yogi who lived on the

banks of a river. He had many disciples and he used to give discourses every day, to which hundreds of people came. He was respected and honored as a master. Now, one day the yogi and his disciples see some activity on the other side of the river, which is unusual. They wonder what's going on and it turns out that a small group of people are preparing a place to stay. The yogi assumes that it must be a few sadhus who are setting up camp, because no one else would live way out there, and he doesn't pay them any mind.

But as the days pass, the small settlement seems to be growing larger, every day there seem, to be a few more people there. What the yogi doesn't know is that it is not a few sadhus who moved in, but a Master and his disciples. Now, the Master doesn't proclaim himself as anything, he doesn't try to set himself up as a teacher, he doesn't give discourses, but because he is perfect, naturally people are drawn to him.

As word of his arrival spreads, more and more people are attracted to him. That is how it is with the Perfect Ones. They don't have to advertise, they don't have to proclaim themselves as anything; their very being proclaims it, and slowly, bit by bit, humanity is attracted to them.

It is like wrapping a lightbulb in a dark cloth. Even if you can't see the light, you can feel its warmth when it is turned on, and people are attracted to the warmth and so they naturally gravitate to the Perfect Ones.

At first the yogi on the opposite bank didn't pay this any attention. What did he care if someone made camp on the opposite side? But over time, he noticed that fewer people were coming to his discourses. When he asked his disciples why this was, they hemmed and hawed. "Oh, have there been fewer recently?" they said. "We hadn't noticed." "No, I tell you, there aren't as many. Where are they?" "Maybe they've gone to the other side of the river," one of the disciples finally suggested. "Why? What's there that they should go?" "There is someone there, and the people have taken to visiting him."

"Why? What does he teach?" "He doesn't teach anything, exactly." "Well, what does he say in his discourses?" "He doesn't give discourses exactly." "Well, what yoga does he practice?" "He doesn't practice any yoga." "Harumph," the yogi said on hearing this. "Doesn't practice any yoga at all? Why do the people go to him, then?" "We don't know," the disciples said, "but they seem to think he is someone great." The yogi brushed this idea aside with his hand. After all, how could someone who didn't even practice any yoga be great, and he felt, "It is only because he is new here. People are always attracted to anything new. But after a while they will see that he has nothing to offer them, and then they will return to me. Not only that, but they will then begin to appreciate just who I am."

But as the days passed, instead of fewer people going to the Master, even more went. And the yogi's discourse groups got smaller and smaller. "Who is this man? Who does he take himself to be?" the yogi demanded of the loyal disciples who were still with him. "It seems the people take him as a *sadguru*," one of the disciples answered. "A *sadguru*. He has the nerve to call himself that?" "No, he doesn't say that, he makes no claims for himself, but that is what the people are saying." "But why should they say that? What is his teaching?" "I don't know." "Well, go over there and find out exactly what he is preaching so I can know what it is and show everyone the fallacy that exists in his teachings."

So the disciple went over and joined the crowd that had taken to staying around the Master. But the disciple was so captivated by him that he never returned to his master. Now this really upset the yogi and he realized that if he didn't do something soon, he would lose all his followers. It never occurred to him to go across the river himself and visit the Master. He had too much pride and arrogance for that. He just automatically assumed that this man must be an imposter, a fraud, and he was determined to show him up so that his followers would return to him.

One morning, before retiring for the day, some dancing girls who are followers of the yogi come to visit him and the yogi suddenly gets an idea of how he can show up this other master as fake. By now, he has heard a fair amount of gossip about the goings-on at the Master's camp and he knows that the Master is not orthodox in his ways. He doesn't seem to insist that his followers meditate at regular hours or repeat God's name so many times a day or do yoga practices. He doesn't seem to be careful that their diet is only according to what has been laid down in the ancient scriptures; in short, he doesn't seem the least spiritual. So the yogi asks the girls, "Have you heard of this so-called Master who has taken up residence on the opposite bank? I want you to go over there tonight and entertain him. I will give you some baskets of meat and wine to take also."

"And then?"

"Entertain him and his followers as only you can, and in the morning come back here and report on everything that's happened."

The yogi sent one of his disciples into town to buy some wine and some non-veg snacks like patties and cutlets, and that evening when the girls came, the provisions were taken down to the shore and put in a rowboat, and the girls got in and they rowed across the river to the Master's camp. The noise of their rowing could be heard and the Master sent one of his mandali down to the river to see who was coming. When they landed and stepped out of the boat and the disciple could hear their bangles jingling, he was surprised. "Is this the hour to come visit?" he asked them, for in those days women would not be out after dark. "Yes," one of the girls answered, "our day begins now."

Baba's acting was so fine. He would show the look of surprise on the disciple's face when he saw the girls get out of the boat, and then He would act out the way the bangles would jangle and the haughty looks of the dancing girls. "We have come to dance for your master," the girls said, and so the disciple led them to the Master's quarters.

The Master greeted them warmly and made them feel

welcome. "What brings you here at this hour?" he asked. "We wanted to see you," they replied. "But aren't you worried about being out so late?" "No, we are used to it," they answered. "We are often out after dark and it doesn't scare us."

"I'm sorry, I can't offer you much, but if you would like something to drink or eat to regain your strength after rowing across the river, I would be happy to share with you what I have." And the Master tells one of his mandali to go fetch some sherbet for the girls, and to heat up some rice and dal. "Oh, we brought some things with us."

"You did?" the Master asks. "I don't see anything." "We left it in the boat," one of the girls replies, and the Master instructs one of his mandali to go down to the banks of the river and bring the provisions from the boat. After a while all the wine and meat is brought in and the Master exclaims as he sees it, "So much? This is wonderful. We can have a picnic," and he starts giving orders that his followers should come and the food should be distributed and they will have a party.

"Bring a harmonium and the tablas and we will have *ghazals*," the Master declares, "and have a real party." It is at this point that one of the mandali goes up to the Master and whispers in his ear, "Master, don't you know that these are common dancing girls? You can't let them stay." The Master turns to the girls? "Is that right? Can you dance?"

"Yes," they admit shyly, because the Master's honest affection for them has made them somewhat embarrassed. They have lost that coyness which they usually use when talking to men, and are reacting not as to a potential customer, but to a friend. So they look down and say, "Yes, we can dance." The Master is delighted at this and claps his hands, and announces, "We will have a party tonight. Come, bring some music to accompany the dance," and he starts asking the girls what sort of accompaniment they would like.

All the details are worked out and the girls begin dancing. And the Master is delighted with it all. Every now and then he claps his hands or cries out, "Wuh," or "Shabash," to express his appreciation. And the girls have the feeling that never has anyone truly appreciated their skill as this man has done. They try even harder to please him, and he seems to know exactly when they have done something extraordinary, or when their grace has been especially fluid, and he never fails to comment and compliment them on it.

After an hour or so, they stop, exhausted, and the Master is unstinting in his praise. "But now you must surely be hungry and thirsty," he observes and he sees that they are given some of the wine and food. "Now, you rest and we will entertain you," he says and he gestures to one of his mandali who had a good voice to sing a ghazal. Partway through, he gestures to another one of the mandali to bring some blankets to give to the dancers. They look up in surprise. "You've just been exerting, and it's getting cold now and your clothes aren't designed for the cold, so put the blankets on and stay warm."

This was the only time the Master seemed to notice that in fact the girls were wearing very little. They were dressed, but with diaphanous outfits which were supposed to make them more alluring. But the Master's only concern seemed to be with their well-being.

And the Master gestures, "Listen, this is a particularly good verse," and he's sitting in his chair, swaying with the music and enjoying everything. The girls too are enjoying themselves and, after a while, they get up and dance again, and the Master sees to it that the wine and meat continue to be passed around to them and the mandali, and the Master himself partakes of it as well. In short, the Master sees to it that everyone enjoys the party and it continues for the whole night.

Finally, it is dawn, and the Master thanks the girls for coming and tells them they are welcome to see him any time they want, and he personally escorts them down to the banks of the river, to make sure that they get off safely.

As soon as the girls get to the other side, they report to the yogi who has been waiting for them. "Well?" he asks. "Did you go?" "Yes, we have just come from there." "And did he receive you?" "Oh yes, he was most welcoming." "Did you give him the wine and meat?" "Yes, we had a great party and everything got consumed." "And you danced?" "Yes, we danced. We danced and danced and everyone had a good time and now we are exhausted, so please let us go."

"You heard," the yogi told his disciples. "He accepted the wine and meat and let dancing girls perform for him. It's an outrage. How can anyone think he's a master. Call the elders, it is time to expose this imposter and drive him out before he corrupts innocent people with his degenerate ways."

So the disciples go out and tell everyone that their master is calling an important meeting and all should come. When they arrive, the yogi denounces the Master as a fraud and holds up the evidence of the dancing girls, the wine, and the meat to prove that the other man is an imposter.

The people are shocked to hear this and many swear that they will stop seeing him. "But that's not enough," the yogi says. "It is our duty now to expose him publicly, and to drive him from here." "Yes, yes," the people agree, and plans are made for a great procession with the yogi at its head, to cross the river and confront this man and denounce him and insist that he leave the place immediately.

But then they realize there's a problem. How to cross the river? Although the river is wide and fairly fast-flowing, it is not very deep and they can easily wade across it, but they feel this isn't befitting the dignity of their master. And if they have the yogi sit in a boat while they row him across, it won't look very impressive. So they finally decide that while they will wade across the river, their master should ride before them, on a big horse. That will be fitting, they feel, and then he can properly denounce this upstart and drive him away.

So the biggest, finest horse is brought and a fancy saddle is put on and the yogi is made to sit on it, and then the procession begins to cross the river for the confrontation. But all of this commotion, this hubbub, reaches the other side and the Master asks his disciples to see what is going on. They report back that a large procession is crossing the river to see him. So the Master walks down to the edge of the river to see this sight for himself.

Meanwhile, the yogi, who is proudly leading the whole procession on his horse, is now about halfway across the river. Just then, his horse suddenly stops and begins to piddle. Did you know that horses have to stand still to piddle? I never knew that, until Baba told us this story. "Horses, unlike bullocks or cows, cannot piddle while moving," Baba told us, and I had never heard that. When I thought about it, I realized that I had never seen a horse piddling while moving, but it had never occurred to me that they couldn't. See sometime, see if you ever see a horse piddling while moving; it will always be standing. You'll see these bullocks piddling while they are pulling the carts, but you won't see a horse do that.

So because the horse had to piddle, it came to a stop in the middle of the stream. The Master knew what the horse was doing, and he suddenly calls out in a booming voice, "Hey you, what are you doing? Your horse is polluting the river." The yogi turns to the crowd of villagers and smiles at this absurdity, as if this only indicates that this man doesn't have any worldly sense at all, much less spiritual knowledge. With great arrogance he shouts back, "Who ever heard of the piddle of one horse being able to pollute such a wide river?"

"Who ever heard that a few bottles of wine and some patties and a few dancing girls can pollute the entire Ocean?" the Master yelled back. And then it came home to the yogi what true Perfection was like, and he realized the error of his ways.

Baba would often tell people who hesitated to come to Him because they felt they were unworthy, "I am the Ocean. Just give Me everything, nothing can pollute Me." And it's true. We have to give Baba not just our so-called strengths, but our weaknesses as well.

We have to give Baba everything. Even our darkest sins are like the horse's piddling in the river; it cannot pollute the Ocean.

So never hesitate to go to Baba. Never feel you are unworthy. Which of us is worthy? If it comes to that, none of us is worthy of Him, but none of us is ever barred from His company because of our unworthiness; that is His compassion. And only by giving Him our unworthiness do we become worthy to remain in His company. For that is what He wants. He wants us to give Him our weaknesses and failings and so-called sins.

💠 A S K   F O R   L O V E

WE WERE IN ANDHRA, but whether this was '53 or '54 I don't know. I think it was during Baba's first visit there, but I am not sure. At any rate, we were in Andhra, that much I know. And while we were there Baba traveled from place to place. And wherever we went, there was one man, a Baba lover, who used to follow Baba and attend all the programs. There was more than one man who used to do this, there were many who took advantage of every opportunity they could get to be in the company of the Avatar, but there was one man in particular that this story is concerned with.

Now, some of you may have seen films, or been here when some of our family from Andhra have visited, so you have some idea of the way in which the Andhras express their devotion. Nothing is too good for Baba as far as they are concerned. They used to serve

Baba out of silver trays. Really, I am not exaggerating. Andhra is a prosperous area, unlike the North which is so poor. It is fertile, and there are rivers and there are many well-to-do people there. And they would do things on a grand scale for Baba.

So you can just imagine the garlands they would have for Baba. They had every imaginable type of garland. They had garlands made just out of roses, they had garlands made out of camphor, they had garlands of sandalwood chips, gold and silver threads, cloves and cardamoms, and even garlands of rupee notes. So many garlands that I used to have to be quick to remove them so Baba wouldn't be smothered under their weight. At practically every *darshan* program Baba used to allow people to garland Him. And at every program, this man that I am telling about would stand in the crowd and gaze at Baba lovingly and think, "How lucky those garlands are. How fortunate that they get to adorn His neck, even if only for a few moments. Their petals get to caress His cheeks. They are able to embrace His form!"

This man had been allowed to have Baba's *darshan*, he too had had Baba's embrace, but for some reason it got into his head to think about how fortunate the garlands were. He was right. The garlands were fortunate, but how much more fortunate he was to consciously adore the God-Man. That is the supreme blessing of this form, of human form, that we can consciously adore and love God. In no other form can one love God. Baba has told us that even angels envy us because they do not have form and cannot love Him. None of the beings who inhabit the higher worlds can love God. It is only in the human form that we are blessed with this opportunity and capacity.

But this lover, for some reason, got it into his head to start envying the garlands. And from there it was only a short step to wanting to have one of the garlands for himself. The more programs he attended, the more he started to think about how wonderful it would be if Baba were to give him a garland. It became almost an obsession, you may call it. This is what we have been led to understand from things this man told us afterwards. Till by the end of Baba's *darshan* tour, his attention was focused much more on the garlands that it was on Baba. His emotions got more and more built up, his heart more and more set on getting a garland.

And Baba did use to give garlands away to His lovers. Periodically He would call someone up and give him or her a garland. Or spontaneously, as someone was passing by in front of Him, He would remove a garland from His neck and give it to them. And every time this man saw that happen, his own desire to receive a garland from Baba was intensified.

Finally it was the last day of the *darshan* tour. Baba gave *darshan* and then retired to His room. As usual His body was drenched in sweat. People often talk about how much love Baba used to give out during a *darshan* program. That may be, I don't know anything about that side of it, but I do know that, whatever else was involved, on a purely physical level, giving *darshan* was an exhausting business.

Although it was wintertime when Baba visited Andhra, Andhra is farther South from here, it would still be hot during the days. And Baba would sit on the dais for hours at a stretch wearing the heavy garlands that people would give Him, greeting His lovers as they filed by, personally handing out *prasad* to thousands of people. By the time He was finished, Baba's sadra would be sticking to Him. So, after a program, Baba would usually retire to His room where He could relax by Himself.

It was so here, too. A room had been put at Baba's disposal, and after the *darshan* program, Baba went there. I helped Him remove the garlands He was still wearing and these were placed on the heap that was already there. Sometimes Baba would want to change into clean, dry clothes; sometimes He used to simply sit quietly for a while. I was with Baba and almost as soon as we entered the room, Baba ordered me to call this man. I didn't know what man, but Baba described him, so I went outside and told some of the local Andhra lovers that such and such a man was wanted by Baba. They recognized him from the description I gave and they called some others who in turn called someone else and eventually this man was located and told to go to Baba's room.

When he heard this, he rushed to Baba's room, and I still remember it, as soon as he opened the door, Baba reached down and picked up a garland made of roses and tossed it to him, gesturing, "You wanted this, here, take it."

I didn't know anything about what this man had been thinking. I didn't know the background to this incident at all. I only saw him open the door and take one or two steps inside and Baba immediately flung a garland at him and he went away. But later he sought me out and told me the story. He told me how he had been longing for a garland at Baba's hands. He said that as the last *darshan* program ended, and it seemed that his last chance to be given a garland by Baba had also ended, he was crushed. He was completely devastated because he had built this up in his mind to such an extent that he felt that he just had to have a garland.

He couldn't believe it when Baba called him and without a word picked up a garland and flung it at him, remarking, "You wanted this, here, take it." The man went away feeling convinced that Baba not only could hear the cry of his heart, but responded to it.

Of course, when I tell this story, I often add that it is true, Baba does hear the cry of our heart. Which is why it is so important that our hearts cry out for Him. You know, one time Charles had come with a group of his students, most of them coming here for the first time. And one of the girls in the group heard so many stories about Baba that she began to long for a glimpse of Him. The more she heard us talk about Baba, the more she wanted to experience what it would be like to be in His physical presence. You may say she "fell in love" with Baba.

As the days passed, she yearned and yearned and prayed that she be given a glimpse of Baba. She didn't tell us what was going through her mind; we weren't aware of her great longing, her yearning to see Baba in physical form. But her longing was so great that one day, as she was sitting here in Mandali Hall, she saw Beloved Baba sitting in the chair. She was overwhelmed with joy, but at the same time, it seemed so natural for Baba to be there that she didn't call out. She didn't say anything, she just took it for granted that Baba was sitting in His chair.

I didn't know any of this. The days passed and one day I told this story about the garland. The girl who had had the vision of Baba started thinking about it and became depressed. This was just before the group was due to return, and on their last day I suddenly found this girl crying. "What's the matter, Jane?" I asked, thinking to myself that she's probably crying because she's sad to be leaving here. But she looks up and blurts out, "I should have asked for love. I should have asked for love." "What are you talking about?" I asked, and then she told me the whole story. That, just as that man had wanted a garland and Baba had given him one, so too she had asked Baba for a glimpse of Himself and He had given her that glimpse. "But if I only had asked Him for love," she said, "then He would have given me that. Why did I ask for so little?"

If God never granted us our desires, it wouldn't matter much what we longed for. It is because He does give us what we ask for with all our hearts that we must be so careful. Of course, this is just words. We can say we want love, but it is not what we say that Baba listens to, but what our heart cries out. We may think we want to love Baba, but if we really wanted to love Him, He would give us this love. He is more anxious to give us the gift of love than we are to receive it. That is a fact. We may say we want to love Him, but we really want to love ourselves. That is why we are still here. That is why I am still Eruch. If I truly wanted to love the Lord, I wouldn't be Eruch any longer, and I wouldn't be talking about love for Him.

But even if we can't honestly long for love, we can long to long for love. That much is always open to us. If our prayers for love are insincere and mechanical, we can at least pray to become more sincere when we pray. If we cannot run towards the Lord, at least we can walk, and if we cannot walk, we can crawl. And even if we cannot crawl, we can pray for the ability, someday, to be able to crawl. And we may find, to our surprise, that even crawling is not necessary, because the Lord Himself has come to us and is carrying us on His back.

But the point is that we should try to remember that it is the Lord we want, and not His garland. If you want His garland, He will give it to you. But then what? What will you have? That is why I say He will grant you your prayers. These are not just idle words, I have seen it happen so often here. So take care, and pray for something worthwhile. Let me give you another example.

This occurred in Guruprasad. How I wish you all had seen Guruprasad so you could picture it in your mind. So you could get some idea of how vast the crowds used to be that would gather there for Baba's *darshan*. How long the queue lines used to extend as people stood for hours waiting for their chance to pass before Baba. And it wasn't a question of people spending a long time before Baba. No sooner did you get there than there were people pushing you on so the next person could take *darshan*. You would stand for hours, so you could have not even a minute, a few moments I should say, before Baba, and then you were pushed along and your turn was over.

Now in this *darshan* queue there was a man, a Baba lover, who was waiting for his chance to greet Baba. As he stood in line, from a distance, he would notice that sometimes when people were before Him, Baba would caress their cheeks, sometimes He would pat them on the shoulder; some He would ask about their families, with some He might crack a joke. The man watched this. He had plenty of time. What else had he to do but look at Baba? You see, the long *darshan* queue did have this advantage. While your time spent immediately before Baba was small, you were given the opportunity to spend hours gazing at Him as you slowly inched forward.

Even now, at Amartithi time you hear some people complain

about the lines. You know that this last Amartithi it took over five hours to take *darshan* at the *Samadhi*. For the elderly this is a hardship; just standing for that length of time is physically difficult for some people. But I've found that it is not these people who complain. It is the young ones. The old ones have learned the secret of patience, it is the young who want everything to be instant. And they would complain, not all, not even most, but a few, here and there. There would be those who would complain about having to stand in line for five hours. For what? To spend only a few seconds bowing down in the *Samadhi*. Because even then, after all that time in the *darshan* queue, they are not allowed to spend any time at all with Baba in the *Samadhi*.

It is as it was when Baba was in the body giving *darshan*. There are even people stationed inside the *Samadhi* whose duty it is to see that no one spends too long bowing down. One is not even allowed to prostrate before Baba because that would take too much time. Imagine! But it is right; we have to do this or otherwise instead of five hours in line it would take twice that. You would arrive on the 30th, immediately get in the *darshan* queue, and, if you were lucky, you might be able to have *darshan* once before Amartithi was over. It's coming to that, I tell you. Soon people will not be allowed inside the *Samadhi*, they will have to pay their respects from the threshold only. But what are we to do? It is His fault. He is the one drawing so many to Him. We worry about the size of the crowds, but this is nothing. In the future instead of thousands coming, there will be *lakhs*. Why *lakhs*? There will be *crores*, and what we experience now at Amartithi, that will be the everyday occurrence at the Tomb. So just imagine what it will like at Amartithi time!

But what I was saying was that even though some people complain about how long the *darshan* queue takes, I heard one woman, an older woman, saying how happy she was that the line was so long, because that gave her so much time to spend facing Baba, thinking about Baba, preparing to meet Baba. You see the difference? Why not see things the way this woman does? Instead of being upset that you get so little time inside the *Samadhi*, be grateful that you get so much time outside of it, standing at His threshold. That is the charm. That is what Baba would always tell us.

What will you get when you get Realization? You will only realize what you already are. But you are that! You are that already, so what will you get when you get Realization – nothing. The whole charm is in the game that's played before Realization. When you can enjoy the apparent separation between you and God. That's where the charm lies, provided you become aware of it, otherwise it's a drudgery. Once you realize who you really are, the game is finished. There is no longer love because there is no longer separation. You need a Beloved and a lover for love to flourish, and once you realize God, the Beloved and the lover become one. That is why all of this came into being, so that God could enjoy the game of love. That's the purpose behind creation. God means Love, and for God to enjoy the game of love, there must be love, loving, and being loved.

What will you get once you're inside the *Samadhi*? You will get the opportunity to bow down. But then what? Then you have to leave. It is always like this. You never get the chance to stay at His feet. You never get the chance to simply sit and gaze at Him and adore Him for as long as you want. The moment passes and you must move on. But in approaching Baba, that's where we get the opportunity. That's when we can think about Baba, when we can gaze at Baba as much as we want. That's when we can enjoy the anticipation of meeting Baba. That's why all of you are so fortunate. Because you still have this to look forward to. Someday you will all get the opportunity to be with Baba. This is assured. That is why you are here now. You are in the *darshan* queue, as it were. You are inching ahead slowly, so slowly that sometimes it seems as if you are not moving at all, or that you will never reach His feet, but you will get there. Baba once told us, He gave us this figure, He said that life was like an unending procession marching along. The people at the back have no idea what is happening at the front, or even where they are going, for that matter.

In this unending procession of humanity, every now and then the God-Man, the Ancient One, the Avatar appears. His appearance is such that those in the front of the ranks stop and stare at Him. Those just behind crane their heads forward to see what is happening. Those behind them start asking each other, "What is going on? Why have we stopped?" And those even further back don't even realize that the procession has stopped. You know how it is, you have seen a long procession. Even after the front stops, it is quite some time before the back rows have to halt. And this procession is unending, so the back rows never stop moving. They don't even realize that anything has happened at the front of the procession.

Baba said this is what it is like for all of us. Only those in the front are aware of His advent, and only those in the very front get to actually see Him and be with Him. But once they have seen Him and been with Him, the procession ends for them. And then those who were behind them become the front ranks. So the next time the same Ancient One returns, they are the ones who see Him and get to be with Him. The fact that you are here, that you have heard of Baba, that you have felt drawn to come here, means that you are approaching the front of the ranks. Maybe you have not seen Him, but you are the ones who know that the procession has stopped. You are craning your necks trying to get a glimpse, asking those just before you in the line, "Can you see? What does He look like? What is happening?"

That is why I tell you that you are fortunate. I know none of you believes me when I say this, you think I am just throwing out words, trying to make you feel better, but it is not that, brother, I tell you, it is not that. You are fortunate. Now is the time to make the most of this opportunity. That is what this man in the queue did. He spent his time staring at Baba. Watching the expression on Baba's face. Watching the way Baba would relate to each person who came before Him.

And as he stood in line, he began to think, "I wonder what

Baba will do when my turn comes? Will He pat me on the shoulder, will He caress my cheek, will He ask me something? What will He ask me? Will He inquire about my family, my job, my health?" And so the time passed with him alternately gazing at Baba and wondering to himself what his reception would be like when it was finally his turn to greet Baba.

Finally, his turn came. And just as he stepped in front of Baba, Baba turned to the side to say something to me. I don't remember exactly what it was all about, but Baba was wondering whether one of His lovers had managed to get a train ticket for his return journey. He was asking me whether there had been any problems, whether the person would be able to return now without difficulties. Something like that, something completely extraneous. And then, before Baba could turn back, this man was pushed along, his turn was over. He was stunned. He couldn't take it in, that after all that time, his turn had come and gone and Baba's hadn't even looked at him. He was completely crushed. He went to the very back of the crowd and stood there feeling dejected, miserable. And as he was standing there, the *arti* was sung, which signaled the end of the program. After *arti*, Baba would gesture, "Now go," and everyone would disperse.

People were always reluctant to leave Baba, so He would have to resort to various ways to get them to leave. Sometimes Baba would give a stirring talk about obedience and then ask those assembled whether they were willing to obey Him. Of course, having been inspired by Baba's words on the subject, everyone would raise their hand, yes, they would obey Baba. "Then go," Baba would say. "I want this hall to be empty in two minutes." And then the people would realize that they had been outsmarted. Having just promised Baba that they would obey, they had no choice but to leave.

Why was *arti* sung to Baba? Does Baba need us to do His *arti*? What is *arti* anyway? *Arti*, in its truest sense, is simply the spontaneous cry of the heart. If Baba were to suddenly appear here now, what would you say? You would gasp, "Oh, Baba!" And that would be your *arti*. But people wanted to do *arti* for Baba. It is traditional here, it is the way we have been brought up to worship God, and taking Baba to be God, His lovers would want to worship Him properly. So Baba would permit His lovers to perform His *arti*. But see how practical Baba was? Baba would use the *arti* as a signal that the *darshan* program was over. He conditioned His lovers to accept the fact that once *arti* was sung, that was it, they had to leave. Otherwise they would have stayed and stayed.

So when this man heard the *arti* being sung, he knew the program was over and he felt totally rejected and downcast. As soon as *arti* was over, people began to leave the hall. They knew that that was what Baba wanted and expected of them. But Baba pointed to someone at the back of the crowd and He indicated to me, "Call that man." "Which man, Baba?" I asked. "The one with the red shirt?" Baba shook His head and pointed, and I would describe the people I saw at the back until Baba indicated that I had found the right man.

And it was the man who had been made so wretched by Baba's turning His head aside when it was his turn to have Baba's *darshan*. I called him forward and Baba started asking him so many intimate questions, about his family, about himself. Baba greeted him so lovingly, poured so much attention on him, that the man started weeping. It always comes to that. First Baba gives His love and then the lover weeps. Mani often says that it is not weeping, it is melting, the lover's heart is melting under the rays of Baba's love. Whatever it be, we know from experience that the human heart cannot endure the God-Man's presence without flowing over with tears. Why this is, I don't know, but it is a fact. We are used to it after all these years.

This man came to me afterwards and told me the whole story, everything that had been going through his heart, and then he started weeping again, saying, "Eruch, you have no idea what love He has for us." And it's true. How can you explain it? Baba simply asked this man how he was, how his family was doing, and it overwhelmed him, he couldn't contain himself and started weeping. Such a little gesture on Baba's part, but see the effect. And why does it have such an effect? Because it is not a gesture on Baba's part, it is not a pose that He is adopting to make His lovers feel good. No, it is something much deeper than that. Sometimes to us, to someone like me who was an observer, who was watching all of this as a detached observer, I would feel, "Baba is just being polite. Baba is humoring this man." But now I know that it is not that. There is something behind this. Baba was the perfect host, there is no doubt of that. But the reason such a simple gesture could have such an effect was because this gesture was in response to the cry of the lover's heart.

That is why I say call out to Baba. Don't be afraid to ask Baba for something. If you can't call out to Baba, then whom can you call out to? Baba always said you must never hesitate to ask Him for anything, but, at the same time, you must never expect an answer. Ask, but don't expect Him to answer. But I am telling you, that He will answer. He will not only hear the cry of your heart, but He will give you whatever you ask for from the bottom of your heart. And that is why, instead of asking for a garland, or for a caress, ask Baba for love.

🔅 MEDITATION

WHAT IS THE PURPOSE OF MEDITATION, after all? It is to concentrate one's attention on God. If meditation makes one think of oneself and not God, then the purpose of meditation is not served and there is no point to it. When we were with Baba we did not meditate. Where was the need, we were already with God; we did not need to artificially focus the mind to think about God because we naturally were thinking about Him every moment. Baba would not stop people from meditating but He never encouraged any of us to do it.

In the early years, in the Manzil-e-Meem period, Baba used to have the mandali meditate early in the morning, for an hour. I wasn't there at the time, but I gather that the focus of the meditation, as far as the poor mandali were concerned, wasn't so much God as it was trying to stay awake. Baba would keep them all very busy, all day long, and then they would have to get up at four or five in the morning and they weren't used to it. It was very hard for them to stay awake. If Baba had had them get up that early and do some sort of physical labor, they could have done it, but to get up early and then sit quietly for an hour was too much and they would start to nod off. That is how Pendu got his name. You know that Pendu is the name Baba gave. His real name is Aspandiar. But in those early hours, the mandali used to resort to different tactics to stay awake. Some used to pinch themselves, some would hit themselves, and Pendu would rock back and forth. When Baba and the mandali came to Happy Valley for the first time, before moving to Meherabad, Baba saw Pendu rocking back and forth and nicknamed him "Pendulum." After a while, He shortened this to "Pendu" and that has been his name ever since.

And that Manzil-e-Meem period was, as far as I know, the only period when Baba ever had His mandali meditate. Sometimes people see how many pages are devoted to meditation in the Discourses, and they think that Baba must have placed great importance on meditation, but Baba dictated those discourses for posterity, for the time when the Avataric period is over and His immediate presence starts to fade. That is when people will once again have to resort to meditation to concentrate on the Lord. But now, if you ask me, I would say there is no need. Now all that is needed is to determine to become His, to make Him your constant companion, and if you do that, then you will find that you are always thinking about Him, and that is meditation in its most natural and highest form.

But Baba did have us meditate once. Would you like to hear about it? We were in Satara. There were five of us and we were playing cards with Baba. It was evening time, I remember that because Baba had called the five of us to be with Him at 5:00 or 5:30, I don't remember the exact time. We all came and Baba suggested a game of cards. We were playing and there was the usual sort of good-natured conversation going on concerning the cards when Baba suddenly stopped the game and said that He wanted us to meditate. This took us all completely by surprise.

Baba must have seen how startled we were because He began to explain how He wanted us to meditate. He said He would clap His hands three times. First, we should go out into the compound area and each of us was to find a suitable spot to sit. When Baba clapped the first time, we were supposed to settle down, relax, quiet ourselves, and try to be calm. When we heard a second clap, we were to close our eyes and begin to meditate. And when we heard the third clap, we were supposed to get up and return to Baba.

But we still didn't have any idea how we should meditate, so Baba came to our rescue. "How will you meditate?" He asked us. "To meditate you must think about God. But God is infinite and eternal, so how will you be able to imagine this? You can't, it is beyond the mind. So think of God as all-pervading effulgence. Try to bring before your mind's eye a picture of an ocean of infinite, all-pervading effulgence, which is God. A shoreless, bottomless ocean."

Baba looked at us then and asked, "But if this ocean of effulgence is infinite and all-pervading, where will you be? What will your position be?" We had no answer for this, but Baba went on and said, "If you imagine this ocean in front of you, then it is not infinite. So try to bring before your mind's eye this infinite ocean of effulgence and imagine yourself in it. You are in the midst of this infinite ocean of effulgence. Try to picture this when you meditate."

So, with these instructions we went outside and we each found a place to sit, and got ourselves comfortable as Baba had said. After a moment or two, I heard Baba's clap. I relaxed, and was breathing very evenly when, after some time, I heard Baba's second clap. I closed my eyes and began to try to meditate as He had just instructed us. I pictured an infinite ocean of effulgence all around me, with me floating in the middle of it. The image came easily to mind and I found that quickly I had lost myself in this ocean. I was just beginning to enjoy the feeling of being lost in this ocean. I don't know how much time had elapsed. It seemed like only a minute or two. I was just beginning to really enjoy the sensation, when I heard Baba's clap again. So I opened my eyes and got up and rejoined Baba as did the others.

Baba told us, "Don't ever meditate like that again," and we resumed the card game. That was the first and last time I ever meditated.

⊲⊳ T R A V E L I N G   W I T H   B A B A

YOU ALL HAVE HEARD ME TELL STORIES concerning railway trains many times. I don't know why it is, but so often it seems my memories of Baba have to do with trains. God knows what work Baba was doing with trains, but it is good because now every time you ride on one, you can think to yourself, "Baba rode on trains all over India, perhaps He rode on this one as well." Think of all the millions of people in India now who are unknowingly taking Baba's *darshan* every day by riding on trains that Baba might have ridden on at one time. Of course, this is an unknowing and unconscious *darshan*. But with Baba lovers, it is conscious.

That is what Baba means when He says that all of creation should be a constant reminder of the Creator. In almost anything you do, you can think to yourself that at some point in this Advent, Baba also shared that experience. That is the power of the personal advent, of the Avatar. By taking human form, and living so completely as a human, it is easy to associate everything we do in our daily lives with Baba because Baba too has shared the human experience.

But now I have gotten side-tracked, I have gotten off the train, as it were, and am wandering away into the station. But before getting back on board, let me just say something about traveling with Baba. If you were to ask me what was Baba's favorite mode of transportation, I would not be able to answer. Baba traveled by train, He flew on airplanes, He traveled by boat, by bullock cart, by car. He walked long distances on foot, He's been ferried in rowboats, in dugout canoes, He's ridden camels and elephants and donkeys.

The one thing I can say, however, from my experience with Baba, is that He never liked to travel in comfort. However we traveled with Baba, we were always uncomfortable. When we traveled by train, we almost always went third-class, especially in the early years. From hearing some of you talk, you think even first-class train travel can be difficult, but believe me, traveling by third class in those days was a constant battle. First you had to fight even to get on board the train. And once you got on, you had to fight to secure a place to sit down and a place to store your luggage. And finally, having attained that, you had to be constantly on guard that someone didn't steal your space from you. At each station you had to be ready to do battle to see that others didn't invade your area and overwhelm you.

Of course, for us, this task was more serious than for others because we were not fighting for ourselves but to protect the physical form of the God-Man, Meher Baba. That is why we found it so nerve-wracking to travel by train with Baba, because there was the constant anxiety of whether we would be able to get Him safely on the train or not. For ourselves, we didn't care. We were young and strong and could make do with whatever we found. But for Baba's physical comfort, we had to take care, and it used to be a kind of torture for us because we never knew whether we would be able to protect Baba adequately or not.

And for some reason, Baba seemed to travel most when there were signs put up all over the train stations in India reading, "Only travel when you must." All during the war years, when the trains were always overcrowded and most of the cars were reserved for the military, we traveled throughout India. After partition, when the trains were piled high with corpses and it wasn't safe to go anywhere, we traveled all over. Again I don't know why this was, whether Baba traveled so much because of the conditions, or it was just coincidence that when conditions were worst for traveling we traveled the most.

Nor was it just the train travel which was difficult. I think some of you may have heard me tell about the time we had just completed a long and arduous journey by train. As usual we were completely exhausted. For even once we managed to find space on the train and were settled in, we couldn't completely relax. Baba never wanted us to sleep when we were traveling with Him. "Don't doze," He would gesture to us. "Don't doze, don't even close your eyes."

Sometimes it would be so hot, and our train rides were not two- or three-hour affairs. We would travel for long distances – which means we would be on the train for hours altogether – but Baba always liked us to keep awake and stay alert. For me it wasn't so bad, because I was young. But for Gustadji and Baidul and some of the older ones it became difficult. Especially in the summer, when it was so hot, and we had been sitting for hours and hours and the train's rocking motion tended to lull you into drowsiness.

Baba would lie down. Not all the way, but we would make room on the seat and Baba would sort of curl up and lie down with a scarf over His face. "Don't doze, keep awake," He would gesture and He would lie down, and we would have to sit there and try to stay awake. Poor Gustadji, just keeping his eyes open in that heat for so long used to irritate them, and he would have to soak a handkerchief in water and put it over his eyes to give them some relief.

So, after a long and exhausting train trip, we returned to Bombay, and we were now driving back to Meherazad in a car. I think Meherjee's driver may have been driving the car, but I don't remember. But after this arduous journey we were at last returning home. But to say that it was much better in the car would be to exaggerate, for there would usually be four of us, and sometimes even five, crammed into the back seat of a car which could only comfortably hold three.

And why were we in a car in the first place? Not because Baba preferred it, but because His lovers were concerned about Baba's comfort. They didn't like to think of their Lord walking all over India, or traveling by third class trains, or being jolted about in a bullock cart. So, out of their love for their Beloved, they purchased a car and gave it to Baba for His use. And because of their love, Baba accepted. I tell you it's all because of love. Everything is because of love. The good and the bad, it's all because of love.

Anyway, because of their love for the Lord, and because of His love for His lovers, the Lord happened to be in a car coming to Meherazad. Of course they had gotten the car for Baba thinking He would be more comfortable that way. Perhaps He was, but the rest of us certainly were not, because it was Baba's way to pack as many of us into the car as He could.

Naturally, we didn't like to crowd Baba, so there would be the driver and Baba in the front seat and sometimes one other member

of the mandali who always tried to take up as little room as possible
so as not to crowd Baba. But in the back seat we used to be packed
like sardines, and we were hefty people, we were like wrestlers, not
like this Lazarus of a fellow Bal Natu that you see there. And what
made it worse, Baba never liked to have a draft on Him, so we had
to keep all the windows rolled up. It would be so hot and stuffy that
you couldn't breathe.

Why did it have to be that way? I still don't know. Why Baba
couldn't just put three people in back I'll never know. If He wanted
to have more people, why didn't He allow His lovers to give Him
another car? I don't know. I only know that this was Baba's way.
Perhaps He was only comfortable in discomfort. Whatever it be, we
were traveling to Meherazad after that long and exhausting train
journey and the car was packed even more than usual. For not only
did it have to carry all of us, but so many of our belongings as well.
And it was so hot and stuffy, and we were so tired, that, in short, it
was enough to make you long for the ease of the bullock cart.

As we were driving along we passed an old man walking along
the road with a large bundle on his shoulders. Baba stopped the car.
"Let's give him a ride," Baba gestured. "There's no room, Baba," I
protested, but I knew it was hopeless. Baba always had a special soft
spot in His heart for venerable old men. And this old man walking
along the road had a long white beard and was just the type of person Baba was fond of. So I knew it did not matter much what I said,
but still I blurted out, "Baba, there is no room, where will he sit?"

Baba gestured that there was plenty of room in the back with
us and insisted that we give the man a lift. So what could we do? I
got out of the car and, walking up to the man, asked him where he
was going and if he would care to go in our car. The old man was
delighted. I took the huge bundle off his shoulders and carried it to
the car. Now there was barely room for me to sit in the car as it was;
I had been sitting on the very edge of the seat near the door. But I
opened the door and the old man gratefully sat in the spot where I

had been sitting. I didn't see how I was going to be able to squeeze back in. And I still had the big bundle.

There was no room for the bundle on top of the car or in the dickey because they were already overloaded with our luggage. So what to do? For me this was the last straw. If Baba wanted to try and squeeze one more person in the car, that was His prerogative, but I didn't see why Baba insisted on picking up someone who had such a big bundle with him.

So I said, "Baba, what about this bundle, there's no room." "Put it in back with you," Baba gestured impatiently. So I took the bundle and by brute force managed to jam it inside. Now there wasn't an inch of space left. So I slammed the door shut and said, "Okay, Baba, now everything's in, go on, I'll walk." And I went storming off.

I had just become completely fed up with it. If Baba wanted to overcrowd the car, that was fine, but I didn't see why I had to endure it; I felt it would be more comfortable to walk the whole distance than to ride any further in such an overcrowded car. Of course, Baba got upset and ordered me back. He pricked my ear and told me to get in the car. Baba indicated that I should sit in the front seat with Him, so I got in and we drove off.

Baba was always so compassionate with us; He let us have our moods, He let us express ourselves. But after these little outbursts, He expected us to quickly regain our senses, if not our moods, and continue to live as free men, men who had become free by exercising our free will to become slaves at His feet. And what is more, Baba helped us regain our senses, by little gestures of thoughtfulness, such as making room on the front seat for me to sit.

But now, to get back on board the train, let me tell you of one incident I remember which amused Baba. Again we were traveling on a train, but this time Baba and I happened to be traveling second class. In those days, at the time of the British and for a while afterwards, there were five classes. There was first class, which was for the V.I.P.'s, the big shots. There was second class, and then there was interclass which was intermediate between second and third. Then there was third-class and lastly there was servant class. For every ticket in first class, you were given two tickets in servant class, and for each ticket you bought in second class, you were given one in servant class.

Again, this incident took place after some of Baba's lovers began to become a bit prosperous. They never liked to think of Baba undergoing the rigors of third class travel, so they would prevail upon Him to sometimes travel by second class. On this occasion Baba and I and another of the mandali were traveling second class. And the rest of the mandali who were with us were in servant class. We were in a four-person compartment. During the day more people would squeeze onto the seats, but at night the seats would be converted into four sleeping berths and then there would only be four of us. As I said, there were three of us and one stranger in the four-person compartment.

It was the dead of night, so we had latched the door to the train compartment so no one could enter, and we had shut off the lights and were "sleeping." Of course, we couldn't really sleep, but at any rate, we were resting. When we traveled with Baba, He always liked us to keep the light in the compartment on at night, but out of consideration for the stranger who was with us, Baba allowed the light to be turned off. But still we had to keep alert, to be ready in case Baba should need us for anything.

Now it so happened at one of the stations, that someone must have reached in through an open window and flipped the latch so he could open the door. For, after a while, someone came into our compartment. I started yelling at him, "What are you doing? All the berths are occupied. There is no room here, get out." I don't know what I said, but that was the gist, that every berth was taken and he should try to find a place somewhere else. And I was within my rights to yell at him, because the berths were all reserved. You had to have a ticket to get a berth, you were not allowed to simply enter such a compartment and try to find an empty one.

But when I yelled at this intruder to get out, I happened to wake up the stranger in our compartment. Because it was so hot, he was dressed only in his shorts. And he began haranguing the stranger, but what a scene it was. He was standing there saying, "Just wait until I put on my pants and then I'll show you something." He kept threatening to fight the stranger, but the whole time he never made a move to get dressed. He would just repeat, "Just wait until I put my pants on and then I'll thrash you." It was so comical, so ludicrous, the way he was standing there pretending to prepare to thrash this fellow and acting as if the only thing which prevented him was the fact that he didn't have his pants on. Baba was very amused by it all. Even the next day, Baba would refer to it and smile. "Just wait until I have my pants on and then you'll see!"

This reminds me of another funny incident concerning trains and Gypsies. Did you know that Gypsies were always allowed to travel free? They never had to have tickets? I didn't use to know that either, until on the New Life we were taken for Gypsies once, so the conductor let us go without attempting to collect our tickets. That's when I first learned that Gypsies never had to pay.

Of course, we had seen Gypsies traveling on the trains many times. In fact, when we were on the platform, if a band of Gypsies came along, we used to groan inwardly and think to ourselves that it would be better to miss the train and travel by the next one than to have to travel on the train with the Gypsies. That's because as overcrowded as the trains were, they were nothing compared to how crowded they could get when an entire band of Gypsies with all of their animals and belongings packed into a compartment. So whenever we saw Gypsies traveling, we always tried to avoid them if we could.

Usually, when we traveled, there would only be a handful of us. On the New Life there were how many of us, twenty, twenty-one counting Baba, but on our mast expeditions, there were usually only four or five of us traveling with Baba. Sometimes Baidul would be there, Gustadji, Kaka, Donkin, myself; it varied. Sometimes Chhagan would come along, or Baba would bring Nariman or Meherjee just to give them a taste of what it was like. At different times different ones would come with us, but usually, at any one time, there would be no more than four or five of us traveling with Baba.

And most often, whenever we traveled with Baba, Vishnu would stay behind to see to the marketing for the women. He always had another duty as well; it was his job to send Baba a cable each day telling Baba if anything important happened. Before we left, Baba would see that Vishnu was given an itinerary of where we would be going and what dates we were expected to be at each place.

Now, since we would be going *mast* hunting, we never knew exactly where we would be. We knew, for example, that we might be traveling to Miraj and would be getting down there to search out a *mast*, but we didn't know where exactly we might find the *mast*. So when I say Vishnu knew how to reach us at all times, what I mean is that Vishnu knew the general route we would be traveling, what big towns we would be stopping at, and what stations we would pass through on the way.

In those days, you could send a cable care of the postmaster or care of the stationmaster and be sure of it getting there. So if Vishnu needed to notify Baba about anything, he could. And even if there was no real news, Vishnu was supposed to end a cable saying, "All's well." And he would. Vishnu would faithfully send cables to the postmaster or the stationmaster along our route. Whenever we pulled into a city, Baba would send us out to get Vishnu's telegram.

This one incident I recall happened at the station. There used to be boards on the station platforms right outside the stationmaster's door covered with glass doors, and the telegrams would be stuck up on the board. You would look through the glass, see if there was a telegram for you, and, if there was, you would open the door and remove it.

I remember one day, we were traveling and we got to a big station, and Baba sent me to pick up Vishnu's telegram. I went but there was no cable on the board with our name on it. Baba said, "Are you sure? Better check again." "Yes, Baba, I'm sure. There's no cable." "But there has to be a cable. Go see the stationmaster and find out what's happened to our cable."

Baba knew that Vishnu must have cabled. He always cabled. And in those days, if you sent a cable, you knew it would arrive that same day at your destination. Now you can send a cable and it can take days to arrive, or never arrive at all. But back then, the service was so good that Baba knew that someone must have taken our cable; there was no question of it not having arrived.

So I went to the stationmaster and put up a big show about the telegram. I told him that we knew the telegram was sent and should have been waiting for us and that it was vitally important that we receive it. It was all a show. What would the cable say, after all, but "All's well." I knew that, but Baba wanted the cable and the stationmaster wasn't likely to help us unless I put up this front. That's what our life with Baba was like, putting up a big front, play-acting.

But I convinced the stationmaster that it was important, so he agreed to check. You see, they used to have a big book which recorded every cable the station received. So the stationmaster checked this book and sure enough, there it was written that a cable for M. S. Irani had arrived. "That's it," I said, "that's my cable. Where is it?"

The stationmaster was sure that it must be in the glass display case but I assured him that it wasn't there. He couldn't understand it, and he checked with the man at the station who was responsible for actually receiving the cables and putting them out.

"Oh yes," the man said. "I put that cable out, but it's been claimed." "Claimed? What do you mean claimed? We've only just arrived, so how could we have claimed it before?" "No, not you, there are a lot of Iranis here and one of them must have claimed it."

"A lot of Iranis?" I asked. I don't remember where we were

exactly, but I know it wasn't in an area where you would expect to find many Zoroastrians. Irani is a common name for Zoroastrians, but it is not at all a common name for Hindus or Muslims, so I was puzzled when the telegraph officer said that there were a lot of Iranis at that station. But it turned out there was a band of Gypsies there and they called themselves Iranis. Gypsies used to always have their camps near the tracks in those days. "The cable's probably been taken by one of them," he said.

I explained all this to Baba, and He emphasized that we must get the cable, that it was very important and that He had to have it. So Baba and I walked over the Gypsy camp. Of course, as soon as we entered, there was a big tamasha, the dogs all started barking and the women and children gathered round and it was a big commotion. Baba was at my side, and He indicated, "Get the cable," so I started saying that someone there had taken my cable. The Gypsies didn't speak the same languages I spoke. They only knew a few words, so communication was difficult. And they are very suspicious of outsiders anyway; I could feel the hostility as they crowded around me. But I kept insisting that one of them had taken my cable. The cable for M. S. Irani.

As I was yelling at them that they had my cable, all the women started yelling at me, the dogs kept barking, it was really quite an altercation. And, it was all being conducted in pidgin since we really couldn't communicate. But when I said I was M. S. Irani, the man who seemed to be the chief came forward and pointed at himself and indicated that he was M. S. Irani. "No, no," I insisted, "I am M. S. Irani." You see I had to pretend that it was my cable. I couldn't involve Baba in this. But all the time, Baba is at my side, urging me on, indicating that it was critical that I put up a big show in order to get the cable.

I said, "I'm M. S. Irani and the cable is mine." But the Gypsy chief said, "I'm M. S. Irani. My cable." For a while we just continued to insist that we were both M. S. Irani, but finally I managed to make them believe the cable was mine because I told them where it was sent from. Now, I don't remember, but I have the vague memory that it was from Satara, that the women and Vishnu and the others were staying at Satara at the time. So I said, "Do you know anyone in Satara? The cable is for me."

It was such a scene, it was really a sight to witness, but so picturesque – the Gypsy camp, the dogs, the children, the tents, the women in their colorful saris, and all their ornaments. Have you ever seen Gypsy women, seen all the ornaments they wear? And everyone yelling the whole time at the top of their voices. But finally I convinced the chief that the cable belonged to me and he gave it to me. Baba was very pleased that we finally got our cable.

Of course, all it said was, "All's well," but Baba, for some reason, was eager to get that particular cable from Vishnu and we did get it. I'll always remember that.

☙ GURUPRASAD INCIDENT

SPEAKING OF GURUPRASAD, I'll never forget one incident that occurred the last summer we went there. This was 1968 and Baba wasn't seeing anyone. From 1965 onwards, Baba continued to go to Poona each summer for three months, but fewer and fewer people were allowed to see Him. And this last summer, no one was supposed to come. Of course, those of us who lived with Baba would see Him, although there were times when Baba went into seclusion within His seclusion, you might say, and then even we were not supposed to see Baba. This would occur when Baba was involved in His universal work.

How to explain it all? There were different levels to Baba's seclusion. Sometimes Baba would be "in seclusion," but would not only be with us, but would even allow outsiders to see Him. These would be general periods of seclusion, which Baba would step out of to be with people. Sometimes Baba would be "in seclusion," which meant outsiders were not allowed to see Him, but with us, it would almost be like any other time. Baba would sit with us, play cards with us, joke with us. There wasn't that much difference from the usual. Then again, there were periods of seclusion during which Baba would assign one or two of the mandali to see to His personal needs and none of the rest of us were supposed to see or disturb Baba in any way.

The time I am speaking of we were allowed to be with Baba as usual, but no outsider was supposed to see Baba. Baba was very strict about this, and if people came to see Baba we had to turn them away. Of course, most of Baba's lovers knew that He did not wish to see them that summer in 1968, as this sort of "seclusion" had been going on, more or less, for several years at this point. They were patiently waiting for Baba to call them and He kept promising that He would do so soon. In 1968, the plans for the *darshan* program in the spring of 1969 were already being chalked out. For the last year or so Baba had been indicating that His seclusion would be over soon, and He would be giving *darshan* to His lovers when it was. The date of this expected *darshan* program kept getting changed, postponed, but finally it was made definite that it would be in March and April of 1969.

All of this is only background for my story, however, as we are not concerned now with the 1969 *darshan* program. We are only concerned with Baba's stay at Guruprasad during the summer of 1968. I used to stay at one end of the verandah, that was my "office," and I used to sit there and work on the correspondence and the other duties I had when I wasn't actually with Baba. Guruprasad was a big palace and it had a verandah along two sides of it. I was at one end, and Baba's room was around the corner and at the other end of the verandah. From where I was sitting I couldn't see Baba's room, but I could see the approach road which led up to Guruprasad, so I could see if anyone was coming. And one day, after Baba had retired to His room after lunch, I was surprised to see a man coming down the path to Guruprasad on crutches. Baba had told us that He would be in His room for a while and that He didn't want to be disturbed and that He would be coming out in an hour or so.

Nana Kher used to sit on the other side of the verandah, as a watchman, to see that no one should disturb Baba, and I called out softly to Nana, to alert him that someone was coming. And then I went to see what this man wanted. It turned out that he was a retired army captain, and he had one leg amputated. He was approaching on crutches, dressed in an ochre-colored robe. I whispered to him to stop and to go away as no one was allowed to see Baba.

"Please, I just want a glimpse," he said. "Impossible," I replied. "These are Baba's orders. There is nothing we can do, you must leave." All of this in whispers, mind you, so we wouldn't disturb Baba. The man pleaded his case but we had to harden our hearts, there was nothing we could do, for it was Baba's orders that none should see Him. Finally the man begged, "At least let me sit here for a while so that I can meditate on Him when He is nearby. Just for a few minutes."

I knew it was a risk, but I couldn't refuse him. So I said, "For five minutes only, then you must leave." Even at that I was taking quite a chance, because Baba could come out of His room soon and if this man were still there, He would not have been pleased. So I said, "Five minutes only," and this man agreed and sat down and began to meditate.

He seemed sincere. I didn't think that as soon as my back was turned he would jump up and try to make his way inside, so I went back to my corner and continued with my work. After a while I looked at my watch and saw that five minutes had passed. But I decided to let him have another five minutes. And then I went to the front to make sure he had left, but I found that he was still sitting there, deep in meditation. Now what to do? I didn't want to disturb him, but I couldn't let him sit there forever, and the longer he sat, the greater the chance was that Baba would come out of His room. I decided to let him have another five minutes.

I say this now very matter of factly, but I wasn't calm then. My heart was beating fast because I was afraid of what would happen if Baba came out of His room. This fellow had his eyes closed, he might not even notice it if Baba came out, but Baba did not walk with His eyes closed. Baba was bound to see him meditating there on the ground and He would want to know what he was doing, and who gave him permission to do it and so on, and so I was nervous about letting him stay so long, and yet I took the risk and let him have another five minutes.

I went back to my corner, but I was too restless now to do any work. I kept looking at my watch, my ears straining to hear any sound from Baba's room. Of course, it was too far for me to hear anything anyway, but I was alert in case Baba clapped. Every few seconds I would glance at my watch, and when another five minutes had passed, I felt, "It's too much now. He asked for a few minutes and it's been twenty. Now he must go."

So I went back to the front and walked up to the man and tapped him on the shoulder gently. He didn't respond. I whispered, "Sir, you have to go now. Your time is up." But there was no response. He was really absorbed in meditation. He was unconscious of his surroundings, of me speaking to him. Even when I shook his shoulder he wasn't aware of it.

So now what to do? He was a big fellow. I couldn't carry him by myself. I couldn't wake him from his meditation and I knew that at any minute Baba would appear. So I went back up on the verandah and I got Nana, and maybe Bhau was there, and I grabbed this man under the armpits and they took his legs and we bodily lifted him, still deep in meditation, and carried him and his crutches down the long approach road.

"Where should we put him?" they asked. "Out on the side of the road," I answered. "The noise of the traffic will wake him up." And that's what we did. We carried him out of the gate and onto the street itself and left him at the side of the street. When we got back to Guruprasad I turned around and saw that, sure enough, he had finally been startled out of his meditation and was walking away. I breathed a sigh of relief. And it was right after that, say a few minutes or so, that Baba called.

〰 BAIDUL

YOU'VE HEARD ME TALK ABOUT BAIDUL many times, about his inquisitiveness. We will call it that; some might give it another name, they might say that Baidul just couldn't refrain from sticking his nose into everyone else's business. But this weakness of Baidul's served Baba well and Baba made it into a strength. See how Baba makes use of our traits, our nature? If a truck delivered supplies to Meherazad, within minutes Baidul would have found out everything about the driver, not only about him, but about his family as well. And this proved very useful for Baba because it was just what was needed for tracking down *masts*.

Baidul was king of the *masts*, but why was he given this title?

Because he had some mystical affinity, some special occult power to find *masts*? No, it was his inquisitiveness, his asking everyone questions all the time. Baidul would go out and would not feel shy about approaching anyone and asking anything. We were not that way. There might be some reticence on our part, especially if the other person was older, or was saintly and deserved respect. But Baidul didn't care for anyone. He was a crude sort of person in this respect. He didn't care so much for social conventions. He was very direct and forthright.

But this stemmed from his conviction in Meher Baba as the Emperor. Since Baba was the Emperor, and he was carrying out Baba's orders, why should he worry or care for anyone else? All others were vassals before Baba. This was Baidul's attitude and it was this which permitted him to have no qualms about ordering *masts* to come out in the middle of the night because Baba wanted to see them. You know that story, don't you, about the time we were traveling and Baba wanted to contact a *mast* late at night? I think it may have been printed somewhere. Anyway, this attitude of Baidul's served Baba well on many, many occasions.

I have told you before about Baidul's inquisitiveness and his *mast* hunting. What I want to bring home to you today is that Baidul also could be quite an imposing figure when he wanted to be. He was a big man, and he held himself in such a way, his manner was such, that you may call it regal. Really, he was an imposing personality. His clothes might have been shabby, and his manner too direct, but he did have this aura about him, this innate dignity.

On top of all this, Baidul was a simple man. I don't mean feeble in intellect or anything of that sort; I mean he was without pretense. You may have heard me tell you about his poetry, how Baba once complimented him on something he wrote and how ever since then he got it in his head that he was a great poet. That is how he got his name, "Aga Baidul." But that is a different story. If you want I will tell you it later.

One day Baidul picked up a book on medicine. It was one of those books that people sell on the street. You must have seen them, they sit on the pavement with books spread out in front of them, books about how to cure every known disease, how to live for hundreds of years, how to ensure that you will have only male children, those sorts of books. They cost only a few rupees, and back then, probably only a few annas. Anyway, somehow, somewhere, Baidul got hold of such a book in Urdu on how to make your own medicine to cure anything and everything, and read it through and began practicing.

Of course, the rest of us didn't mind. We were used to such crackpot doctors. At different times it seems we had so many of the mandali practicing their own versions of homeopathy, naturopathy, biochemistry and this and that. We didn't mind. What harm did it do? And it made them feel good, that they were helping others. And Baba would even encourage such harebrained doctors. In the early years, if anyone got bitten by a scorpion, Baba told them to go to Homi, Gustadji's older brother, who supposedly knew a mantra that would effectively counteract the pain. It never seemed to, but at least Homi felt happy.

So it was that Baidul began practicing his own version of medicine. As I said, we didn't mind, but that is not completely true. There were those who did mind, and who were they but the real doctors, Nilu and Donkin. They used to get wild every time they heard of Baidul attempting to treat anyone with his crackpot medicine. And they were right. Baba held them responsible for seeing that all the mandali stayed in good health. And they took their duties very seriously. You may have heard how in '69 Donkin saw to it that the Westerners who came for the big *darshan* in Poona should stay healthy. On his own, he would inspect the kitchens of the hotels where the Westerners would be staying to make sure that proper sanitary procedures were followed. Don took this duty so seriously that he cleaned the latrines of the hotels himself to make sure they were done properly. That was Don's nature. People would come here and think Don was a servant, never realizing that he was one of Baba's close ones and a British gentleman, an orthopedic surgeon. That was his way. He would never push himself forward, he would always be in the background seeing to everything himself. What a gem he was. It is too bad you didn't get to meet him. Then you would know what real service was like.

But to get back to our story, Don and Nilu took their duties very seriously and they were not amused or appreciative of Baidul's efforts to dispense his own brand of medicine. Now we were staying in Satara, so this was probably in the '40s. I don't remember any more. And Baidul was with us. Now whenever Baidul was with us and wasn't out reconnoitering for *masts*, Baba would assign him guard duty. In Satara we stayed in a lovely property owned by an aristocratic Parsi lady. It was a huge property, with a big bungalow and gardens and a guest house some distance away on the property, and she rented this guest house to us. That's where Baba and the women stayed. It was called Grafton. The men mandali stayed maybe a third of a mile away at Rosewood.

And Baidul would sit at the gate to the property, by the roadside, to see that no one entered and disturbed Baba. But you know Baidul's nature. If anyone happened to be walking by, Baidul would call out to them and ask them who they were and where they were going and how long they had lived there and how many were in their family and so forth and so on. In those days Satara was sparsely populated, very sparsely I should say, so there was not much traffic on the road. It was only every now and then that someone might pass, but even so, this was the perfect job for him. Someone else would have gotten bored, but the prospect of seeing new people and talking to them was always one that appealed to Baidul, so he didn't mind. He would sit there for hours, keeping watch.

And when someone did go by, when they stopped to answer his questions, Baidul would ask, "Why are you sniffling? Have you a cold?" Or, "Why is your voice hoarse? How long has it been like this?" And in that way he would get the symptoms out of the person and before long would be prescribing treatment of some sort.

Now it so happened that every day the aristocratic lady who owned the property would go out for a stroll and Baidul would call out to her, "Good morning," in Gujerati. And she would politely answer, "Good morning," back to him. Because this woman was a lady, an aristocrat, she would wear the clothes of someone in that stratum of society. She would wear dresses that were cut low in the back. And Baidul noticed that she had a patch of scaly skin on her back.

If anyone else had noticed, he no doubt would have kept quiet and pretended that he hadn't seen, but this was asking too much of Baidul. He had a different nature, as I have told you. So one day he calls out to this woman, "I have a cure for that which you have on your back." I don't know the word for it, not eczema, but the skin would get a hard sort of scaly crust over it, like the bark of a tree, and would flake off. There is a word for it, but I can't think of it. Anyway, Baidul called out to her that he could cure her.

"Are you a doctor?" the lady asked. "No, not exactly," Baidul replied, "but I have the cure for what you have."

"But I have been to so many doctors, specialists, and none of them can cure it; what makes you so certain that you can?" You see, she wasn't offended at Baidul's presumptuousness in mentioning her affliction. She had been suffering for a long time, and so when he said he could cure it, she was very interested.

"That may be," Baidul agreed, "but nonetheless I have something with me which I am sure will cure you. Anyway, what harm can it do you? Just take it in Meher Baba's name and you will get better."

Of course the lady had heard of Baba because she was the one renting the property to Him. And, as I said, for all of his coarseness and shabby clothes and all that, there was a certain bearing that Baidul had, so the lady agreed to try his medicine. I don't know what it was. Some sort of pill that he had concocted. He used to always carry around with him a few little bottles of pills, and whenever he found anyone suffering from anything he used to say, "Baba," and pop a pill down their throats.

So Baidul gave her some medicine and told her to take Baba's name and she would be cured. Every day she would go for a walk, and every day she would see Baidul. "Well," Baidul would ask, "are you feeling any relief yet? You must be feeling some relief now. Aren't you feeling that it is a little bit better?" This was Baidul's way with all his patients: psychological treatment, telling her that she was definitely getting better, and every day Baidul would prescribe some medicine or other and, taking Baba's name, would give her the pills. It went to such an extent with the mandali, that whenever Baidul would ask us whether we were getting better, fearing we would get more medicine if we said no, we would tell Baidul, "Yes, it is much better."

But in this lady's case, after some days, she did get better! She was so pleased, so happy that at last, after all this time, she was cured, that she asked Baidul if there was anything she could do for him.

Baidul said no, he was just pleased that he had been able to help. "But no, really, you must let me give you something," the lady insisted. Now, this was a very wealthy woman; Baidul could have asked for something expensive, but see Baidul's nature, it did not occur to him to do this. After all, what use did he have for any such thing, living with Baba?

Perhaps you've heard about the time Baidul was given a camera. One of Baba's lovers wanted to get some pictures of the *masts*, to keep a record. So naturally, since Baidul was the king of the *masts*, they gave a camera to him so he could take photos. It wasn't one of those fancy cameras that all of you have, with the giant lenses and fancy light meters, it was just an old box camera, a Brownie that Nariman or Meherjee or someone gave to Baidul so he could take some pictures of the *masts*.

So one day, I remember, we were driving in a car and Baidul had hung the camera up by its strap on a little hook that was there near the window. As we drove along, the camera would bump against the side of the car and make a noise. Baba turned around and gestured, "What's that noise?" "Just the camera, Baba," Baidul answered. "Whose camera is that?" Baba wanted to know, and Baidul explained the whole thing.

Baba did not seem pleased. "Who will pay for the film?" Baba asked. "Baba, I have already a roll of film in it." "But who will pay to develop the film?" This was the way Baba went on, and then He ordered, "Throw it out." So Baidul rolled down the window and threw the camera out as the car was moving. He never even got to take one photo with it.

But again, see Baidul's nature. He obeyed instantly and threw the camera away without arguing with Baba or trying to convince Baba that it would be useful. Baba said get rid of it, so he instantly rolled down the window and tossed it out. That was Baidul's great strength; he was a character, there is no doubt about it, but his love for Baba was something to behold.

So when this wealthy aristocratic lady offered to give Baidul something as a token of her gratitude for his curing her, Baidul said that he didn't want anything. "But if you really insist on giving me something," he added when he saw she was determined to repay him for his help in some fashion, "you may simply give me a certificate testifying to the fact that my medicine cured your condition."

"Certainly, most certainly I will do that," the lady replied and, sure enough, she had a little certificate written out on her letterhead which stated that it was owing to Dr. Baidul's treatment that her skin condition, which no other doctor had been able to treat at all, was entirely cured.

Baidul was overjoyed with his certificate and immediately lost no time in showing it to the mandali, especially Nilu and Donkin. They were always giving him a hard time about his practicing medicine, and now he had the opportunity to turn the tables on the two doctors. And, as you can imagine, given Baidul's nature, this was not done with great subtlety.

Donkin and Nilu went wild. They were afraid that someday something might happen to one of Baidul's patients and that it would all come on Baba. So when they discovered that Baidul had been treating the lady whose property we were renting, they caused quite a scene. Eventually the news of all this reached Baba. Baba agreed with Donkin and Nilu and ordered Baidul to stop practicing medicine at once.

But now, see how cleverly Baba designed things. If he had simply ordered Baidul to stop practicing his medicine, it would have pleased the doctors, Nilu and Donkin, but it would have hurt Baidul. So what Baba did was tell Baidul that he was not allowed to go outside the property to treat anyone, but he could treat anyone who came to him. This made everyone happy.

Donkin and Nilu knew that, at least in the future, no outsiders could be injured through Baidul's treatments, and Baidul still had the scope to practice on any of the mandali that were willing to submit to his ministrations, and so a sort of harmony was established. But, and this is where the beauty of Baba's order comes in, after curing the aristocratic lady, news of Baidul's prowess spread, and soon villagers were coming on their own to Baidul to have him treat them. This was entirely within the scope permitted him, as the villagers were coming to Baidul, he was not going outside to treat anyone.

So, although Baba's orders would seem to have prevented Baidul from continuing his practice, in fact it grew more than ever. Nilu and Donkin were not aware of this, but Baidul now had a booming business, as it were, treating everyone who came to him with his own peculiar brand of medicine.

One day, as Baidul was on watch duty, a peon came to him and asked where he could find the man responsible for curing Lady so-and-so. Baidul said he was the man, and the peon asked him if he would come and see the chief medical officer of the Government Hospital. Baidul got Baba's permission, and he went to see the doctor, who greeted him very cordially.

"Are you the one who treated Lady so-and-so?" "Yes," Baidul admitted. "But how did you do it? I saw her many times and hers was a hopeless case, I tell you." "That may be, but I have my own medicine and I take Baba's name and I have good success." "You have treated others as well?" "Oh yes, I have treated hundreds of people." "Would you be willing to come to my hospital and make rounds with me?"

You see, there was a hospital in town and it was filled with chronic cases. You can call it a repository for all those who couldn't be cured. And the chief medical officer hadn't been able to do anything for these people, and he knew it. So he thought maybe Baidul could help. Baidul said he would have to ask Baba's permission first.

Baidul asked Baba, and since it was the chief medical officer who suggested it, who came to Baidul and asked him to make rounds with him, Baba gave His permission. This, of course, only made Nilu and Donkin all the more outraged when they heard about it, but they couldn't say anything because Baba had told Baidul to do this.

So each day, Baidul and the CMO would make rounds in the Government Hospital. Baidul would wear his usual black coat with his pockets stuffed with his own special pills and they would walk from bed to bed. "This is a special doctor from Iran who has graciously consented to assist me," the CMO would say as he introduced Baidul to the patients. And Baidul's bearing was such, this is what I was trying to impress upon you, that everyone accepted him. His clothes may have been shabby, but he held himself with such dignity that no one objected to his being there. Baidul would ask the patient a few questions, reach into one of his four pockets, pull out a pill, take Baba's name, and toss it down the patient's throat. And, you won't believe it, but he effected cure after cure after cure. He emptied the hospital, you may say.

So one fine day– no, it was nighttime, I remember because it was Pendu's birthday, it must have been around 7:30 at night and we were all sitting around the room – there was Gustadji and Pendu and Donkin and Nilu; Murli Kale was there, I remember. We were all there remembering Pendu's birthday and grumbling because there were no sweets or special preparations and we couldn't celebrate it properly, when there was a knock at the door. A servant all dressed up in livery was there holding a tray in his hands that had some sort of gift resting on it. "Is the doctor here?" he asked. "I have a gift from the CMO for him."

Naturally Nilu got up and went to the servant, who said, "No, not you. Is there another doctor here?" So Don got up, but again the servant replied, "No sir, not you." "Then who do you want?" Don asked. The servant looked around the room and then he spotted Baidul sitting there and he said, "There, there's the doctor I want," and he went up to Baidul to give him the gift.

This was the last straw for Nilu and Donkin and gave Baidul the last laugh, as it were.

⬙ W H A T   S H O U L D   W E   D O ?

YOU WANT TO KNOW HOW YOU CAN KNOW what you should do? It's simple, haven't I told you all before, just do what Baba would want you to do? I know, I know, you say, "But what does Baba want us to do?" Or you say, "That's easy for you to say, you were with Baba,

Baba would tell you what to do." So many times I've tried to explain to you all that our life with Baba was something quite different. Yes, Baba told us to do certain things, but these were day-to-day orders concerning our work. Baba might tell someone to write a letter, another would have to go to town to buy something, another would be told to mop a floor or clean the latrine. These are the sort of orders Baba gave us.

Baba assigned specific tasks to each of us, but how we were to do them, and how we were to behave when we weren't doing them, that was up to our own judgment. And today, do you mean to say that Baba is telling me what I should be doing and He is not telling you? Brother, how many times do I have to say it, we are all in the same boat. We are no different from you. Our life with Baba, yes, I concede that that was different, but not in the way all of you imagine. There was something about Baba's presence, about being in His presence which words cannot describe. That was there. It fell to our lot to have the blessed good fortune to spend time in His company and that, I agree, was something unique, I should say. But do you mean to say that when Baba dropped His body we suddenly had no idea what to do?

No, we went on doing what we felt would please Baba because Baba had trained us not to follow specific orders, but to anticipate His wants, to learn to be sensitive to His moods, in short, to dance to His tune. People often tell me that to live with Baba you have to be this or you have to be that, but I always say the only thing you have to be is a good dancer, you have to learn to dance to His tune. And you learn how to do this by following the inner voice which we all have been blessed with. Baba once said that this inner voice is His voice. So, you see, you too have the opportunity to obey Baba's direct orders if you simply listen to this voice.

Sometimes when I say to someone, "Why do you do that? Is that the way to behave?" they will reply, "It was easy for you. If I were with Baba I could obey Him too, but it's not knowing what to do now that's so difficult." But I tell you there's no difference. We had the same temptations, the same difficulties you have. Do you think that because we were with Baba that we suddenly became blind and deaf to the world? Haven't I told you all about the time I became attracted to a woman in Baba's presence? Here I was, standing here, introducing people to Baba, when a beautiful woman came into the hall. I was struck by her beauty. I was captivated by it, you may say.

And Baba knew what was happening to me. Not because He could read my mind, but because I was so preoccupied with the woman's beauty that I lost my concentration on Baba's gestures. You see, I had to concentrate very hard to make sure that I could interpret correctly for Baba. It wasn't just a case of reading Baba's gestures, but I had to look at Baba's face at the same time to see what sort of expression He had. I had to know what sort of intonation to use to speak out Baba's words. It wasn't enough to merely throw out the words, I had to put the emphasis that Baba wanted. And this would be indicated by the expression on Baba's face, whether He was smiling, or looking stern, or serious or whatever. So it took tremendous concentration to do this properly. I had to put my whole mind into it. That is why I often tell people when they ask me about Baba's physical appearance that I never had the opportunity to look at Baba. I saw Him so many times, it is true, but I was never free to simply gaze at Baba, I was always too preoccupied with looking at His hands, looking at the board, and reading the expression on Baba's face to ever be able just to look at Baba to adore Him.

So when my mind got distracted by this woman's beauty, there was an interruption in the interpretation of Baba's gestures. Not a big one, but Baba could tell that something had happened to me. There's always a human explanation for Baba's behavior. It wasn't that Baba was reading our minds, it was that Baba was extraordinarily sensitive and perceptive. He was God. He is God, I should say, but His knowledge was always based on His perfect humanity, not His omniscience.

So Baba, seeing that something was wrong with me, quickly put two and two together. He could see that this young woman was exceedingly beautiful and He guessed what must have gone through my mind. The woman had had her chance to be introduced to Baba and was about to pass by when Baba reached out and took her face in His hands. He held her chin and turned her head slightly and gestured to me, "She's very beautiful, isn't she?" "Yes, Baba," I said, "she is." The woman got very embarrassed. She blushed at being held up to public scrutiny in this fashion, but Baba continued praising her beauty.

"But where will that beauty be in fifty years? She will be old and wrinkled then. The luster will have gone from her skin. Her back will be bent and she will walk with a shuffle. She won't have any teeth and her glossy black hair will be white and dull. Nobody will stop to give her a second glance. What you think of as beauty is just a matter of muscle and bone and flesh, and that will all change with time.

"Why get so enamored of something which is so transitory? It will fade, the greatest beauty in the world will fade like a flower, it has no permanence. But does this mean we shouldn't appreciate the beauty when we see it? No, we should. But we should remember that it was the Creator who created this beauty. We should not get attracted to the beauty for its own sake, but should be reminded of the One who created such beauty." Baba was saying this to everyone; my temptation provided Baba with the excuse to give everyone there this discourse. But what I am trying to bring home to you is that, right there, in Baba's presence, I was dazzled by this woman's beauty. Being in Baba's presence did not automatically make us immune to such things. Wherever you go, it is the same mind and the same heart. And as long as we have the same mind and the same heart, we will all have the same temptations, the same difficulties in obeying Baba.

To be honest, in this particular instance, Baba made it easy for me by bringing home to me, and to everyone else there, how fleeting this beauty is. Baba gave us the guideline that we don't have to turn our face away from worldly beauty. We have eyes, we should notice such beauty and we should appreciate it, but it should make us glorify Him and not the one who has been blessed with such beauty. But now, you too have the benefit of Baba's words. And even without them, you know this. We all know this. Who is there in this room who doesn't know that beauty fades with age? It is axiomatic. What saved me, what saved all of us with Baba, was not so much these explanations, or discourses, or any orders Baba gave, but our determination to be His.

That's all it is. We are no different from you. We had the same problems, the same difficulties, the same temptations and frustrations and desires, but we had one desire which, fortunately for us, was stronger than all other desires, and that was the desire, the determination to be His. Once you have this, you will be safe, and without it, even with Baba giving you direct orders, you will be lost.

Let me give you another example from my own life with Baba. Baba had retired to His room at night and was going to lie down. This happened here, at Meherazad. Baba was staying in what is now Pendu's room, and I was sitting outside under the tree that used to stand there. Baba told me not to disturb Him for any reason, not to enter His room unless He clapped and then I was supposed to enter immediately to see what He wanted. That was straightforward and there was no confusion in my mind about what I should or should not do. I stayed outside the room and waited for Baba's clap. But as I was sitting there, I felt something crawl over my leg. It was a snake and it was heading towards Baba's room.

I rushed forward and, with my flashlight I managed to pin the snake's tail just as it was disappearing in the crack under the door. Only the tail was left outside of Baba's room, but I held it down with my flashlight so it couldn't get completely inside. I knew that Baba's bed was just inside the door to the right, so that the snake was only inches from Baba's bed, so I couldn't let go of the snake. But in pinning the snake, I must have made some noise, because Baba clapped. Now what to do? Baba's order was that when He clapped I was to drop everything and rush into His room. Baba had not said, "When I clap, drop everything, unless you are holding a snake in your hands." You see, Baba had given me an order. A very specific order, yet even so, I felt that my first responsibility was to kill the snake.

Now what happens if you hold a snake by its tail? It curls around to attack whatever is holding it. I knew this. So I just stood there with my flashlight on its tail and it wriggled its body round and slithered back out the door. Mind you, the whole time this is happening, Baba is clapping. But I waited until the snake was outside Baba's room and then I took my *chappal* and beat it to death. Only then did I finally heed Baba's clap and go inside.

"Where have you been?" Baba demanded. "Didn't you hear me clap?" I explained to Baba what had happened. "You should have come. You should have let the snake go and come immediately. That was my order to you and you should have obeyed."

I did what I felt was right. I did what I felt I should do to protect Baba's body, even though this contradicted an order Baba had given me. And Baba told me I did the wrong thing. But if it were to happen again, I would do the same thing. The point I am trying to make is that even when we had direct orders, we still had to use our best judgment, we still had to examine our conscience and try to figure out what would please Baba. We were not always right, we made mistakes, but it was no different then than it is now.

You have to do your best. It is difficult, I know, but there is this consolation. Baba one time told us that although we would not necessarily know what would please Him, we would always know what would displease Him. So we have this built-in compass that points the way.

Baba stressed selfless service. And I've noticed that many Baba lovers are involved in service of some sort. But is this selfless service? Even in Baba's time people would come and tell Baba about the selfless service they were doing. But as soon as you are aware of having served another, then you haven't served them. I don't say don't do good deeds, but it is better not to do them than to dwell upon having done them and thereby tighten the bonds of attachment you have for those deeds.

Some people come here and they say they feel guilty because they are earning so much money. Why feel guilty if you are earning it? If you are not cheating anyone and are coming by it all honestly, why feel guilty? Did Baba say we should all be poor? There is nothing wrong with having money, as long as you know how to use it. Baba has said, "Really rich is he who knows how to spend his wealth well." But, on the other hand, it is not good to earn more and more money, to become preoccupied with earning money, with the idea that you are doing this only so that you will be able to do "Baba work" all the more. It is presumptuous on our part to think of ourselves doing "Baba work." It only feeds our ego.

Again and again it comes back to the same truth: live a normal life. All these questions, what is good, what is bad, should I do this, should I refrain from doing this, will it feed my ego if I do it, but if I don't, isn't that simply being selfish? And so on, ad infinitum. There is no end to questions, and there is no end to answers to these questions. Don't get involved in trying to figure it out. Meher Baba wants us to lead an ordinary, normal life, in accordance with how you are guided inwardly. Do what you feel intuitively prompted to do, but all the time this should be based on the solid foundation of being His.

Whatever you do, whatever you undertake, dedicate it to Him. Don't even think is it right, is it wrong, is it good or bad, is it a strength or a weakness. Just dedicate everything to Him. Gradually dishonesty will fade. Gradually other things will fade, and more and more unadulterated love and honesty will grow.

You cannot begin with a clean slate, as it were. You must begin from where you are. We all have weaknesses. But analyzing and dissecting our motives, trying to understand whether we are being prompted by selfishness or unselfishness will not eliminate our weaknesses. It will only drive us crazy and make it impossible for us to do anything. The only way to get rid of our selfishness is to go ahead and do something, but dedicate it to Him.

For example, say you decide to pick up junk from the street so that the streets will be kept clean and tidy. This is a "good," a "worthwhile" enterprise. So you start to do it. But you notice very quickly that there is a strong desire in you to have others notice you doing this. You find yourself thinking, "What a good example I am setting. I am not doing this for money. I am doing this for everyone's welfare, and people should be grateful to me." Perhaps, after a while, you even want to call attention to yourself, or you get angry when others don't notice what you are doing. You may even become resentful that you are not being properly appreciated. Or then again, your ego might fasten itself upon the fact that others are not noticing you. "See how spiritual I am, that I am doing this even though no one is noticing or praising me for it." In short, the ego is very much present.

But so what? The ego is always present. It is the nature of the ego to seize upon whatever we do and use it to strengthen itself. So what is the solution? The solution is to simply keep on doing what you are doing. After a while that initial zeal may be gone, you may lose your enthusiasm, but if you continue, even if it is mechanical on your part, the selfish aspects of your behavior, with time, will fade. Eventually you will completely forget about all those other considerations and you will find yourself picking up the junk from habit, solely from the desire to keep the streets clean. It honestly won't matter to you whether others notice you doing it or not. You won't expect them to praise you. And it won't bother you if they condemn you. The action, by being dedicated to Him, becomes purified.

◈ SUFFERING

YOU ASK WHY, IF GOD IS COMPASSIONATE AND LOVING, should there be suffering? This is a question many people have asked for centuries. And the answers the great ones have given over the years seem to suggest that suffering is necessary. That it is only through suffering that we are able to reach that place where suffering no longer exists. Of course, so much of our suffering is self-created. We bring it on ourselves, and much of that can be avoided, but as long as we are in a human body, we will suffer; that is what the human body means, it is a vehicle of suffering.

But no matter what I say, it will not satisfy you. It will just be throwing out words until you experience for yourself that this is all illusion, and that you are really infinite knowledge, power, and bliss. No matter how much you tell a man he is dreaming, he will not be able to believe you unless, and until, he wakes up. That is why Baba says that He has not come to teach us anything – what can you teach a dreaming man about the real world – He has come to awaken us. And, He assures us with His divine authority, that when we wake up, all of our suffering will be as if it has never been.

One time someone asked Baba why, if He could give us all Realization in an instant, and if this was our eventual goal, did He not do so? Baba replied by talking about the mountains, how beautiful the Himalayas are. "Have you seen them?" Baba asked. "Yes, Baba, they are indeed beautiful," the man replied. "What if, after seeing them, you became full of the urge to climb those mountains, to scale them yourself? And you set out and you struggled and sweated and slaved and finally you succeeded, you conquered them and were at last at rest on the very summit. How would you feel?" "Exhilarated, Baba. Exalted." "Wouldn't all of the effort that went into scaling the peaks seem worth it?" "Yes, Baba, definitely."

"But now," Baba asked, "what if, instead of climbing the mountains yourself, you got into a helicopter and were whisked to the very top in no time and you climbed out and had the same view. Would it feel the same?"

"No, Baba, there would be no sense of triumph, the exhilaration would not be there." Baba nodded and gestured, "That is why I do not simply take you to the heights of Realization; you would not have the same sort of appreciation, of satisfaction, as you would if you scaled the peak yourself."

That is what Baba told someone when he asked, but whatever it be, I don't want to get into a long philosophical discussion about suffering, I just wanted to tell you a story about one particular person's suffering, and if it is any help to you, if you feel it answers some questions about all suffering, fine. If not, disregard it and we'll go on to something else.

The story I want to tell you concerns a *sahavas* program Baba was giving at Meherabad. I think this was probably the '55 *sahavas* program but I am not sure. It doesn't matter. But it was a long program, that I remember. I used to drive Baba to Meherabad in the morning, and in the evening I would drive Baba back again to Meherazad, where He would spend the night. The program went on for days, so every day I would drive Baba to Meherabad and He would spend time with His lovers who had gathered there.

Now, in addition to all of His lovers, there were also workers there who saw to all the many things that had to be done to make such a large gathering possible. Pendu used to be in charge of such gatherings, but he would have people working under him to see to everything. And this particular *sahavas*, Pendu had engaged one of the boys from the village to be in charge of bringing Baba His meals every day. This was the same boy I was telling you about who used to bring Baba His cream every morning.

He was a local boy, and though he was working for Pendu, he also loved Baba and he tried his best to please Baba. The first day we arrived, he brought Baba a tray with some tea and some toast. I don't remember exactly what it was, but it had a few things on it for Baba, and Baba accepted it very graciously and gave the boy a loving look and that was that.

But I noticed that, after that, every time the boy came, Baba always found something wrong. The tea had spilled out of the cup onto the saucer, the cup wasn't clean, the food was cold. Every time there would be something wrong. And Baba wouldn't just point this out gently, Baba would take the boy to task. He would reprimand him in no uncertain terms, and make him feel that he had been negligent in his duty.

To me, however, seeing all of this as an observer, I felt that the boy really was trying his best. It did not seem to me that the boy was being negligent at all. In fact, I was struck by how conscientious the boy seemed. How hard he was trying to do everything perfectly to please Baba. But every day Baba would find fault in what he did, and every day He would reduce the boy to tears. Every day the boy would silently vow to do better, but the very next day, Baba again would find something wrong and would criticize the boy, "What are you doing? Don't you take any care at all? Can't you see that this cup is cracked and needs washing? Does someone have to show you how to do everything? Can't you put your heart into your work just a little?" On and on it would go, and the boy would cry, and I would feel for the boy, but I couldn't say anything. And if Baba turned to me and demanded, "Isn't this an outrage, have you ever seen such terrible service?" I would have to shake my head and agree with Baba. But then, when we were alone, I would say to Baba, "But Baba, it seems to me he is try-ing hard." And Baba would reply, "I know what I'm doing, be quiet."

So what could I say? Anytime I said anything, Baba would reply, "I know what I'm doing." Well, to make a long story short, the *sahavas* program finally ended. And Baba was going to go to Meherabad one last time to spend time with the workers. That was Baba's habit. After every large program, Baba would spare some time to spend with the workers who had missed having Baba's company during the programs. As we prepared to go that morning, Baba asked me, "How did the *sahavas* program go?" "It went well, Baba," I said. "Do you think My lovers were happy?" "Yes, Baba, you gave so much that I think all of Your lovers are happy, except one."

You see, we couldn't just come out and say, "Baba, why are You doing this?" or "I don't think you should do that, Baba." It didn't behoove our status as slaves to make such comments. But we had hearts, we had to act as if we had none so often, but we felt for people, and when the opportunity presented itself, when we were given a little scope, then we would, in a natural way, put in a little prick here or there to give vent to our feelings. So when Baba asked if I thought He had made everyone happy, I said, "Yes, Baba, everyone, but one of Your lovers You did not make happy."

Baba looked surprised. "Oh, which one?" "You made all Your lovers happy, Baba, but that boy from the village who was serving You every day, him You made most unhappy." Baba looked sad and gestured, "He really loves Me." "Yes, Baba, that's what I felt." I said, "so I could not understand why, when You were giving Your love to everyone else who came, You seemed to go out of Your way to make this one lover unhappy. Every day You made hundreds of Your lovers happy, but every day You made this one lover cry."

Baba shook His head. "What you say is only half true. Every day I gave My love to My lovers who had come to be with Me, but every day I also gave My love to that boy as well. But what is My gift of love? It is the sowing of love in your heart for Me. When anyone loves Me, it is because I have given him that love. That boy had already received My gift of love, and he loved Me. But if I had been pleased with his service every day, what would have happened? He would have been happy, but he would have been complacent in his love for Me. He would not have had the same urge each day to try to do better. Yes, I made him cry, but I made him cry in order to increase his love, care and concern for Me. That was the gift I was giving him."

And when we went to Meherabad that day, before all the other workers there, Baba called the boy over and embraced him and told him how pleased He had been with his service.

⚙ ANCHORED TO THE WORLD

THE OTHER DAY I WAS SAYING that we are all in the same boat. That we are no different from any of you. I was reminded of that this morning, because I was talking to someone and she said she was getting discouraged because after all these years of following Meher Baba, she was still full of weaknesses. "If we don't get any better, then what's the point?" I was asked. And I had to laugh. I hope the person didn't find me rude; I wasn't laughing at her, I was laughing because the exact same thing happened to those of us who stayed with Baba.

I wasn't looking for God when I came to Baba. I wasn't searching for spiritual answers, I was happy in the world. I had everything. Really, I tell you, my life was like a paradise. I had boy friends, I had girl friends, my family loved me, my friends loved me, I lived in a huge estate with a beautiful garden, I had the best of schooling, I had tutors, in short, I had everything I could have wanted, we lacked for nothing. And we gave that all up to come to Baba. How I came, that's a different story and one I've told many times before. Suffice it to say that my family and I left everything and joined Baba. He called us, and we came.

But, after leaving everything and coming to Him, what did we get in return? Not that we came with the idea of getting anything, not that we expected anything, but others would bring it up. They would say, "You've lived with Baba for so many years, and what have you gained?" And once they said this, we thought, "They're right. We have given up the world, we have given up everything, and we have spent years living by Baba's side, in intimate contact with the Avatar, the God-Man, and what have we gained? We don't seem to be any better than we were when we first came. In fact, sometimes it almost seems as if we have gotten worse."

And not only would such thoughts go through our minds, but we would even express them to Baba. Not that we would come to Baba and start complaining, but you know how it is, when you're unhappy about something there are many ways of bringing this to someone's attention without just blurting it out. There would be mumbling, little asides thrown out when Baba didn't appear to be listening, there would be frowns, a certain air of sullenness. You know how it is when a child doesn't get its way, it sulks, it has a long face; it doesn't have to say anything for you to know perfectly well that the child is unhappy. And that's what we were like, little children.

Baba let this go on for a while and then one day, while we were sitting with Him, He suddenly brought the subject up on His own. He gestured, "You have been living with Me all this time and you still have so many weaknesses. Why is this? You have left the world, you have left everything, you have truly renounced it all and are living right by My side, obeying My orders, and yet you seem no different from when you first joined Me. Why should this be?"

Of course we couldn't say anything, because these were the very questions we had been muttering under our breaths for the last so many weeks — months, you may say. But Baba continued, "It reminds me of a story." And He then proceeded to tell us the following story.

It seems there was a Master who was living with his mandali in a certain area of India. The life of the mandali, because they were living with a real Master, was comprised of mundane chores and activities. From dawn until night they were kept busy seeing to various things at the Master's behest. They did this without complaining and everything was fine.

But as the years passed, there began to be a certain lack of enthusiasm amongst the mandali. Not that they were unwilling to do what the Master said – they still obeyed Him one hundred percent – but some of the former zeal, the zip, was missing. Life seemed flat and uninspired. The Master noticed this and one day he called his mandali to him and said, "You all have been working very hard for years now without a break. What do you say we have a vacation?"

"A vacation? What sort of vacation?" the mandali asked, somewhat bewildered by the Master's suggestion. "A vacation," the Master explained. "Twenty-four hours when you are free to do whatever you like. No work of any kind except the duty to see to it that we enjoy ourselves to the fullest." "Enjoy ourselves to the fullest," one of the mandali grumbled, "that means we can have two servings of rice and dal instead of one." "No, no," the Master insisted. "I mean a real vacation. No restrictions of any sort on us in any way. We can eat whatever we wish, we can . . ."

"And drink?" "Yes, didn't I say no restrictions? We can have whatever you want. The only condition is that you all have to agree amongst yourselves what you most want to have and then we'll have that."

When the mandali realized that the Master was completely serious, they began to take an enthusiastic part in planning their twenty-four-hour vacation. After much discussion, it was decided that a sort of picnic outing would be ideal and all started making suggestions. Some were very concerned with the food and drink; others didn't care much about that but wanted to make sure that they had the picnic in nice surroundings. Others protested that they didn't want to have to go hiking for miles to find a nice spot. And so on and so forth.

The Master took an active part in all this and listened to the suggestions with great interest and occasionally made some of his own from time to time. Finally, it was decided that on a certain date, at the time of the full moon, three weeks from then, they would spend the day playing cards. They would have music and good food and drink and then, as evening approached, they would walk to the nearby river and get on the Master's boat that was kept there so they could get across to the other side to go into town for supplies and such, and spend the night rowing up and down the river under the moonlight, enjoying themselves with wine and chicken and patties and all manner of delicacies. Then, at dawn, they would return to shore, walk back to their quarters and so would end their glorious twenty-four-hour vacation.

One of the mandali was put in charge of the music, making sure the gramophone was in working order, selecting the records. Another was in charge of the food. Each mandali was deputed a specific duty.

Everyone got very excited at the prospect, and the Master always seemed to be looking forward to it. For the next several weeks, he would remind the mandali about it. If someone wasn't feeling well, he might say, "Better start taking some medication, you want to be well for our vacation." Or he would ask another, "Don't forget to order enough wine, we don't want to run short. Are you sure that will be enough patties? Do we have a big enough *bagulla* to carry everything? Will it stay hot if we have it cooked right before we leave, or should we make arrangements to cook on board the boat?"

In short, the Master oversaw every detail and kept everyone's interest in the upcoming vacation at a high pitch. The spirits of the mandali picked up once more, and once again there was a lot of good-natured teasing and liveliness predominating in the Master's camp. Before long, they were all so involved in their day-to-day duties that it was something of a surprise when the Master remarked one morning, "The moon will be full in two days."

Of course they hadn't forgotten about the vacation, but they had been so busy with their usual chores that they had lost track of the time. Now that they realized their vacation was coming up in only two days, they all became very excited.

And finally the day itself arrived. They got up and had a good breakfast, which, for the first time, they could enjoy at their leisure. There were no duties so they could relax and enjoy themselves. Some even slept in, but for the most part they were so eager for their vacation that they were up bright and early.

After baths and breakfast they went into Mandali Hall and began their card game with the Master. Meanwhile, the mandali member in charge of the music set up the gramophone, while those in charge of the food brought a basket of sweets into the hall so they could eat while playing cards. And so it went.

The Master was true to his word, and there had been no skimping. As the day wore on, there were cutlets and patties and kababs. Everything they had wanted was there, and in copious quantities. They had sherbet and iced drinks and, in the afternoon, they started opening the wine. Some of the mandali got out a harmonium and tablas and began to sing along with the records. In short, they all were enjoying themselves to the fullest, and the Master was in the midst of it all.

By the time evening came, they were already a bit tipsy as they walked down to the river and boarded the boat. Then a discussion cropped up. Should they keep some food for a meal later that night, or have their dinner then and there and then spend the night drifting down the river, under the stars and moon, listening to music and having more wine? It was decided they might as well finish the food then so they wouldn't have to be bothered about trying to serve it when it was dark. So they sat on the boat and had their dinner.

Now it was dark and the moon was rising over the horizon as they finished. It was truly a magical setting, to be on the river, to hear the water lapping against the sides of the boat, to see the moon peeking through the leaves of the trees which lined the bank and to see it rippling on the water itself. More wine was opened, and again the harmonium and the tablas were brought out and they began to sing *bhajans*. Meanwhile, other members of the mandali took turns at the oars and rowing the party downstream.

Everyone there was delighted with their vacation. After working hard for so long, even this little bit of a break was considered something great, and with the Master to keep them company, with the night and the river, the songs and the wine, no one had any complaints.

Just as dawn was breaking, the Master clapped and said it was time to return now. So, somewhat reluctantly, they set to turning the boat about and returning, when suddenly a commotion broke out. "What is it?" the Master asked. And what it was, was that now that it was beginning to be light and they had been brought out of their dreamy reverie by the Master's clap and ordered to return, they were astonished to see that they were still tied to the shore! They had never cast off the previous night, and the whole time they were rowing the boat and admiring the beautiful scenery, they were sitting in the same place without moving. They all had had the illusion of having spent the night drifting along the river with the Master, but in fact they hadn't gone anywhere.

Baba then turned to us and gestured, "And with all your talk of leaving the world behind, of having given up everything, in reality none of you has cast off your lines. You are still firmly anchored to the world."

When Baba said this, what could we say? All of our complaints vanished, because, of course, we knew it to be true. We had given up the world, we had left everything, in a sense that was true, but inwardly, we had to acknowledge the truth of Baba's statement, that we were still firmly anchored to the world. And still are. I admit it. If I were not firmly anchored to the world, I wouldn't be here now telling you this story. The fact that I am here, sitting in Mandali Hall, passing the time by talking to you goes to prove that I have not yet cast off my line.

IS THAT SO?

PART III

◬ A GOOD LAUGH FOR BABA

SOMETIMES PEOPLE ASK, "What was the most humorous event you can remember with Meher Baba?" There were many humorous incidents I can recall. And Baba's sense of humor was so perfect that even relatively minor things could become a source of great amusement for us all. But I happen to recall one time when Baba was greatly amused at something. Would you like to hear it?

It so happened that we were on a *mast* tour. On this particular occasion we were traveling by car, and I was driving. Baba sat beside me on the front seat. We were driving through a town and we were just on the outskirts when the crowd on the road became very dense. There were so many people in front of us that we could barely move.

I was concentrating on inching the car forward, trying to find a path through the sea of humanity, impatient because Baba was always in a hurry when we traveled, and I thought He would not be pleased at this unexpected delay. But as I was driving I suddenly became aware of Baba's body shaking. I could feel the vibrations of the car seat, and I glanced over and saw that Baba was laughing heartily.

In fact, more heartily than I had ever seen Him laugh before. Of course, Baba made no sound when He laughed, but He would go red in the face and His body would shake with the laughter contained inside. When I saw Baba in such a mood, I was so surprised that I asked Him why He was laughing. Baba pointed to the side of the road.

Up ahead, where Baba was pointing, was a shrine of some saintly person. That was why there were so many people on the road. Apparently it was the anniversary of this saintly person's death and so many people were coming to bow down and pay their respects.

"Yes, Baba," I said, not able to see what was so funny. Baba pointed to someone in the crowd. There were so many people it was hard for me to know whom Baba was pointing to. Baba gestured that the man was wearing a hat and a coat but there were many who were. "That man?" I asked as I described the man I thought Baba meant.

Baba shook His head, "No," and pointed again, "Oh, that man who's just about to bow at the shrine?" Baba nodded, "Yes," and then gestured, "He is bowing down to himself."

From this I understood that in a previous life, that man had been the saintly person that all had come to honor. But see the fun. The saintly person, in a new incarnation, had also come and was now bowing down in reverence to his own tomb! This fun in illusion was a great joke for Baba.

🕮 QUAKER OATS

IT SO HAPPENED THAT IN 1958, two of my cousins were to marry each other. Meher Baba told me to attend the wedding, which was unusual. As it turned out, this was the last wedding I ever attended, but I didn't know that at the time. I just thought it would be an outing for me and I was happy to go. Little did I know what was in store for me.

The time for the occasion was four o'clock. We were staying in Poona at Guruprasad at the time, and as I prepared to leave for the Zoroastrian temple where the wedding was to take place, Baba gestured, "Have a good time. Come back soon."

As I entered the large compound of the temple, I noticed that all the invited Baba lovers were grouped together. There were, in all, some six or seven hundred people there. Some were Baba lovers and some were from the Zoroastrian community and some were friends of the wedding party. Naturally I went to join the Baba group and, as I did so, someone came to me, hugged me and greeted me by saying, "It is good that you have come." I said, "Yes, Baba permitted me to come today." "Will you please come over here?" he asked and then led me to a group where a heated discussion seemed to be taking place.

At the center of the group was the editor of the local paper and he was saying, "What is this? I hear that Meher Baba is trying to draw people to him. His lovers go to people and say, 'You are a devotee of Rama? Forget about Him, He is dead and gone. Now you are to hold to Meher Baba.' So too the devotees of Krishna are weaned from Him and told to only follow Meher Baba. To devoted Christians, the Baba lovers say, 'This is all past history. Now you need Meher Baba. You have to believe in Him. He is the same Ancient One, come yet again.' Is it fact that Meher Baba says this? Why does He do this? Why does He try to wean others from their devotion?"

I said, "So this is the discussion? But we have come here for a wedding, not for a lecture or study group."

"But I would really like to know," the editor replied. And some of the Baba lovers from the local center said to me, "This has been going on for an hour or so. It is good that you have come. Did Baba say anything on this?"

"Whatever I have gathered," I replied, "I will tell you. The fact is that what you say is absolutely wrong. Meher Baba has never said such things, and He has never told His devotees to do so. He does not send people out to the marketplace, or ask them to visit people and tell them that they should forget their devotion to Krishna, or Rama, or Jesus, or Zoroaster, or anything of that sort. On the contrary, Baba says, 'You belittle Me if you do that. I am that same Ancient One. If others are devoted to Jesus, Rama, Krishna, and if you drag them out of their devotion and try to divert it to Me, you belittle Me in their devotion because I am that same Rama, Krishna, Jesus,' This is what I have heard from Meher Baba."

"Is that so?" the editor asked. "Then why are Baba people saying such things?"

"I don't know," I said. "But this is what I have gathered from Meher Baba. In their fervor, some Baba lovers may say something else, but this is what I have heard from Baba Himself."

The editor seemed very happy to hear this. So then I added something else, a little anecdote Baba had told us once and which possibly some of his devotees had misconstrued. "Are you familiar with Quaker Oats?" I asked the editor.

"Yes," he answered, "as a child we used to have them, and we still give them to our children."

"I, too, was given those oats as a child," I said. "So when Baba asked us if we knew the brand, we did. Baba went on to explain that the oats were good for children, as they gave nourishment and enabled the children to be strong and vigorous. He then told us the following story."

"Let's say," Baba began, "that a mother has been feeding her son with Quaker Oats. She has been doing this for years and is quite convinced that the oats are beneficial for her son. Well, one day, as she pours some out for her son's breakfast, she notices that she only has enough left for one more serving. It is just after the war and there is a scarcity of consumer goods, there is rationing. So the woman is very concerned. She doesn't know whether she will be able to find any more tins of Quaker Oats in the stores.

"After breakfast, she rushes down to the store, and to her great relief, she notices that there is one tin left on the shelves.

Immediately she goes over to get that precious last tin when the storekeeper appears and says, 'Don't take that tin.' The woman is startled and says, 'But I have to have this tin. I am almost out of Quaker Oats at home, so I need to get more.'

"'I understand that,' the storekeeper replied, 'but please don't take that tin.'

" 'But I'm your old customer,' the woman pleads, 'I have been shopping here for years. Surely you can sell that to me.'

"'I know you are my old customer, that is why I am asking you not to take that tin. I can sell it to you but . . .'

"'I will pay extra,' the woman suggests, thinking that this is what the storekeeper has been leading up to. 'I don't care what you charge; I have to have that tin.'

"'No, no, you don't understand. It is not a question of paying extra at all. You see, I have just received a new shipment of Quaker Oats. That is the last tin from my old stock. Let me get you a tin from my fresh stock.'

Baba then asked us, "What mother is there who would insist on buying the old stock when she could purchase a tin of the fresh new stock? I am the fresh stock," Baba added. "It is all Quaker Oats, the ingredients are the same, but I am the fresh stock."

◿ HELPING OTHERS

OVER AND OVER AGAIN Meher Baba talks about selfless service, about serving others, about making others happy at the cost of our own happiness. But helping others is not easy. You have to know how to help.

People come here to India and they see so many beggars. This raises all sorts of questions in their minds: "Should we give money to these people? Shouldn't we try to help them in some way?" and so on. By all means, give if you feel prompted to do so, but you should know how to give first. It is better to give than to receive, but you must know how to give. It is not just a question of reaching into your pocket and pulling out some money and giving it to a beggar.

Let's say you do that. And let's say the beggar has a wife and children and takes your money and spends it on drink and then goes home and beats his family. Who have you helped by giving him the money? Perhaps you've helped ease your conscience, but that's all. You haven't really helped at all.

That's one reason Meher Baba was always very particular when He sent us out to find the poor that we take pains to ascertain whether the people we were contacting were really poor. We just couldn't take any beggar off the street. We had to make sure those we were contacting needed help. And usually those who needed help the most were the most shy about asking for help.

Even now, if we are moved to try and help someone on our own, we know that Baba would want us to make sure that our help is given in an intelligent manner. That we don't just blindly give money but try to see that the help is given in a way which will truly help. But the issue, of course, goes even deeper than that. What do we mean by help? Who are we to help anyone? Really speaking we cannot help anyone unless and until we have become perfect ourselves. Only then can we be of real help to others. Anything else, short of that, is just lip sympathy. We cannot even help a crow get a morsel of food. To talk of helping is presumptuous. No sooner we feel that we have helped than we haven't.

Why is this? Because if we have the feeling that we are helping another, then our attitude binds us to that person. Suppose you are traveling to Ahmednagar and a beggar calls to you. You see how frail he looks, and you take out money and give it to him. Your mind then feels satisfied, and while you travel, you think, "I have given him money. It will be of help to him. It is good that I was of some help to that man."

But let us look at this for a moment. Who have you helped? You certainly haven't helped yourself, because those thoughts you are entertaining about having helped another only create a binding for you. The ego takes pride in having "helped," and this only reinforces the illusion of separateness. Whether you are bound with an iron chain or a gold chain, you are still bound.

Nor have you helped the beggar. Because when you give with any sort of motive, with any sort of consciousness of "I am helping," the other person is automatically made to feel obligated to you. It doesn't matter whether you say anything or not, it is more subtle than that, but where your ego is present, the other person's ego will react to it, and new binding *sanskaras* will result. This is one reason why people who receive charity so often dislike those who give it; unconsciously they are aware that they are being put under an obligation when they accept the charity.

Only when in serving others you feel you have helped yourself can it be said that you are beginning to be of "help" to them. Only when you can give with your right hand in such a way that your left hand does not know it, can you truly help. You must totally forget that you have given. Remember what Baba says about the "Real Gift"? Read the beginning of the "Real Gift" from *Life at Its Best*. What does it say?

"If a gift is to be real, then both the giver and receiver of the gift must forget the transaction completely. To forget completely would mean that the giver should not feel he has given, and the receiver should not know he has received. If the giver does not forget, then he has obligated the receiver, and if the receiver does not forget, he experiences a sense of obligation towards the giver."

When Baba says that things that are real are given and received in silence, part of what He is hinting at is the silence of total forgetfulness. But does this mean that we should forget about helping

278 ⚙ THAT'S HOW IT WAS

others? Not at all. But how to help them? When you see someone
suffering and you honestly feel for that person, when your heart
goes out to them, your genuine empathy, your feeling of their suffering is, in itself, a help. Baba said that. Baba told us that. That our very
impulse to help, to do something to alleviate the suffering, does, in
fact, on a spiritual level, help.

This doesn't mean that we can't try and help on a material
plane, but we should be aware of how to help so we can go about it
in the right way. But when we see what Baba says about giving help,
we realize we are helpless to give as He wants us to. And this only
intensifies our empathy with those who suffer, because we too feel
helpless before their plight, and this feeling helps them.

But until we become perfect, the only real way to help another
through material means is to give in the name of the Lord. This is the
avenue which is open to us. For when we give in His name, we will
remember Him, and the more we remember Him, the more we will
forget about ourselves and about our having given anything. If you
can do this, then by all means go on doing it and your life will be a
perpetual benefit to others. But notice the shift of emphasis, you are
no longer concentrating on "helping" others, but in serving others
you are helping to remember the Lord and to forget yourself. And
when we completely forget our self, we find our Self as God and then
we are able to truly render help to all humanity.

This reminds me of a story that Sam Kerawala told recently
which deserves to be told again. It seems that after the battle of
Kurukshetra, the five Pandava brothers performed a great sacrifice
and made very large gifts to the poor. All people expressed amazement at the greatness and richness of the sacrifice and said that such
a sacrifice the world had never seen before.

After the ceremony, there came a little mongoose. Half his
body was golden, the other half brown, and he began to roll on the
floor of the sacrificial hall. He said to those around, "You are all liars;
this was no sacrifice." "What!" they exclaimed. "You say this was no

sacrifice! Do you know how much money and how many jewels were poured out to the poor? Everyone became rich and happy. This was the most wonderful sacrifice any man ever performed."

But the mongoose said, "There was once a little village and in it there dwelt a poor Brahmin with his wife, his son, and his son's wife. They were very poor and lived on small gifts made to them for preaching and teaching. There came in that land a three-year famine, and the poor Brahmin suffered more than ever. At last, when the family had starved for days, the father brought home one morning a little barley flour which he had been fortunate enough to obtain. He divided it into four parts, one for each member of the family. They prepared it for their meal and, just as they were about to eat, there was a knock at the door.

"The father opened it and there stood a guest." Now, in India, a guest is a sacred person; he is as a god for the time being, and must be treated as such. "So the poor Brahmin said, 'Come in, sir, you are welcome.' He set before the guest his own portion of food, which the guest quickly ate. But instead of expressing thanks, the guest said, 'Oh sir, you have killed me. I have been starving for ten days and this tiny morsel of food has only increased my hunger.'

"Then the wife said to her husband, 'Give him my share,' but the husband said, 'No.' The wife, however, insisted, saying, 'Here is a poor man. It is our duty as householders to see that he is fed, and it is my duty as a wife to share with you your obligations. You have no more to offer him, so it is my duty to now offer my portion.' And so saying, she gave her share to the guest, who hungrily devoured it.

'I am still burning with hunger,' the guest complained after eating the wife's portion, so the son said, 'Take my portion also. It is the duty of a son to help his father to fulfill his obligations.' The guest ate the son's portion also but was still not satisfied. The son's wife then offered her share, and the guest ate this as well and, at last, felt satisfied. Blessing the family, the guest left the house.

"That night, all four in the family died of starvation. A few specks of the barley flour had fallen on the floor, and when I rolled my body on them, half of it became golden as you see. Since then I have been traveling all over the world, hoping to find another sacrifice like that, but nowhere have I found one. Nowhere else has the other half of my body been turned into gold. This is why I say this was no sacrifice."

◁▷ S A N S K A R A S

MOST OF THE TIME WHEN WE WERE WITH MEHER BABA, we did not talk about God, or spirituality. We talked about whatever work we were engaged in at the time, or we talked about commonplace things; it was not often that Baba was in the mood to give a discourse. But in the early years, Baba would repeatedly bring up the subject of *sanskaras*. He would explain how it was our *sanskaras* which kept us from realizing our oneness with God. Because of the emphasis Baba put on it, many in the mandali became convinced that their goal should be to get rid of their old *sanskaras* and avoid talking on any new ones. And Baba did not discourage them in this.

But as Baba explained more and more about the nature of *sanskaras*, the mandali were forced to adopt more and more desperate measures to avoid taking on more *sanskaras*. It reached the point where people were reluctant to sit near each other, or to have someone look at them while they were eating – it became almost impossible for anyone to do anything, and it was then that Baba told the following story.

There was a notorious bandit, a highwayman who not only robbed but also murdered people. This was how he supported himself and his family. In the course of earning his livelihood, he had killed ninety-nine people. It was at this point that he experienced a sudden and intense change of heart. He realized for the first time what terrible karma he was creating for himself through his occupation. Deeply tormented with the thoughts of his evil deeds and in great despair, he left his family and wandered the country seeking peace of mind.

He grew more and more desperate, constantly beseeching God to forgive him his sins. One day it so happened that he had the great good fortune to attract the attention of a Perfect Master. The Master asked him what was troubling him, and he told the Master his whole story, poured out his heart to him, and pleaded with him to help.

The Master agreed to do so and led the repentant man into the surrounding jungle. He took him to a certain spot and instructed him to sit there and repeat God's name. "Never leave this spot, except to beg for food or to attend calls of nature, and even then return to this exact spot immediately and stay here." The man was overjoyed that there was the possibility of escape from his karma and immediately began following the Master's instructions.

Well, years went by, and because the man was sincere in his quest for forgiveness, he continued to sit where his Master had instructed him and repeated God's name. In fact, he became lost in the repetition of God's name and gradually left the spot less and less. Although he seldom came into town now to beg for his food, the people there began to respect him and eventually to revere him for his dedication in repeating the Lord's name.

It so happened that the jungle where the man sat lay in between one town and another. The king decided that a path should be cut through the jungle so that his messengers could more speedily travel from one town to the other so, accordingly, townspeople were hired to cut a track through the jungle. When they reached the spot where the man sat, they stopped and waited until he had gone off to beg for food, and then they worked hurriedly so that the section would be done by the time he returned.

Absorbed in his repetition of God's name, when the man returned, he simply resumed his spot which was now in the middle of the king's highway. Years went by and the man continued to sit there. Travelers respected the man and would always edge to one side of the path so as not to disturb him when they passed. And always the man held to the repetition of his Beloved's name.

Now it so happened that one day the king sent a courier on this road to deliver a message to a neighboring king. The messenger was full of arrogance and self-importance, and he reacted to the spectacle of a man seated in the middle of the track, forcing him to slow down and go around. He reined in his steed and called out to the man, "Hey, you, are you blind? Move aside, and at once!"

The man was so absorbed in his repetition that he didn't even hear the messenger, who continued to yell at him and to abuse him. The messenger got so angry at the man's lack of response that he reached down and slashed the man across the cheek with his riding whip. In a flash, the highwayman's old skills reasserted themselves and instinctively he reached up, yanked the messenger from his horse, and throttled him, thus making him his one hundredth victim.

But the messenger happened to be carrying an order from the king for the execution of one hundred innocent people. Thus, the one hundred people the highwayman had killed were exactly balanced by the one hundred people he had inadvertently saved, and because his *sanskaras* of killing and saving were thus so balanced, he instantly became God-Realized.

This was the story Baba told us. But of course its point was not that it is okay to kill, but rather that balancing one's *sanskaras* is such an exceedingly subtle operation that there is no way one can hope to do it on one's own. The intricacies of the path are finer than the finest hair. So be natural, Baba urged. Simply do as I tell you to do, obey Me, and don't worry about *sanskaras*.

⚑ THE TEN CIRCLES

THIS REMINDS ME OF ANOTHER, SIMILAR SITUATION. In the early years, another theme Baba often brought up for discussion was the circles. Baba had explained that while a Perfect Master has a circle of twelve intimate disciples, the Avatar has ten circles of twelve disciples each. The mandali got intrigued with this explanation and began trying to figure out which of them belonged to which circle. There was much discussion and speculation amongst them as to their places in Baba's circles.

It was around this time that Pleader, who had come to Baba for God-Realization, was informed that he wasn't in any of the circles. Pleader took this very hard and eventually went to see Baba to complain. "Baba," he exclaimed, "the others say that I'm not in any of Your ten circles!"

"That's right," Baba agreed, "but would you like to know why not? It's because you are My chargeman." Well, naturally, Pleader was delighted to hear this. As chargeman he was Baba's spiritual heir and as such his position was more exalted than any in any of the circles. He was overjoyed to hear this and, after making him promise not to show it to anyone, Baba even gave him a piece of paper with the names of all of the members of the circles on it. I never saw it, but some of the early mandali told me that Pleader used to carry this in a small pouch which he wore at all times as a "seal" of his office.

When the others heard that Pleader was the chargeman, this was too much for them. "But, Baba" they protested, "how can he be your chargeman? He doesn't even love you! He just wants God-Realization." And others would say, "We've been with you all these years and now you make Pleader, who has only just come, your chargeman?" If anything, the bickering only got worse.

I think Baba must have been amused at all the petty squabbling. At any rate, Baba later explained when He was dictating *God Speaks* that the Avatar, unlike a Perfect Master, does not even have a chargeman.

I remember I joined Baba in '38 in the middle of the circles controversy. One day Baba asked me, "What do you do when you're not with me?" "I go listen to the others, Baba." "And what do they talk about?" "Circles, Baba. But not like any circles I've ever heard of. I've had geometry and trigonometry, but I can't make heads or tails of the kinds of circles they're talking about."

Baba laughed and then gestured, "Let it go in one ear and out the other." And before too long, the whole question of who was in what circle was totally forgotten. Baba always gave us room to be ourselves, which meant occasionally indulging in such silliness as worrying about what circle we were in, but eventually Baba always put things into perspective for us, and we came to realize that loving and obeying God was the only thing which has any real importance to it. Nothing else mattered.

⚜ I N T I M A C Y

I CAN RECALL TWO ESPECIALLY INTIMATE MOMENTS with Meher Baba. The one occurred one day at lunchtime. All the other mandali had gone to have their meal. It has been my habit for a long time to not have lunch, and this proved most useful in giving me more time for my work for Baba. On this particular occasion, Baba was sitting in the hall, and I was standing in my usual place, facing Him. Baba gestured for me to get a chair. So I did, and Baba gestured for me to put it near His chair.

I thought that Baba must be tired of sitting in His chair. This was after the accident and Baba's hip gave Him a lot of pain. I thought Baba wanted to switch chairs for a while. But when I went to help Baba, He gestured, "No, you sit." So I sat there, near Baba's chair, looking at Baba. Not a word was said. I just sat gazing at Baba and He looked at me.

Although I spent so much time with Baba, I almost never got the opportunity to simply stare at Him. I was always too busy. Even when I looked at Him, I usually had to concentrate so hard on His fingers, at first to read the board, then His gestures. I would look at His face to catch the vivid expressions which passed with incredible rapidity across it so I would know the right inflection to put on the words I was speaking out, but I never got the opportunity to simply stare at Baba this way.

So I sat in silence gazing at Baba, and He sat in silence staring at me. And I found cool tears streaking down my cheeks. Nothing was ever said, but that remains one of my treasured memories of my time with Baba.

Another intimate moment occurred when we were staying on the coast, south of Bombay. It was in 1949, after the Great Seclusion and before the New Life. Baba had wanted a short period of physical relaxation, and the women and I had gone with Him to a secluded house on the coast. One day we all went swimming. There was an isolated stretch of beach, and the women used that. Baba and I walked further down the beach and went swimming ourselves.

Of course when I say that, you understand that Baba didn't know swimming. But He enjoyed the waves, and I took Him out and held Him by the waist and showed Him how to paddle His arms, and in this fashion Baba had His swim. Afterwards He looked at me and gestured, "What about you? Wouldn't you like to have a swim?" Now, I had learned swimming as a youngster, but living with Baba I never got the chance to swim. So Baba told me to go out by myself and enjoy myself. And I did. I went out and had a good swim for a few minutes, and then Baba called me and I joined Him on the beach.

Baba instructed me to yell out to the women that we were leaving and that they should stay until they were ready to go and then should make their way back to the house by themselves. In the meantime, Baba wanted to walk into town to contact a *mast* who lived there. So I walked over to where the women were swimming and yelled out to them until I got their attention and then briefly relayed Baba's instructions. They signaled that they had heard and understood, and then I rejoined Baba and we began walking along the coast towards town.

We could see the town from the beach, but in between us was a stretch of backwater, a tidal area which formed a sort of creek we would have to cross. The alternative, however, was to walk a long way around the water and then approach the town. Baba suggested we take the short-cut. There were some boys, sons of the local fishermen, playing in the water. There were also a couple of canoes there, tree trunks, really, that had been crudely hollowed out to form primitive canoes, and Baba gestured that we could get in one of these and thus cross the water.

I didn't like the plan. I knew how tippy those canoes were, and the water was filthy. You know how backwaters are, they are full of filth, and I thought it was too dangerous to attempt crossing. But Baba gestured that it would be such a long walk the other way and the sun was so hot, it would be better to cross this way. He pointed to the boys, "See, they are crossing. They will ferry us across." "Baba," I replied, "we can't trust these urchins. And those boats are very unstable. They tip easily."

But Baba persisted and assured me that all would be well. So I went and spoke to the boys and asked if they could ferry us across. They said they would, but I said, "Now, no mischief," and impressed upon them how careful they had to be. I promised them a good tip if they would get us across safely, and they promised me they would, but I still had misgivings about the whole affair.

The boys brought the canoe to the shore and Baba got in first. As soon as He stepped in, the boat began to rock from side to side and I said, "See, Baba, it isn't safe. Let's walk." But Baba nimbly took a few steps and sat down, gesturing that it would be all right. I was carrying the small satchel I always had with me when I was traveling with Baba. It had two bottles of water in it, an extra pair of *chappals*, some soap, an alphabet board, a face cloth. A sort of emergency kit I carried because you never knew when a strap might break on one of Baba's sandals, or when we would be somewhere where there was no fresh water available. I stepped into the boat and again it rocked, but I also managed to sit down and then the boys pushed off into the water.

There were two boys taking us. The canoe wasn't big enough for them to sit in it with us. They swam alongside, one at the front, one at the back, and pushed us along. Everything was going fine until some of their playmates spotted them. This seemed too good an opportunity to pass up, so they swam over and began making mischief. One of the boys went underwater and pulled the legs of one of the boys who was guiding us, pulling him underwater. But as the boy went under, since he was holding on to the boat, he jerked the boat down as well and the unstable canoe quickly capsized, spilling both of us into the water.

We both went under and the water was so dirty, so murky, that I lost sight of Baba. I couldn't see anything, and I desperately began thrashing about with my arms, and fortunately, I felt Baba's arm. I grabbed it and, still holding the satchel, I sank to the bottom, clutching Baba to me. Baba didn't know swimming, and I knew it would be difficult pulling Baba to the surface, especially encumbered with the satchel, so I allowed us to sink to the bottom and then I gave a mighty push with my legs and we shot up to the top and broke through the surface.

I held Baba as best I could and I told Him to paddle as I had shown Him earlier, and then we began swimming for the far shore. Eventually, with great effort we touched the bank and walked up onto dry ground. We were both covered with filth. There was no one around, but we were on the outskirts of town, and I didn't want people to see Baba in that condition. So we walked a little towards town and found a nice secluded spot behind a dilapidated building, and I had Baba sit underneath a tree there. Baba told me to go back to our house and get some clean clothes for Him. I didn't want to leave Baba alone, but I had no choice. "Now stay here and don't move until I get back," I told Baba. He gestured that He would be all right and that I should go get the clothes.

So I left Baba and ran back to the house. It was the first time in many years that Baba had been left entirely by Himself. I ran all the way back to the house, going the long way, and found that the women had not returned yet and the door was locked. There was no time to waste, so I broke in through the bathroom, got some fresh clean clothes for Baba, and then ran all the way back to Baba. Baba was still sitting there, relaxed and happy under the tree.

I got some clean water and helped Baba bathe and change into his new clothes. Then Baba set off to contact the *mast*. As always, Baba contacted the *mast* in private and I waited a little distance away. When Baba clapped I came to Him, and I could tell right away that the contact had been a good one. Baba was never happier than when He had a good contact with a *mast*. He even walked differently. There was something triumphant about His stride after a successful *mast* contact. There was such radiance, such happiness about Him. So I was very happy, and we began walking back to the house.

After a while, Baba stopped and looked at me with a smile on

His face. "Look at yourself," He gestured, with a humorous twinkle in His eye. "You're a sight!" "I know," I answered, for it was true. Baba was now resplendent in fresh white clothes, but I looked like something out of the garbage heap. I stank from my dunking and there were still dried bits of algae and filth on my clothes, in my hair. "I told you, Baba, it was very dangerous to attempt that crossing." Baba nodded and we walked on.

After a while Baba stopped and conveyed, "It was fortunate you caught My hand." "Yes," I agreed. "It was most fortunate." Baba then added, "As you gave Me your helping hand today to help Me out of the filth of the creek, so a day will come when I will give you My hand to get you out of the filth of illusion."

◈ THE JEWELER AND THE CON-MAN

THIS IS A STORY THAT WAS TOLD TO US BY BABA HIMSELF. Of course, His was a unique way of telling it and I cannot do it justice, but this is the gist of the story as I have gathered it and which I am now sharing with you all.

There was once a diamond merchant who was very famous. He traveled widely to all the different courts and wealthy people round the country and even to other countries. He did not seek fame, he did not want to attract attention, so he traveled on foot, alone, like an ordinary man. To go on camel was not safe because wealthy merchants used camels, and thus a camel was a sure sign to a robber that its rider had something worth stealing. Yet the merchant became very famous, his fame spread far and wide, because he dealt only in the best of diamonds and gems and with great honesty and straightforwardness.

Equally famous for his skills was a certain con-man. He had heard of the diamond merchant and he determined to steal his gems. So he began watching the merchant, studying his habits. He found out the exact date that the merchant was leaving on his next journey and, that morning, he stood at the gates of the city.

As the gem merchant started to pass through the gates, the con-man greeted him and struck up a casual conversation. "You're traveling somewhere?" he asked the merchant. "Yes, I am going to such and such a city," the merchant replied. "What a wonderful coincidence! I am also going there and would be very happy if you would travel with me."

Now, the gem merchant did not know the con-man, nor did he know that the con-man knew he was carrying gems, so he said, "Certainly. Two is company, let us go together." And so the two began their journey.

As they traveled, the con-man used all of his arts to impress the merchant with his simplicity and faithfulness and honesty. And the merchant, for his part, made out that he was just an ordinary businessman. They chatted happily about this and that while they traveled, and the con-man was satisfied because he felt he had gained the confidence of the merchant and the merchant did not suspect that he was really after the gems.

They came to the first place of business, and each went off by himself after arranging to stay together in the inn that night. After the evening meal, they said good night and lay down to sleep. The merchant quickly fell asleep and began snoring, but the con-man stayed awake, eager to achieve his goal of the gems. Slowly, quietly, he rose from his bed and began looking for the jewels. He carefully went through the merchant's belongings, taking care to put everything back exactly as he had found it so that there was no evidence of his search, but he did not find any gems. He went through the merchant's coat, searched under the bed, and finally, in desperation, silently slid his hand under the merchant's pillow. But nothing was there.

The next morning they resumed their journey, the con-man continuing to be a lively companion, and the merchant and he were happy together. But that night, again the con-man stayed awake and again searched for the jewels, but once again he could not find any. The days passed and each night, as the merchant slept soundly, the con-man searched for the jewels. He explored every nook and cranny of the merchant's clothing, bedding, and satchel. He was constantly awake, tormented by the fact that he could not find the jewels. He knew they must be there, somewhere, but he could not find them. He got so that he knew almost every stitch in the merchant's clothing, and he even began to worry that maybe he had made a mistake and his companion was not a gem merchant after all.

By the end of the journey the con-man was exhausted. He had had no sleep, as every night was spent searching for the merchant's gems, while the merchant was in good spirits. He had successfully conducted his business and was now preparing to return home. "Thank you for traveling with me," he said to the con-man. "You have given me good company and made my journey more pleasant. I wish you every success as you continue your journey."

This was too much for the con-man, and he was unable to contain himself any longer and he fell at the merchant's feet. "Today, I become your disciple," he announced. "Do you know who I am?"

"You are my good companion."

"Yes, I have been your companion, but I had a motive in being that. When I joined you, I knew you were the famous gem merchant. But you did not know me, the famous con-man of the country. Yet today I become your disciple."

"What makes you say that?" the merchant asked, surprised at this strange confession.

"For three months we have been traveling together, and every day you do your business, and every night you lie down and sleep soundly without giving a thought to the treasure you carry with you. Every day, I too did my business, trying to cheat people, and every night I sought to cheat you by searching for your packet of gems so I could take them. But I never found them. Where are they? Where did you hide the gems? I looked everywhere, but I never found any. Today, I take an oath that I am your disciple. I am a con-man of great renown and I acknowledge that you have defeated me. I surrender to you. Now please, tell me your secret. Where did you hide the gems?"

The gem merchant laughed. "But how will that help you now?"

"It will help me. Please, I take a vow that I won't deceive you. I have been deceiving you this whole journey, but not now. Please, tell me where you hid them."

"You say you searched everywhere and everything, but did you search your own satchel? Each evening before retiring, I slipped the treasure in your own satchel, knowing well that should you want to rob me, you would not look there for the gems."

So Meher Baba reminded us that He, the treasure, was to be found within ourselves; not to be found searching outside ourselves, but to be found within ourselves, within our own hearts.

⚙ MAD AND *MAST*

I DON'T REMEMBER THE EXACT OCCASION, but there must have been some talk about the difference between mad and *mast*. Baba explained that there are some people who are mad, completely mad, some who are only mad after God, and there is a world of difference between them. Then Baba announced that He would tell us another story of Bahlul, the king who became mad after God, and who gave up his throne and left his palace in search of God.

Bahlul spent most of his time in seclusion in a remote isolated spot, but occasionally he would appear in the streets of the capital. Apart from his having been the king and leaving his kingdom, Bahlul had become famous because eventually people realized that he had not just left his kingdom, but had left it for God. At first they thought him mad, but, in time, they came to see that he had won God's favor and he was therefore much honored and respected.

Now it so happened that one day Bahlul was wandering in the streets of the capital when a merchant passed him, then stopped and said, "Oh wise Bahlul, please tell me, guide me, as to what type of business I should do this season?" Without stopping, Bahlul replied as he walked, "Store sugar." The merchant took this as a divinely inspired tip and began to buy all the sugar he could.

He used whatever money he had to buy sugar and eventually was able to acquire a good supply. As it turned out, the season was a poor one for sugar cane, the crop was ruined, and the price of sugar rose heavenward, as you say. The merchant made a fortune. He was very happy and, now that he felt that he had the whole world in his hand, he turned his back on God. Such is the nature of man. When man is helpless he turns towards Him, and when he is not, he turns his back on Him.

After some years, it so happened that Bahlul and the merchant again passed each other in the street. But this time the merchant had many friends with him and was intoxicated with his wealth. In front of his friends the merchant was not about to say, "Oh wise Bahlul," and instead, showing off he said, "Oh mad Bahlul, what business should I do this season?" Bahlul answered as promptly as before, "Buy onions."

The merchant did so. He put all his wealth into onions and

loaded up warehouse after warehouse with onions. As time passed, however, the onions began to go bad. At first, only a few, but finally the entire crop was affected and all the onions had to be destroyed. Almost overnight the merchant had become a pauper. His friends deserted him, and to anyone who would listen, the merchant ranted and raved that it was all the fault of that "madman, Bahlul."

Some time later, Bahlul came into the city again and the merchant sought him out. "Hey, Bahlul," he cried. "You've ruined me." "What have I done?" Bahlul asked. "Don't you know? I asked you what business to go into and I followed your advice and stored onions and lost everything." "But why did you do that?" Bahlul asked. "Don't you know that a madman's advice should not be taken? How can sound advice come from a madman?"

When the merchant called Bahlul "wise," the advice given was sound, but when he called him "mad," Bahlul had advised the merchant accordingly.

This was a story Baba told us.

◁▷ PALACES IN HEAVEN

ONCE MEHER BABA ASKED US TO DEFINE GOD. We made various attempts, but Baba was not satisfied. He said when the question "What is God?" is asked, the answer is "What is not God?" He then continued, "Age after age, from time immemorial, you have been trying to find God, but you do not do so. Only one in tens of millions somehow or other realizes God. But why do so many sincerely, wholeheartedly strive to find Him and so few do so? If God exists, and He does, then why cannot we find Him?"

Baba answered His own question, "It is foolishness on the part of man seeking to find Him. How can anybody find something which is never lost? God eternally is. Stop your search to find Him, lose yourself and you will realize Him." That is what Baba taught us. No sooner do you lose yourself than you realize God: not by search, but by effacing ourselves; not by asserting ourselves that we are the ones searching for God, positively asserting ourselves, but by losing ourselves in His love.

Lose yourselves by remembering Him more. We here are the same; now we remember Him. When He was physically with us, His presence was such that there was no room for remembering. Our presence here now with each other is quite different from being in His presence. There is ample scope in my mind now in your presence to remember aspects of His life, but His presence was so overwhelming that it enfolded everything. There was nothing left for us. Nothing. Not even a thought that we should remember Him.

But, mind you, thoughts were there — yet they were thoughts revolving around Baba, His welfare, His comfort, His work. We were disturbed with thoughts, you could say, but all that was really no disturbance because it was a game where we spent the whole time associating ourselves with Him, heading towards Him.

Meditation has to serve but one purpose: to steady the mind of the aspirant, to make him think less of his life and eventually to make him forget totally his false self. If, on the contrary, meditation were to remind one of himself or herself, the purpose of meditation would not be served. One has to beware of getting attached to any form of meditation. Meditation then becomes a ritual.

Meher Baba has revealed to those who lived with Him that true meditation is to remember Him constantly in our everyday life. Whether we eat or drink, feast or fast, attend to nature's call or take a bath, whether we are busy in an office of business, or relaxing in bed, whether we are meditating in a place or making merry, sleeping or moving about, we should always think of Him. We should have Him always as our constant companion. There is no better way of meditation than this. This is spontaneous meditation. There is no set time, place, posture, principle, or austerity for this meditation where every breath is dedicated to His remembrance.

Eventually we totally forget ourselves, and act and live in His Grace alone. Blessed indeed is such a life.

This is what we have gathered about meditation. After all, what is meditation? There was no scope for meditation while we lived with Him. Meditation needs some separateness. All the time, everything involved us with His presence. We could not meditate on Him when He was never absent.

One day Baba asked the mandali which was more difficult, to give one's life or to lose one's life. Each was asked, and then one said, "Of course losing, Baba." Baba answered, "You are right. What is there in giving one's life? It is comparatively easy to give your life for a great cause, for honor, religion, or country. Even cowards may, under a sudden impulse, give up their lives. But to lose one's life is to die every moment. Every second one suffers the poignant pain of ego elimination, to culminate in utter resignation to the Divine Will."

In Baba's presence there was the continuous process of losing your life to Him. We were alive and at the same time dead. We had to be, as it were, not there, our self not present, alive and yet, in His presence, not allow our selves to be present.

Of course, there were times when we would take Meher Baba for granted. And yes, there also were times when we would be despondent, and so Baba, in His compassion, told us this story. Baba did not refer to our moods or our attitude towards Him, He simply asked if we would like to hear a story, and then began.

There was a certain emperor in Persia and his kingdom was extensive. He ruled justly, peace prevailed, and his subjects were very happy. One day, without warning, the emperor took to the streets of his capital, instead of sitting on his throne. For a time the courtiers and officials took it as a capricious whim, but days went by and the emperor continued to wander the streets. They began to suspect that there might be something wrong.

They went to the emperor and requested him, "Sire, will you not now return to your palace?" But he replied, "Palace? Which palace? Here is my palace, here is the dome of my palace," he said, pointing to the sky. They realized that something had gone wrong with the emperor's mind, and they were unanimous in their decision that his younger brother and wife should now be king and queen.

The emperor continued to wander the city, begging for food, indifferent to his condition. He was familiarly known now as Bahlul, and soon people forgot that he had been the king and he became the butt of jokes – an object of teasing by the children. Yet the wife of Bahlul's brother, now the queen, always maintained a soft spot in her heart for Bahlul, and never even considered that he had gone mad. Rather she respected him as somebody who has been struck with love for God.

The years passed. One day the queen was strolling along the seashore with her ladies, and she came upon Bahlul playing in the sand. He was sitting there, scraping the sand with his hands into a huge pile, and then brushing it aside and then scooping it back together again, chuckling all the while to himself. The queen was drawn to talk to him.

"Bahlul, do you recognize me? Do you know who I am?" "Sure, I know who you are. You're the empress of this kingdom." "What are you doing, Bahlul?" "Oh, I am very busy. I am building castles in heaven for those who deserve them." "You are building castles here?" "Yes." "Do I deserve one, Bahlul?" Bahlul looked at her a moment. "Yes," he replied. "Will you build a castle for me, then?" she asked. "Sure, but you will have to pay the price." "What price?" He pointed to a necklace of precious gems she was wearing.

Although it was an heirloom given to her by her husband, she promptly took it off and gave it to Bahlul. He looked at it and then, laughing as he did so, he tore it apart and threw the gems, one by one, into the ocean. After throwing the last jewel into the sea he looked up at her and said, "Now go. It is all built in heaven for you. Go."

The empress and her maidens went happily off and enjoyed themselves on the seashore. It never occurred to the empress that she might have done something wrong. To her it was just a simple necklace of precious stones, that's all. She forgot all about it. But after a few days the king noticed that his wife never wore the necklace anymore. "Don't you like the necklace I gave you?" he asked her. Suddenly she remembered the incident. "Yes, I liked it, but I gave it away," she confessed. "Gave it away! To whom did you give it?" "Bahlul." "What! Bahlul, that madman!" "Yes, he asked for it," and then she related the whole episode.

The king was furious, and a good verbal fight ensued between the two. He tried to impress upon her that she had no right to give the necklace away, for it did not really belong to her but to the kingdom, it was part of the royal treasure. She replied that one little necklace didn't matter. And besides, what harm had been done? Bahlul, after all, was the real emperor, and he was entitled to the necklace if he wanted it.

As you can imagine, one word led to another and eventually they became so angry with each other that they stopped speaking entirely. Days passed and neither would say a word to the other. Until one night, in the middle of the night, the king had a terrible nightmare. He tossed and turned on the bed, moaning and calling out loudly, obviously in great distress. Even though she was still upset, the queen's heart melted and she took pity on her husband and woke him up.

He came to with a groan, drenched in perspiration. "Oh, what a nightmare I had!" he exclaimed. He sat up in bed and recounted the dream.

I still remember Baba's gestures so clearly as He went into all these details. The way He would turn His face aside to show how the queen refused to talk to her husband. The way He acted out the part of the husband, having a nightmare and then waking up trembling. I can't give you that vivid picture that Baba gave us of all this, but I am giving you the gist of the story, the food, as it were, without the spice, the seasoning.

"I dreamt," the kind said, "that I was dead and was led through the gates of heaven. For some time I wandered around, enjoying the sights, but gradually I began to grow tired and longed for a place to settle down. There were many castles all around, but each time I tried to enter one, the owner would stop me, saying, 'This is mine.' Everywhere, every time, it was the same story. I grew more and more tired. I became despondent and finally even frightened. When would I ever find my own place?

"I came to yet another castle, but as I approached, a window opened on the first floor and I saw your face. I was so relieved that at last I had found my own castle. I rushed up to enter, but as I did you stopped me and said, 'Here, no one can share a castle. Each to his or her own.' And so I was left outside once more. The experience was terrifying. Nowhere was there any place for me. And that's when you woke me."

The queen comforted the king, helped him to calm down, but then reminded him. "Do you remember what happened last week?" She couldn't resist giving him a little dig. "You were so furious with me that I had given the necklace to Bahlul when he offered to build me a castle in heaven in exchange, but now see!" But the king was too miserable for the queen to enjoy chiding him so, she relented and suggested, "Why don't you ask Bahlul to build you a castle in heaven? He is your brother, surely he will do it for you if you ask."

The king readily assented, and Bahlul was brought to the palace. He was given a good scrubbing and then adorned with royal clothes and made to sit opposite the throne of the king. "Bahlul, do you recognize me and this lady here?" the king asked. "Yes," Bahlul replied, "you are my brother. You are also the king and the lady is your wife, the queen." "Do you recall, Bahlul, that you said to her on the seashore that you were building castles in heaven for those who deserved them?" "Yes, that is what I do all the time." "Do I not deserve a castle in heaven? Would you not build one for me?" "Surely I can do that, but you will have to pay the price," Bahlul answered.

The king immediately took a string of pearls from around his neck and handed it to Bahlul. Bahlul merely looked at the king and said, "What else?" The king added another necklace but again Bahlul replied, "What else?" The king added more and more jewelry but Bahlul remained unimpressed and kept asking, "What else?" The king took of all his jewels, and even sent to the royal treasury for some particularly fine pieces, but Bahlul's answer never varied, "What else?"

Finally the king burst out, "Why is it that my wife gave you only one necklace and you built a castle for her, but with me you keep asking for more and more, saying, 'What else?' Why is it that my castle costs so much more than her castle?" Bahlul laughed, "Even if you were to offer me the whole of your kingdom, it would not be enough."

The king was dismayed. "Why? What have I done?" "You know the worth of a castle in heaven," Bahlul replied. "On the seashore your wife just took my word that I was building castles in heaven. Whatever price I asked, she gave immediately. She did not bargain, nor did she give in a calculated manner. But here, now, with you, there is bargaining, because you know the worth of what you're seeking. Even if you were to part with your whole kingdom it would not be enough. Part with the kingdom and with yourself, only then may you have your own castle in heaven."

Here Baba finished the story and commented, "Do you all realize what this story means? When I first asked you to leave everything and stay with Me and obey My orders, you did so without knowing what you were doing. You were drawn to do so, and you willingly parted with all the things you had in the world in order to be by My side and to live with Me. But you did not know the worth of what you were doing.

"But there will come a time when the world will know of Me, who I am. Then, even if the emperors of the world want to part with their kingdoms to be with Me, that price will be too little. The little price you paid to be by My side was enough for Me, because you did it not knowing what you were doing, but trustingly relied on My word without giving a second thought to what you would gain by doing so."

That is why we sometimes tell all of you who come how lucky you are to come now when it is only love which brings you. The day will come when the whole world will recognize Baba. When people will be flocking here. When so many will come to Baba, but why will they come? They will come in a spirit of bargaining, to get something out of it. Even those who are sincere will have a hard time keeping such motives out of their mind, for at that time it will be to one's advantage to come to Baba, it will be good for one's business, for one's reputation to have it be known that one follows Baba. So it is good now to be able to come to Baba when the only incentive is love.

⚛ EARLY YEARS

IN THE EARLY YEARS, not long before leaving Upasni Maharaj, Meher Baba used to work in His father's shop. On the footpath outside the shop, there dwelt an old man who was an opium addict. The footpath was his home.

He would sleep there during the day and then, about sunset, he would wake up. In the night he acted as a watchman for the shops, and in the early hours of the morning he would go from shop to shop to awaken the shopkeepers for their morning prayers. They would give him tea and a little money. That was how he earned his livelihood.

With the money he earned he would buy opium, and the effect of the opium was such that he would sleep the remainder of the day. But he slept standing up. He would fall asleep while standing and, as he slept, he gradually would bend over more and more until he was doubled over. He slept the whole day that way. Then, in the evening, as he woke, he would slowly straighten out.

Now, this old man had faith in Merwan (as Meher Baba was then called). He came to Him one day and said, "Merwan, I have some savings. I would like You to keep the money with You for my funeral. I don't trust anyone else, but I know You will see to my body. Otherwise, when I die just standing here on the footpath, I will be dragged away like a dog and thrown somewhere. I would like a decent funeral, so please keep this money and see to it for me."

Merwan had a soft spot in His heart for this man, who was a good man, despite his weakness of opium addiction, and so He agreed to the old man's request.

When the old man died, Baba kept His word. He saw to the man's funeral, and He did so on the most wonderful scale. He invited everyone possible, hired numbers of different bands: brass bands, Indian bands, dancers, entertainers. There was a huge procession of people, with music, dancing, noise, gaiety. The city thought it must be a marriage party, not a funeral procession, so splendid were the arrangements. For days it was the talk of the town.

So it was that Baba, the God-Man, fulfilled His promise to the old opium addict and gave him a right royal funeral farewell. But nobody knew at the time that Baba was the God-Man; to them He was only Merwan Seth, a prosperous businessman helping his father in his father's old age.

This reminds me of another story of Baba's early years. This was one He told Himself. In 1956 when Baba was in Myrtle Beach, there was a large gathering held one day at the Barn. I don't remember exactly what was being discussed, but it was probably something to do with the nature of illusion, for I know that to illustrate the illusory nature of heaven and hell, Baba told the following anecdote.

He said that one day, while a young boy, He saw several men coming down the footpath, obviously intoxicated. One of the men was commenting rather loudly and enthusiastically that he was in heaven at the moment. He felt so good that he was in heaven.

As they were walking, they came on a small puddle that blocked their way. But since they were intoxicated, the puddle took on the dimensions of a huge obstacle. They stopped and surveyed the seemingly endless expanse of water. After much deliberation, the man who had declared that he was in heaven decided to leap over the water. Thinking he had to jump a considerable distance, the man made a mighty leap. He sailed over the puddle with ease, but in the process of landing, managed to break his ankle.

So there he lay, clutching his foot and moaning in pain. "Oh, I'm in hell," he cried. "I'm in hell."

Of course, the man was never in heaven or hell. It was only his inebriated state which made him think so. But I remember Baba using that incident from His youth to explain the point years later while in America.

◁▷ A   B E N E F I C I A R Y

THIS INCIDENT OCCURRED during Meher Baba's first tour of Andhra in 1953. We were staying outside of town in a government rest house. The mandali were staying in a nearby building, and at the time I am speaking of, only Baba and I were in His quarters. It was early in the morning, before the *darshan* program began for the day, and Baba wanted a bath. I looked everywhere but I couldn't find a big vessel for heating the water in. I also couldn't find any kindling to make a fire. There was nothing in or around the house. Baba was waiting, and I was becoming desperate. How could I arrange for Baba's bath?

I found some old newspaper or something of that sort and I lit it on fire and held a small *lota* of water over it, hoping to get a little water at least lukewarm for Baba in this way. Obviously this was not a very efficient method, but I didn't know what else I could do. Just at the moment, as I was trying to warm the water, I saw someone approaching from a distance. It was a man with a big brass pot on his head. I went out to intercept him since it was my duty to see that no one disturbed Baba's privacy. I stopped him and asked him, "Why have you come here? What do you want?"

It turned out that the man was one of the local Baba lovers. He was a poor man, and not at all a prominent man in the community or in the work connected with Baba. I asked him what he wanted, and he explained that he had brought some hot water for Baba in case He wanted to bathe. I was wonderstruck at how timely this man's intervention was – Baba had just expressed the wish to have a bath, and within minutes this man appeared with a large pot of hot water on his head. Not only that, but I learned later, he had come from quite a distance carrying the water. No one had told him to bring the water, he had just felt prompted to do it. I thanked the man sincerely, as you can imagine, since this hot water had come just at the right moment, and I sent him home and then immediately took the hot water in to Baba so He could have His bath.

At the time I was deeply impressed that the man had brought hot water at precisely the moment Baba wanted it, but I thanked the man and forgot all about it. Years later, when the Avatar Meher Baba Trust Deed was being drawn up, Baba named the various beneficiaries of the Trust. Most of these people were well known to us. They were those who had surrendered their all to Baba, and, being perfect in every detail, Baba was now seeing to their needs in the event that He dropped His body. As I said, we were familiar with all of the beneficiaries, but suddenly Baba added a name that surprised us. It was the name of this poor man from Andhra who had brought the hot water so many years before. He was one of only two Baba lovers from all of Andhra to be named as beneficiaries. See how the Lord is. I had thanked the man and forgotten all about him. Baba hadn't thanked the man because He had been inside the house when the hot water had arrived, but He hadn't forgotten him. Man thanks and forgets. The Lord does not always thank, but remembers.

⚜ THE SECRET

MEHER BABA WOULD OFTEN TELL US that there was no smoke visible with the fire of real love. "The flame of love within does not even give out smoke for others to see," He would tell us. "When you love Me, you burn within yourself and yet appear cheerful with a broad smile. You bear the pangs of separation calmly and quietly. Even the sigh of the pang of separation is an insult to love."

Baba would tell us to, "Attend to all your duties and you can still love Baba by dedicating all good and bad to Me. Just as you dress your body with clothes and then forget all about the dress you wear during the day, similarly dress your soul with thoughts of Baba, and Baba will then be with you all the time, even without your paying any further attention."

The following story reveals something of the nature of this love, this real love that Baba was talking about. It concerns a king and a queen who lived and ruled some centuries ago. They loved each other and were happy together. The king was a wise and just ruler, and under his reign his kingdom flourished and peace and prosperity prevailed over the land. The king's subjects were happy and content. In short, it was almost an idyllic existence, but there was one flaw, one minor thing which prevented the queen from being completely happy. And this was that the king seemed to have no interest in God. It was not that he was against God. He had no objection to his subjects or his wife worshipping God as they saw fit, it was just that he never seemed to join in.

Because the king was such a good man, whose life seemed naturally full of virtue, it was not immediately apparent that he was not a believer. But, as time passed, the queen noticed that the king always seemed to make some excuse so as not to attend religious festivals. And while she understood that the nature of his duties prevented him from worshipping as regularly as she did, she realized after a while that not only had she never seen him perform worship, she had never even heard him utter a short prayer. In fact, she had never heard him mention the Lord's name.

Now, the queen was very religious, and when she began to suspect that her husband, the king, was not a lover of God, she became quite upset. She did her best to persuade him to join her in her devotions, but no matter how hard she tried, he always found some excuse for not joining her. This was the only thing that marred her happiness, but as time passed, it became a bigger and bigger thing. She would think to herself, "My husband is such a good man, his kingdom is peaceful and prosperous, his subjects are happy. Just think how perfect life would be if only he loved God." Or sometimes she would fear that because her husband did not love God, the peace and prosperity might be taken away, and the more she thought about it, the more upset she got.

She began to lose interest in her duties as queen. Uppermost in her mind was the thought that her husband was not loving God as he should. Next to that, nothing else seemed important. She began to spend more and more time by herself in the palace temple. Her eyes, which previously had always twinkled with delight, now seemed pensive and brooding. Her constant cheerful smile was replaced with a frown. The king observed this and was sad, but whenever he asked the queen what was wrong, she would say, "Nothing." For she had already told the king she would like it if he worshipped regularly, and he had said, "Ask me for anything but that."

And so life went on, with the king attending to his duties, and the queen becoming more and more despondent and withdrawn.

Now, it so happened that one day, after this had been going on for some time, the king awoke and went to the ramparts of his palace. This was his usual custom. He would rise early and climb up to the ramparts and look out over his kingdom. He used to feel that he could ascertain the pulse of his kingdom from there. He had learned to tell, just from standing there in the early morning hours, whether there was any unhappiness or sorrow in the kingdom that needed attending to.

Well, this morning, as he looked out, he was surprised to see that many people were already awake and were busy putting up decorations. Others were cleaning the streets or their homes, and it was clear that some sort of major celebration was about to take place. This puzzled the king. He couldn't think of any festival or celebration which took place at that time of year. He called his prime minister and asked him what was happening.

"It is the queen's order, sire," the prime minister replied. "The queen's order?" "Yes, sire. Early this morning she got up and ordered that today was to be a day of rejoicing. She instructed that orders were to be given to all your subjects that today was a day of celebration."

"Why did she do that?" "I don't know, sire. She didn't say."

The king was puzzled at this. Of course it was in the queen's power to pass such an order, but as she had taken no interest in the affairs of the kingdom for some time, this was a complete mystery to the king. Why had she suddenly given such an order? He went to see the queen, who greeted him in her best clothes and with a dazzling smile on her face.

"Did you order this celebration?" the king asked. "Yes," the queen admitted. "Why? What is it? What has happened that has made you so happy all of a sudden?"

"Oh my king," the queen exclaimed, "I am so happy. At last what I have been praying for all these years has come true. Last night, while you were sleeping, you turned over and I heard you utter the name of God. That is why I have ordered this celebration."

"What!" exclaimed the king, "has my Beloved escaped from my heart and passed through my lips!" And with that the king sighed and dropped dead.

⚶ HONOLULU ENCOUNTER

THIS INCIDENT NOW RETURNS TO ME. We were on our way from the U.S. to Australia with the God-Man, Meher Baba. So this must have been in 1956 or 1958, I don't remember which year it was. We had stopped at the Honolulu Airport and we had to wait for several hours before our plane left for Australia.

There were four mandali sitting with Baba watching the crowds go past. Half an hour passed. We had already been sitting for hours on the flight to Hawaii, and we knew we had hours more of sitting on the flight to Australia. So Adi suggested we get up and take a walk along a path outside the building and close to the beach. But Baba gestured, "No, stay put."

We sat for a while longer and then again a walk was suggested, but Baba insisted we just sit there. Not long after this a well-dressed couple, not Hawaiians, approached Baba. They bowed respectfully and asked Baba if He would care to come to their house for some food and rest. Baba seemed very pleased at this invitation and expressed His happiness, but conveyed that we would have to catch our plane shortly, so we could not accompany them. With this, the couple departed.

"Aha," we thought. "This is why Baba insisted on sitting here.

He wanted to have that contact with the couple. But now we can go for a stroll." It wasn't just our own comfort we were thinking of; we knew that Baba would also be forced to sit for a long time on the plane, and we felt it would be good for Him to be able to stretch His legs for a while. Again the idea of a walk was suggested to Baba, but, to our surprise, Baba insisted on remaining where He was. There was nothing we could do but continue to sit there with Him. After a while the couple returned. This time they were carrying large brown bags, filled with food for Baba and the four of us. Baba accepted the food in a warm and loving way, gently stroking their cheeks and blessing them. The couple then left with no further words. As soon as they left, Baba stood up and gestured, "Now let's go for a walk," although by then there was only a little time left before our flight.

Then we felt we knew why Baba had inconvenienced Himself – for the sake of His lovers. But the odd thing was that we never heard from the couple again. We would ask people, "Have you ever heard of a couple of Baba lovers in Hawaii?" But no one else had ever heard of them either. To this day, we have no idea who those two people were.

◈ A N G E R

DO YOU ALL WANT TO KNOW what Meher Baba said about anger? Do you all get angry? Once I remember a man confessed to Baba, saying, "I don't know what to do. I get so upset at times and just burst into anger." Baba conveyed, "Why are you so upset about that? I don't want stones around Me, I want human beings. It is natural that you feel anger."

Meher Baba went on to explain that while it is natural for a human being to feel anger, it is also expected of a human being to control the expression of that anger; to flare up, go into tantrums and kick out – that is not good. If someone bullies you, you should hiss at them so they do not take advantage of you, but hissing does not mean striking the person. Express anger, while not actually becoming angry within.

This distinction can sometimes be difficult to understand but Baba gave us a very good story to bring the point home to us. Would you like to hear it?

This story is from the time of Muhammad the Prophet. Muhammad had a disciple named Ali. Ali was very strong, but he also had a very short temper. At the time of Muhammad, there were only a few followers at the beginning, but many thousands were opposed. The faithful few were persecuted by the many who not only taunted and ridiculed them but, in some cases, even molested them.

This would infuriate Ali and he would thrash anybody who molested one who believed in Muhammad. Over time, the persecution became less because all were afraid of Ali's wrath. It was well known that there was no one as strong as Ali, no one able to oppose him physically, and if Ali ever came to hear that someone had attacked a believer, he would be sure to beat the offender. Thus, due to Ali's strength and courage, life for the small community of believers became more bearable. But at the same time, Ali's ego started to become inflated. He began to take pride in his great strength.

Muhammad, observing this and holding Ali very dear, called Ali to him. "I am well pleased with your strength," he said, "and with the way you put that strength to use in defending and protecting the flock. That is good. But you must remember that you should not strike or kill anyone in anger. So now I give you an order: maintain your image as protector of the flock and, when necessary, strike others to protect the weak and defenseless, but never strike anyone in anger."

Ali, of course, accepted this order and determined to do his best to obey it. But he soon discovered that it was almost impossible for him to protect others without getting angry. And because he was so determined to obey his Lord, Muhammad, he began to avoid those situations where he might be tempted to strike an adversary. At first, Ali's renown was enough to keep the opponents at bay. But over time, the adversaries noticed that Ali did not seem as vigorous in his defense of the community of believers. Someone would throw a stone at one of them, and Ali would let him get away with it. The adversaries slowly began to become more aggressive. They discovered that while Ali might yell at them and threaten them, he seemed to be reluctant to actually raise his hand against them as he used to. They wondered at this strange meekness of Ali's and eventually they found out about Muhammad's order.

There was jubilation in the camp of the adversaries when they heard of Muhammad's order because they knew that now there was no one to oppose them. They decided to take full advantage of this situation, and they immediately issued a challenge to Muhammad's followers. They suggested that each camp send forth a champion to do battle on their behalf to settle the dispute once and for all. "If our champion wins, then we know that Muhammad is false and you must all stop following him. If your champion wins, then we will bow our heads, believe, and keep faith in Muhammad."

Muhammad's followers had no choice but to accept the challenge, but they were in an uproar. Who was going to be their champion? Apart from Ali, there was no one in their camp who could face any champion the adversaries would put forward. Without Ali, they were doomed to certain defeat. The only solution was to convince Ali to fight. They all went and begged Ali to fight, but he replied, "The Prophet has bound me not to strike in anger, and without anger how will I be able to fight to the finish? I do not want to break an order of the Prophet." "But it is a matter of defense of the faith. We must have someone meet their challenge." And eventually they persuaded Ali to be their champion.

Now, the day of the fight had been fixed and, as was the custom, it was to be a fight to the finish. The day arrived and it was like a giant fair. All had come from both camps to watch the fight. When the adversaries saw Ali, they became frightened. They had never expected Ali to fight, and they knew their champion didn't have a chance against Ali. Still, they couldn't back out now, they had to go through with it.

The fight began, and because of his superior strength, Ali was able not only to defend himself, but to disarm his opponent and to pin him beneath him without ever getting angry. Ali sat on his adversary's chest and prepared to thrust his dagger into him and slay him. The adversary knew all was lost, but he remembered Muhammad's order, and so he resolved to make Ali lose his temper – only then might he be saved. He spat on Ali, but Ali just smiled and raised his dagger high.

So he began abusing Muhammad, using the foulest possible language. Ali lost his temper at once and, in his anger, almost plunged his dagger into the man's throat, but at the last moment he checked himself and stabbed the dagger into the ground. The Prophet had said he must not strike another in anger, so Ali stood up and walked away from the fight. It meant that he lost, but obeying Muhammad's order was more important to him than winning or losing.

Seeing this, the crowds were astonished. They could scarcely believe it was happening. "If Ali is willing to lose everything just to obey an order from Muhammad, then Muhammad must not be an ordinary man. Only the Prophet could command such unusual respect and obedience." This was what those in the crowd thought, and they were so impressed with what they saw that instead of holding Muhammad's followers to the terms of the challenge, they, on their own, became followers.

It was not really a combat between two champions, but a combat within Ali between his physical strength and his tendency to become angry. He became angry in his fight, but he obeyed his Lord, he did not express his anger. He overcame that weakness. A battle can be fought and won, Baba has told us, but the moment you experience anger, beware, for you become bound.

There is another good illustration of the nature of anger given by the Perfect Master Ramakrishna. He was from the area around Calcutta, and the Ganges flowed by his ashram. One day Ramakrishna was standing by the river with his disciples and, pointing to a boat moving upstream, he gave this parable on anger.

The boatman rowing upstream sees another boat, far off, moving downstream towards him. He shouts, "Hey, watch out! Change your course, look out!" But the boat continues to rush towards him and, as it comes closer, he sees that there is nobody in the boat. Now is he going to continue to yell at the boat to change its course? No, he is simply going to change his own course and steer around the onrushing boat. Ramakrishna said, "The one who is angry is like a boat which has no captain. When you see there is no captain, steer away. Don't stand and throw words back at the boat in anger. Steer aside. Otherwise neither boat has a captain."

Our nature is such that we do get angry. But then try to control it, try to curb it. It is natural to feel anger, but try to control its expression. Try to be rational and calm and not create hatred. If you should lose your temper and yell at someone, then immediately afterwards go up to that person and apologize. We have a tendency when we get mad at someone, or there has been some sort of argument, to turn away from that person, to have nothing to do with them even after we have calmed down. But that is not good. Even if you have closed the door, at least keep a window open. Otherwise the whole relationship stagnates and a stench arises.

The best thing is to go to the other and say, "Forgive me." Even if it was the other who lost their temper first, even knowing this, say, "Please forgive me. I lost my temper. Forgive me, it is not good that I have done that."

Perhaps it is your father. Beg of him to forgive you. Sure enough, he will melt like butter. The important thing is that one has to become childlike. One has to become small. One has to efface oneself. We have crossed the animal stage of asserting ourselves and we are humans now. So now we have come to the stage of effacement. But it is not natural to remain always humble, loving and kind towards all. Every so often we will burst out. This is natural. Even if we try to control the expression of our anger, invariably the time will come when we will not be able to do so and we will burst out. But when we have calmed down, we should go and beg pardon. That is what is expected of a human being.

⚛ P L E A S I N G   B A B A

SOMETIMES WHEN PEOPLE HEAR ABOUT OUR LIFE with Meher Baba, they express amazement that we could have put up with all the hardships. But it is only now, looking back at it, that we can say, "Yes, that was a hardship," for at the time it did not seem that way to us. We were too busy simply living our lives to be aware of whether it was a hardship or not. We didn't think in those terms.

Of course, I can't speak for everyone. There were some who came to Baba, no doubt, wanting God-Realization, or powers or such, and invariably they found the life with Baba to be a hardship. It was not to their liking, and so, sooner or later, they left. But you see, those of us whom Baba permitted to stay with Him, we didn't come for anything, we only came for Baba.

When Baba told us to do something, we didn't stop to figure out what we were going to get out of it, we simply did it. We weren't there to get anything, but simply to try to please Baba. That was the key for us. We tried to see to Baba's pleasure. This meant not only doing whatever He told us, but, more importantly, trying to anticipate His needs.

And invariably when talking about this, someone will ask me, "Well, did you ever please Baba?" And that reminds me of a funny story. One time there were four or five of us traveling with Baba—it must have been a *mast* tour – and we arrived at a dak bungalow late one afternoon to discover that it was completely full. The manager, however, knew us, as we had often stayed there and so he said to me, "I can't give you any rooms, but you can give me all your luggage and I'll lock it up for you so it will be safe, and you can sleep here in the courtyard."

We had all slept out in the open often enough that that was no hardship, and I went and explained to Baba what the manager had suggested. Baba thought it was a good idea, so I spread Baba's bedding roll out in the compound and put mine next to it so I could be near Baba in case He wanted anything during the night. The other mandali put their bedding some distance away so their snores would not disturb Baba.

It was dark now, and, as usual during our travels, we were all exhausted, and everyone soon settled down to sleep while I sat on my bedding keeping watch. As I sat there, I saw a comet in the sky. It had a long tail and was moving very slowly across the sky. I was fascinated by it and my first thought was, "Oh, Baba would love to see this." But Baba was sound asleep. I sat there and watched the comet and thought how much Baba would enjoy it. Finally I said softly, "Baba, Baba, Baba."

Baba sat up and gestured, "What is it?" "There's a comet, Baba," I said excitedly, and pointed it out in the sky. Baba turned His head, looked at the comet for a fraction of a second, and then lay down immediately and pulled the covers over His head with a decisive gesture as if to say, "What's there to see in that?" I still remember the way Baba pulled the covers up as He went back to sleep – as if only an idiot would have awakened Him to look at the comet.

But we did occasionally please Baba. I remember one time some years later, when Baba had given me some work to do. There was a Baba family who lived around two hours from where we were staying with Baba. There had been a family dispute and Baba sent me to try and effect a reconciliation and, at the same time, get the various family members to agree to certain conditions He had laid out. Baba wanted me, in fact, to get them to sign their names to an agreement He had drawn up.

I knew this would be a difficult thing and would take a long time, as family disputes are always complicated and take a great deal of patience to resolve. So I left around six in the morning on a bicycle. As I left, Baba repeated to me several times that I should be sure to return by six that evening.

I got to the family's house at eight in the morning and called everyone together and immediately began trying to thrash things out. As I had expected, progress was very slow. As it neared four o'clock that evening, I knew I would have to be leaving soon if I were to make it back to Baba by six. But, on the other hand, I knew that this particular work was very important to Baba, and I felt that matters were slowly but surely resolving themselves. I decided to stay on.

And sure enough, although it took another two hours, a little before six I got the family members to agree to everything and to sign the agreements Baba wanted. As I was cycling back I was very happy. I knew that Baba would be pleased with the outcome of the day's work. Of course, I also knew that I was going to be late, but I felt that compared to getting the signatures that Baba wanted, it wasn't so important. Better to arrive late with the work accomplished to Baba's satisfaction than return on time with nothing to show for it. So, as I said, as I cycled back I was sure that Baba would be very happy, and I was happy that I had accomplished this.

But when I got back I found that Baba had already retired for the night, and one of the mandali told me very brusquely that Baba was furious with me. "Don't you know Baba said to return at six? What do you mean by coming back so late? If you aren't going to obey Baba, you aren't good for anything. You might as well go eat shit."

Hearing this, I went to my room and took off my sweaty clothes and then, wearing only my shorts, walked across the compound to where our latrine was. In those days, our latrine consisted of a raised platform with a hole in it. Under the hole was a small open metal box which collected our deposits. The box had a handle on it, and the sweeper would bend down and grab the handle and slide the box out from under the latrine so he could empty it, clean it, and then return it. I now went into the latrine and began to bend over to reach down through the hole to the box. After all, if Baba had left word that I should eat shit, it behooved me to obey, and so I was bending over to scoop some out with my finger when another one of the mandali called, "Eruch, Baba wants to see you immediately."

"Just a moment, I said, "I have something I have to do first."

"No, now," the other replied. "Baba said you were to drop whatever you're doing and come at once."

And so I went to see Baba, who immediately began taking me to task for returning so late. As Baba reprimanded me, all the feeling I had had cycling back that I deserved praise for accomplishing something was washed away. And there was nothing I could say, for I had broken Baba's orders. He had reminded me Himself to come back by six, and I hadn't done it.

Baba seemed very angry with me, but after a while as I stood there without saying anything, Baba asked me why I was so late, and then I explained how difficult the negotiations had been but how I had finally gotten all to agree and to sign the papers Baba had given me. Baba's face lit up. "You did?" He gestured. And when I gave Him the completed forms, Baba clapped me on the back and then embraced me and I knew at that moment, I had truly pleased Baba.

But see how compassionate Baba is. If He had complimented me on a job well done when I had first returned, I would have accepted it merely as my due, as something I deserved, something I had earned. Not only would this have been reinforcing a lurking egoism, but by feeling I merited Baba's praise, it would have been tarnished when received. Whenever Baba expressed His pleasure, it was always clear that it was coming as a gift from Him, that it wasn't something our behavior had forced.

You see, sometimes our love for Baba could be a burden to Him. We wanted to help Him, to serve Him, so He permitted us to do so. But think how awkward it must have been for Him to have us help Him wash His hands, for example. Someone holding the soap, someone holding a towel, as if Baba were not perfectly capable of washing His hands by Himself. He was capable, but He let Himself be inconvenienced so we could have the opportunity of thinking we served Him. This was one of the ways our love was a burden to Him.

People would sometimes sing for Baba who had no musical talent, no voice, no ear, only the desire to please Baba. And Baba would listen to this screeching with a rapt smile on His face, swaying to the music as if it were the most delightful sound in creation. Baba was responding not to the singer's voice, but to the love which prompted the song. Being the slave of the love of His lovers (you know that Baba often stressed that He is not the slave of His lovers; He is the Lord of His lovers, but He is the slave of the love of His lovers), Baba would respond with great love by expressing His delight and enjoyment.

Every day it seems I am made aware of some new way in which our love for Baba forced Him to suffer. In the ordinary course of events, knowing this, some of us might have begun to suspect that when Baba expressed His pleasure with us, that then too He was only doing so in response to our wish to please Him. And this would have been a weight on our hearts. But Baba's pleasure was always a pure gift when He gave it. We always felt that Baba was indeed genuinely pleased, and He always saw to it that we knew it wasn't in response to our needs that He was expressing that pleasure.

HUMILIATION AND GLORIFICATION

MEHER BABA WOULD TELL US, NOW AND THEN, about His humiliation, and of His glorification which would follow the humiliation. But we all missed the point. We thought that the New Life period was His period of humiliation, a time when there were many humiliations – such as gossiping and backbiting, being mistaken for bandits or political agitators, and so on – and that His period of glorification was the period following the New Life, when hundreds of thousands throughout the country hailed Him as the Ancient One. We felt that was His glorification.

We had led a life of great seclusion, and we were quite unprepared for the spectacle, time and again, of a sea of humanity adoring and worshipping Him as the Highest of the High, the Expected One. I remember one occasion that gave me a fright. We were in the South of India, considered the stronghold of orthodoxy. Brahmins, the highest class, have greater power here and control the minds and hearts of the people. Baba was seated on a dais, I was with Him, and we were surrounded by an immense sea of humanity. It would have been impossible to escape if the mob had turned against us, or even if they had all sought to hug and kiss Baba.

As usual on these occasions, the locally prominent people, the leaders in each profession and branch of life, gave Baba welcoming speeches. Then Baba conveyed, "Remain seated. I am going to bow down to you. Do not think that this bowing down is for you individually; I bow down to your love for Me. That will avoid any necessity for each of you to physically bow down to Me."

After doing this, Baba had me read out a short message which He had prepared beforehand. On such occasions, Baba might give a further impromptu message. This is what now happened, and that stands out in my memory of my life with Baba.

For the first time in public, Baba conveyed, "I am the Ancient One." And he went on, "I am the same Ancient One come once again in your midst. My message is of love. I have come now, this time in your midst, to do away with all rites, rituals and ceremonies."

As I read out Baba's gestures, I became frightened. I was aware of all those people, that sea of humanity surrounding us, and I knew that many of them were Brahmins whose power rested in those very rites, rituals, and ceremonies. I shuddered to think what might happen next.

But Baba seemed to know what was going through my mind, for He pulled a corner of my coat and gestured, "Don't be frightened," and He gave me a reassuring smile. So I continued reading out Baba's gestures, and because I was speaking out Baba's words for Him, I made them as forceful as I could, as was appropriate for the message, and when I was finished giving this message, there was pin-drop silence.

And then, as if with one voice, there was a mighty ovation as all hailed Baba. We thought such occasions, when thousands hailed and accepted Baba, were part of His glorification. But Baba smiled when I suggested this and gestured, "This is not My glorification. Wait, wait, My humiliation will come, then My manifestation, and My glorification. This enthusiasm and emotion that you witness is not My glorification."

I wondered then, "What will be His humiliation? What form will it take?"

Our life with Baba continued, and there were no signs of a new form of humiliation. But once in a while a report would come to us that ones close to Baba had gone to see and pay homage to a saint or guru, or such ones were expressing thoughts of seeing a saint or a master. Out of the blue, not in connection with His humiliation, Baba told us a story.

A woman, judged guilty of adultery, was sentenced to death. Before her execution, according to law, she was placed in the middle of the market square, and everyone who passed was required to throw something at her. The passers-by threw stones, or filth, or rubbish at her, but the woman never cried out in complaint or pain. She made no sign that she was being hurt; she just stood there, radiant and beautiful as ever.

Now, it so happened that her daughter passed by and, by law, she was also required to throw something at her mother. She had no heart to throw a rock or anything like that, so she bought a rose, and as she passed she threw the flower. When the flower hit her, the mother shrieked, although no filth or stone until then had caused her pain. She had not uttered a single sound, but the light touch of a rose thrown by her daughter brought forth a cry from the depths of her being.

"How much that mother felt the accusation when it came from her own daughter!" Baba gestured. "How much more," he continued, "will I feel, when My own ones hurt me, even if with the petal of a rose!"

We said that we did not understand, and Baba continued, "Although you all have been with Me for many years, if, in your ambition to aspire more and more for the truth, you seek the blessings of a saint – that action will be the equivalent of the daughter throwing a rose at the mother."

Later, when we did hear about some close lovers of Baba coming to Baba meetings irregularly and instead going to see this master or that saint, we would feel sad because this had saddened Baba. We would ask ourselves, "How can this be when Baba repeatedly stressed that He is the root of all creation, and that once we have contacted Him there is no need to go anywhere else?"

Isn't this an aspect of His humiliation or a foreboding of it? There is no need to go even to the Perfect Masters, because Baba is the eternal Perfect Master of all Perfect Masters.

☙ PIR FAZL SHAH

MEHER BABA DID NOT LIKE US TO SIT IDLY while traveling by train. And one of the reasons for this was so that people around us were diverted from noticing Baba. Without that diversion, people would naturally have been drawn to Him, to stare at Him, and would even have intruded themselves on Him. Even in disguise, Baba's presence was such that people could not help being drawn to Him.

I remember one time when we were traveling by train and there was an Englishwoman in our compartment. She kept looking at Baba, and, after a while, Baba gestured to me to ask her if there was anything she wanted to ask Baba. Now, in those days it was not common for an Englishman to strike up conversation with an Indian, and almost unheard of for a *memsahib* to begin talking to an Indian she hadn't even been introduced to, but when I relayed Baba's message to this woman, without any hesitation, she began pouring out her tale of woe to Him.

It seems this woman's husband was an officer in the government and, as such, traveled around the country a good deal. Often she accompanied her husband, but her problem was that she was terrified of snakes, and it seemed that wherever they stayed, there would invariably be snakes there.

Baba listened very patiently and then told the woman not to worry. All she had to do was to take an eggshell and burn it and then put the ashes from the eggshell into a locket and wear it, and she wouldn't be bothered by snakes. The woman seemed very relieved to hear this, although I never saw her again, so I don't know if she did it or if the eggshell talisman worked. I have sometimes wondered about her karma, that she should be blessed to have a moment with the God-Man, should be fortunate enough to have the God-Man, on His own, ask her if there was anything she wanted to ask Him, and then to use that precious opportunity to inquire about charms to ward off snakes! But maybe the whole incident was only a means of establishing contact, of deepening her link with the Ancient One. At any rate, although on that occasion Baba on His own responded to the woman's unvoiced interest, in general He did not like it when people were drawn to Him because it interfered with His work.

There was another reason, however, for us to talk to the other passengers and that was to find out whether there were any *masts* or advanced spiritual pilgrims in the area.

On one particular journey we were traveling and we heard of a very advanced pilgrim. Baba wanted us to find out all that we could about this man, what his habits were, his characteristics, his likes and dislikes. So we started asking our fellow passengers if they knew anything of this man. Some had seen him. "He must have likes and dislikes," we asked. "Oh yes," they replied, "and he has a very short temper." "Is that so? Violent?" "No, not violent, but he is very blunt. And if you are going to him, he is fond of one thing —

coconut creams. But are you going to see him now?" "Yes." "Oh no! Don't go as you are. You should have baths first and change into neat, clean clothes. He will like that and be very happy. But otherwise, if you go as you are, he will be very short-tempered and will have you thrown out."

We were very dirty from our travels. The soot and smoke from the steam engine was in our hair and clothes and in our very skin. We told Baba about what we had found out and asked what He wanted to do – did He want to go straight to this saint or did He want to stop first so we could bathe? Although Baba usually would do everything He could to see that a *mast* or sadhu's whims were respected, He said that we didn't have enough time to bathe first, and if the saint threw us out, well then, we were thrown out. So we went straight from the station.

About two miles away we found the big bungalow where the saint stayed. The door was ajar, and we of the mandali hesitantly entered, each saying, "You go first," to the other. But to our surprise the saint welcomed us with great respect and cordiality. He directed his people to get a chair for Baba and a bench for us. We were very surprised.

The saint moved the chair and made Baba sit. He said that he was very happy to see Him. Baba gestured for him to seat himself, but the man said that he was happy to stand. In short, he appeared to know of Baba's spiritual status, and Baba looked really uncomfortable, as He always did when His secret, as it were, was revealed. Baba gestured to me and I said to the saint, "My elder brother has come a long way and would like to be with you alone. He wants to see you personally. Would you mind being with Him in that room?"

"Oh no," he replied. "I don't mind. I have been waiting since morning." Baba then looked pleased, and we all heaved a deep sigh of relief. If Baba is not pleased, then the whole world is dead, as it were, to us.

After Baba and the saint left, the saint's followers began to chat with us and to ask us what we did in life, where we were from and the like. "Your elder brother seems quite different from other people," they observed. 'Where is he from and what does he do?" "He is from Bombay side and he is a businessman," we replied. (As an aside, I might mention that while this seems like a lie, actually it is not. While in America, Baba once defined Himself as a businessman who was eternally, "turning His liabilities [sinners] into assets [saints]."

The saint's followers then expressed their astonishment by noting that ever since the morning, the saint had been saying that someone was coming whom they would not know but that everything had to be clean for him. And we could see that everything had indeed been cleaned. The place was spotless, the floor had been washed, and everything was nice and tidy. "We heard on the train that your master likes things to be clean and won't see anyone who has not washed well," we commented. "Yes, this is most unusual. He had us clean the place so thoroughly but then did not insist on your cleanliness. That is what astonishes us."

And so we went on chatting about this and that until Baba came out, in a very good mood. He gestured to us to leave, and we immediately turned to go. We did not hesitate; the emperor had called and we obeyed, that's all. But then what happened?

Baba was already past us, but the old man, the saint, but still a pilgrim on the spiritual path, came out of the house and said, looking towards Baba, "No one, until You came, has touched my heart with the arrow of Divine Love. You have the power to destroy and flood the world; no one fully knows the limits of Your greatness; You are the spiritual authority of the time, and if I were to die, I would take another body to be close to You."

A small footnote to this story is that as we were walking to the railway station, the saint sent one of his men running after us with a message. "My master says," this man reported to us, "that on your arrival home, he would like it very much if you would drop him a postcard of your safe arrival." Baba told me to remember to do this, and when we finally returned to Ahmednagar I sent the saint a post-card saying that we had arrived home safely. What significance this had I don't know, but Baba was most particular that the saint's wishes be observed.

⟨⟩ BEAUTY AND UGLINESS

IN THE BOOK, *LISTEN HUMANITY*, Meher Baba enumerated the different types of death. Later He said that there was one more type of death that had not been included in Listen Humanity – this He called circumstantial death. There is only one case of circumstantial death among the Perfect Masters, and that is with Dnyaneshwar.

Dnyaneshwar was very beautiful physically. His personality was also dynamic and captivating. His presence was such that everyone flocked to him. They could not be persuaded to leave him, even though Dnyaneshwar would take great care to tell those people who had a connection, a link, with other Masters, to go to them and not stay with him. As Baba explained, in spirituality the most important point is the link that one has with the Master. You may go to any Master and, of course, you will derive benefit from the contact, but if you have no connection with that Master, you will eventually have to go to the one with whom you do have a link. This ensures further progress on the spiritual path.

So Dnyaneshwar would dissuade people from staying with him

when this was a barrier to their spiritual progress. But his beauty, his language, and the expression of his personality were such that they persisted in staying with him. Eventually, so his personality would no longer be a hindrance in the spiritual development of some people, he asked that he be sealed alive in a small crypt. That is the case of circumstantial death amongst Perfect Masters.

It is said that many years later, a certain person had a persistent dream of Dnyaneshwar telling him to open the crypt. The dream or vision continued to occur, and so, in time, the elders of the town decided to open the crypt. Dnyaneshwar was still there, inside, but a root of a nearby tree had entwined itself around his neck and was choking him. It was cut off. It is also said that Dnyaneshwar said that the crypt was not to be opened again.

But then we might ask, do not all Perfect Masters have appealing personalities? Why should one have more appeal than another? It seems, from the story of Dnyaneshwar, that some do.

The answer is that our gross eyes see the surface, but not that which is inward. So some personalities are more appealing than others, even though all are One in consciousness. This reminds me of a story, a story of a saint, mind you, not a Perfect Master.

There was once a saint of great repute. No one knew that actually he was saintly, because he was totally silent about himself. He was also one of the most ugly people alive on the earth, and so horrible was his ugliness that people used to make a joke of it. He was very close and very dear to the Lord, yet he must have been the ugliest man on earth at that time. The children would tease him, the elders played practical jokes on him, and all would treat him as an object of mirth and ridicule – yet he would never retaliate, he simply smiled and kept himself aloof from them.

Now, it so happened that he decided to visit a town some distance from where he lived. To do so he had to board a ferry and travel some hours across a very wide river. The ferryboat was crowded with passengers, most of whom knew the saint. The youngsters immediately started to taunt and tease him and play practical jokes on him. Their parents and older passengers thoroughly enjoyed the spectacle, and this went on and on.

Eventually the patience of the Lord Himself was exhausted, and He spoke to His lover: "Why do you allow these people to do these things? I cannot tolerate this behavior towards you any longer. I will sink the ship and everyone on board!" These were the words that the saint heard, but within himself, and no one else heard. What the people heard, however, was the saint talking to himself in reply to the Lord, "Oh my Lord! If you love me so much, drown them in the Ocean of Your Love. If You sink the ship, I will be the cause of the disaster. If You love me, please do not do that. Drown them in Your Ocean, make them see Your Divinity and Your Beauty; that would be real drowning."

Immediately there was a total transformation in the hearts of all the people – the saint's ugliness disappeared and the people became aware of the beauty within.

This reminds me of another story about a saint who was very ugly. This saint's body was covered with nodules, with fleshy growths, and so grotesque was his appearance that people couldn't bear the sight of him. And yet this saint, unlike the saint in the previous story, was loved by the people around him. This was because the saint was very compassionate, and he used to use his powers to heal those around him. Although people could not bear to look at him, they loved him, because he had cured so many of them of their afflictions.

The years passed and, despite his ugliness, crowds began to gather round the saint wherever he was, begging to be healed or cured. Patiently, the saint would go from person to person, healing them as he went. This went on for years and years and one day, someone called out to him, "You've healed so many of us, why don't you use your talent and cure yourself of your disease?"

"Shut up!" the saint demanded, and the people were shocked because they had never seen the saint angry before. "Don't you realize," the saint continued, "that these growths are the rungs of the ladder by which I reach the height?"

And then there is the story of Raja Gopichand. He was not ugly. In fact, he was exceedingly handsome. So handsome that it is said that sixteen thousand women fell in love with him.

One day his mother was standing behind him and contemplating his extraordinary physical beauty. Suddenly she realized that his physical form was impermanent and that his beauty would vanish with the coming of old age. With this realization, she wept, and the tears fell upon his bare back. Feeling her tears, the Raja turned around and asked her the reason for her tears in spite of all his care to see that she had all the comforts the palace could afford. She told him of her realization, and such was the power of her vision that he immediately gave everything away, became a *sannyasi*, and devoted his life to the search for Eternal Beauty.

⚙ A Y A Z

MEHER BABA WOULD SOMETIMES TELL US STORIES of Ayaz, a true slave to his lord. Ayaz was a slave in the court of the emperor; he had been purchased as a slave and he remained one. His integrity and honesty and attitude to life, however, brought him closer and closer to the royal family. In time he became the favorite of the emperor and would constantly be in attendance on him. He was the true slave to his lord, his master.

Even in open court, when lengthy and intricate legal cases were brought to the emperor, before judgment he would turn to Ayaz, and the two would whisper back and forth, and then the emperor would give judgment according to Ayaz's opinion. This went on and, while once or twice or even three times would have been all right, when every time it was the same, it seemed that Ayaz had become the ruler of the kingdom.

The ministers, officials, and courtiers all became very jealous of Ayaz, and many stories were circulated about the slave and about his relationship with the emperor that sought to discredit him, and even the emperor. In short, all connected with the emperor's court and government could not stand the sight of Ayaz.

The emperor felt pity for Ayaz, for the taunts and ridicule and rejection that he had to endure, and he determined to reveal the truth. He called everyone, all his ministers and courtiers and officials, to the palace and said, "I have a whim. Here is my signet ring, the royal seal, a ring that can bring death to people or free them from death. I want to know what it is worth. This is my whim."

The ring was placed on a table, and everyone filed by and stated a price. Some said, "Five thousand dinars." Others said, "Thirty thousand." The estimates varied tremendously, and finally one minister spoke up and said, "But sire, why waste the time of the court on this? A simple solution would be to call for the royal jeweler and ask him for an estimate. He can give you the correct valuation." The emperor agreed, and the jeweler came and quoted the correct market price. All those in the court seemed satisfied with this judgment, and then the emperor turned to Ayaz. "Ayaz, what do you say? How much is this ring worth?"

Ayaz came forward and looked at the ring. He picked it up, examined it, and then put it back on the table. "Sire," he said, "to me this ring, as it is now, lying on the table, is worthless. It has no value at all. But as soon as it is on your finger, sire, the ring is priceless."

Baba then finished the story by concluding, "Know once and

for all, as long as you hold fast to My daaman, you are priceless. But if you let go, you have no worth, no value at all. So beware, and hold on to My daaman until the very end."

Baba told us another story concerning Ayaz and the emperor, and the emperor's attempts to bring home to his court why Ayaz was so special to him.

One day the emperor announced that he wished to make a show of the royal treasury. "I want my subjects to know just how much wealth I have," he declared. "But sire," urged his courtiers, "what of the dangers? What about loss, or bandits? How can we be sure the treasure will be protected?" "Nothing will happen," the emperor assured them. "It is my whim to do this and there is no danger. I myself will head the procession."

So the diamonds and rubies and gold and silver and pearls and precious stones and all the other treasures were loaded into large baskets which were hung on camels, one basket on each side. The camels made up a long procession, so great was the treasure, and at the head rode the king and his courtiers and guards and, of course, by his side, the faithful Ayaz.

Slowly the long caravan set off through the capital, and the citizens lined the streets to get a look at the treasure. But the emperor was not content with simply going through the main streets; he led the procession through all the little alleyways of the capital as well. These streets were so narrow that the baskets on the sides of the camels rubbed against the walls. Soon holes began to appear and gems and coins began to spill out on the roadside. The king was at the head of the caravan and Ayaz was walking by his side. Suddenly he stopped and looked around. "Where are all the courtiers?" he asked Ayaz. "Nobody is following us anymore. Where are they all? Go and find out." Ayaz left and he did not have far to go. Back a little distance he found all the courtiers and subjects fighting and squabbling over the treasure lying around.

When Ayaz returned and told the king what was happening, the emperor said, "But why don't you go back and try and pick up some of the treasure yourself? This is your opportunity to become rich. You don't have to stay by my side." "To stay by your side and have you is my treasure," replied Ayaz.

When the emperor returned to court, he used this incident to reveal the worth of Ayaz. In the same way, Baba went on to tell us, "When you have Me, you have everything. What need have you for anything else? Just hold fast to Me with both hands."

⟁ KRISHNA MAST

IN NORTH INDIA THERE WAS A CERTAIN RAILROAD TRAIN GUARD, an important position involving responsibility for the whole train, who was most conscientious in his duties. He was also a great devotee of Lord Krishna, and whenever possible, he would attend evening programs of devotional music in praise of Lord Krishna.

One night while attending such a program, he lost himself completely in repeating Krishna's name and in singing His glory. He forgot everything except his joy in praising his Lord. At dawn the program ended and he came to with a shock. In his rapture he had totally forgotten the time and he was supposed to have reported to the station for duty at two A.M. and now he was hours late.

He rushed to the station in great anxiety. The train might have been a minute or two late, but he knew since he was hours late that he would have missed the train. This was a most serious breach of duty, and he was sure he would lose his job because of it. When he reached the station he rushed straight for the stationmaster to explain and apologize. But before he could say a word, the stationmaster, seeing him rush in, exclaimed, "What's happened? Where is the train?"

The guard began to apologize for missing the train, and the stationmaster interrupted him and insisted, "Has there been an accident? What's happened?" "I don't know," the guard replied. "I missed the train." "What do you mean, missed the train? Where did you miss it?" "Here. I didn't get here in time last night to leave with the train," the guard explained. "What are you talking about?" the stationmaster demanded. "You took the train out last night. Now what's happened? Has there been an accident that you're back again so soon?"

"But I never left," the guard insisted. "I'm only arriving just now for duty." "What nonsense!" the stationmaster exclaimed, "We had tea together last night before you left. Look, look in the duty book if you don't believe me. You signed your name when you took charge of the train!" The stationmaster called a clerk, who brought the duty book, and sure enough, there was the man's signature. The clerk also testified that he had served them both tea last night. Then others came in who also swore that they had seen the guard when he came in and took the train.

Suddenly the guard realized what must have happened. He knew that he had been at the *bhajan* program. Therefore it could only have been the Lord Himself who had come in his place, had tea, signed the duty book, and taken charge of the train. While he was singing the praises of the Lord, the Lord had come to attend to his duty for him. This realization made the man a *mast*, and he resigned on the spot and spent the rest of his life restlessly roaming from place to place, remembering his beloved Lord, Krishna, glorifying Him, and writing His name, "Krishna, Krishna," wherever he went.

Well, during our travels we came to hear of this *mast* who was known by the name of Krishna *Mast*, and Baba expressed the desire to contact him. Baba traveled all the way from Ahmednagar to northern India to see him. Krishna *Mast* was found most often in a small

town in Nahan State, and for several days we scoured the area looking for him. But he was so restless that he never stayed long in any
one spot. We would hear that he was somewhere, but by the time we
got there, he would have left for someplace else. For two days we
trailed him, just missing him time and time again. Baba became more
and more anxious to contact the *mast*, and, meanwhile, the *mast*
was spending all of his time searching for his beloved Krishna. We
could always tell where the *mast* had been, because we would see
"Krishna, Krishna" written on the walls of the buildings of any street
he had passed by.

We spent the night at a rest house and we were going to go out
the next morning in search of Krishna *Mast* once again when, early
in the morning, just as we were getting up, from afar we could hear
the distant chant, "Krishna, Krishna, Krishna." Baba was quickly out
the gate and into the street, and then we saw him, Krishna *Mast*, at
last, walking down the street towards us. He caught sight of Baba
and instantly he started running towards Baba even as Baba quickly
ran toward the *mast*. They rushed together and embraced. It was a
sight for the gods to see! – the lover and the Beloved locked in a
seemingly inseparable embrace. So intense was their meeting that
they fell down and rolled together on the road, locked in each other's
arms. I will never forget that demonstration of Real Love. Such is the
love of the Lord for His lover, and such, when the longing is intense
and sincere, is how the lover gets drawn to his Beloved.

That is the story of Krishna *Mast*, who lost all consciousness of
the world in the search for his Lord and eventually found Him. Baba
used to call the *masts* His beloved children, and we could see why.
Their love for Him was so great, so pure, so touching,and Baba's love
for His children was even greater. That is how it is. The Divine Beloved
comes for us, wanting us to love Him, longing for our love. And when
He creates love in us, we then long for and search for Him. And when
our love reaches a certain intensity, He comes in person, searching for
His lovers, to receive His love. It is all the interplay of love.

◁▷ **T H E *D H U N I***

EVERY MONTH, ON THE TWELFTH, the *dhuni* at Meherabad is lit. And every month, when there are pilgrims here, right around the twelfth, someone asks, "What is the *dhuni*? Why do we light it? What does it signify?"

Well, the story of the *dhuni* goes way back in time, back to the Sat Yuga, or Golden Age, thousands of years ago. In those days, when a man reached sixty years of age, he was considered to have completed his worldly duties. His children had been raised and they now had children of their own. His labor was not needed to support the family, and he was now free to dedicate the remainder of his life to finding God.

This was a sacred obligation, and the family did not object to his leaving them to find God; for finding God, ultimately, was the duty of everyone, and it is said that even if one member of a family realizes God, all members of the family for seven generations are benefited.

So, at the age of sixty, the head of the household left his home, renounced the world, and headed off, usually into the jungle or forests to search for God. But what did this seeker find? He found that with no house to shelter him, no blankets to wrap around him, it was cold at night. And the mosquitoes would bite him and distract him and make it difficult for him to concentrate on God. And there were wild animals in the jungles, especially at night, so his search was made very difficult for him because of all these worldly considerations. He had left the world to find God, but he found that it was hard to think of God because of the world.

So these seekers would light a fire at night. The flame kept them warm, and also kept the animals away, and the smoke would keep the mosquitoes away. And the ash from the fire they would rub over their bodies as protection from the elements, so the fire was truly a friend to them, a companion to them in their search for God. Over time, the fires that these seekers would build near their seats of meditation became associated with the search for God. If someone went hunting in the forest and saw the remains of such a fire, the person would think, "Oh, a holy man has been here," and the place would be respected because the search for God was respected. If one came across the remains of such a fire, it automatically signified that someone had sat there repeating the name of God, thinking about God, meditating on God, and so the fire, the place, was respected, in much the same way that if you were to come upon a church or a temple, you would be respectful; it was a place of worship.

Now, the word *dhuni* itself might have evolved in several different ways. It might be based on the root word *dhoon*, which means repeating the name of God aloud. Or then again, possibly it is based on the root word *dhyan*, which means meditation. *Dhyani* means one who meditates, and *dhuni* might have evolved from it. At any rate, eventually the word *dhuni* came to be associated with these fires.

And, over time, as the tradition of all men once they were sixty renouncing the world and seeking God became less universally observed, the *dhuni* fire began to be associated specifically with the fires kept near the seats of holy ones, the saints and sadhus and Perfect Masters. When Meher Baba first came to Meherabad in 1922, there was no such fire. But a few years later, the monsoons had failed and the farmers were getting desperate. This area has always suffered from a shortage of water, and drought or a bad monsoon meant severe hardship, possibly even starvation for the villagers, who were mostly farmers.

Now, as you know, we have two monsoon seasons here. The first monsoon season, which is supposed to come in June, had been very poor. Now it was September and the second monsoon season was ending, and still there had been no life-giving showers. So the farmers were desperate. They knew that Meher Baba was living at Meherabad, and they considered Him a saintly personality, so they came to Him to seek His blessings for rain. They came in a large crowd to beg Baba for rain.

Baba received them very lovingly but encouraged them to leave for their homes immediately because their love and faith in Him might bring about a downpour that would drench them if they didn't hurry home.

Now, it was a bright and sunny day and there was no sign of rain whatsoever. The villagers did not know whether to take Baba seriously or not. They thought perhaps Baba was only trying to get rid of them by urging them to leave so quickly. But eventually, with much coaxing from the mandali, they were persuaded to leave.

When all had gone, Baba turned to His men and told them to collect wood and to dig the pit that you still see to this day by the side of the road, under the neem tree. Baba ordered this *dhuni* lit, and very soon clouds gathered in the sky and it began to rain. It rained so hard, in fact, that the villagers got thoroughly drenched on their way home. This was not an act of Baba's greatness, but of His compassion, and the *dhuni* pit has remained as a sign or symbol of this.

For a while, the *dhuni* was lit regularly, but in those early years Baba traveled frequently, and during the long periods when all were away from Meherabad the *dhuni* obviously was not lit. Returning one time from one of the travels in the Blue Bus, Baba had the *dhuni* lit. This was on the twelfth of December, 1941. Baba then ordered that thereafter the *dhuni* should be lit on the twelfth of each month.

So that is why we do it, because Baba told us to continue to light it on the twelfth of each month. It was His order to us, so it is our pleasure to obey and light the *dhuni* each month on the twelfth.

But what about the sandalwood, and the burning up of *sanskaras*, you ask? Well, during a Sahavas program in 1955, Baba asked each one there to take a small piece of sandalwood and throw it in the fire. This piece of wood was supposed to symbolize some attachment we had, some attachment which was a hindrance in our journey to God. Each was to throw the piece of sandalwood in the fire with the thought that that attachment would be consumed. But there is nothing magical about it. You don't need to wait until the twelfth to start burning up your attachments in Baba's divine love. For that ultimately is what the *dhuni* symbolizes – the fire of Baba's divine love. That love consumes everything, and if anyone is brave enough to throw themselves into the fire, they are consumed, their false self is burnt away, and what is left is the Real Self, and we call this God-Realization.

The *dhuni* is only a symbol of this. But does that mean that there is no point in going to the *dhuni*, that the whole ceremony is simply an empty ritual? Not at all. It is a means of remembering Baba. Baba told us to light the *dhuni*, so when we light it in obedience to His wishes, we are remembering Him. When we take a piece of sandalwood and throw it in the fire, that will not automatically burn up one of our attachments, but if we think about Baba, if we sincerely dedicate ourselves to becoming His, then indeed we may start a fire in ourselves which is far greater than the fire we see in the *dhuni*.

Everything is a ritual, and nothing is; it all depends on how you approach it. If you go to the *dhuni* and throw in a piece of sandalwood because someone tells you you should, or because you want to get rid of one of your attachments without making any efforts, then it becomes a ritual, a bit of magic mumbo jumbo, and yet, even so, if your faith in Baba is great enough, you might just find that your attachment has been lessened. But what is the point of freeing oneself from attachments? It is so we are free to remember our Lord, Meher Baba, the Avatar, with all of our heart and soul. And we can begin to remember Him now, where we are. Baba said that all of creation is only a reminder to humanity to remember the Creator. So the *dhuni* is one more opportunity to remember Baba.

It is an opportunity to focus more concentratedly on Baba. But the real *dhuni* is the human heart. And the real fire is the fire of love for God. And if we had the courage, the daring, every day, every moment, we would be attempting to throw our attachments on this fire. Not just attachments, we would be throwing ourselves onto this fire. That would be the real *dhuni*.

A farmer from near Meherabad came to Baba, very distraught and in a desperate state. He implored Baba to help him and poured out his story. It seems he had spent every penny he had in digging a well on his farm and there was no water. He was now penniless, his farm was mortgaged, and his situation seemed hopeless. So he had come to Baba seeking His divine intervention.

Baba, as usual, expressed Himself as the most ignorant one. As I have said many times, ignorance was the weapon Baba used most in His battle to win the hearts of humanity. So, pretending not to know anything, He asked the farmer for all the details, how far had he dug, how much had he spent, what was the soil like where he was digging, and so on. The farmer told the whole story and said that he had come because he had full faith in Baba, he knew that Baba would be able to help him get water in his well.

Baba listened and seemed to be moved by the man's plight and said, "Just dig another five feet and you'll get water." Now, the man had been at his wits' end. He was exhausted, he was broke, he was going to lose everything, but when Baba said to dig another five feet and he would find water, he had renewed hope, and he went home determined to dig another five feet.

As soon as the farmer left, Baba turned to the mandali and said, "Now, why did I say that? I just made a bad mistake. Why did I tell that man he would get water if he dug another five feet? I don't know that he'll find water. I shouldn't have said that." And the mandali tried to reassure Baba that it was all right, that He had to say something, and now the man had renewed hope and would continue digging and, after all, he might find water.

"But I didn't tell him he might find water," Baba objected. "I told him he would find water. I shouldn't have said that because I don't know whether he will find water or not. I don't know why I said that. I shouldn't have told him that."

Over the next few days, Baba kept worrying about what He had told the farmer. He seemed very upset. "What if he doesn't find water?" Baba would ask the mandali. "What then?" "Then he will be in the same situation he is in now," the mandali replied. "But I told him he would," Baba said. "If he doesn't find water, he may turn the whole village against us. They may come here and drive us out. They may decide we are responsible for the drought, that we bring bad luck. We may have to leave here." And so it went. Baba kept bringing the subject up and the mandali did their best to reassure Baba that there was nothing to worry about, but nothing they said convinced Baba. Finally, the mandali took to avoiding Baba because they knew if they were around Him, He would only start worrying about what He had told the farmer again.

After a few days of this, the farmer reappeared. There was a large crowd accompanying him, but they had not come to drive Baba and the mandali out of Meherabad. They had come with garlands and sweets to express their gratitude for Baba's divine intervention. For the farmer, with the help of his family, had dug his well deeper, and even before they went five feet, they hit water, and a good supply of water at that. The man was overjoyed because now he and his family were saved.

Baba had the man retell his story before all the mandali and then revealed to the farmer that it was his faith which had made the water appear. Baba explained to all who had come that He did not perform miracles. It was not He who had brought the water, but the man's faith in Him. He had merely said, "Go another five feet and you'll find water," but it was the man's faith in Him that had produced the water. It was the man's faith which had worked this miracle. The God-Man, Baba explained, does not do miracles. He has no need to do them, because He has already arranged everything in creation with such precision that there is no need for Him to interfere with His own creation. In His original whim the entire universe was laid out in precise detail. Baba would tell us that He is the one with infinite leisure, because He has nothing more to do.

At any rate, the farmer and his friends and family and neighbors were overjoyed, and they paid their obeisance to Baba and distributed the sweets and left singing Baba's praises. When they left, Baba turned to the mandali and began expressing His wonder that the man had actually struck water. "It was his faith, and his faith alone that produced the water," Baba said. "I did nothing. I didn't know there was water there. Remember how worried I was? It was the man's faith in Me which produced the water. It was his faith which made this miracle." And Baba went on to extol the farmer's faith.

The more Baba praised the farmer's faith, the more disgruntled the mandali felt. Meherabad also had water problems, even back them. At first, when there were only a few people living there, the well sufficed, but as the population expanded with the clinics and schools and *dharamshalas* that were built, the need for water became more and more acute. The mandali dug new wells, but time after time these proved to be dry holes. So they pestered Baba to show them where they should dig to get water, since none of their efforts to find water had succeeded. Finally, one day as they were walking across the fields at Meherabad, Baba pointed to a spot and said, "Dig here." The mandali took a stone and put it on the spot to mark the place Baba had pointed out. But as they were all very busy, it wasn't for another day or two that they had the time to begin digging the well. When they went to the spot they found that someone had moved the stone in the meantime. Still, they knew the general area, if not the exact spot, and they began digging a well.

Baba took great interest in their efforts and would ask them how it was going. As time went by, the well got deeper and deeper, but still they didn't strike any water. Baba encouraged them to keep at it, and eventually they ended up digging much farther than the farmer had without ever striking water. Finally, Baba told them to forget it. So this was the background to the incident with the farmer. And the more Baba praised the farmer's faith, the more irritated and upset the mandali got, especially Rustom, Adi's brother. Rustom was in charge of Meherabad; he was the manager of the property and, as such, was also in charge of the well-digging operations. Finally Baba's praise of the farmer became too much for him to take.

"What's this injustice?" he demanded before Baba. "What have we done to You that You don't give us water, yet You give it to that farmer?" "I did not give water to that farmer," Baba replied, "it was his faith that gave him the water." "Do You mean to say that we have no faith in You?" Rustom demanded. "What's the use of our living here with You if we have so little faith? We have given up everything to be with You. We put up with every hardship to be here, and now You tell us we don't have faith in You? Then what's the point in our staying? We might as well pack up and leave!"

Baba smiled. "When that farmer came to Me for water, I told him to go another five feet. It was as a man comforting another man that I told him that. I didn't know that he would actually find water, but his faith produced the miracle and he found water. But what would have happened had he not found water? His faith would have been destroyed. He would have denounced Me to everyone in the village. He had faith in Me, it is true, but only for water. When he found water, his faith was strengthened, but if he hadn't found water, his faith would have been destroyed. With you, My mandali, I know fully well that whether you find water or not, your conviction in My divinity is such that nothing will shake that conviction.

"That farmer is blessed because of his faith. But you are far more blessed, because even though you do not find water, you continue to do your best and remain convinced in Me. Because you have come not for water but for Me."

Baba continued, "There is a world of difference between those who have been blessed with conviction and those who have been blessed with faith. Those who have been blessed with conviction are doubly blessed. Faith carries you through to a certain extent, but faith falters; if circumstances go against you, your faith can weaken and even be lost entirely. Conviction is independent of circumstances, however. Conviction carries you through all situations until you find Me as I am. Faith is the fruit of one's devotion to Me, whereas conviction is My gift of grace to you. That man came for water, and he got water. But you have come for Me, and you have Me."

❁ J A L K E R A W A L A

YOU KNOW, JAL KERAWALA WAS TRULY ONE who lived for God and died for God. His father worked in a factory which my father inspected. Through Papa, Jal's father heard of Meher Baba. When Baba came to Nagpur in 1937, Jal was informed, and Jal met Baba for the first time then. Jal was a brilliant man, and after his schooling he went into government service. He quickly rose to a high position and eventually was made commissioner for a large district in what is now Madhya Pradesh.

In 1945 we were with Baba in this area. Baba expressed the wish to do some special seclusion work in Darjeeling. I was sent to Raipur with a message for Jal Kerawala, and then I was to proceed to Darjeeling to find a suitable site for Baba's work. As I recall, there were five conditions which had to be met. Baba wanted a spot which was completely secluded and which was in the mountains. There also were supposed to be caves nearby where Baba could stay. Baba wanted to do some important work, and He wanted the place selected to have a spiritual atmosphere and, if I remember correctly, He wanted the place, if possible, to have some connection with previous saints. I was to go ahead and send Baba a cable when I found a spot which seemed suitable to me. But when I arrived at Raipur and explained my mission to Jal, Jal said there was no need to go so far, that there were plenty of places in his district which met those conditions. "Why make Baba travel so far?" Jal asked. "Can you wait a day or two?" I said I could, and Jal immediately summoned all the heads of the departments under his jurisdiction and started asking them if they knew of any such place in their areas. They discussed it and said that there was the famous place at Sarguja, Sinahawa, situated in the forest. There were mountains there and caves, and it was said that the famous sage Angiras had undergone severe penance in this area. In fact, one of the hills in the area was known as Angarishi Pahad after him.

"Sounds perfect!" Jal said. "The problem," the department heads replied, "is that it is very difficult to get to the cave and impossible by car, as there is no road." "Well, let's make a road, then," Jal suggested. "Up a mountain!" "What if we just make one to the foot of the mountain?" "But it's impossible, it is all very thick, dense forest. There's no way to make a road there." "Nonsense," Jal replied, and he called for the geodesic maps of the region to be brought in and immediately began plotting a road through the thick sal (teak) forest to the base of the mountain.

The area was wild, but there was a small camp in the woods which had been set up to aid logging operations. Jal decided that they would begin the road from there. He would use all the lumberjacks that were already there to help cut the new track in the woods. This would make it somewhat easier, but it still involved cutting a road through miles of dense forest.

As he chalked out the route, the department heads who knew the area, would comment on the difficulties before them. "But there are streams there, how are you going to have the car cross?" "We'll lay logs over the tiny streams." "But some are too big for that." "Then we'll station two water buffaloes there and they can tow the car across." When it was pointed out that a certain stream was too wide even for a pair of water buffaloes to tow a car, Jal would reply, "Then we'll get six pairs if two are not enough."

While Jal's department heads were looking for reasons why it couldn't be done, Jal was determined to do his best to do it. He arranged for petrol for the cars which would bring Baba's party to be stored at the lumber camp. As there were no villages in the area, all the supplies would have to be sent to the camp and then ferried to Baba's place of seclusion as well. "That reminds me," Jal said, "we should have a buffalo for the mountain so Baba can have fresh milk."

"It won't work," the department heads objected. "The scent of the wild animals will scare the buffalo and she won't give any milk." "We'll get the forest rangers in the area to go there before Baba arrives and drive the wild animals away." "But they will come back again whey they smell the water buffalo there." "Then we can station the rangers around the mountain so they don't come back. We'll have them build fires, too, to keep the animals at bay." In short, every objection that was raised, Jal dealt with.

"So you think you can do it?" Jal asked. Reluctantly all agreed that it could be done if they were given enough time. "How about twenty days?" "If everyone cooperates." "Don't worry, I'll see to that," Jal assured them.

"Well," Jal asked, "what do you say? Should we send a cable to Baba saying it can be done?" "If you want us to, we will try," the department heads replied. "Yes, I want you to try, because I am committing myself to my master." And Jal went on to impress upon them Baba's importance, that this was all being done for Baba. I remember all these details because I was there while all this was going on. Jal was always very conscientious, and if he told Baba he was going to do something, he would always make a point of seeing that it got done. His men all said they would do their best so Jal turned to me and said, "Why don't you wait until we hear from Baba? Maybe He will agree to change the work from Darjeeling to Sinahawa."

A cable was sent to Baba explaining the situation and saying that all the conditions were met and the place of seclusion could be arranged in twenty days. Baba sent word back that Jal should go ahead and start work immediately and that I should return to Baba without going on to Darjeeling.

I did so, but a few weeks later, I returned with Pendu, Baidul, Chhagan, and Gustadji. We came in a truck with luggage and supplies which Baba would need, like gunpowder, food, dry wood, etc. We went in advance of Baba to make sure that everything would be ready for Him when He arrived. Having been there when the plan was first proposed, I had some idea of the difficulties Jal faced, but the full enormity of the task he had undertaken did not come home to me until I traveled the roads myself. The forest was very thick, and there were countless streams which had to be forded. Just going to the lumber camp, we were amazed at how primitive the area was and we hadn't even started on the new road yet! Even as we drove on the regular road we could see leopards in the woods and hear the roars of the tigers. We couldn't imagine what it would be like at the mountain itself.

We stopped at the camp for petrol. We had large jerry cans we had brought to be filled. At the camp they had a small storeroom, maybe ten feet by ten feet, which had huge petrol drums inside. It was night when we arrived, and I walked into the storeroom with my jerry can to fill it. The big drums had valves at the bottom, and I opened the cock and started filling my jerry can. Because it was night, it was very dark. One of the men in the camp brought a lantern

into the room so I could see better; I had only a small torch with me.
I don't know what he was thinking of, because, of course, as soon as
he brought the lantern in, the gas fumes ignited. The jerry can I was
filling burst into flames.

Somehow I had the presence of mind to turn off the cock so
the huge drum wouldn't explode, but the jerry can was blazing away.
I looked around and picked up a rug and threw it over the jerry can
to try and smother the flames. Then I began dragging the can backwards out of the room so the whole place wouldn't explode. It all
happened so fast that no one knew what to do. I managed to drag the
jerry can out of the room, but as I was walking backwards, backing
out of the room, I couldn't see where I was going and I stepped right
off the verandah, and fell backwards onto the ground. The jerry can
might have fallen on top of me, burning me badly, but Baidul rushed
over as I fell and gave the jerry can a mighty kick. I think I've told
you before about Baidul's strength. Well, this one kick not only sent
the jerry can off the verandah, but it went sailing over my head and
onto the ground behind me.

But even then our problems were not over, because this was
essentially a lumber camp and there was wood and kindling piled up
all over the place. It would not have taken much to set the whole
place on fire, but fortunately we were able to throw dirt on the jerry
can and put out the fire before it spread. After putting out the fire,
we went back and refilled our jerry can, making sure that no one
with a lantern came near, and then we set out on the newly con-
structed road to the mountain.

By dawn we reached the foot of the mountain and found that
Jal had arranged for a long line of people to meet us there and to
begin carrying all the supplies up the mountain to the camp he had
arranged for Baba. We walked up the mountain, and were amazed to
see all that Jal had done. He had built a small hut for Baba on the
very top of the mountain. Near the side of the hut was a small
natural cave, from which one had a magnificent view of the

surrounding forest. There was also another cave nearby which was approached by a different path. One felt secluded from the whole world sitting in this cave. Jal had also made a hut some distance away for the mandali and another hut for Ali Shah, the *mast*, whom Baba was bringing with Him.

We learned later that Jal had worked incredibly hard to see that all the arrangements were made for Baba's stay. But then, that was like Jal; once he decided to do something for Baba, he wouldn't stop until it was done. And making the whole job even more difficult was the fact that partway through, Baba sent word that He was coming earlier than planned, so Jal didn't even get his twenty days. On hearing this, Jal started laboring alongside his crew to make sure things got done on time. In India it is not common for government officials to work like laborers, and you never find the commissioner of the entire district working with his hands in this way. But Jal worked day and night to get the work done. Jal worked hard not only to make Baba's hut, but also to make a place where we could cook our food, and to make huts where we could store our fuel and our grain.

Once it rained heavily and Jal got drenched to the skin. The laborers felt pity for Jal and begged him to change clothes with them (they were inside the huts while he was working outside). They had never seen anything like this. They were impressed by Jal's dedication. They thought to themselves, "Jal is so great, he is such a big man, but then how much greater must his guru be. Who could this guru be?"

When Baba arrived, along with Ali Shah and Adi and Kaka, he was very pleased with all the work Jal had done. Baba liked the place very much. He was amazed at all of Jal's work. But Jal simply said, "You did it, Baba."

Years later, we heard that the villagers who had labored to help Jal arrange for Baba's stay still remembered Jal. They told how "Saheb" himself had worked to help build the huts, and they remembered "Saheb's father," too, who was, according to them, a very saintly person. That is how Baba is remembered by these people, as "Saheb's father."

And that is the story of how Jal Kerawala arranged for Baba's seclusion at Angarishi Pahad. And that reminds me of another story, a humorous little incident connected with Jal. We were traveling with Baba by train. Now, wherever we went, the trains were always very crowded. Baba always seemed to like to travel when conditions were at their worst, like during the war, or at the time of partition. The government used to urge people not to travel unless it was necessary, and it was then that Baba did so much of His traveling.

This meant that we always had difficulties when we traveled. It was hard for us to find room in carriages for Baba and for all of our luggage. There was such a crowd and rush for seats that we were afraid that one day Baba would be injured. Well, Jal knew of this, so when Baba was traveling through his district, he arranged for Baba to have a special compartment. One whole carriage was reserved for Baba and the mandali. We were very grateful because it was always such an anxious time for us in the mandali when a train came in, we were never sure we would be able to get Baba into the carriage safely, or that we would find sufficient room for Him. Each time our train would pull into the station was a time of great nervous strain for us, so we were happy with Jal's arrangement, and Baba also seemed pleased. In fact, Baba stretched out on a seat and relaxed.

Well, it seems that somewhere along the line someone erased the chalk markings on the outside of our carriage which said that it was reserved. We didn't know this at first, all we knew was that at one station suddenly a lot of soldiers started piling into our compartment. We pointed out that this was a private carriage, but they came in anyway. That's when I went out and saw that someone had erased the reserved sign.

Well, after a while the soldiers got settled and again all was well. But one of the soldiers sat down on the bench that Baba was resting on. Baba had drawn his feet up so there was room for the soldier, but soon the soldier decided to stretch out and started to put his heavy boots against Baba's foot and pushed, to make more and more room for himself. I couldn't tolerate this, so I reached over and swept the man's feet to the floor. The soldier got mad and started yelling at me, and I yelled right back at him, and a fine old row ensued until Baba gestured to me, "Be quiet, not another word out of you."

I kept quiet after that, but soon the soldier put his boots back up on the seat and again started pushing against Baba. I finally couldn't stand this insolence and I said to him, "If you persist, I'll throw you out of this moving carriage." You see, it wasn't our pride which made us say things like that, it was our duty to look after Baba's physical welfare. When it came to ourselves, we had to be lambs in the world, but when it came to Baba we had to be tigers. But Baba was not pleased at my outburst. Baba gestured, "If you will not be quiet, I'll pull the emergency cord and simply get out wherever the train stops." So I had to be silent. But I didn't like it. None of the mandali liked it, we were all so upset with this fellow's insolence, but none of us could say a word because we dared not disobey Baba. So we all sat silent and glum. In fact, when the ticket examiner came and observed us and saw how unhappy we all looked, he asked us if were going to attend a funeral. Such was our plight!

🪷 THE HIJARA

OVER THE YEARS MEHER BABA WOULD, every now and then, needle His men mandali about their lack of love for Him. "You men don't know how to love Me as the women disciples do," He would tell us.

Or, if a difficulty occurred in some task He had set us, He might point out that the difficulty would not have occurred if we had the same love for Him that the women had.

This was not a constant refrain of Baba's, but every so often, over the years, He would refer to our lack of love compared to that of the women disciples. After this had been going on for some time, I finally became so exasperated that once I blurted out, "Oh Baba, you talk of the love the women have for You, but if You really want to have a taste of love from men, then let there be an Advent where You are in female form and then You will see how we love You!"

But Baba replied, "That can't be because it is so ordained that I always come in human male form. The Perfect Masters can be either male or female – Babajan, one of the five Perfect Masters who brought about My Advent, was in female form – but it is so ordained that the Avatar always descends as man amongst humanity."

Nowadays, when some women hear this, they think it is sexist. But actually it has nothing to do with sex; the Avatar is completely beyond sex, as are the Perfect Masters. And Babajan, who was in female form, used to get very angry if anyone referred to her as a woman; "I am man," she would insist. So the outward form of the body is not very important. In fact, one time Baba told us a story about a Perfect Master who was neither male nor female.

The story concerned a Perfect Master who lived in Lucknow, in Northern India. I have forgotten his name, but he was a *hijara*. I am not sure exactly how to translate that term. I guess "eunuch" probably comes closest. In India there are tribes of such people. They are men, but they have long hair and they dress themselves in women's garments, in saris, skirts, bangles, and necklaces and so on. And they have the gait and characteristics of women, so if you saw one, you would think it was a woman you were seeing.

As I said, there are tribes of these people who live together, and their position in society is very low. They are outcasts. No community will accept them; they are looked down upon. They are almost excluded from society entirely, and yet, not completely. For these people traditionally are good musicians. They tend to walk through the streets while their leader drums, and the rest of them clap their hands and dance and keep time with bells and tinkling anklets. And at the time of a wedding or a funeral, these people are paid to come and create a certain atmosphere. At a wedding they sing and laugh and entertain. At a funeral they march through the streets and cry and wail and beat their breasts. They are paid to do this, and so they earn their livelihood that way, and yet they are not respected. If a mother sees her children watching them as they pass by, for children are always attracted to anything colorful and out of the ordinary, she will quickly run and pull her children away. In short, we can say that they are considered the lowest of the low.

Baba told us that in such a community in the city of Lucknow, there was a Perfect Master. In order to uphold this utterly rejected section of humanity, it was ordained that one from that tribe should become a Perfect Master. And so it was. One of this tribe became Perfect and so, naturally, all of his disciples were also of the tribe. This Perfect Master became the leader of the tribe. Although he did not play the drum, he simply walked at the head of the tribe as they marched through the streets.

One day as they were walking through the streets they saw a crowd approaching them from the other direction. It was a group of wrestlers returning from a title fight, surrounded by the fans. Now, wrestling in India is very popular. And in that group was the winner of the match, the champion, so there was a large crowd following him. When the champion saw the small group of the despised *hijaras* walking towards them, he started to ridicule them. He was full of his victory and very arrogant, and the knowledge that he was surrounded by hundreds of people only inflated his sense of self-worth, so he began sneering at the *hijaras* and making fun of them. As they passed by, the wrestler pointed to their leader, who was calmly walking at the head of the group, and remarked, "Look at him! He thinks he is someone great. Just see the way he is walking as though he were the leader of all, although we all know he is only a *hijara.*"

The Perfect Master did not say anything but continued to walk by. When the group had passed, he turned back to the wrestler, who was still standing there pointing at him. "Yes, you have pointed me out already," the Master called to the champion. "But I have passed now, so why don't you put your finger down?"

But the champion was unable to lower his arm. He continued to stand there pointing, but no matter how he tried he could not move his arm. The Perfect Master called out to him, "You are so strong, yet you do not have even enough strength to lower your arm."

As the crowd watched in amazement, they saw that the champion could not lower his arm, and they realized that the leader of the *hijaras* must have done something to the champion. They realized for the first time then that the leader of the *hijaras* was not an ordinary person. Word went around town, and soon everyone knew of what had happened in the streets that day.

Still, most of the community continued to look down on the *hijaras.* It was the youth in the city who were drawn to the Perfect Master. Maybe they came at first out of curiosity, to see this man who had made a laughingstock of the champion wrestler, but they stayed because there is always a special atmosphere around one of the Perfect Ones. As Ramakrishna once said, when the flower is ripe, the bees come of their own accord. And so it was. The youth began to flock to the Perfect Master.

The elders in the community were upset. To them the Master was only a *hijara,* and as such, only fit to be ridiculed and despised. They couldn't tolerate the fact that their children were spending time with such a one, neglecting their studies to be with him. What was the world coming to, what would happen to society if the youth was polluted by listening to that man's ideas and philosophy? The situation was intolerable to the elders, and they decided they had to do something to expose the Master as a fraud.

Because they thought of him as a *hijara*, a certain idea came to them. They decided they would get two young men and dress one of them up as a woman. Then they would present them as a bride and groom to the Master and ask for his blessings for a child. The Master would naturally give his blessings, and then they would expose him as someone who was not all-knowing and they would drive him out of town and then their young would return to their studies. It seemed to them like a good plan.

Accordingly they selected two young men, one of whom was particularly slight and feminine-looking. They dressed them up in the traditional garments of a bride and groom and tutored them on what to say to the Master. When the young couple was ready, they went to the Master, who was sitting on the roadside with his disciples as usual. The couple approached the Master.

"Yes, what is it?" the master asked. "We have just been married," the couple replied. "Yes?" "We would like your blessings for a son." "A son?" "Yes, we would like to be blessed with a bonny boy. That is our longing, please bless us."

The Master looked pointedly at the boy who was playing the part of the bride and asked, "Are you sure you want a son?" The "bride" shyly repeated, "Yes, we really want that." The Master told the couple to think about it. He pointed out that it is a big responsibility to raise children and they were only newly married. They could afford to wait. But the couple insisted that they knew what they were doing and they wanted a son and they wanted the Master's blessings, so finally the Master said, "So be it. You are blessed."

When the elders heard this, they were full of glee. "Now we have him," they thought. So they called a meeting of all the leading people in town and then questioned the couple before everyone. "You are a man but you dressed as a woman?" they asked the boy who played the part of the bride. "Yes." "And you asked the leader of the tribe to bless you to have a son?" "Yes." "And did he?" "Yes." "Were there witnesses to this?" "Yes."

And so the interrogation went. At the end the elders turned to the congregation and announced, "See! It is confirmed that the man is an imposter. It is impossible for a man to conceive and have a son. The man cannot be all-knowing to give such a blessing. He is a fraud and he is duping others into believing that he is of high spiritual status. But we have proved that this is not so!"

Over time, word of the Master's blessing spread through the town, and everywhere it was proclaimed, "The man is a fraud!" But meanwhile the boy who had been the bride started to feel strange. He began having stomach pains, a strange bloated sensation in his stomach. When the sensation didn't go away they took him to a doctor, but the medicines given had no effect.

As time passed, the boy grew more and more uncomfortable, more and more miserable, dull, and disturbed. So the parents took the boy to one who was regarded as the best doctor in town, one trained in Greek medicine. The doctor examined the boy and was astonished. How could it be? There were unmistakable signs of pregnancy.

The doctor was confounded; it was not possible for a male to conceive and carry a child, and yet it was happening. But the parents were shocked. They knew what had happened. So they went to the elders and denounced them. "See what you have done!" they exclaimed. "You have led this boy astray. You have put him in this terrible situation. Now you must take full responsibility. He should not have to suffer this shame by himself."

The elders couldn't believe it. They went to the doctor, but there was no mistake in the diagnosis. And each week that went by made it clearer that he was indeed pregnant. The elders knew now that there was only one way out – they must repent and seek the Master's forgiveness.

So the elders set out to find the Master to ask his forgiveness, but instead of sitting by the roadside, the Master was walking with his disciples and the tribe of *hijaras*. Baba, when He was telling the story, gave a delightful picture of the Master leading all the elders, with their long beards and dignified, pompous manner, a merry dance through the streets of Lucknow as the elders sought to contact him and he managed to evade them. Baba seemed to enjoy telling the story; I still have that picture in my mind of Him.

Finally, after much undignified scurrying and haste, the elders, together with the young couple, parents, and onlookers, managed to catch up with the Master on the corner of the main street in town. All settled down and the parents pushed the young "bride and groom" forward to seek the Master's forgiveness. But the couple protested, "Why should we do so?" they said. "It was all the elders' idea, they should be the ones to seek his forgiveness!"

So it was the elders who were pushed forward. They approached the Master and said, "You remember this couple came for your blessings, and you blessed this one that he might have a child?" "No," the Master replied, "I blessed a woman, not a man. I asked her a number of times whether she really wanted the blessing. I brought home to her the responsibility involved in asking for such a boon. Now what can I do? My word has passed my lips; I cannot take it back."

The elders began to plead, "Please withdraw your blessing. Can't you see what calamity has befallen this youth?" "I cannot," said the Master. "It is not in my power. Once I have blessed someone, I cannot take it back. I am indeed sorry for the youth, but there is nothing I can do."

At this, all began to weep, especially the "bride," and they all fell at the feet of the Master begging his forgiveness and pleading with him to do something. Finally the Master spoke, "There is one way out. I cannot retract my blessing, so there is nothing I can do, but my friends, my colleagues, these *hijaras*, they may be able to help." "Help? How?" "Ask them to pray to God to have the blessing removed. Beg them to pray to the Lord and maybe He will hear their prayers and He may do something for you."

So the elders, the parents, the youngsters, everyone, turned to the tribe which they had always despised and rejected, and they begged them to intercede on their behalf, to help them, please, please, help. The Master turned to his people and said, "Yes, pray to the Lord that the youngster be relieved of his condition." So the *hijaras* prayed in accordance with the Master's wish and the pleadings of the community, and it came to pass that the boy's pregnancy gradually disappeared and he became normal.

This is a story that Baba Himself told us, and one of the main reasons for His doing so was to remind us to treat the friends of God with respect. Of course, we do not know if this one or that one is a friend of God. It is just that others say so. But because we do not know, and yet people say of these ones that they are great, Baba told us to just salute them from a distance. Have no ill feelings towards them, Baba told us, but do not go too close. To go close is to get involved – favorably or unfavorably.

Baba gave us this instance as an example. He once told one of His disciples to observe fast. I forget the exact period of time but I think it was for seven days. That was all Baba had said, fast for seven days. But the disciple on his own then proceeded to run ahead of Baba by not only observing fast, but by doing it at an ashram where there would be quiet and seclusion and a better atmosphere for fasting. Or so the disciple thought. So he went to this ashram and began fasting. After a few days the spiritual preceptor of the ashram came to this disciple and said that he had fasted enough and should eat something now.

The disciple had respect for the preceptor, but he explained that he had to fast for the full seven days that Baba had set. The preceptor, however, perhaps knowing that this man was not used to fasting, arranged for some food to be sent to him and given to him with instructions that he should eat. Since the food came from the spiritual preceptor, the man did not know how he could refuse it, so he ate it.

Later when he was with Baba, Baba asked him about the fast.

As always, Baba appeared to be completely ignorant, so Baba asked if this man had observed the fast as ordered. "Yes, Baba, it was fine." "Did you observe the full period of seven days as I asked you to?" Baba asked. "No, Baba, I broke the fast after a few days." "What? But I ordered you to fast for seven days. What happened?" "I went to an ashram and was fasting there and broke my fast because the spiritual preceptor there told me to eat some rice and dal. Because it was the preceptor telling me to eat, I thought it was tantamount to Your telling me to eat, so I broke my fast."

"Oh," Baba gestured, "so that is how you obey My orders! You broke the fast simply because a spiritual preceptor asked you to. But why did you go to an ashram in the first place? Why didn't you stay at home and go about your usual work? You say you love Me, but what is love if there is not obedience to the wish of the Beloved? This is why I have said, salute from a distance the ones whom others hold as great. All are good in their own place, but where I am concerned, keep aloof from them, and do not vitiate your love for Me by involvement with them."

⬙ QUICK THINKING

YOU HAVE HEARD ME SAY MANY TIMES that one had to have one's wits about one to stay with Meher Baba. Just as in the story I told the other day about the snake who was allowed to hiss but not to bite, so those of us living with Baba were not allowed to lie, but we had to be able to think quickly and use our wits. For example, when we were traveling with Baba, Baba went to great lengths to see that no one recognized Him. He would tuck His hair up under a hat and wear glasses and disguise Himself. For years and years, decades actually, Meher Baba traveled throughout India, covering thousands of miles by train and car and bus and bullock cart, and yet never disclosing His identity. So those of us who traveled with Him knew that He preferred to remain incognito. But even so, sometimes people would recognize Baba in spite of the precautions He took.

We might be sitting in a train compartment and someone else on the train would nudge me and say, "Is that Meher Baba?" Now, what could we do? On the one hand we couldn't simply lie and say, "No," because Baba would not like that. But on the other hand, if we said, "Yes," that too would displease Baba because it interfered with His work when people recognized Him. So what we would do in that situation was to look at the person quizzically and say, "What?" as if we were hard of hearing. "Is that Meher Baba with you?" "Who?" "Meher Baba." "What's that you're saying?" and so on, and the person would conclude that if we didn't recognize the name Meher Baba, then we certainly couldn't be traveling with Him, and so they would stop asking questions and wouldn't try and approach Baba.

You know, when Baba gave us an order, He never told us how we were supposed to carry it out; that was up to us. It was our duty to figure out how we could accomplish the tasks He would give us. And often we had to use our ingenuity. You just can't be a lump if you're going to serve the God-Man, you have to use your intelligence. You have to be shrewd and clever. One time we were traveling in the summertime and we were staying at a *dak* bungalow. Now, these bungalows were reserved for government officials. Technically we had no right being there at all. But my father was a high official. He was Inspector of Boilers and Factories, and he used to travel widely in the course of his job. So when we arrived at a dak bungalow, we would act as if we belonged there and I would sign the register book, "Jessawala and party."

Well, this one time we all signed in to the *dak* bungalow, and I was with Baba because it was my job to stay with Baba and see to His personal comfort. The other mandali usually stayed in another room, or in the courtyard so their snoring wouldn't disturb Baba. It was summertime, so it was very hot. You know, Baba never liked drafts. He would always have me close all the windows so there wouldn't be any breeze on Him. This made it unbearably hot, but this was the way Baba liked it. Well, this night, after a while, Baba gestured that He couldn't sleep, there was too much noise.

I listened, but couldn't hear anything at first. Then I put my ear to the floor and could hear the vibration. I said, "I think that's the noise of the fan from the downstairs room You hear, Baba." Baba instructed me to go downstairs and ask the man to turn the fan down.

Now, see the situation I was put in. We were not supposed to be staying in the *dak* bungalow to begin with. And now Baba was asking me to go tell someone who did have the right to be there to turn his fan down on such a hot night. Not only that, but as it turned out, the man staying beneath Baba was the executive engineer for the whole district, the man in charge, as it were, of the *dak* bungalows – who decided who got to stay there and who didn't.

I went downstairs, dressed only in my shorts, because it was so hot and because once Baba had given me the order, He wouldn't be pleased if I waited until I put my clothes back on before carrying it out, and I knocked on the man's door. I explained that my elder brother was staying in the room above and that He had been traveling and working very hard and desperately needed a good night's sleep but the sound of the fan was keeping Him awake and would it be possible for him to turn his fan down?

The man seemed to think this a rather unusual request, given the temperature, but I pleaded with him and he consented. I went back to Baba and reported what had happened. Baba lay down but after a minute or two sat up and gestured that there was still too much noise.

I should go and ask the man to turn his fan off completely. Now, I knew if I simply went down and asked him to turn his fan off that he probably wouldn't even open his door once he heard my voice. A high government official doesn't like being disturbed at night, and he had the authority to kick us all out of the bungalow since we didn't belong there. So I had to use my wits. I went and knocked very smartly and when he said, "Who's there?" I replied as officially as I could, "Message for you." "Slide it under the door," he said. "It won't fit," I replied. So, reluctantly, he got up and opened the door.

"Oh, it's you again, what do you want now?" "I want to thank you for turning down your fan, but I was thinking how hot it must be for you now, and I've come to suggest that you might be more comfortable sleeping out in the open. Since you were so nice as to turn your fan down for us, my companions and I will move your bed, and your nightside table and all your belongings out into the courtyard where you will be able to take advantage of the nice breeze. It will only take us five minutes, and I think you will be much more comfortable."

The man was completely taken aback by the suggestion, but I emphasized that it wouldn't be any bother to him, that we could effect the switch in only a few minutes and then he wouldn't be disturbed again for the rest of the night, and he agreed. So, with the help of Pendu and the other companions, we set up the man's bed under a tree in the courtyard, and he had a comfortable night's sleep. More importantly, by using my wits, I was able to see that Baba got what He wanted, which was the man's fan turned off completely.

The story has a nice little twist at the end of it, however. The next morning this man saw me and asked how my elder brother was feeling today. I said much better, that he had gotten a good night's sleep. "I wonder if I could meet your elder brother," the engineer asked. "I don't know. I'll have to ask him," I replied, and I reported the conversation to Baba, who surprised me by granting the man's request. I went back to the engineer and told him he could see my elder brother and thus he had Baba's *darshan*.

"I thought it must be Meher Baba," he told me afterwards. "Your requests were so unusual that I suspected that your elder brother was not an ordinary person. And this morning I checked the register and saw 'Jessawala and party, Ahmednagar,' so I was pretty sure it must be Meher Baba."

And so the man had the good fortune to have Baba's *darshan*. I sometimes wonder if the whole complaint with the fan hadn't been staged by Baba so this engineer would get curious and be prompted to seek Baba out.

I remember another time when Baba was staying at Lonavala near Poona. I was with Baba one night when He suddenly expressed the wish for some coriander. It must have been around one A.M. and Baba asked if I could get him some. "Sure," I said. "I'll wake up the kitchen staff and get some." Coriander is a common ingredient, and we always had some with us. I knew there was bound to be some in the kitchen, but Baba said, "No. Don't wake anyone up here. Can't you get it outside?" Now, at one o'clock in the morning, where was I to get coriander? But I said, "I'll try, Baba," and left.

At that hour, the market, of course, was closed but, as it so happened, I had had a big fight with the supervisor of the market a few days earlier. As I recall there was an open sewer near the market, or people were washing the vegetable in filthy water or something of that sort, and I had gone to the supervisor to complain about this unhygienic situation. So I knew where the supervisor lived. I now went to his house. Even though I had just had a big argument with him a few days previously, I had no choice but to go to him now. I knocked loudly at his door and succeeded finally in waking him up. I knew, as soon as he saw me, he would be furious, so before he could say anything I started apologizing for waking him at that hour and explained that it was an emergency, that I needed to get some coriander. I explained that my elder brother's last wish as he lay on his bed had been to have some coriander. I didn't lie, I never said it, but I managed to create the impression that Baba was on His deathbed. Finally the man's heart was softened, because he got dressed, came out and took his bicycle, and then led me to the market, which he unlocked and went inside and gave me a big bunch of coriander.

I returned, washed it, and gave it to Baba, who ate and relished it. Baba seemed pleased that I had been able to get Him some coriander at that hour of the night.

Another time there were four or five of us with Baba at Aurangabad. Baba expressed the wish to do some seclusion work in a cemetery there. Baba did not want to be disturbed by anyone, so we posted ourselves around the wall of the cemetery, each of us taking a different side so we could stop anyone from entering. Baba wanted a quiet, undisturbed atmosphere.

Unfortunately, as it so happened, I was keeping watch at the main gate and after only five or ten minutes I saw a funeral procession coming towards the gate. Baba had said we should see that no one entered, so I knew I had to stop the funeral procession. But how? I couldn't simply step forward and order them to halt. So I went to meet them when they were still a little distance away and began engaging those in the procession in conversation.

First, I commiserated with the people. I comforted them, giving condolences to the ones who were weeping, expressing my sympathy and sorrow for their suffering. It was a natural thing to do, and they didn't find it odd. But now that they had stopped to accept my condolences, I asked the name of the person who had died. Then I asked how old he was and under what circumstances he had died. What about the family, I wondered? How will they carry on? How many children are there? Are his parents still alive? And so on.

Then, after learning all about the man's family, I began asking the members of the procession about themselves. What their relation to the dead man was, what they did for a living, whether they had had any deaths in their families recently. In short, all manner of questions and random conversation. Whatever I could think of. Meanwhile, those at the back of the processions were wondering what was holding things up. I must have talked to the people for at least half an hour until, finally, I heard Baba's clap. What a relief that was. Midway through a conversation I stopped and turned my back on the procession and ran to the cemetery. There must have been some bewilderment on their part at this strange conduct of mine.

Baba had finished His work, and so we left the cemetery with Him through the main gate. As we were leaving, the funeral procession was coming in. Baba remarked, "How blessed is that body that I am here while it goes to its final resting place."

⚛ THE NEW LIFE

DURING MEHER BABA'S LIFE OF HOPELESSNESS AND HELPLESSNESS called the New Life, Baba decided to establish Himself at Motichur, from where He could attend the Kumbha Mela at Hardwar. The Kumbha Mela is held on dates connected with certain astronomical positions of celestial bodies and is attended by thousands upon thousands of sadhus and hundreds of mahatmas. Meher Baba contacted over ten thousand sadhus and sannyasis during this period. He did so by touching their feet with His hand or, in some cases, by placing His head on their feet. Each day He and His companions walked from Motichur to Hardwar, a distance of about twenty kilometers round journey, and then He moved around that area throughout the day on foot. The following three stories are from those days.

Meher Baba played the role of a perfect seeker during His New Life. Particularly during the period of the Mela, Baba would bow down to and touch the feet of each and every sadhu, regardless of whether the person was a rogue or a saint. These sadhus were contacted on the roadside or in their camps. Baba also contacted the many ashrams that were located on the banks of the Ganges.

In one of His visits to an ashram, after Baba had bowed to the head of the ashram, the Mahant (head of that sect of sannyasis) offered Him prasad. Baba turned away swiftly, as He always did after making contact. At the end of the day, before returning to Motichur, Baba suddenly said that He should have accepted the prasad offered by the Mahant. I replied, "Yes, Baba. I thought at the time that it was not in the spirit of the New Life not to accept." Baba asked if I could find that ashram and if I would recognize the Mahant again. I said I could and Baba told me to go back and accept the prasad on His behalf and express His apologies that the prasad, so lovingly offered, had not been accepted.

I found the ashram and contacted the Mahant, and he was happy to reoffer the prasad, which I then took to Baba. In a happy mood Baba distributed it to His companions.

Another incident from this time illustrates the way Baba could make use of the smallest incidents from our daily life to bring home the meaning of true spirituality. One day while we were walking between Motichur and Hardwar, we saw two crows mating. Now, this is a rare event. It is so rare that tradition has it that if anyone ever happens to see it, it means that the one nearest and dearest to the observer will die.

Now, when we saw the crows mating, Baba acted like an ordinary man and wondered whether something couldn't be done to ward off the death of one of our near ones. As with most superstitions, there is usually a traditional antidote, and in this case it was generally agreed that if we announced a "death," we would be able to avoid a real one occurring.

A lively discussion took place while we discussed this, with Baba provoking and stimulating it. He suggested that we send a telegram to Keki Desai, a Baba lover in Delhi, to inform those concerned that He, Baba, had died. But we companions felt that the shock of getting this news might prove too much for Keki. Knowing his love and devotion for Baba, we feared he might have a heart attack on receiving such a cable. We also didn't know how his family would take the cable, or other Baba lovers that he informed. Would people try to contact us when they heard the news, which was against the New Life orders? It seemed the cable might produce serious repercussions. Meanwhile, throughout this discussion, it seemed that Baba took the whole thing as a game, and yet at the same time was serious throughout, playing to the hilt the role of an ordinary man.

It was finally decided that instead of announcing Baba's death, we would send a cable saying that Pendu, one of the close companions who was with us, had died, and that an hour later we would send another cable announcing that Pendu had not died. When we reached Hardwar, the two telegrams were sent.

As it turned out, although we didn't hear about this until sometime later, the cables arrived in reverse order. First Keki received the cable announcing that Pendu had not died and to disregard the first cable. Keki was still puzzling over this when the cable arrived that Pendu had died. So no serious confusion or alarm occurred.

Everything that Baba does, no matter how apparently trivial, has immense significance. What the deep inner meaning behind this episode of the cables was I cannot say, but on an ordinary worldly level, the conversation about what to do now that we had seen two crows mating helped pass the time on our long journey by foot to Hardwar. It was a diversion for us all, the humor of it kept us amused and, who knows, perhaps getting those two cables in such quick succession (and out of order at that) helped Keki and his family realize the impermanence of life in Illusion and helped them ground themselves in the never-changing Truth of God as the only Reality.

This period of contacting sadhus at the Kumbha Mela was a very strenuous and exhausting period for us and especially for Baba. It was a long walk to make on foot, and then Baba would spend hours every day bowing down to hundreds of sadhus and then make the long walk back again in the evening. Our meals during this time were, as usual during the New Life, quite meager. We ate only once a day and only dal and chappatis then. But since we spent all day with Baba, it was some time on arriving back in camp before we could arrange to cook even this simple meal. It was suggested that a local boy be engaged to watch our camp during the day and to cook the evening meal for us.

Baba agreed to this, and a simple, good-hearted lad from the hills, named Satpal, was engaged. But when he saw how limited our diet was and the amount of physical exertion being expended every day, he began to worry that we weren't receiving sufficient nourishment. He suggested that some oil be purchased and added to our dal to make it more nourishing. Baba thought this was a good idea, and so the tin of oil was bought.

The next night when we returned, the dal wasn't cooked. We wondered why this was, and Satpal explained that he had wanted to make sure our food was fresh, so he waited until he saw us coming before beginning to cook. No one could fault him for such consideration, but even when the dal was finally served, it wasn't completely cooked. It wasn't soft and it tasted different from usual. But we ate it anyway, and after dinner Baba sent me to a nearby farm to get some grass for the bulls.

On the way I had violent diarrhea, but I didn't think much of it until I returned and saw that the whole camp seemed affected. The companions were all having attacks of diarrhea and Baba was complaining about stomach pains. I went to Satpal and asked him how he had prepared the evening meal. It turned out that instead of cooking the dal as usual and then adding a bit of oil, he had soaked the dal in the oil before cooking, instead of soaking it in water. When I went to examine the tin of oil, I saw that three-fourths of it had been used. No wonder we all got so sick!

After this incident, we discussed the food situation again, and it was decided that instead of oil, we should purchase some ghee. Baba never said no to these ideas. He always took an interest in such discussions and seemed to like the idea. So the next day, we carried back from Hardwar a large tin of ghee. It was extra work carrying such a heavy tin all that distance, but the meal that night made it worthwhile. Satpal added just a little ghee to the dal as it cooked and it tasted delicious to all of us. All were pleased at this experiment, which seemed to have turned out so well. That night Baba warned Satpal to guard the ghee well.

The next day, as usual, we walked with Baba to Hardwar so He could contact the sadhus. On the way back our minds naturally started thinking about the delicious food we would soon be getting. It was with great anticipation that we received our dal, but when we started to eat, we found that the extra flavor of the ghee was missing. We asked Satpal, and he said there was no more ghee left. We knew this couldn't be because we had brought a full tin back yesterday, so we asked Satpal what had happened, and sorrowfully he told us the sad tale.

A dog had come into camp and managed to drag the tin of ghee away. Satpal had looked for the missing tin but hadn't found it at once. In the meantime, the dog had knocked the tin over and, in the hot sun, the ghee had melted and run out of the tin while the dog licked it up as best he could. By the time Satpal found the tin, it was empty.

After this, Baba suggested we simply stick to our old routine. It seemed that on the New Life, even when we tried, austerities were not to be avoided. But this was Baba's way. Typically Baba would not say no to requests from His close ones for additional comfort, but then circumstances would arrange themselves so that eventually all agreed it was simply easier to do without.

For example, when Elizabeth Patterson was driving Baba during the Blue Bus tours, she found it very difficult to get up so early in the morning. But not only did she have to get up, she had to drive as well, which took a great deal of concentration. Elizabeth never complained, but she worried that in her drowsy state she might have an accident and asked Baba if she might not be allowed to have some coffee in the morning to help her wake up.

Baba thought this a very good idea, and at the first large town we passed through, he had a good thermos purchased and each morning it would be filled with coffee. Baba then ordered Elizabeth that anytime she felt drowsy, she had to pull over to the side of the road and help herself to the coffee. Now, Elizabeth knew that Baba did not like to stop unnecessarily on His tours, but on the other hand, it was now an order from Baba that when she felt drowsy she had to stop to have some coffee, so the first day she had the thermos, when she felt drowsy she pulled over to have some.

Elizabeth kept the thermos on the floor of the car near her feet, and when she opened the door of the car to get down, the thermos rolled onto the ground and smashed. Elizabeth was upset because she felt she had been careless, and she knew that Baba had gone to some trouble to get her the thermos. But Baba assured her that it was all right and not to worry about it, and that the very next time we went though a big enough town we would get another one. Which we did.

But the next time Elizabeth stopped and opened the car door, the same thing happened. I don't remember how many thermoses we bought, but each time the same thing happened until Elizabeth agreed that it was simpler not to worry about it and not buy any more. So it was. Baba wouldn't say no to us, but we would eventually decide, on our own, to do without.

This also did not happen on the New Life, but if you will permit me to digress some, this reminds me of an incident that occurred with Baba's mother, Shireenmai. In the early years, she would periodically come and stay with Baba. One time we were staying at Lonavala, which is not far from Poona. As always our diet was very simple, meager, one might say, and Shireenmai, who was a very good cook, Mani says, found the fare insufficient.

Now, Shireenmai happened to love pomfret, a type of fish. My mother knew this, so my mother arranged for some pomfret to be sent to us at Lonavala. She did this without telling Baba because she knew Baba would not approve of this extravagance, but on her own she arranged for some pomfret to be called for. The fish came, and my mother and Shireenmai were very happy. The fish was cooked and put on the table for Shireenmai to eat, but before she had even a bite, a cat jumped in through a window and ran off with the fish. Shireenmai, of course, blamed this on Baba.

But it was through such little incidents that we learned to accept our situation, to not be attached to our desires and even to find humor in the very way that our desires were foiled. Real spirituality doesn't consist of going off to the Himalayas and meditating, but in being content with what life gives us each moment.

⚜ MEHER BABA'S DIVINITY

YOU HAVE ALL HEARD ME SAY that for many years when I was with Meher Baba, I lived here as an observer. Baba had called me and my family to come to Him, and we had come. I did my best to obey Baba; in fact, when I was young I took pride that whatever Baba asked me to do, I could do. But I did not accept Baba as the Avatar.

Indeed, in the fifties when Baba first started proclaiming to the world, "I am the Ancient One. I am the same Ancient One come once again to live in your midst. I am the Avatar," my mind would say, "Is He that?" It was ironic because I was the one who used to speak out Baba's words to the crowds. I would say before thousands of the Lord's lover, "I am the Ancient One," and I would say it with authority, because that was the way Baba wanted it said (you see, it wasn't enough that I simply read Baba's board, or put His gestures into words; I had to put the proper inflection and emphasis on the words too), yet at the very instant that I would be saying these words into the microphone, my mind would be whispering to me, "Is He that?"

This went on for many years. But there were two incidents which helped finally convince my mind that Baba was who He said He was. One story I've told before, and it's even printed in Naosherwan's book—the one about the man who worked for the railways. He came to Baba and said he was accused of embezzlement, and Baba assured him, "Don't worry, Truth will prevail. Not a hair on your head will be harmed." I was there. I was interpreting Baba's gestures during this interview, so I remembered Baba's words very well.

So, when this man was later found guilty and sent to prison, my mind said, "What is this? Baba has said, 'Truth will prevail,' and now this man is sent to jail." I never said anything to Baba about it, but it upset me. You see, I was just an observer. I would watch everything and think about it, and it seemed to me that something wasn't right here. Baba had promised that Truth would prevail and that not a hair of this man's head would be harmed, and yet he had been found guilty and sent to jail!

Baba arranged for the man's family to be taken care of while the man was imprisoned, but the fact that he was sent to jail at all bothered me. In 1962 this man came to the East-West Gathering. He had been released from jail at that time and he was now standing in the *darshan* queue waiting for his chance to pass before Baba. His turn came, and Baba greeted him with great love as the man put his forehead on Baba's feet and then moved on. Baba gestured to me to call the man back. I did so. Baba gestured for me to help the man onto the platform.

Baba could have very easily just talked to the man while he stood in the queue, but He did not do that. The God-Man does not come to expose our weakness in front of others. There were some five thousand people sitting there in front of Baba, so Baba had the man brought up on the platform so that even though there were thousands there, Baba could have an intimate conversation with this man. Baba is always willing to put a curtain around our weaknesses, to accept us as we are, with infinite love. So it was that Baba now asked, "Now you are free?" The man said yes. Baba gestured for him to come close so there would be no possibility of anyone else over-hearing the conversation. And then Baba gestured, "Now tell the truth. Did you do it?" The man admitted, "Yes, Baba." Baba called the man nearer still and gave his ear a tight twist and then gestured, "Never do such a thing again. Now go, I forgive you."

It was a small incident and went unnoticed by the thousands who had assembled there for Baba's *darshan*, but it made a great impression on me. Truth had prevailed. Baba's words had not been mere idle reassurance but had reflected His true understanding of the situation. And I was struck by the extent of Baba's compassion, for Baba had known all along that the man was guilty, and yet He had still taken such pains to see that the man's family was provided for, that the children received a good education, and this had gone on for some time. Knowing that the man had lied to Him, knowing that the man had committed a crime, Baba's compassion was so great that He had looked after the man's family for years and then received the man Himself with great love. This was not ordinary compassion I had witnessed. This was infinite compassion. The compassion of the God-Man.

The other incident which made such a big impression on me

was also something which was kept secret from all but those most directly concerned. Baba was staying in Bombay, and a young man and woman came to see Baba. The man said, "I have come a long way to have Baba's *darshan*." I said that I would see if Baba would see him and went and told Baba that this young man had come to see Him. Baba called him in.

The young man was well dressed, he was wearing a suit and seemed to be well educated from a good family. But the instant he came inside, he fell at Baba's feet and began sobbing. "What do you want?" Baba asked. "I want your help," the man replied, and he went on to relate his story. He had gotten involved with a woman and now she was pregnant. He didn't know what to do.

"Are you married?" Baba asked. "Yes." "And the woman?" "No, she was a virgin. She also comes from a good family. Neither family knows. It will ruin all of us and the woman's pregnancy is far along." "Where is the woman?" "Outside." "Call her in."

When the woman came in, Baba asked the two of them if they would do exactly as He said. Both folded their hands and said yes. Baba then turned to the man and instructed him to leave, to go home and stay with his family and forget everything. "Leave her behind and go," Baba ordered. "Never do this again." The man promised and then left to return to his family.

Baba then turned to the woman and began comforting her. "Don't worry," Baba told her. "Will you obey me?" "Yes, I will," the woman answered. "Do one thing, then. Write a letter to your parents saying that you are here with me and feeling happy. Tell your parents you wish to stay here for some time." The woman wrote the letter as Baba directed and it was sent to her family. Then Baba called one of the mandali and arranged that the woman should go to an institution where she might have the baby. Baba arranged for her stay and for the baby to be adopted after it was delivered. This was all done very quietly. No one knew about it.

After the woman gave birth she returned and Baba told her,

"Remember what I have done for you. Remember Me, love Me, and never do anything like this again." The woman's family never knew, nor did any of her friends or associates. In fact, to this day, both the man and the woman lead good lives, totally dedicated to Baba, and no one in the Baba community has any idea of what happened in the past. This made a big impression on me. It was another example of Baba's infinite compassion. It wasn't just that Baba forgave and forgot, but the way He saw to every detail – the minute aspects of His concern.

You see, I was the one who was with Baba. I was given the opportunity to observe Him, not just during public *darshan* programs, but at all times, and I never saw the time when Baba didn't manifest this love, this compassion, this concern. At first I might have thought, Meher Baba is really an extraordinary person to manifest such attributes. But as time went on I realized that these were not the attributes of an extraordinary person, but the attributes of the Lord Himself. And I was struck by Baba's compassion and patience that He allowed me, who didn't believe, to be near Him all those years. He knew the doubts in my mind but He never sent me away, He never insisted I believe, He gave me the opportunity to be with Him day and night until His attributes finally convinced me. It was not His saying that He was the same Ancient One come again that convinced me, it was the divine attributes He manifested. No one other than the God-Man could have such patience, could demonstrate such love, such forgiveness, such compassion.

And that is how I came from being an observer who would think, "Is He that? Is that so?" to one who can now declare with full conviction, "He is the Avatar. He is the same Ancient One come into our midst."

⚜ T H E   P O O L   O F   L O V E

IT IS TRUE THAT WE MAY BE CONSCIOUS of our weaknesses and say that it is not possible for us to love Meher Baba, but we should not be defiant about this. We should remember that Baba says, "I love you and that is enough. If you cannot love, do not worry, remember I love you. I am here to love you."

Every now and then Baba would give us a description of what real love was. And sometimes, after explaining what love was, Baba would ask, "Do you love me?" Well, after just hearing about the saints, the *masts*, those who possessed real love, what could we say? Some of us might say, "I try, Baba," or "I would like to, Baba," or simply, "I don't know, Baba." Baba might ask me, "Do you love me?" and I would say, "I don't know, Baba." And Baba would look sad and gesture, "Well, can't you at least say, 'I love you'?" So I would say, "I love you, Baba." And Baba would gesture, "Give me a kiss." So I would go forward and kiss Baba lightly on the cheek, and He would gesture, "No, not like that, like you loved Me. Give Me a kiss like you loved Me." And I would kiss Baba again.

And this whole time, my mind would think, "What is it with this old man? Is He so desperate to be loved that He has to make us tell Him we love Him?" You see, I didn't understand at the time what Baba was doing. Why does the God-Man take birth? He comes to love His creation and to accept the love of His creation. The entire universe was created so that love could be freely expressed. Baba wants us to love Him, because through loving God we achieve our proper position in creation, and we experience the full charm of the love-game that God-Man has created. Baba wants us to love Him, and yet, on our own, we are not capable of loving God. So Baba tells us, "Say you love Me," knowing that if we simply say it, in obedience to His wish, whether we feel it or not, our very saying it in obedience, will help it come true.

Once someone said to me, "Eruch, aren't we kidding ourselves when we bow down to Baba's chair and pretend that He is here?" And I said, "Yes. But this is significant kidding. Because this kidding will one day make us see that we are only kidding ourselves when we say that Baba is not here. One day we will experience for ourselves the Truth that Baba is always here, that nothing is really here at all except for Baba, and then we will see that we were only kidding ourselves that Baba was not here."

This reminds me of an incident that occurred during Baba's visit to America in 1952. Baba was in Myrtle Beach and one of the people who came to see Him was a woman who had first met Baba in the States in 1935. She felt very bad that her way of life had displeased Baba and caused Him to suffer. Baba assured her that He loved her and not to worry about anything else. But the next day when she saw Baba she once again was upset that her weaknesses had caused Baba to suffer. Again Baba told her, "I love you," and then went on to assure her, "Do not worry about your weaknesses. Eventually they will go; even if they linger, love will one day consume them. Everything disappears in the Ocean of Love. Because I love you, you have a pool of love within you. When you feel wretched, when you fall in your weakness, have a dip in that pool of love. Refresh yourself in that pool of My love within you. It is always there. Even if you wash your weaknesses every day in that pool, it will remain clear. Don't worry. Baba loves you, that is what really matters."

Baba would comfort us, "You fall, you stumble, falter, but if you don't fall, how will I be able to exercise My infinite compassion? Remember, when you stumble, My hand is extended to lift you up."

All that matters is to remember Baba. Do not harp on and brood over your weaknesses, your failings, and your failures; that will lead you nowhere. What counts on the path of love is to begin to remember Baba more and more.

⚛ PRAYERS

MEHER BABA GAVE US THE PRAYERS that have become known as the Parvardigar or Master's Prayer, and the Prayer of Repentance. At times Baba asked us to recite these prayers, but when we were with Baba we did not have the urge to say them on our own. His presence, as I have told you, is something quite different from the concept of God. Baba has told us, "My work is greater than God," and, although we cannot understand this, and I do not know what God is, yet His presence is really overwhelming and everything – prayers, God, everything – fades into insignificance before Him.

But sometimes Baba would want us to recite the prayers, and He would ask me to say them. Baba would stand as one of us, in our midst. He would first wash His hands and face and then join His hands together in prayer; His appearance and His gaze would be that of one deep in the act of adoration, totally absorbed in participation in the prayers.

Because Baba would ask me to recite the prayers, I tried to learn them by heart. But as soon as we started praying, I completely forgot them. I became so absorbed in the first line, "O Parvardigar, the Preserver and Protector of all," that after that my mind became completely blank. Baba would look at me with displeasure and gesture for me to go get the book in which the prayers were written. So after that I stopped trying to say the prayers by heart, and every time Baba wanted them recited, I would go get the book and simply read them out.

Baba would wash His face and hands, using that blue basin and small pot you see by His chair. Water from the pot would be poured on His hands; He would wash His face, then dry Himself and stand up and worship with us standing around Him.

Time passed by, the seclusion work increased, and Baba became weaker and weaker, and He wanted the prayers recited more and more frequently. It became an everyday matter during the seclusion, and Baba, especially in the last year, could not stand without difficulty. Eventually the stage came where He needed to be supported on each side by two of us, and there He would stand as a worshipper. The Lord Himself prayed.

But because it was such a strain on Him, Baba would have me read the prayers faster and faster. I have already told you the story about the time I was reading the prayers so fast I started laughing because the prayers sounded to me just like an express train rumbling through a station with no time to stop. I could not understand why Baba was subjecting Himself to such physical strain. Finally I said, "Baba why do You do this? Can't You sit down?" Baba gestured, "Why should I sit down? Do you know what I am doing? My participation in the prayers will help every individual saying the prayers after I drop the body. My body is so weak I cannot stand. But it doesn't matter how you pray. The important thing is My participation in the prayers. After I drop this body, whosoever recites these prayers will be helped, because of My participation now. And when anyone repeats the prayers, I am there with them. My presence is there."

Now, this reminds me of a very good incident concerning Dr. Deshmukh. Deshmukh was a professor of philosophy, a Ph.D. and a brilliant scholar. He was also completely devoted to Baba and whenever he had vacation he would come to spend time with Him. In the earlier years Baba would not have us repeat the prayers regularly as He did in the last years. He had the pleasure sometimes and would ask me to recite them, but this was not an everyday occurrence. So it was that Deshmukh, who was one of Baba's close ones, did not know about this practice at all. He did not know that every now and then Baba would ask for the prayers to be read out. Or that afterwards, Baba would have the mandali file by, stand on a little stool, and He would bow to us, touching our feet with His head. As He did so, we had to call out a certain name of God, a name dear to one according to one's religion.

Thus some of us would say, "Ya Yezdan," others, "Ahuramazda," or "Parabrahma Paramatma," or "Allah-Hu," or, "God Almighty," depending on what religion we had been brought up in. But we were not allowed to say, "Baba." I remember when Baba first told us to repeat the name of God most dear to us, one of the mandali said, "Baba, Yours is the name of God most dear to me." But Baba instructed us not to use His name; to repeat one of the traditional names of God.

Now, one year, Deshmukh arrived for his vacation just as Baba had asked for the prayers to be read out. Baba had washed His hands and face, and we were all standing at attention, and I was just about to read when we heard someone jiggling the door latch. It was Deshmukh trying to open the latch to come in. As soon as he stepped inside Mandali Hall, Baba gestured, "It is good that you have come. You are fortunate, you are blessed to be with Me now. Come in and stand there with the others and be quiet."

Poor Deshmukh did not know what was happening, but he came and stood with the rest of us and I began reading the prayers. During the Prayer of Repentance, Baba would follow the common Eastern practice of *tasubah*, which means making the gesture of repentance, of softly slapping one's cheeks with one's palms, signifying, "Oh God, I will not do that," or "I repent, I repent."

Deshmukh was stunned at all this. In his heart he had always enthroned Baba as the Lord of Lords, the Highest of the High, the one who is prayed to, the one who redeems us when we repent, not one who prays Himself or repents like an ordinary man. He was very confused by this. His philosophical mind could not reconcile Baba's status as Highest of the High with His behavior of praying like an ordinary man. Deshmukh thought, "I take Baba to be God incarnate, but then who is it that Baba is praying to? If Baba is praying, then doesn't it follow that there is a God who is higher than Baba? But how can this be?'" Deshmukh was very upset and confused, but he never said anything to any of us. We noticed that he was more withdrawn than usual, but none of us had any idea what was going through his mind.

Well, not long after that Deshmukh's mother died. In India we have the custom that when someone dies, the family will take their belongings and wrap them up. Then on the anniversary of the death, a year later, the eldest child will open the bundle. So it was a full year later that Deshmukh opened the bundle and came upon a book which he remembered his mother was fond of reading. It was a book on Krishna.

Being a philosopher and scholar, it was natural for Deshmukh's attention to be drawn first to the book. So he picked it up and decided to see what it was that had caught his mother's interest so, and he opened it at random. He looked down and saw the chapter heading was, "The Lord Prays." The Lord prays? Deshmukh's attention was immediately caught and he started to read.

The watchman replied, "He said he wanted to pray." "Pray? My Lord is praying? To whom does He pray? Who is greater than my Lord?" Narada demanded and accused the watchman of blasphemy. But the watchman persisted in keeping Narada out, saying, "I am only telling you what He told me. He said He wanted to pray and that I should not let anyone in because He did not want to be disturbed while He is praying." Narada had no choice but to wait, and all sorts of confused thoughts were going through his head, just as similar thoughts had gone through Deshmukh's head when he had first seen Baba pray. Deshmukh read on with avid interest – how would it end, to whom was Krishna praying?

After half an hour or so, Krishna came out of his room and saw Narada waiting outside the door. He greeted Narada warmly, but Narada was so agitated that he made only the most perfunctory of greetings. "What's wrong?" Krishna asked. "You seem upset." Narada was so upset, in fact, that he totally forgot about the message he had come to deliver, he totally forgot that that was why he had come in the first place, and he blurted out, "The watchman said You were praying."

"Yes, that is so," Krishna affirmed. "But to whom do you pray?" asked Narada, whose confidence in the Lord was shaken by Krishna's admission. Krishna laughed. "Do you really want to see to whom I pray? Come with me." And Krishna led Narada to His prayer room. "Here, here is My God," Krishna said.

And what did Narada see? He saw little figures, little images of Krishna's mandali. There was a little figure of Narada, of Arjuna, of all the close ones. "These are the ones I pray to," Krishna explained. "I pray to My lovers. You see, the whole purpose of creation was so that My love might flow. I eternally love my creation, but periodically I take birth to receive the love of My lovers. My lovers worship me and I worship their love for Me."

When Deshmukh read this, he felt very much relieved. Now he knew why Baba prayed. All his confusion vanished. The next time he came to Baba, he confessed all that had happened, how the doubts had started in his mind and how they had been dispelled, and that was how we came to know of it.

ᗺ S L A T E S

I JUST TOLD A STORY IN WHICH I MENTIONED Meher Baba using a slate. In the early years, when Baba first stopped speaking, that was how He communicated. My first memory of meeting Baba occurred not long after He had started observing silence.

I have told that whole story before so I won't go into detail now, but one of my vivid memories from that meeting was of Baba sitting crosslegged on the ground with a pile of slates on either side of Him. Baba had a slate pen. I don't think you have slate pens nowadays, but in those days we didn't use chalk, we had special pens, known as slate pens, which were made for writing on slate. Baba used to take a slate and write on it to communicate with His visitors. When the slate was full, one of the mandali used to clean it. Baba used the slates for several months.

Padri used to tell the story how, in the early days, Baba would stay at night in the hut known as the Jhopdi at Lower Meherabad. During the night there was always one of the mandali sitting outside the hut, as a watchman. Baba would write messages on a slate and pass it through an opening, a small window in the hut if He wanted to communicate with the watchman.

One night while Padri was on duty, he fell asleep. After a while he woke up feeling refreshed and very happy that Baba had not discovered him sleeping. But when he went to the opening in the hut, he noticed the slate. On it was a message from Baba calling Padri an ass for sleeping on duty and saying how thirsty Baba had been while

Padri was asleep and there had been no one to get Him water.

According to Pendu, it was probably early in 1927 that Baba stopped using the slate. One day Pendu and Vishnu were with Baba and for some reason He didn't have a slate with Him. Perhaps one of the mandali had gone to clean it and hadn't returned. Anyway, Baba couldn't "talk" to the mandali, so He picked up a piece of newspaper and tried pointing out words on that. But you know what a newspaper is like. The print is too small. It was impossible to tell what Baba was pointing at. But this gave Vishnu and Pendu the idea of putting the letters of the alphabet on a board, with enough distance between them so that Baba could point easily and there would be no confusion. So they made the first alphabet board. Baba liked it so much that He never used the slates again.

☙ M E H E R   B A B A ' S   *C H A P P A L S*

GABRIEL PASCAL WAS A FAMOUS MOVIE DIRECTOR, and in 1933 Princess Norina Matchabelli had talked with Pascal in Paris about the possibility of his directing a film based on certain ideas of Meher Baba. Baba expressed great interest in having a film which expressed spiritual themes made, and many people were contacted, and we even have a copy of a screenplay that was done for Baba, but no film was ever made.

Anyway, in 1934, Norina arranged for Pascal to come to Zurich, Switzerland, to meet Baba for the first time. Pascal was more than a little skeptical about Baba and full of his own self-importance when he arrived. But after meeting Baba it was a different story. As one of the mandali remarked, "He went in as a lion and came out as a lamb." Pascal wrote about this meeting, "I was at once his devoted servant. Anything he wishes me to do, I will do. I shall not need a script. I shall go out with my men one day into the jungle and there we shall start on the film. It will be made on the spot. I shall show how God lives with men."

As I said, nothing came of the film, but Pascal met Baba again later on in India and a year later returned to the United States. As a farewell gift, Baba gave Pascal a pair of His *chappals* (sandals). These sandals and a small weatherbeaten suitcase were all the luggage Pascal had when he was put ashore in San Francisco by a sea captain Pascal had befriended in Bombay. Although Pascal, at different times in his life, made a good deal of money, he also spent quite freely and often was broke. So it was when he landed in the U.S.

This did not stop him from going to the Saint Francis Hotel, the finest hotel in San Francisco, and staying there, in the best room, as always. After a short stay, Pascal decided it was time to go to Hollywood and make his fortune, but the manager of the hotel, an Italian man who knew Pascal, demanded that he pay his hotel bill. Pascal assured the man that soon he would have millions and would pay the bill, but the manager was firm, if Pascal could not pay at once, he had to leave his suitcase behind as collateral.

Pascal then offered the manager Baba's sandals instead. "You have to realize," Pascal said, "that these sandals are worth millions of dollars. They belonged to a Master in India. I tell you, they will bring you good luck and you are fortunate to have them. Just being able to have them for a while is worth far more than the piddling little sum you are charging me for the hotel room!"

The manager was charmed with the idea of possessing, if only temporarily, such magical sandals and accepted them and let Pascal go. Sometime later, Pascal was once again back in the money and returned to San Francisco to retrieve his sandals. He went to the

Saint Francis, but the old manager no longer worked there. Apparently he had become quite successful, was a multimillionaire, in fact, and had quit being a hotel manager and was now a shareholder in a big company. Pascal went to see him and demanded the sandals back, but the man would not part with them. "But I have the money now to pay you for the hotel bill," Pascal explained. "It doesn't matter. Those sandals have been lucky for me. I wouldn't part with them for anything. All that I am now I owe to them." "But I will not only pay you. I will pay you my bill with interest."

But the manager refused to part with the sandals, no matter how much Pascal argued that the sandals belonged to him. Finally it was clear that the ex-manager was never going to part with the sandals, so Pascal asked if he could at least see them. The man agreed to this and had the sandals removed from the safe where they were kept. Baba's worn cowhide sandals, the work of an Indian village cobbler, were brought in lying on a solid gold platter. Such was the respect the ex-manager had for them, and for him, they were merely lucky sandals, he didn't even appreciate that these were the sandals that the God-Man had worn during His life. If he kept the sandals on a golden platter, then how should we display Baba's sandals? Shouldn't we treat them with even greater reverence?

This reminds me of another story about Baba's sandals which perhaps puts the question of the respect and reverence due to the sandals of the Lord into proper perspective. It seems that during the early years at Meherabad, Baba had instructed the mandali to follow Him any time He left Meherabad, no matter what the mandali happened to be doing at the time.

One day, Baba suddenly left Meherabad and began walking towards the family quarters near the village of Arangaon. Vishnu, one of the early mandali, saw Baba leaving and immediately rushed after Him, even though he was barefoot at the time. On catching up to Baba, Vishnu realized that Baba did not have any slate or a slate pen to communicate with. Baba sent Vishnu back to Meherabad to fetch a slate and a slate pen. He instructed Vishnu to wear His sandals in the meantime.

Vishnu hesitated. Who was he to wear Baba's sandals? He stepped back, but Baba insisted. Vishnu protested that he couldn't commit such a sacrilege, that Baba's sandals were holy and that he couldn't defile them by wearing them for his own use. At this Baba asked," Have you come here for Me or for My sandals? You are attaching more importance to My sandals than to Me. If you think My sandals are more important than obeying My order to you, then what's the use of your staying with Me?"

Vishnu saw his mistake, put on Baba's sandals, and rushed back to Meherabad to get the things Baba wanted. So yes, we should respect and revere anything associated with the Lord, but we should not allow our respect for any physical object to come in between us and our obedience to the Lord.

🔸 LOST IN HIS OCEAN

YOU HAVE ASKED, if you fail to carry out Meher Baba's order, His wish, His precepts, are you lost?

But lost where? In His infinite Ocean? Is there any room for us to get lost there? No, there is no room for us to get lost; He is there. But then, on this particular occasion or that, we displease Him, and then, so to say, we are lost. We have fallen and we should cry out for His help. Yes, it behooves us to obey Him, and if we do not, then, in a sense, at that moment, we are lost. Can I give you an instance, my own instance, where I should have been lost, yet now I find myself still amongst you all? Would you like to hear that instance?

It so happened that Baba called me and my family (that is, my mother and father, brother and sisters) in 1938 to be with Him, to leave everything and follow Him. Naturally we came and, by His grace, by His help, we followed Him. Somehow or other, we maimed ones, weak ones, could, by His grace, struggle, crawl, walk and even run sometimes. Years passed by. For myself I say that, well, I tried my best to please Him, to carry out His wishes.

Many things happened. We went on tours, *mast* tours, tours hunting for needy families, work to do with the poor, the mad, the *masts*, and the lepers. Then we were with Him in the New Life. He assured us we would not return, and we went out through India and then, somehow, we found ourselves back in the place where we had started, at Meherazad. There Baba completed the phase of the New Life called *manonash*.

The New Life was an exhilarating time because we had great freedom living a life of utter hopelessness and helplessness. But physically, it was exhausting. I was strong as a young man, stronger than any of you, but strength is finite, and Baba will push you to the very limits of your endurance. So it was that each morning when I got up, I would tell myself, one more day, just make it through the day. Because Baba had laid great emphasis on the *manonash* work and seemed to indicate that if He completed it successfully, the burden of work would be lifted somewhat. At least, that is the impression I got. So I struggled through, one day at a time, until at last, on January 31, 1952, Baba had the *dhuni* dug behind what is now my cabin and declared that He had completed the work one hundred percent to His satisfaction.

I heard that with a great sigh of relief, like a horse that has finally reached the stable and at last can have some sort of rest and relaxation. But no sooner had Baba announced that His work was completed than He started a new phase of work, which included traveling to the West, and Baba told me I was to accompany Him.

I said, "But Baba, it is impossible for this body to be of use to You, it is struggling, it is about to fall. It cannot stand the constant stress and strain. I will only be a burden to You if I go." Baba replied that He wanted me to come. But what was my job? To look after Baba's physical comfort, and I felt I wouldn't be able to do that. That Baba would have to take care of me instead of me taking care of Him, so I pleaded with Baba to excuse me, saying that I would only be a drag, a burden on Him.

"You must come," Baba answered. I fell on my knees and asked His pardon. "Please, Baba, do not do this. I know I will only be a drag on You." I knew within myself that it was not possible for me to go. The exertion on my body had been too much, the extreme fatigue I was experiencing made it difficult for me to stand up, my legs would tremble; I knew I was in no condition to travel to America and look after Baba there, so I begged Baba to release me, to let me stay behind. Finally Baba got upset at my attitude and gestured, "Well, what is the use then of your living with Me? Get out from here! Get out! If you don't obey Me, what's the point of living with Me?" Saying this, Baba left His seat to retire to His room for the night.

I quietly went to my cabin to prepare myself to leave. Baba was right, if I wasn't going to obey Him, then I should leave, so I started to sort out my things to leave. I went to pack up my belongings and picked up my blanket, but then I realized, this blanket isn't mine, it was given to me by Baba. The sheets were also given to me by Baba. We had come to Baba as refugees and everything we had had been given to Him. Now, everything I had had been given to me by Baba. Even the clothes I was wearing had been given to me by Baba.

I realized that I couldn't take anything, it all belonged to Baba. I would have to leave naked. It would be embarrassing, but that didn't bother me. What did bother me was the thought that someone would see me and think poorly of Baba. It wouldn't look right if I just walked naked away from Meherazad. I didn't mind for myself, but I didn't want to do anything which might put Baba in a bad light, so I decided to wait a little longer until it was dark, and then I would leave.

But I had no sooner made this decision than another problem confronted me. I thought, "Even this body is not mine. I have surrendered completely to Baba, not just my possessions but my body too. How can I now take it away? It doesn't belong to me but to Baba." As these thoughts were assailing me, one of the mandali knocked at my door with a message from Baba. I was to stay at Meherazad, eat supper, go to sleep, and Baba would talk with me in the morning.

But during that night, the Compassionate One had someone type up a long circular, and first thing the next morning, Baba gave it to me to read. To this day I don't know who stayed up that night typing the circular, but Baba just handed it to me and told me to read it. It said that not long after Baba left for the West, Pendu and I would be going out all over India and Pakistan to give Baba's message of love to all. We were to travel around the country, telling people about Baba and seeing who wanted to join Baba on the Life, the new phase of His work which was starting. I read the circular and I thought, "This is worse than if I had gone to America. Traveling in America would be easy compared to this." This was much more strenuous, would be much more exhausting, there was no doubt about it, but then I deserved it.

Baba asked if I had any questions. Nothing was said about the previous day, about Baba's ordering me to get out. Baba merely asked if I had any questions. I said, "But Baba, what should I say? I am not a public speaker. I have never given any talks, I don't know anything about spirituality. How am I supposed to tell people about You?" For since coming to Baba I had swept Baba's floor, I had made His bed, in short I had been Baba's valet; I was not cut out for public speaking.

But the incident in the cabin helped me, for I realized that nothing belonged to me, that I did not belong to myself. That helped me. If we lose ourselves completely, then He is there. It all depends on how far we lose ourselves. We need to lose ourselves totally, and then we become His. So He handles us. Sometimes we get blunt, sometimes too sharp, sometimes crooked; Baba just mends us and uses us as His instruments. So that all helped.

But still, when Baba asked if I had any questions, I said, "But what message should I give out?" Baba said, "Well, you have been living with me now for many years. Your eyes and ears have been open. Simply tell people about what you have seen and heard while living with Me for so many years." "But Baba, I am not a public speaker. I have never done anything like this." "What makes you think that you will be speaking? Before you begin to speak, stand there and remember Me. Say, 'Baba, You want me to speak, so speak,' and then just open your mouth and don't worry about it."

And after Baba left for the West in April 1952, Pendu and I set out to tour the country, and I did as Baba instructed. And I continue to do that now. Even today, as I sit here, I do what Baba told me to do. And being infinitely compassionate, Baba instructed me in one other thing which otherwise might have been a problem. As I have told you many times, although I lived with Baba, I was an observer, not a lover or a believer. Knowing that it would be difficult for me to say, "Baba is the Avatar," or "Baba is the Ancient One" with one hundred percent conviction, Baba instructed me to say, "Baba says He is the same Ancient One come once again in your midst." Even in this little thing, Baba's compassion rescued me.

So we get lost, there is no doubt, but He is always there to find us. If we fail to carry out an order, then we are lost, no doubt about it. But He is the one who will find us. It is never too late, and we are never lost forever.

Those who turn their backs to Him and on Him must, eventually, face Him because He is in all directions. He is the infinite One, He is infinite compassion, and in His compassion He tries to accelerate our facing Him. But we are free to remain adamant, inflexible.

We are free to turn our backs to Him, and He says, "All right, take your time, I am not in a hurry."

It is in His love that is always flowing that He is impatient. If we do not recognize this impatience, then we continue our path away from Him, and He will permit us to do so. But eventually we must face Him because He is everywhere. He is everywhere. There is no place where He is not. He is everything, there is no thing in which He is not. One time Baba asked us, "What is hell?" As usual, we all gave different answers, and then Baba gestured, "Whatever you take hell to be, know that I am there too. I cannot be excluded from hell because I am in all existence. So as soon as you grant hell existence, I too am there."

From the point of view of Reality, there is none but Him. So who is getting lost? Who is being punished? Who turns his face away from Him? None but Himself. There is none but Himself. So, really speaking, He is the one who turns away from Himself, He is the one who makes us fall, but unless we fall, how can He exercise his compassion? Yet, as human beings, it behooves us to take upon ourselves our weaknesses. Even if it is He who makes us fall, it is presumptuous of us to say that. It behooves us to take our weaknesses upon ourselves, to accept them as our own. And to struggle to overcome them. We must not brood on our weaknesses, or think, "I am so weak," all the time. But we must not become complacent either and say, "Well, I am only doing this because Baba wants me to." We must do our best to obey Baba, but we must also realize that it is impossible for anyone to lose His love and compassion. That is what we should concentrate on, not our failings, but His love. For His love is eternal and invincible.

◢◣ H O N E S T Y

MEHER BABA WANTS US TO HAVE ABSOLUTE HONESTY IN OUR LIFE. But now, if I were to be most honest at this moment, I would lie down and go to sleep. Honesty demands that I blurt out that I would like to go to sleep. But then there is also duty, and in the execution of my duty, honesty demands that I stay awake. Which honesty should we follow? Should we be honest to ourselves, or honest to the demands of duty?

I am reminded of a lawyer, a disciple of Baba's. He came to Baba very distressed. Baba had been emphasizing at this time that the only thing that God cannot forgive is hypocrisy, and the lawyer was stunned with shock. He said to Baba, "I am absolutely dishonest. In the course of my vocation I tell so many lies. I know many of my clients are scoundrels, but I have to endeavor to protect them, and so I tell lies. Baba, should I give up my work?"

Baba gestured to him, "To follow Me, you have not to give up anything. Begin to remember Me from where you are, from what you are and how you are, because I cannot be excluded from any area, any vocation, anything. If there is such a thing as hell for barristers, then you will find Me there. So continue with your vocation. Defend your clients, do your duty, and see that your clients gain victory. You have taken their brief and you must honor your pledge to them. If you shirk this responsibility, then you are being dishonest."

But, of course, a lawyer does not have to take a brief. If he feels a potential client is guilty, he does not have to defend him, he can simply refuse to take the case. And even once a lawyer accepts a case, he does not have to lie, but he does have to do his best to defend his client. That is what Baba was bringing home to the lawyer, that he has certain duties and responsibilities to those he chooses to defend.

Now, this reminds me of a story from the time of Prophet Muhammad which I told the other day, but it seems so appropriate that I will tell it again, and anyone who heard it and is bored can leave the room.

Muhammad was sitting with His lovers, and they were talking about this and that when a young man came forward and offered his obeisance to Muhammad. Muhammad blessed him and went on talking, as before, with the others. But the young man did not go away. He continued to stand there, so Muhammad turned to him and asked, "Yes, you want something? You have something to ask me?" The young man said, "Yes, I have a question I would like you to answer." "Speak out." "Can you tell me what work I should do?"

Muhammad laughed. "That is simple, follow your father's vocation," and saying that, He turned back to the gathering. But the young man continued to stand there, obviously distraught and unhappy. The others were intrigued. Here was a man who came to ask the Prophet what vocation he should follow, and the Prophet in His loving kindness had given him a simple straightforward answer, and yet he seemed very upset at this reply.

Muhammad said, "What is the matter? You do not seem happy. What did your father do?" The man was distressed but answered, "He was a thief." Muhammad looked at the youth and then replied, "So what? I tell you to follow your father's vocation."

At this the gathering was even more intrigued and astonished. What was the Prophet saying? They found it hard to believe, but Muhammad continued, "Continue with your father's vocation, but always remember two things. First, always do justice in your life, and second, whenever you hear the call to prayer, you must drop whatever you are doing and join in the prayers. Do you understand? Always observe these two conditions and you will not be bound by your vocation. Now go." So the young man bowed to Muhammad and left.

As he walked home, he took a route that would lead him through the prosperous section of town. He walked slowly, carefully noting the layout of each house, studying them with the practiced eye of a thief to determine which ones he might be able to plunder and how best to do it. For the young man had been a thief when he had been touched by the Prophet's call and decided to live a straight life. But he didn't know any other profession, and without stealing he soon was without money and was slowly starving. That was what had led him to Muhammad to see what profession he could do to survive. But now he had been told to go back to being a thief, and so he studied the houses as he walked by until he found one which seemed just right to him.

That night, he returned to the house and threw a rope with a hook attached to it over the parapet surrounding the roof. The hook caught and the thief silently climbed up the rope and was soon standing on the roof of the house. Now, he knew that it was the habit of wealthy folk to hide their money in the kitchen. Why was this? Because in those days the kitchen always had someone in it. Women were kept in purdah, and the kitchen was usually in the back of the house where the women were, and throughout the day there would be someone there, so no stranger could simply walk into the house and enter the kitchen without causing a big commotion.

So the thief now climbed down the stairs of the roof to the inside of the house and silently walked to the kitchen. He got down on his hands and knees and, in the dark, began running his hands over the floor. After a while he felt a minute difference in the surface, as if someone had dug a hole and then covered it over again, so he began to dig there, and sure enough, very soon he had uncovered twenty-five bags of gold.

The thief unwrapped a large cloth from around his waist and spread it on the floor and then piled all the gold bags on the cloth and tied it up. He slung the cloth over his shoulder and started silently walking to the stairs when he remembered what Muhammad had told him – always do justice. He thought, "I am alone in the world, I have no wife, no parents, no children, I do not need much. On the other hand, whoever it is that I have robbed tonight has a very large household. From the number of rooms I can tell that the family is large and there are many dependents." Thinking this, he untied the cloth and took out two gold bags and put them on the floor and then retied the cloth and started to the stairs.

"But is this justice?" he asked himself. "That I should take twenty-three bags for myself and leave only two for this household?" So he untied the cloth and took out two more bags. But again, after only going a few steps, he had to admit to himself that he still had not done justice, so he took out three more bags. "Now I have left seven bags," he thought. "That is enough to see that the household does not starve, and obviously the head of the house must have a prosperous business and in no time can save more."

Yet he was only partway up the stairs when he remembered Muhammad and felt in his heart that the Prophet would not consider that he had done justice, so he took out three more bags. On the one hand, he told himself, "With what I have taken tonight, I will not have to steal again for a long long time. So the other people I might have stolen from will also benefit." But on the other hand, it kept occurring to him that there was no way he could really justify taking more than half of the household's wealth, so he took out another few bags.

By the time he reached the roof's parapet, he had only five bags left in the cloth. "I have left twenty behind. That is still a considerable fortune, so the family will not suffer too much," he thought. "I have only kept five for myself. That is just." And thinking this, he took the rope in his hand and was about to descend to the street when the early morning call to prayers could be heard issuing from the mosque. He had spent so much time deciding how much gold to take and tying and untying his cloth that it was now almost dawn. He stopped. He remembered the second condition Muhammad had laid on him — whenever you hear the call for prayers, you must stop whatever you are doing and join in. The man let go of the rope, put the cloth down, and began praying in his normal voice on the roof.

Immediately the man of the house was awakened. "What's that?" he asked his wife. "It sounds like someone praying." "Impossible," his wife answered. "Nobody prays in our house. What need have we for prayers? Go to sleep." (Because, of course, we only pray when we need something from God.) "No, no, listen," the husband insisted. "I tell you there is someone praying." So they listened and it sounded like someone was praying on their roof, so they both got up and walked to the stairs. But as they did so, the husband tripped over something. "What's this?" he exclaimed. For it was one of his bags of gold. "We've been robbed!" he shouted and started hurrying up the stairs. But every few feet he found more bags of gold, and by the time they reached the young man who was kneeling by the parapet in prayer, he had recovered most of his gold.

The man was bewildered. What had happened? He had been robbed, that much was clear, but then why did the thief leave so many bags behind? And who had robbed him? He saw the bundle next to the youth praying and guessed that the remaining gold bags were tied up inside, but if this man was the thief, then why was he kneeling here praying? It didn't make any sense. But even though he was bursting with curiosity, he dared not disturb the youth's prayers. That was the custom in those days. Another's worship was respected, even if the man was your worst enemy, so the head of the house stood there for ten minutes until the youth was finished and then immediately demanded, "Who are you and what are you doing here?"

"I am sorry," the youth replied, "I am a thief." "You are the one who stole my gold?" "Yes." "Then why didn't you climb down the roof with the gold? Why did you stop here to pray, and to pray so loudly that we were awakened and could catch you?" "It was prayer time, so I prayed," the youth replied. "And this is the proper way to pray." "But if you really are a thief, why didn't you take all the gold? Why did you leave so many bags behind?" "Because I thought it wouldn't be just if I took all the bags, when there is only one of me and you have such a large household to support."

The householder was totally mystified at these responses. "What kind of thief are you?" he asked, and eventually the whole story came out. How the youth had tried to go straight but had been starving and how he had gone to Muhammad and how Muhammad had told him to continue his father's vocation but to always see that justice was done and to never neglect praying whenever he heard the call.

The householder was quite impressed. The youth was a thief, and yet he seemed a completely honest thief. "If you had some other vocation you could do, would you do that?" he asked. "Yes," the youth replied, "but I am not trained to do anything else." The householder thought about this. The youth's sincerity impressed him, and he needed a manager for his business. All the managers he had hired stole from him; there was no one he could trust. He looked at his wife and she nodded, for she knew what he was thinking.

So he turned to the youth and asked him if he would be willing to work for him. "Of course, your salary will be lower than usual at first to make up for tonight," he added, for he was, after all, a businessman, and a businessman is always eager to make the most of every situation.

But soon the youth proved so honest, so reliable, that the businessman was making much more money then he ever had in the past and, at his wife's prompting, began paying the youth a very good salary. In fact, the wife had more than that in mind, for they had a young daughter, and ever since she had seen the youth on the roof that night and been so impressed with his simplicity, and honesty and obvious devotion to the Prophet, she had felt that here was someone who would make her daughter a good husband. That is why when her husband looked at her she had nodded her head.

And before too long, the marriage was arranged and the youth was made a full partner in the business. So it was that the youth's first attempt to thieve, in obedience to Muhammad's wish, was also his last. He obeyed the Lord, had done exactly what he had been told, and his thieving became a blessing. Obey Him without any why or wherefore, and all will be well.

ᐊᕆᐅ *M A Y A*

REALITY NEEDS ILLUSION in order to point out that this is illusion. Baba once gave a good example of why this is so. We were up north, near the Himalayas. It was very, very cold. We did not have heaters or any such thing and we lived in a small room. We were there for more than a month. Baba used this room and our circumstances for His example.

We had our beddings spread on the floor, and we were as neat and tidy as we could be, but there was never time to really sweep or clean the room. Baba kept us too busy for that. One day Baba was trying to bring home to us the nature of Maya, and He used our room as an example. He gestured, "Now suppose, in this room, I point out to you the dustiness, the uncleanliness of the room. You hear Me, but you remain complacent and uncaring. You say to Me, 'Yes,' but you do not rise to the occasion and really feel that it is so dirty. So you continue to live in this room.

"Then I tell you again and again, but you do not take any notice. You say you are very cozy, very comfortable, and that there is nothing wrong in the situation. Now suppose I take a broom and begin sweeping, and all the dust that has accumulated for so long fills the air. You can't breathe, you become choked, and you rush out of the room. That experience of choking dust gives you the conviction that the room you were living in was indeed a dirty room."

This is the way we live our lives in the world. We are so engrossed in whatever it is we are doing that we never have time to clean or dust. We are not even aware that dust has accumulated. Then the time is ripe for Baba, the Awakener, to come as sweeper and enter our lives. He begins to sweep and, in doing so, raises the dust you were not even conscious of. That dust is like the buried attitudes and tendencies of the individual.

When individuals come to Baba, they often begin to experience things that surprise them. They say, "But we never used to become angry, and now it often happens. Instead of not having unpleasant and disturbing tendencies, we seem to have more of them more often." But Baba told us, "In order to get rid of something, first you have to dig it out." Raising dust is like making us aware that we have depths in our being that we smugly thought were not there. Baba uses illusion to make us more aware of illusion and increase our longing for Reality.

This reminds me of a story from the time of Buddha. One day Ananda, Buddha's close disciple, said to Buddha, "Lord, you are always talking about Maya, but what is it? Please show me Maya." A few days passed and it so happened that Buddha and Ananda were traveling through a hot, dry part of India. After walking several miles, the Buddha sat on a rock under the shade of a tree and said,

"Ananda, I am thirsty. Can you fetch some water for me?" Ananda went at once to try and find water.

He walked quite a ways and came upon a small farm. He thought the farmer might have a well and went up the house to ask permission to draw some water. He knocked at the door, and it was opened by the most beautiful woman Ananda had ever seen in his life. Instantly he was spellbound. He just stood there and stared at her, speechless. He had completely forgotten why he had knocked at the door; all thought of water was gone. The woman, for her part, was equally struck with Ananda, for he was a handsome man and his love and devotion to the Buddha had changed him so that all who came into contact with him were struck by his presence.

So the two of them just stood there staring at each other, without saying a word. After a while the farmer returned home and asked Ananda what he wanted. "I was wondering if you had any work that I could do for you," Ananda answered spontaneously, for his only thought was that he had to spend more time near this beautiful woman he had just met. Of course, farmers always have work that needs doing, so the farmer agreed to hire Ananda to help him in the fields. And so the days passed, and Ananda's love for the woman did not lessen in the least. If anything, it increased, and the only thing Ananda knew was that he wanted to stay near her. He also wanted to please her father so he would not be sent away, and he worked hard every day and came home exhausted, but content that for an hour or two, before bed, he could sit near the daughter.

After a while, Ananda got his courage up and asked the farmer if he could marry the daughter. The farmer was happy because Ananda was a good worker and he knew he would look after his daughter well. And, of course, the daughter and Ananda were happy, and so the marriage took place.

The years passed and Ananda and the woman had three children. Ananda continued to work very hard and the farm prospered. After a while, the father-in-law died and Ananda inherited the farm.

There was more work to do now, but Ananda was happy. His life seemed perfect. He loved his wife and his children, and there was enough to eat because the farmland was fertile and it seemed that there was nothing else Ananda could wish for.

Then, after twelve years of contented married life, there came a flood. Overnight the river rose and overflowed its banks and came rushing towards the farm. There was no time to save anything. Ananda put one child on his back and held his wife with one hand and the other two children in his other hand and was swept away by the current.

Ananda started swimming hard so as not to go under, and as they were pushed along by the flood they saw animals drowning in the torrent. Ananda felt his only hope was to try and swim across the current to the other side because there was a hill there which was not submerged, and if he could make it to there they could be safe. But a flood means what? The current is not like that of an ordinary river, and Ananda had not gone very far at all when the child on his back was swept away by the current. His head was seen briefly above the raging waters but then disappeared from sight and was never seen again.

Ananda cried out in despair but kept on swimming. But the current was too strong and before long his two other children could not hold on any longer and were also swept away before their parents' eyes. Now Ananda only had his wife left, and he was determined to hold on to her. They had almost made it to the high land where they would be safe when the flood tore them apart. Ananda desperately reached out for his wife, touched her for a second, but the current drove her under and she too was lost. With his last strength, Ananda kicked and managed to throw himself on the dry land, where he lay exhausted and weeping bitterly about the loss of his family. His heart was broken.

Behind him came a gentle voice, "My child, have you brought the water?" Ananda looked up and there was the Buddha, sitting on a stone, looking at him with great compassion. "The water?" Ananda repeated, unable to take it all in. "Yes," Buddha replied. "You left at least half an hour ago to fetch water, and now that you have returned I was wondering whether you had brought any." "Half an hour!" Ananda exclaimed. "But that can't be. I . . ." and now he lowered his head in shame, for he remembered how he had forgotten his Lord. "But what about my wife? I was married. I had children. Twelve years have gone by!"

The Buddha smiled and shook his head. All of Ananda's twelve years of married life had taken place in less than half an hour. "That is Maya," said the Lord.

KRISHNA NAIR

IT WAS IN 1939, I believe, that we traveled to Bangalore with Meher Baba. It was here that I was first sent out to find *masts* for Baba. It was here that Baidul and I first came across the ghous *mast* and received such a shock. After we reported back to Baba about our *mast* journey, Baba came with us to contact the *masts*. For some reason, this region of South India always had many *masts*.

This region also had many languages. I speak Gujerati, Hindi, Marathi, and English, but the people around Bangalore don't know these languages. And I didn't know Telugu, Tamil, Kannada, or the other languages which the South Indians speak. Therefore, some boys were found who could translate for us. There was Amdu,

Venkoba, and Krishna Nair. They helped us in contacting the *masts*, and with their help a large *mast* ashram was created at Bangalore. Chatti Baba was there, Karim Baba, Phool Baba, and many others.

When we left Bangalore, the *mast* ashram was disbanded. Many of the *masts* were taken to Meherabad. The rest were sent back to their homes. Baba called the boys to Him and told them that they should ask Him for whatever they wanted.

Amdu, I remember, wanted his own *jatka*, a small carriage with a horse, like the tongas you see here. Baba made the gesture, "Granted." Venkoba said he wanted to be a businessman, and again Baba made the granted gesture. When it was Krishna Nair's turn, he said all he wanted was to be able to stay with Baba. Baba granted his wish, and he then joined us and did nightwatch for Baba for many years.

One night, as usual, he was sitting silently outside Baba's room. Baba often emphasized that those during night watch had to remain absolutely still and silent. But that night the mosquitoes were particularly fierce and, try as he might, Krishna finally could not resist moving silently to avoid them. Instantly, Baba severely reprimanded him.

At this, Krishna lost his mood and he started thinking about the unfairness of it all. The more he thought about it, the more unjust Baba's reprimand seemed. He started to wonder, "Can Baba really be God? He says He is God in human form, but He has no pity or consideration for those who serve Him." You know how it is with this monkey mind. It is not content with just suggesting that you have been wronged, but it keeps magnifying the wrong done until you are convinced that only a devil could have treated you this way.

So it was with poor Krishna. But finally his nightly period of watch passed and Baba told him to have breakfast that morning at four A.M. and then get a tonga so that they could go contact a *mast* who stayed about six miles from there. This *mast* was part *majzoob* and part *salik* – that is, sometimes drowned in love for God and sometimes conscious of his love for God and of the world and his surroundings.

Krishna decided to arrange for the *tonga* first, before having breakfast. It turned out that there were complications, and by the time everything was straightened out, he had missed his breakfast. This did not improve his mood, and as Baba and a few of the mandali set out to contact the *mast*, it was a thoroughly disgruntled Krishna who accompanied them.

Now, the *mast* they were going to contact had some unusual peculiarities. For the previous two years he had never stood on both his feet at once. One year he had stood on one leg, and the next year he had stood on the other. He also was observing silence. Baba instructed the mandali to stay well behind Him, at least fifty feet, when they approached the *mast*.

Although this *mast* had a large following, no one was around as Baba approached. On seeing Baba, the *mast* immediately stood on both his feet and, breaking his silence, exclaimed, "Oh, God! I have been waiting for you for so many years and at last you have come!" and then he prostrated himself before Baba.

After the contact, Baba returned to the ashram. The next day, He sent Krishna to contact the *mast* again, but when he arrived, Krishna found that the *mast* had died. The *mast's* followers told Krishna that the *mast's* last words were, "I met God face to face and He blessed me. My life's mission is fulfilled."

This experience restored Krishna's faith in Baba as God in human form. It also restored his mood of willing, cheerful obedience to his Master's orders.

But perhaps I should add a footnote to this story. You remember how I mentioned that Baba had told the boys to ask for whatever they wanted? Well, we returned to Bangalore in 1944, I think it was, although I am not sure of the date. I can't remember dates anymore, but at any rate, you can take it that it was only a few years later. We went by train, and as we were leaving the station someone came up to us. We didn't recognize him but he recognized us and he came running up to us. "Do you want a ride into town?" he asked us. It was Amdu. He was now a *chatka* driver. He had his own carriage, just as he had asked Baba for.

What about Venkoba, you may ask? Well, after we left Bangalore, he came to Meherabad and asked Baba whether he could stay on the property that had been set aside for the Spiritual Center Baba had planned to build at one time. Baba later abandoned the idea, but twelve well-constructed plinths had been erected and although the buildings had never been built, the plinths still stood. Venkoba asked if he could stay there. Baba said he could.

Later, when we returned to Bangalore, Baba went to see Venkoba and asked him what he was doing. "I'm a salesman, Baba," he said. I think he was working for a store or a company in Bangalore. Time passed, and one day Venkoba showed up at Meherabad with the news that someone wanted to buy the property.

Baba seemed very excited at this news and explained that He was in great need of money just then, and He told Venkoba to sell the property immediately. Venkoba did so and returned again to Meherabad with the money. He handed the money to Baba, the money which Baba said He needed so desperately, and Baba gave most of it back to him and told him to keep it. I can't remember how much the property sold for, but if it was 5,000 rupees, then Baba kept 1,000 rupees and gave the rest to Venkoba. Or if it was 500 rupees, Baba kept 100 and gave the rest to Venkoba. And it was with this money that Venkoba set himself up in business and became a very prosperous businessman. Thus Baba saw to it that Venkoba's request was also granted.

Krishna Nair, as I said, was with us many years, but eventually he left. Since this story was first published, he returned and he is now living with us once again at Meherabad. So in this way, all three have had their wishes granted by Baba.

◿◿ IS THAT SO?

SO OFTEN YOU HAVE HEARD ME SAY, "Be determined to be His." Yet people come to me and say, "But Eruch, how can we determine to be His?" What can I say? If you are determined to be a lawyer, do you need someone to tell you how to be determined to be a lawyer? No. You simply are determined to be one, so you study and you work, and you do whatever is necessary until you get your degree and are certified as a lawyer.

If you are determined to be His, then you do whatever is necessary to become His. This doesn't have to be explained. But the mind, oh the mind, what can I tell you about the mind? You know what the mind is like. So the mind says, "But what is necessary to do to become His?" Even in the presence of Baba, people's minds would play mischief this way. Baba would tell a large gathering, "Love Me." And someone in the crowd would stand up and ask, "But how should we love You, Baba?" Baba asked the man if he was married. He said. "Yes." Baba said, "Does anyone have to tell you how to love your wife?" "No, Baba." "So no one needs to tell you how to love God, you just do it." It's that simple and that difficult.

And yet, there are hints, indications, when we are on the right track. And one of these hints that we are on our way to becoming His is when we develop an unshakeable acceptance of His will. By this I don't mean mere lip service, as when people come here and they tell us, "Yes, I left my wife, but what to do, it was Baba's will." I'm not talking about that kind of acceptance that uses Baba's will as an excuse to do whatever you secretly want to do, but a resignation to His will so profound that it remains the same regardless of the circumstances. Maybe this story will help drive home the point I am trying to bring to you all.

It so happened that in a certain area of the country there lived one who loved the Lord. He had settled in an isolated area some distance from the nearest village. There was a small cave in a hill a mile or so outside of the village, and that is where he stayed. You may call him a recluse if you wish, but what need did he have of other people's company when his constant companion was the Lord? But, as Ramakrishna Paramahamsa said, "When the flower is ripe, the bees come of their own accord." And so it was that the villagers started coming to visit.

You know how it is. First, probably, it was just one of the boys herding goats who happened to notice that someone was living in the cave, and he told the other boys and they told their parents, and so people started coming to see who was there, out of curiosity and to pay their respects. For it was obvious that it must be a devotee of the Lord, for who else would choose to live in such an isolated place?

And so, bit by bit, the villagers started to go visit this recluse, and what did they find? They found him absorbed in his devotion to the Lord. So the people would humbly bow, pay their respects, and leave. But every once in a while, they might come when he was just sitting at the entrance to his cave, seemingly lost in admiration of God's creation. And they would seize this opportunity to begin a conversation, as they were naturally curious to know where he had come form, how long he planned to stay, what sect, if any, he belonged to, whether he could give them mantras to protect their livestock, in short, the usual endless questions that worldly people have for those who have given up the world.

But no matter how hard they tried, they could not engage him in conversation. For his response to everything and anything they said was always the same, "Is that so?" If they told him how they had come just to see him, he would look up very serenely and reply, "Is that so?" If they wept and said one of their family members was sick, he would reply just as calmly, "Is that so?" In short, to each and everything his answer was the same, a very gentle, "Is that so?"

This was a disappointment to those thirsting for gossip or words of advice or comfort and yet the villagers found that they were comforted and sustained just by sitting in his presence. They began to send him small offerings of food which they would leave outside the entrance to his cave. And sometimes they would sit there for a while, enjoying the peaceful atmosphere, before returning home. All were happy. The recluse was pleased to be left alone to his worship and adoration of his Beloved, and the villagers were happy that their area was blessed with the abode of a true lover of God.

Now, it so happened that in the village itself we find an entirely different scene. One of the unmarried girls had become pregnant. Her mother eventually discovered this and was horrified. She began weeping and wailing at this calamity. When the father returned home in the evening, he was even more upset at this revelation and began yelling at his daughter, berating her and demanding to know who was responsible for this outrage. You see, in those days people were very strict; such a happening brought disgrace and dishonor on the whole family – even the village felt itself shamed.

The girl began to weep, but she was afraid to name the one responsible for fear that her parents would hurt him, so the more her parents demanded to know who had done it, the more she wept. Finally she blurted out, "Don't keep saying, 'Who is responsible?' If you must know, you are the ones at fault. It is because of you that I am now in such a wretched state." "Our fault! But how can that be?" "Because you are the ones who used to send me every morning with the bowl of curds for the saint living outside of town." "So? What had that to do with . . . you mean he is the one?"

And the girl tearfully confessed that one morning after leaving the curds, the saint came out of the cave and raped her and she hadn't dared say anything until then because she knew what high esteem he was held in by all.

Well, the parents were understandably shocked and outraged at this, and the father began cursing the scoundrel and muttering, "I knew he was up to no good." See how the mind works. Only that morning he had sent the saint a bowl of curds and spoken of him with the greatest reverence, but as soon as his daughter confessed that he had raped her, then suddenly he always knew that the saint was an imposter, a rascal.

So the father goes to the village elders and tells them what has happened. Most are for going to the cave immediately and thrashing the man. But a few, remembering the feeling they always had in his presence, found it difficult to believe that he could have done such a thing and insisted on confronting him first, before taking any action.

Thus, a party of the village men tramp out to the cave and call the saint out. After a while he emerges, as unconcerned and benign as ever. "You rascal," the father shouts on seeing him. "You raped my daughter!" "Is that so?" the saint replied, as if the father had merely said, "It seems like it might rain." The father rushed forward to strike the saint, but one of the elders held him back and addressed the saint himself. "This man's daughter is pregnant and she claims you are the father." "Is that so?" the saint replied with equal unconcern. "She says you raped her!" "Is that so?"

Well, this was too much for the father. "Have you no shame!" he declares. "And to pose as a lover of God, you hypocrite!" and he began beating the saint.

The other villagers are also enraged that the saint showed so little concern at such a serious accusation, and they conclude that such indifference can only reflect callous guilt, and they are also outraged that all these years they have been duped into feeling the man was a saint when in reality he was the lowest of the low, and they all take their anger out by hitting and kicking the saint. Finally, leaving him for dead, they return home, satisfied that they have done what honor demanded.

But the saint did not die. He crawled back to his cave and went on with adoration of the Lord as always. Meanwhile time passes and the daughter gives birth. The parents don't want the child, as it only reminds them of their disgrace, so the father, who has heard from the goatherders that the saint is still living in his cave, goes there and takes the baby with him.

The saint is sitting outside the cave, silently marveling at the beauty of his Beloved, when the father approaches and thrusts the baby in his hands. "Here, this is yours." "Is that so?" the saint asks, looking at the child. "This is the fruit of your evil action, now it is up to you to look after it." "Is that so?" The father stalks off, and the saint, as unruffled as ever, begins to raise the child. Some of the shepherd boys give the saint some milk which he feeds to the child, and so time passes.

Meanwhile the parents feel that the only way they can really get over their shame is to get their daughter safely married. Of course, it is out of the question to marry her to anyone in their own village, but, by promising a large dowry, they manage to arrange for her marriage to an older man living in a nearby village. With great happiness they announce to the daughter that they have found her a husband. But, to their astonishment, the daughter starts crying. "I won't marry," she says. "What are you talking about? You have to get married. You are of age, you can't stay in our home forever, and we have a good man in the next village who is willing to marry you in spite of your past." And they began to extol the virtues of this marriage. But the more they go on, the more their daughter weeps.

She declares, "If you make me marry with any other person, I will kill myself." The parents can't understand this at all. What does she mean, "any other person"? Finally, the girl confesses, "I love another. I have loved him for years. If I marry anyone, it will be him or I won't marry. He is the one who fathered my child, and he will be my husband or nobody will."

The parents can hardly believe their ears. Immediately the

father feels crushed with guilt. The saint had not been responsible for his daughter's dishonor, but he had dishonored the family by abusing the saint. With great embarrassment and shame, the father goes to the village elders and confesses to them what has happened. They are also all abashed at their former treatment of the saint, and they realize there is nothing for it but to go and beg his forgiveness. So once more the father and the village men climb the hill outside the village and stand humbly at the entrance of the cave.

They beseech the saint to come out, and soon he appears, carrying a small happy child in his arms. The father is so humiliated at this that he almost can't say anything, but he falls at the saint's feet and finally blurts out, "Forgive me, I have done you a great wrong." "Is that so?" the saint asks mildly. "Yes, I am sorry. My daughter has confessed. Here, this is not your child," and the father takes the infant back. "Is that so?" the saint replies. All of the villagers join in begging forgiveness and asking the saint's pardon, but all he ever says is, "Is that so?"

After confessing their errors, begging forgiveness, and leaving all the gifts and garlands they had brought, the repentant villagers tramped down the hill while the saint went back inside his cave to continue his worship of the Lord as if nothing had ever happened.

When he was given the baby and told it was his, he said, "Is that so?" When the baby was taken away and he was told it wasn't his, he said, "Is that so?" When he was abused, "Is that so?" When he was honored, "Is that so?"

And why was this? Because the saint, as a true lover of God, took all that happened as His will. As long as we are for ourselves, even if we try to love the Lord, we cannot be resigned to His will. But if we become His, then His will becomes our pleasure and every manifestation of it is a fresh marvel of His divine attributes. If we are His, our equanimity is never disturbed because it is all His doing, and His presence sustains us.

APPENDIX

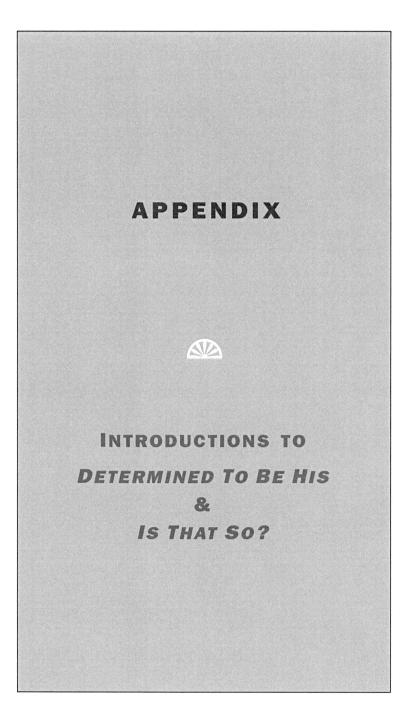

INTRODUCTIONS TO
DETERMINED TO BE HIS
&
IS THAT SO?

INTRODUCTION TO DETERMINED TO BE HIS

AS IN ITS COMPANION VOLUME, *Is That So?*, the stories collected in this book have been narrated by Eruch Jessawala and concern his life with the Lord, Avatar Meher Baba, or are retellings of stories which Avatar Meher Baba shared with His mandali.

These stories have all, at one time or another, been told in Mandali Hall and have been transcribed from tapes or notes which were made at the time. In some instances, however, these versions have also been influenced by private conversations. Although efforts were made to ensure the accuracy and authenticity of the contents herein, it should be borne in mind that all of these stories have been edited to varying degrees. They are not verbatim transcripts of tapes and are intended only to give the general gist and flavor of Eruch's talks, not to reproduce his narration word for word. Also, it should perhaps be noted that although Meher Baba is quoted throughout these stories, these quotes are not intended to represent actual words Baba used. During the time that these stories take place, Meher Baba observed silence, and communicated either through the medium of an alphabet board or through hand gestures. If a story says, "Baba said," it indicates only that the following quote represents the overall meaning of what Meher Baba conveyed through non-spoken means.

While I have tried to be as faithful as possible to Eruch's original telling of the stories, inevitably, in the editing process much is lost. Undoubtedly, at some point, one of the asides or spontaneous comments I have included in an attempt to capture something of the "feel" of the sessions in Mandali Hall will prove distracting, possibly even annoying to readers. While at other times, the reader may search in vain for a digression in a story only to find that I have omitted it for the sake of brevity. The end result may be that the stories here do not correspond very well with the way you remember them. Some of this may be due to the fact that Eruch does not tell the stories the same way from day to day or year to year. But most of it is undoubtedly caused by the editing and my inability to truly capture the moods Eruch is able to create through his superb sense of timing, his intonations, his gestures and even the expressions on his face.

Which might lead some to question the value of printing these stories at all. My feeling is that even shorn of the atmosphere created in Mandali Hall when the stories are told, they nonetheless have a life of their own. And many, I think, will prove to be new and therefore of interest, to the readers while the others, I hope, will be encountered as old friends. If they seem cold, lifeless and irrelevant to one's life with the Lord, then know well that this is due to the well intentioned but awkward hand of the editor. If, on the other hand, any of the stories is able to remind one of Avatar Meher Baba, to inspire one to think of Him, to live for Him, then all the credit must go to the magic of Eruch's story telling, and this book will have proved well worth it.

Steve Klein

◈ INTRODUCTION TO IS THAT SO?

THIS BOOK IS A COLLECTION OF STORIES told by Eruch Jessawala, one of Avatar Meher Baba's intimate mandali. Some of the stories were originally told by Baba to His mandali, others are accounts of the mandali's life with Baba, and some are stories which Eruch tells to illuminate various aspects of the life of surrender to the Lord.

The overwhelming majority of these stories have never been published before. Two or three, in greatly abbreviated form, can be found in *The Ancient One*, but it was felt that the addition of the context in which the stories were originally told, as well as many extra details, made the stories more significantly different and warranted their inclusion here.

In several places, stories united by a common theme or chronological sequence have been grouped together under a single title. Two or three of these stories have been published separately in *Glimpses* or *Tales From the New Life*, but as these sets of stories naturally belong together it was felt it was better to include a couple of stories which have already appeared in print than to exclude over half a dozen which have never been published before. But, for the most part, the stories in this book are being printed here for the first time.

All of the stories were transcribed from tapes of Eruch talking in Mandali Hall, or were written up from notes made at the time. Some of the incidents recounted herein were first shared with Bill Le Page during his visit to India in 1967. Others have been recorded only in the last few years. Great care had been taken to insure the stories' accuracy. Eruch's convalescence from his second cataract operation in the summer of 1985 provided a rare opportunity to have the rough manuscript read out to him, and he made some suggestions and corrections. However, it is important to state that the stories you are about to read have all been edited—they are not, nor are they meant to be, verbatim transcriptions of Eruch's talks.

Perhaps some may wonder why, if accuracy was felt to be so important, we didn't simply transcribe the tapes and let it go at that. The answer is obvious to anyone who has ever transcribed an informal conversation or impromptu talk. What makes perfect sense when heard, will oftentimes be terribly confusing and misleading when written out.

This is because we do not follow the rules of grammar when we speak. We use run on sentences, incomplete sentences, we start a sentence with one thought, pause, and then conclude with a totally different thought and at times will even say the exact opposite of what we mean. The listener is not confused, however, because of the "body English" the speaker uses—the tone of voice, the gestures, facial expressions, and general context of the conversation which he shares with the listener but which may not be apparent to someone only reading the text of the talk.

And Eruch, as an accomplished storyteller, knows how to take full advantage of the significant pause, the shrug of the shoulders, the grimace, the precise tone of voice to evoke a feeling and an understanding in his listeners which far exceeds the content conveyed by his words alone.

Therefore, it was necessary to edit all of the stories in this book. While they are all true and accurate to the essential gist of the stories as Eruch has told them, they are not entirely in his own words. Similarly, although Avatar Meher Baba is quoted throughout, two things must be noted. First of all, as Meher Baba observed silence most of His life, even when the text says, "Baba said," or "Baba explained," etc. it should be understood to mean that Baba spelled out on His alphabet board or indicated through gestures. Secondly, the words given in quotes are not intended to be exact representations of Baba's words, but are meant merely to convey in idiomatic English the gist of what Baba expressed.

Consequently, this book is not to be studied in a scholarly fashion, with great emphasis put on any particular word or phrase, but is meant simply to be enjoyed, appreciating the stories for what they are: entertaining tales whose only real value is their ability to remind us of Him—stories whose worth lies only in the degree to which they inspire us to more fully determine to be His.

Steve Klein

◐ **B I B L I O G R A P H Y**

THERE ARE MANY BOOKS BY AND ABOUT MEHER BABA, His life, and His teachings. For the sake of convenience, only some are included in this list.

BOOKS BY MEHER BABA

Beams from Meher Baba on the Spiritual Panorama. Walnut Creek, CA: Sufism Reoriented, 2008.

Discourses. 7th edition, one volume, newly revised. North Myrtle Beach, SC: Sheriar Foundation, 2000.

The Everything and The Nothing. North Myrtle Beach, SC: Sheriar Foundation, 2003.

God Speaks. 2nd edition revised and enlarged. Walnut Creek, CA: Sufism Reoriented, 1997.

Infinite Intelligence. North Myrtle Beach, SC: Sheriar Foundation, 2005.

Life at Its Best. Walnut Creek, CA: Sufism Reoriented, 1974.

BOOKS ABOUT MEHER BABA

As Only God Can Love by Darwin Shaw: North Myrtle Beach, SC: Sheriar Foundation, 2003.

The Beloved by Naoshwerwan Anzar. North Myrtle Beach, SC: Sheriar Foundation, 2003.

The Dance of Love: My Life with Meher Baba by Margaret Craske. Myrtle Beach, SC: Sheriar Press, 1980.

82 Family Letters to the Western Family of Lovers and Followers of Meher Baba, written by Mani (Manija Sheriar Irani) from December 1956 to August 1969. Myrtle Beach, SC: Sheriar Press, 1976.

Glimpses of the God-Man, Meher Baba by Bal Natu. Vol. I (1943–1948), Walnut Creek, CA: Sufism Reoriented, 1977. Vol. II (January 1949–March 1952), Bombay: Meher House Publications, 1979. Vol. IV (February–December 1953), Myrtle Beach, SC: Sheriar Press, 1984. Vol. V (January 1–March 6, 1954), Myrtle Beach, SC: Sheriar Press 1987. Vol VI (March 1954–April 1955), North Myrtle Beach, SC: Sheriar Foundation, 1994.

God-Brother: Stories from my Childhood with Meher Baba by Mani S. Irani. North Myrtle Beach, SC: Sheriar Foundation, 1993.

The God-Man by C. B. Purdom. North Myrtle Beach, SC: Sheriar Foundation, 2010.

He Gives the Ocean by Najoo Kotwal. North Myrtle Beach, SC: Sheriar Foundation, 2006.

Listen, Humanity, narrated and edited by D.E. Stevens. New York, NY: The Crossroad Publishing Company, 1998.

Love Alone Prevails by Kitty Davy. North Myrtle Beach, SC: Sheriar Foundation, 2001.

Meher Baba's Early Messages to the West: The 1932–1935 Western Tours edited by Avatar Meher Baba Perpetual Public Charitable Trust. North Myrtle Beach, SC: Sheriar Foundation, 2009.

Still Dancing with Love: More Stories of Life with Meher Baba by Margaret Craske. Myrtle Beach, SC: Sheriar Press, 1990.

The Ocean of Love: My Life with Meher Baba by Delia DeLeon. Myrtle Beach, SC: Sheriar Press, 1991.

The Wayfarers: Meher Baba with the God-intoxicated by William Donkin. North Myrtle Beach, SC: Sheriar Foundation, 2000.

RELATED BOOKS

Conversations with The Awakener by Bal Natu: North Myrtle Beach, SC: Sheriar Foundation, 1991.

Flowing Conversations with The Awakener by Bal Natu: North Myrtle Beach, SC: Sheriar Foundation, 2004.

Intimate Conversations with The Awakener by Bal Natu: North Myrtle Beach, SC: Sheriar Foundation, 1998.

More Conversations with The Awakener by Bal Natu: North Myrtle Beach, SC: Sheriar Foundation, 1993.

For further information about Meher Baba contact:

Sheriar Foundation Bookstore

807 34th Ave. S., North Myrtle Beach, SC 29582, USA

or www.sheriarbooks.org